CY YOUNG

CY YOUNG

A BASEBALL LIFE

Reed Browning

University of Massachusetts Press
AMHERST AND BOSTON

First paperback edition 2003
LC 99-088275
ISBN 1-55849-398-0 *(paperback)*
ISBN 1-55849-262-3 *(cloth)*

Designed by Steve Dyer
Set in Bell by Graphic Composition, Inc.
Printed and bound by Thomson-Shore, Inc.

LIBRARY OF CONGRESS CATALOGING-IN-PUBLICATION DATA
Browning, Reed.
Cy Young : a baseball life / Reed Browning.
p. cm.
Includes index.
ISBN 1-55849-262-3 *(cloth : alk. paper)*
1. Young, Cy, 1867–1955. 2. Baseball players—United States—Biography.
3. Pitchers (Baseball)—United States—Biography. I. Title.
GV865.Y58 B76 2000
796.357′092—dc21
[B]
99-088275

British Library Cataloguing in Publication Data are available.

Frontispiece: Cy Young, ca. 1904.
All photographs are from the collection of George Sullivan except where noted.

FOR SAM

who first saw Greg Maddux pitch on May 9, 1999

CONTENTS

Illustrations follow page 144

PREFACE

AS EACH passing season advances the threshold of living baseball memory, men whose legends were once the staple of sports talk fade inexorably into obscurity. Even the "immortality" ostensibly conferred by membership in the inaugural class of Hall of Fame inductees is not proof against the spread of collective amnesia. I can testify first-hand—for I have probed the waters—that such names as Honus Wagner, Walter Johnson, and Christy Mathewson do not register at all with many of today's younger followers of the game. As a professional historian, I don't find that fact surprising. Why should fans today bother with Eddie Collins, Ed Delahanty, Rogers Hornsby, Larry Lajoie, or Tris Speaker when they have the careers of Jeff Bagwell, Albert Belle, Barry Bonds, Ken Griffey Jr., and Mark McGwire to track, and the achievements of Hank Aaron, Joe Dimaggio, Mickey Mantle, Willie Mays, and Ted Williams to measure the current stars against? Sports fans live in the present and the remembered past; except for the occasional history-minded journalist, no one associated with the publicizing of the game has any strong interest in perpetuating tales that antedate living memory.

Three players, however, have defied the rule that consigns distant heroes to the realm of the forgotten. The first is Babe Ruth, who has been dead for over fifty years but whose reputation as a batter of unparalleled power still hovers over the game. The second is Ty Cobb, whose name almost forty years after his death still evokes the image of a player driven by a compulsive need to win. The third is Cy Young. This great pitcher died in 1955, and his case is the oddest of the three, for the average fan today is scarcely able to conjure up any mental picture of this ancient worthy's career, or even to say what skills made him dominant. Yet that same fan certainly knows that Cy Young's name graces the award given annually to baseball's two best hurlers and is apt to conclude that Young must have been a helluva pitcher.

Larger-than-life personalities, both Ruth and Cobb have attracted the attention of biographers.[1] As a happy consequence, we now have superb and challenging studies of these two giants of the game's earlier years. For reasons that may soon become clear, however, Young has been less fortunate. And yet, measured by the durability of their diamond achievements, it is Young who now looms the largest of the three. Ruth's home run records, whether posted for a season or for a career, have been eclipsed. Cobb's lifetime records in base hits and stolen bases have been broken. But Young is an entirely different case. Can anyone really believe that Cy Young's career total of 511 victories—think of it, 511! incredible!—will ever be surpassed? Or that his total of 7,356 innings pitched will be exceeded? Unless the character and rules of the game change even more dramatically in the new century than they did in the century just ended, Young's monumental achievements will still be standing on that distant day when people finally stop paying attention to the game of baseball. It was this consideration more than any other that drew me to the happy task of writing a biography of Cy Young.

Since my focus in the coming chapters will be on Young himself, I want to take a moment before beginning to situate him in his wider national context and to remind the reader that the times he lived in were as dynamic as the game he played—that throughout his twenty-two years as a professional baseball player the turbulent changes that had been surging across the United States ever since the Civil War continued to transform the cultural, economic, and social landscape of the nation. When Young entered the major leagues in 1890, the population of the United States stood at 63 million; by the time he retired after the 1911 season, it had swelled to 92 million—an increase of more than 45 percent over the course of only two decades. And fast as the country as a whole was growing, cities were growing even faster. Cleveland, for example, which served as baseball home for Young in both his first and last seasons, swelled during those years from 260,000 to 560,000. The forces that propelled the Forest City's expansion churned elsewhere as well, so that an America that boasted only seven cities with populations in excess of 300,000 in 1890 had eighteen such cities by 1911. And the change in the nation was not simply quantitative, for while the country grew in population, the texture and quality of its citizens' lives were being transformed. Telephone wires proliferated to bind homes within urban centers, while dirt roads yielded to paved highways as the basic links between these areas. When Young began his career, he had never driven an automobile, attended a movie, sipped a Coca-Cola, or seen a motorized aircraft. Before he retired he owned his own car, he enjoyed watching forty-five-minute films at public theaters, he drank Coke, and airplanes had developed so swiftly that they had been used in combat abroad. In short, we powerfully misjudge the stresses and challenges that our forebears of a century ago confronted if we envision them living in a largely static universe.

Baseball was also undergoing formative shifts in these decades, two of which flowed directly from the demographic growth just noted. First, the larger pool of young men seeking employment as professional ballplayers raised the talent threshold for admittance into the major leagues and allowed owners to be more selective in offering contracts. Second, the nation's expansion afforded the option of professional baseball careers to young men who grew up in the West. A quick comparison makes this second point directly. When Cy Young launched his career, fewer than 40 of his fellow major leaguers had been born west of the Mississippi River and only 8 came from California. Just two decades later, over 120 of his colleagues came from the West, 26 of whom were born in California. Since St. Louis was the westernmost outpost of the major leagues in both 1890 and 1911, the development of the West as a cradle of talent cannot be attributed to franchise shifts. Instead, it was the expansion of the nation that caused the siren call of baseball to reach as far as the Pacific Ocean.

Quite independently of demographic trends, other pressures—often commercial in character—were also transforming the game. When Cy Young reached the majors, home plate was a square and the distance from the pitcher to home was 55 feet, 6 inches; when he ended his career home had become a pentagon and pitchers began their deliveries 5 feet farther back, the present-day distance. In his early seasons he played with both hands uncovered; when he retired, he protected his left hand with a glove. For over half of his career Young faced batters who suffered no penalty at all for fouling off pitches; by the end he was benefitting from the rule, still in effect, that designates the first two fouls as strikes. These alterations in baseball rules and equipment were accompanied by important shifts in baseball strategy. It was during the first decade of Young's career, for example, that the finely honed philosophy of "scientific baseball"—a strategy that placed a premium on contact hitting, skillful bunting, and aggressive base running—became the hallmark of successful clubs. In like manner, management recast its expectations of the pitcher's durability. Thus, while in Young's first year starting pitchers finished almost 9 out of every 10 games they began, by 1911 that number had fallen to below 6 out of 10. Meanwhile, the physical environment and the vocabulary of the game were also changing. When Young launched his career, ballparks were really wooden grandstands, and a crowd of three thousand "cranks" was deemed a pretty good gate; by the end of his career concrete and steel stadiums were appearing, and good games could readily draw twenty thousand "fans." Even the sporting press was transformed. Whereas in 1890 newspapers had only artists' sketches of players' faces to enliven their pages, by 1911 they could incorporate action photographs into their coverage. Baseball's reputation as a game that changes slowly is not entirely undeserved. But that reputation should not lead us to overlook the shifts that have in fact occurred over the years, or lead us to forget that in baseball's early days—and the entire span of Young's career may safely be assigned to the game's early days—the pace of change, especially in playing rules, was swifter than we have come to expect in more recent times.

Before beginning, I want to alert the reader to an assumption I make in trying to understand the personality and character of my subject. A taciturn and poorly educated man, Young left behind very few pieces of correspondence, and those I've seen, though useful in some ways, are almost silent about his thoughts. Public records provide important information about residences, land purchases, health, and vital statistics. But the chief source of information about Young as a private figure must be the reportage of baseball writers, and three considerations oblige the biographer to treat this source cautiously.

First, in the pre-television age, when the baseball writer's central role was to describe what had happened on the diamond for a readership that had no visual sense of the contest, interviews figured less prominently than they do in today's media-saturated environment. The writer's role in Young's day was neither to enrich the context within which the game should be understood nor to memorialize the great achievements on the diamond; it was simply to provide an account of what had transpired. Writers served as the "eyes" of absent fans. As a consequence, players—even great ones—were less frequently quoted than they are today.

Second, many baseball writers weren't very knowledgeable about the game they covered and thus fell back on ritualistic formulas in explaining what had happened: teams and players often faltered because they lacked spirit or even because they were jinxed. Moreover, the fact that many

writers did not leave their home cities encouraged a persistent parochial-
ism in their commentary. Sometimes they were cheerleaders, nothing
more. As a consequence, contemporary accounts are often devoid of useful analysis and riddled with errors.

Third, it was a convention of the day to typecast players and then to
use anecdotes to confirm again and again the reliability of that casting.
That's how we get Rube Waddell the flake, King Kelly the drunk, and
John McGraw the fox. Quite early on, Cy Young was cast as the honest
rustic. Almost everything that is later said of him reinforces that depiction. The biographer may want to pierce the press image, but if the press
is almost the sole source of information, then piercing will not be easy.

Fortunately, it's also probably not necessary. I suspect (and thus oper-
ate on the assumption) that press images, though doubtless oversimplifi-
cations, were not randomly allocated—that the roles assigned to players
gained credibility from being grounded largely in truth. Kelly could
never have been a model of temperance, Waddell was implausible as a
paragon of responsibility, and Young defied depiction as a swaggerer. Too
many people knew the truth about these athletes, and it strains credulity
to believe that baseball writers in all the major league cities would be
complicit in a vast conspiracy to create a false picture of any player's character. Having said that, I must quickly concede that with respect to the
sexual activities of players such a conspiracy did exist. Womanizing was
the great exception, its disguise being deemed obligatory in family publications. Only if one knew the code words—"malaria" for venereal disease,
for example—could one decipher explanations for a particular player's
prolonged absence from the lineup. Otherwise, however, baseball scribes
depicted players much as they perceived them, ignoring complications
certainly and tidying up their language, but faithful to the central point.
In the relative innocence of a century ago such perceptions were not even
mediated by press agents. And so I'm moved to conclude that if Cy Young
was cast as a salt-of-the-earth farmer, it was because the picture was in
significant measure true. My task, therefore, is not to discredit the received view of Cy Young but, by scrutinizing contemporary press coverage and other kinds of testimony from those who knew him, to add detail
and nuance to it.

Two final introductory points are in order. First, insofar as I use statistics in this book, they are basically the traditional ones that fans are familiar with. I do so in full awareness that over the past quarter century statistically minded students of the game ("sabermetricians" is the nifty

neologism they are known by, derived from the initials—SABR—by which the Society for American Baseball Research is usually designated) have devised a whole array of newer statistics that permit sharper and more accurate assessments of player performances. I admire these tools and occasionally, as you'll see, refer to them. But because I want to be understood by an audience that is by and large not familiar with the novelties, I have chosen to confine myself to a vocabulary that does not require elaborate translation. Second, I often use the first person singular in this book. In part, that's because I am imagining myself in conversation with the reader, in part because I want to be able to talk about how and why I'm doing certain things in the book, and in part because writing about baseball brings out the colloquial in me. I have tried not to allow casualness of tone to lead to slackness of thought.

Many people have helped me at various times as I've written this book, sometimes in providing information or background, sometimes in giving me access to sources, and sometimes in critiquing my conclusions. I'm glad to have this opportunity to thank Michelle Arnold, Doris Baker, Ed Bartholemy, Philip Bergen, Sheppard Black, Jean Chapman, Inez Cline, Miller Dailey, Clark Dougan, Mike Dugan, Don Duren, Thomas Eakin, Bob Feller, Richard Gannon, Jim Gates, Joel Gunderson, Fred Hawley, John Hobson, James Keeler, Don Kohl, Mary Ellen Kollar, Joan Krizack, Joseph Lee, Charles Leech, Richard Levin, Marian Mardis, Bruce Markusen, Helen Mathew, Neal McCabe, Jane Meuhlen, Doug Pappas, John Phillips, Carlos Piano, Irene Ransom, Robert Ransom, Dale Robinson, Ralph Romig, Jonathon Rosenthal, Peter Rutkoff, Barbara Scott, Will Scott, Corey Seeman, Ric Sheffield, Lee Sinins, Brad Sullivan, George Sullivan, Cindy Wallace, Joseph Wayman, Mark Wernick, Jay Willey, Frank Williams, Frank Wojcik, and Allan Wood for help they've given me along the way. I am also grateful to Kenyon College for awarding me the Faculty Development Grant that allowed me to do research at the National Baseball Hall of Fame and Museum in Cooperstown, New York.

Since you're with me so far, I'll only add that I hope you enjoy the book.

REED BROWNING
Gaubier, Ohio

CY YOUNG

CHAPTER ONE

⛧

1867–1890:
Life before Glory

O N MARCH 29, 1867, near the hamlet of Gilmore, Ohio, Denton
True Young howled his way into the world. His incontestable claim
on the nickname "Cy" lay a quarter of a century in the future, and
so in discussing the early years of his life I'll call him "Dent," the abbreviated form of his Christian name that quickly sufficed among family and
friends. "Denton" was a common first name among his Young ancestors
and relatives; at least one Denton Young lived nearby. "True," however,
was new to the family, a name chosen out of respect for a Civil War officer
under whom Dent's father had served. "Denton" and "True" are names
that go well together: there is a stoic compactness to the linkage, a hint
of a no-nonsense view of life. And before his life was over, Dent would
prove the particular aptness of his middle name.

Family lore buttressed by census information allows us to trace Dent's
antecedents back three generations. It was shortly after the ratification
of the United States Constitution that three Young brothers migrated
from Britain to America, settling near Baltimore. One of these three,
Denton by name, was Dent's great-grandfather. While in Maryland he
met and married Mary McKinzie. The couple had five children, the eldest
of whom—born in 1799 and named McKinzie—was Dent's grandfather.
When McKinzie was three years old, Denton Young joined the swelling
westward movement, settling his family first in western Pennsylvania
and then leading them farther west across the Ohio River. A pause in
Steubenville allowed the Youngs to secure a land title. They finally put
down roots north of Cadiz, in Harrison County, where, like most other
settlers streaming into the new state, they took to farming. McKinzie
Young grew to adulthood in the hilly country around Cadiz. Like his

father he tilled the land; if he was a typical east Ohio farmer, wheat was his chief crop. In 1820 he married Sarah Northamer, a woman of Pennsylvania Dutch background who, by one later account, was somewhat older than he. At some point in the succeeding decade, McKinzie and his family moved their holdings about forty miles farther west, settling near Gilmore, Ohio, and finally linking the Youngs with the county that bore the wonderfully resonant name of Tuscarawas. (A half-century later, as Cy Young impressed his name upon the nation, one fact that most Americans who followed baseball would know about him was that he was a son of Tuscarawas County.)

In the following two decades, as the construction of canal linkages to Lake Erie and the Ohio River widened the market for the produce of Tuscarawas County, McKinzie and Sarah Young participated in the growing prosperity of the region. They also had twelve children. The eleventh, coming into the world in 1843, was named McKinzie, after his father. This young McKinzie was Dent's father. (From now on I shall distinguish Dent's grandfather from his father by referring to them as McKinzie Sr. and McKinzie Jr., respectively. It's worth noting that the name "McKinzie" goes through an array of spelling permutations in the surviving records from the day. I have standardized these spellings by choosing the version that McKinzie Young Jr. seems to have preferred.) McKinzie Young Sr. and Sarah Young lived the rest of their lives in Gilmore, McKinzie dying in 1875, his wife dying the following year. They and three of their children who died before reaching the age of twenty are buried in the cemetery there.

McKinzie Young Jr. was eighteen when the Civil War broke out in 1861. He did not rush to enlist. He may have been needed at home, or perhaps the health problems that were to nag him throughout his life— measles, for example, had already left him with poor vision—made him dubious military material. And of course he may simply not have wanted to go to war. Still, a young man of the time, five feet ten inches tall and accustomed to doing hard labor, could not ultimately avoid military service in the national conflict, and so in October 1862, McKinzie Young Jr. joined the Forty-third Infantry Regiment of Ohio in the capacity of a medical aide.[1] He left military service just nine months later—those health problems again?—but then, in September 1864, reenlisted for a second tour, this time in Ohio's Seventy-eighth Regiment. We know that he cast his first presidential ballot that same fall for Abraham Lincoln, a vote that supplies the earliest surviving sign of the Young family's longtime attachment to Republican politics. During this second stint in the Grand Army of the Republic, which lasted until the war was over, he sustained injuries that bothered him throughout the rest of his life. Surviving military records show him also to have suffered from diarrhea and varicose veins while a member of the Grand Army of the Republic. He left service as he had entered it, a private.

Upon his discharge, McKinzie Young Jr. returned to Gilmore, apparently assuming chief responsibility for handling the affairs of the 140-acre farm owned by his aging parents. By 1870, under his supervision, the farm had grown to almost 200 acres. Meanwhile, in February 1866, less than a year after returning home from the army, McKinzie Young Jr. married Nancy Miller. The daughter of John and Rebecca Miller, she was one of seven siblings to have survived to adulthood, and grew up on a farm close by the Youngs' property. The eldest child of the marriage between McKinzie Young Jr. and Nancy Miller, born thirteen months later, was Dent.

Over the next eight years McKinzie and Nancy Young had four more children. Jesse Carlton (usually called Carl) was born in October 1868. Alonzo (Lon) appeared in July 1870. Ella came into the world in August 1872. Anthony (improbably called Otto) completed the family in September 1874. McKinzie Young Jr. became a modestly prominent citizen of Tuscarawas County—a successful farmer, a Mason, and an occasional school director. The family attended the Methodist church. At some point, perhaps as early as when McKinzie Jr. married, McKinzie Sr. gave his son the 54 acres of his property that lay inside Washington Township. As the farm prospered, the younger Youngs were able to extend their holdings. Buying from neighbors while selling to relatives, McKinzie and Nancy Young managed between 1870 and 1890 to add about 120 acres to the initial Gilmore core of 54 acres. This rugged but ample homestead served as the training ground for life on which young Dent and his four siblings worked and played.

The foregoing five paragraphs summarize almost all the information about Dent's forebears that can confidently be drawn from available records.[2] It would be especially interesting to know more about the family of Dent's mother. The Millers had migrated from Pennsylvania but there are too many Millers in the records to permit identification of her precise ancestors. Still, thanks to an 1875 map, it is possible to locate both McKinzie Young Sr.'s and John Miller's farms on the outskirts of Gilmore and to understand the topographical significance of some of the property transfers that McKinzie and Nancy Young executed as they expanded and consolidated their Gilmore farm. The information from McKinzie Young Jr.'s army years has let me shape an image of this young man, perhaps his mother's last surviving child, struggling through his youth with infirmities that are more commonly associated with age.

Dent's childhood and adolescence were basically unremarkable. He attended a rough-framed, two-room school in Gilmore through the sixth grade, at which point his formal education ended.[3] He accepted farm chores as part of his daily responsibility and began to cultivate a powerful and lifelong sense of the importance of work and duty in the life of a man. In light of a Sabbatarianism that he displayed as a young adult, it appears likely that he regularly attended church as a child. Since he had many relatives living nearby, it is also probable that he often played with cousins. Many years later Cy Young said that his grandparents "raised me."[4] Strictly speaking the claim was false, but it stands as evidence that he passed many enjoyable hours in the company of grandparents, all four of whom he might have seen on a daily basis. Dent grew into a strapping young man, six feet two inches in height and a muscular 170 pounds in weight. As I say, it was an unremarkable childhood and youth.

Except for baseball.

Conventionally a two-word term in the nineteenth century, "base ball" was an activity whose popularity swept the nation in the aftermath of the Civil War. By the 1870s professional leagues existed to link larger cities, and most small towns had their own informal clubs. The game had even penetrated the recesses of Tuscarawas County. Dent and his brothers discovered that they loved baseball. "All us Youngs could throw," he later told Arthur Daley. "I usta kill squirrels with a stone when I was a kid and my granddad onct killed a turkey buzzard on the fly with a rock."[5] Encouraged by their father, they sought out playing opportunities, sometimes traveling as far as twenty miles from home—presumably on foot or horseback—to find teams needing their skills.

But Dent was the best of them all. And though he was a good hitter, his throwing speed made him even better as a pitcher. Dent devoted long hours to cultivating his ability to throw accurately. During noontime breaks from farm work, he practiced aiming at a target on his father's barn door. He experimented with putting spins on the ball. When he didn't have a ball to hurl, he used walnuts instead. Dent also organized a local Gilmore team, though he had much difficulty finding someone who could catch his hard pitches. Little is known about these early games. But on one memorable occasion in 1884 a seventeen-year-old Dent led the Gilmore nine to a whopping 54–4 victory over a team from much larger Newcomerstown. His fame grew, and in that same summer he played on semipro teams in nearby towns such as Newcomerstown, Cadiz, and Uhrichsville. For his efforts, the team organizers would pay his expenses "and sometimes"—the words are Dent's, from many years later—"a little extra."[6] Baseball, he discovered, was a way to make some money.

The world of Tuscarawas baseball was abruptly shattered for Dent in 1885 when he and his father moved west to Nebraska, near the Kansas border in the town of Cowles. It's not clear why they went. One possibility is that McKinzie Young Jr., who had traveled to Iowa between his two tours of Civil War duty, wanted to return to a region across the Mississippi he had visited earlier. Or they may have moved to be with one of Dent's cousins who had traveled with her husband to the state. What makes the action particularly odd is that Nancy Young and the other Young children remained in Gilmore. In any case, Dent worked as a hand on the farm of Doug Terry, earning $20 per month, and he continued to find opportunities to be paid for playing baseball. The nine from nearby Red Cloud arranged for him to receive $35 per month for playing third base and working part-time in a dairy business. When that team folded, he took the initiative of organizing a team in Cowles, assigning to himself the role of pitcher. Still later on, he pitched for Guide Rock. These semipro games occurred on Saturdays, Dent usually took the mound, and at least according to his own later account, he never lost a game he pitched in Nebraska.[7]

After the summer of 1887, Dent and his father returned to Gilmore. The cause of their return is as mysterious as that of their departure. Perhaps McKinzie and Dent got lonely. Perhaps Nebraska failed to fulfill some promise. Perhaps someone got ill, and the Young family needed to reconvene. Still, although Dent's stay in Nebraska lasted but three years, he remembered the period warmly throughout his life. In 1911 a number of people from Guide Rock sent him birthday greetings. As late as 1955, only eight months before he died, he summoned up a few memories about his days in Cowles for a reply to a letter of inquiry.[8] Most significantly, within just a few years of his return to Ohio, as sportswriters began to inquire into the background of the speedy young pitcher from Tuscarawas, he would regularly identify his years in Nebraska as the start of his pitching career. Guide Rock was not slow to recognize the value of the publicity; by 1905 it was calling itself the place where Cy Young was "discovered."[9]

Ralph Romig has suggested an altogether different reason for Dent Young's return to Gilmore before the summer of 1888: a desire to be near Robba Miller, the sixteen-year-old girl he was hoping to marry.[10] My research has uncovered no explicit evidence to support this view, but it is not improbable. We know that a few years later Dent and Robba got married, and we know—because they lived on contiguous farms—that they had known each other from her early childhood. Moreover, even though 1888 is the last year of this story that has left almost no evidentiary trace, we can speculate with fuller confidence than usual about what was going on in Dent's mind at this time. He was after all, coming home to face his twenty-first birthday—to enter into adulthood, and to make some important decisions about his life. Marriage, of course, was one. But more immediate was the need to decide how he would make his living. With only a sixth-grade education, his obvious options were limited to two: to remain a Tuscarawas County farmer, or to join the ranks of young men who were moving to the burgeoning urban centers of the Midwest to find employment in one of the many newly emerging industries. The latter choice seems never to have attracted him. But if everything in his family experience suggested that he was meant to be a farmer, there remained a third possibility, probably initially viewed as marginal in likelihood but nevertheless intensely exciting in prospect. He had learned in recent years that people would pay him to play baseball. He could spend a few years finding out if his talent was great enough to allow him to earn a living playing the game he so deeply enjoyed. The years 1888–89 can most plausibly be understood as a time in which Dent Young, while working hard to assist his father at farming, honed and tested his ball-playing skills in the hope of using them to make a living.

During 1888 Dent played some ball for the semipro Carrollton team, located in Carroll County, about thirty-five miles from Gilmore. Pitching and playing second base, he received a dollar per game.[11] The next summer, perhaps living some of the time with one of his many relatives in Harrison County, he played for the Franklins based in New Athens. Energized by Dent's arm and bat, the Franklins marched through their schedule with extraordinary success, defeating opponents by scores like 24–16, 29–14, and 50–6. As late as August 8, they were still undefeated, and in October they played a three-game series with the team from Cadiz for the championship of Harrison and Belmont Counties. The earliest box score I have discovered containing the name "Young" comes from this season and details a 9–2 victory by New Athens over Brownsville. Dent handled second base that day and went 2 for 3 in the rain-shortened contest.[12] Many years later, Cy Young reminded people of the primitive character of these semipro games: "Most players played barehanded. Only the few who were 'better fixed' "—that didn't include Dent—"had gloves of their own."[13] Still, rough as the game was, Dent made his mark for New Athens in 1889, and as a consequence he received, according to an account from three years later, "several flattering offers" from teams seeking his services for 1890.[14]

One of those teams was the Canton club, the defending champion of the Tri-State League. This circuit was a full-fledged minor league, one of the associations of baseball clubs that, in cooperation with the National League and the American Association (the two major leagues), had established a set of arrangements designed to let all participating club owners purchase and (with limitations) protect ballplaying talent within a hierarchical structure of organized baseball. Early in the spring of 1890, someone representing Canton traveled to Gilmore to explore with Dent and his father the possibility that Dent might play for Canton during the upcoming season.[15] It was a particularly difficult spring for club owners everywhere, for the creation over the previous winter of a third major league—the Players' League—had generated a national search for new talent, forays to skim skilled players away from teams they had been playing with, and, more generally, an upward pressure on salaries throughout the hierarchy. Like all clubs, Canton was scrambling to secure talent wherever it could find it. When an initial offer of $40 per month was insufficient to get Dent Young to sign, Canton raised its proposal to $60. This was more money than Dent had made even when he was moonlighting at dairy work to complement his ballplaying in Nebraska, and so McKinzie Young Jr. approved his son's acceptance.[16] While the venue and timing of this conversation—by one account it occurred in the Gilmore pasture with Dent behind the plow—may have caught the Youngs off guard, the fact that such a conversation would some day occur probably had long been understood by father and son. By signing the contract, Dent Young, his twenty-third birthday at hand, became a professional baseball player.

Within a few weeks he began to acquire a new name to go along with his new career. It happened innocently enough. Eager to impress his new manager and his new teammates, who had some doubts about the awkward-looking hayseed in his blue overalls, Dent fired some of his fast balls against a fence at Pastime Park, home grounds of the Canton nine. "I threw the ball so hard," he later explained, "I tore a couple of boards off the grandstand. One of the fellows said the stand looked like a cyclone struck it."[17] The name stuck, and by late April a Canton newspaper account not only referred to Young twice as "the Cyclone" but even listed him as "Cyclone, p" in the box score.[18] Perhaps the meteorological term suggested itself because it was on many Canton tongues at the time, for the same newspapers that celebrated the arrival of the new hurler were also describing destruction caused throughout the county by recent cyclones and advertising performances of a theatrical production called "The Comedy Cyclone." The abbreviation of "Cyclone Young" to "Cy Young" lay two years in the future. With the baseball season at hand in April of 1890, however, the longer nickname served the purpose of emphasizing the "cannonball speed" of the newcomer and redoubling the interest of Canton's baseball-loving public in the season that was about to begin.[19]

Canton played a few exhibition games before the official season began, and in one contest Dent pitched a one-hitter against Columbus. Then on April 30, Cyclone Young pitched and won Canton's season opener by a score of 4–2, holding Wheeling to 3 hits in its home park and striking out 8. Four days later, he won his first game in Canton, besting McKeesport 4–3. The press praised both his speed and his curves. But he quickly learned that the team he had joined was a feeble one, with no chance of defending its league championship. By the middle of June, Canton had lost 27 games and won only 15. Cyclone Young had been the winning pitcher in all but 4 of those victories. In July the team became so stretched for players that on one occasion Dent caught and on another his offer to play first base was happily accepted. In an effort to reverse the club's fortunes, its directors installed a new manager every month during the first half of the season, but nothing worked. Meanwhile, however, Cyclone Young plugged away. For much of the season he pitched every second or third day, usually starting but occasionally relieving. He was not always sharp; on June 2, for example, his motion hampered by an ankle injury, he gave up 17 hits to Springfield. Moreover, he regularly received poor defensive support; on June 30, the victim of wretched fielding, he yielded 10 unearned runs in the last two innings and lost 14–4. Still, Cyclone Young slowly caught the attention of a wider audience. By midseason, with as many victories as losses to his credit and more strikeouts than hits on his ledger, he was being widely saluted as the best pitcher in the Tri-State League. Rumors circulated that several major league teams were scouting him and interested in securing his services.[20]

If any curious scouts were present among the six hundred spectators at Pastime Park when Cyclone Young took the mound against McKeesport on July 24, 1890, they were not disappointed. Young felt good as he warmed up and predicted he would pitch "the game of his life" that day.[21] He proceeded not only to win the game 4–1 but also to shut down McKeesport without a single hit. He walked none and struck out a remarkable 18. He was so sharp that only one batted ball reached the outfield. Canton errors in the ninth inning deprived him of his shutout—Canton's defense was so feeble that Young never pitched a shutout in 1890—but the game was unquestionably his finest of the year. With it, he evened his season record at 15–15 though playing for the worst team in the league, and took his seasonal strike-out total up to 201 while keeping his seasonal bases on balls total at a lowly 33. Has any pitcher ever concluded a minor league career with a more stunning outing?

Had 1890 been like most years, Cyclone Young's opportunity to break into the majors—"fast company," as it was called—might not have come quite as early as it now did. But competition among three major leagues was hurting attendance almost everywhere, and in smaller market cities like Cleveland, which was being asked to support clubs in both the National and the Players League, the search for players who might both help the team and pull in fans was intense. For Cleveland teams, therefore, Cyclone Young was doubly attractive. He was a fastball pitcher, speedier, it was said, than Chicago's great Bill Hutchison. And he was an Ohio boy, able perhaps to stir a regional loyalty and draw the curious to ball games. The most eager of the suitors was the Cleveland National League team, improbably called the Spiders. "Cash" Miller, their informal Canton scout, had alerted the Spider ownership to the Tuscarawan's ability.[22] The Spiders' task was to persuade the Canton club to sell the contract of the man who was clearly its greatest asset. Their advantage was that the season had gone so poorly for Canton that the club needed money.

Davis Hawley represented the Spiders in these conversations. A prominent Cleveland banker, he was also secretary of the club. Canton hoped to get $1,000 for Cyclone Young's contract, but Hawley thought that price far too steep.[23] Faced with Hawley's refusal to pay the asking price, and presumably disappointed that no rival bid had appeared, the Canton management relented fairly quickly, accepting a Cleveland offer of $300.[24] On July 30 word was released that Young was joining the Spiders. The new pitcher accepted contract terms that increased his monthly salary from the $60 that Canton had been paying him to $75 for the remaining two months of the 1890 season. On August 2, in the company of a Canton team official, he traveled to Cleveland and began daily pitching practice at the Spiders' ballpark. Davis Hawley bought Young a suit of clothes to replace the outgrown attire he had sported at an earlier meeting. Cy Young's own later and inaccurate story that Canton had been so desperate for income that it had accepted a suit of clothes in exchange for his contract is probably grounded in the confusion of an old man's memory.[25] (Other accounts note, as a mark of Canton's impecuniousness, that the team disbanded within a week of losing Young. The truth is less dramatic; the team disbanded, but only because the Tri-State season was over.) As for Cyclone himself, as a young man unacquainted with big-city ways, he was nervous. "Well, I'll pitch a game," he reportedly declared on the morning of his first start. "And if I win I'll stay; If I lose, I'll go home this evening."[26] Thus, even at the moment when he had achieved what he had been dreaming of for at least four years he was ready to return to farm life if he failed.

Pride alloyed with realism: that was a yoking of attitudes that would accompany Cy Young throughout his life.

CHAPTER TWO

1890−1892:
The Cyclone Blows into Town

THE CLEVELAND CLUB that Cyclone Young joined in 1890 was among the most embattled franchises in the National League. Founded in 1887 as a member of the American Association, the team transferred its affiliation to the National League two years later. At the same time it acquired its popular but unofficial nickname of Spiders, reportedly a reference to the gauntness of some of its players. The chief owner of the franchise was Frank DeHaas Robison, a Cleveland trolley magnate with ties to the Republican Party.[1] A prominent sports enthusiast, Robison believed that he could serve both of his financial interests by creating an attractive professional baseball team and building a playing field for it along his Payne Avenue streetcar line. The difficulty facing Robison and his colleagues was the relative paucity of high-quality ball players, a problem greatly exacerbated in 1890 by the appearance of the Players League. Not only did this league draw players away from the Spiders and other teams in the National League and American Association, it also challenged the Spiders directly by locating a franchise in Cleveland.[2] It was a fight that the Spiders were losing; while neither Cleveland entry was competitive in its own league in 1890, the Players League club, by featuring league batting champion Pete Browning and the popular local lad Ed Delahanty, was outdrawing the Spiders.[3] The Forest City could not support two major league teams, and the Spiders seemed the feebler of the contenders.

In this competitive climate, and preceded by a flurry of newspaper hype about the marvelous new "Canton Cyclone," Dent Young pitched his first game for the Cleveland club on August 6, 1890. Though the Spiders' opponent was the powerful Chicago Colts club, led by the already legendary Cap Anson, the day was a total triumph for the rookie, who wore a uniform manifestly too small for his large frame. Supported by an increasingly noisy crowd, Young yielded only three base hits and defeated the Colts by a score of 8–1. In the process he outpitched Bill Hutchison, who was well on his way to winning 42 games during the 1890 season. The next morning a *Cleveland Plain Dealer* headline trumpeted the happy news to the Cleveland baseball public: "Chicago makes but three hits off the cyclonic pitcher."[4] Not to be outdone in celebrating the occasion, the *Cleveland Leader and Herald* asked rhetorically, "Can Mr. Young pitch?" "Can a fifer fife?" came its pointed rejoinder. Trawling for tropes, the *Leader and Herald* writer noted that Cyclone Young "sends lessons in geometry up to the batter with a request for a solution." In the pre-television age the press had a responsibility to provide its clientele with a memorable visual image, and the writer provided one—the rookie, he wrote, was a "tall, very well put together, and athletic young man."[5]

For a full generation after Cy Young became a celebrity, the story of this first game remained one of the staples of baseball lore. A parable of rustic virtue trumping urban arrogance, its key elements come down to us in several forms.[6] At the heart of all of them, however, lay Cap Anson's misjudgment of Young. According to some versions, Anson had heard about Young's successes at Canton and had made a trip to watch him pitch. (Given Anson's playing schedule and the remoteness of Tri-State League cities, this strikes me as unlikely.) According to others, Anson did not see Young until the rookie took the field on August 6 in his ill-fitting uniform. What matters for the purposes of the tale is Anson's comment before the game: Cyclone Young, he declared, was "just another big farmer." By Young's account, that dismissal cut him deeply, and he went to the box determined to show Anson up. As the game proceeded, the Colts, hoping to unsettle the farmer, lavished a fiery dose of major league vituperation upon him. But nothing upset the imperturbable rookie, who was "as cool as though he were home in Canton."[7] Though some stories go so far as to report that he managed to strike the great Anson out, the box score shows otherwise. But the Colts' leader was held hitless, and when the game was over, he approached Davis Hawley, offering to pay Cleveland a sizable sum, perhaps as much as $1,000, for the young pitcher. Having just seen Young make fools of Anson's team, Hawley naturally enough refused the offer. A year later—here is the coda to the tale—with his Colts beginning to slip into what was to be a decade of mediocrity, rueful Anson stated that "if I had Young I'd win the championship in a walk."[8] Young himself savored the occasion for years. "I've won many more important games since then," he told a reporter fourteen years later, "but none that gave me half the satisfaction that victory did."[9]

The day was important for another reason. The Spider who caught Cyclone Young in his first major league game was Chief Zimmer, a player who may well have been the finest catcher of the 1890s and who was a friend of Young's for almost the next sixty years. In 1890 the twenty-nine-year-old Zimmer set baseball writers clucking by being the first catcher in history to handle more than 100 games in a season. His success at throwing out base runners was already well known. At first Zimmer's ability astonished Young, who had become accustomed at Canton to working with catchers who could not cope with his speed. Though standing closer to the plate than most backstops of his era and wearing, as Young described it, "an ordinary dress glove with sole-leather tips sewed on the fingers," Zimmer handled the rookie's shoots with apparent ease.[10] By some accounts (but it's an anecdote attached to many catchers who handled fastball pitchers) he gave his calloused hand further protection by padding his glove with beefsteak. As Young's career progressed, no major league pitcher was more outspoken than he in expressing how much a fine catcher enhanced his performance on the mound. Young and Zimmer quickly became the most famous battery of the 1890s.

As long as the Spiders remained at home, Young continued to win. But when the team took to the road after mid-August, his fortunes turned. Perhaps the fatigue of rail travel and grimy hotels affected him. Perhaps the tendency of nineteenth-century umpires to give close calls to the home club cost him an edge. We may be confident that as major league hitters saw more of the rookie, they quickly made some adjustments to the heat of his speed and the dinkiness of his curve. In any case, Cyclone Young stumbled, and by mid-September he had an overall losing record.

In an era of small pitching staffs Cyclone Young quickly saw and even faced some of the outstanding hurlers of the day. On September 1 he lost 5–0 to New York's hard-throwing star Amos Rusie. On September 11 he lost by the same score to Chicago's Bill Hutchison, who probably savored his revenge. But Cyclone Young enjoyed some victories too, including a 5–4 triumph over Boston's sensational rookie hurler Kid Nichols. Another satisfying game occurred on September 18, when Cleveland shifted a home match to Canton, hoping to profit from the city's enthusiasm for the talented rookie it had graduated. Many of Young's Canton fans turned out to cheer him on in a game he finally won by a score of 11–10. (This victory brought Young's pitching record back to even, at 6–6; never again would his career record fall below .500.) On balance, Young was impressive—"possessing more skill than any youngster seen here this season," read one newspaper account.[11] And Young certainly ended his rookie year with a bang. On the last day of the season the Spiders had a home doubleheader against Philadelphia. With nothing at stake except pride, Young, having won the first game 5–1, persuaded his manager to let him handle the second as well. It too was a victory, by a score of 7–3. Though pitching both ends of a doubleheader was far from unknown in this era, Young never attempted the feat again. His one go at it apparently persuaded him that there was a fine but important line between assertive self-confidence and career-threatening bravado.

When Cyclone Young returned home to Gilmore in October for a winter of farm chores and rail-splitting, he had a signed contract for the 1891 season in his pocket. The club's readiness to pay him $1,430 for the coming year showed that though he had been with the Spiders for less than two months, he had already established himself as the team's most promising new pitcher. Additionally, at some point very early in his Spider career—possibly on the signing of his first full-year contract—he received a gift of stock in Cuyahoga Savings and Loan, Davis Hawley's company, which he held for the rest of his life. We now calculate Young's won-lost record for 1890 as 9–7; at the time it was reckoned as 10–7, though it's important to note that the won-lost record of pitchers was not a carefully scrutinized statistic in the 1890s.[12] Whichever count is used, Cyclone Young was the only Spider pitcher with a winning record in the 1890 season. The other conventional mark of a pitcher's ability is his earned run average. Although this figure was not regularly derived before the second decade of the twentieth century, knowledgeable observers were able to distinguish roughly between hurlers who were good at preventing runs and those who were not, and some sporting publications printed the cruder statistic of earned runs per game. Recent calculations of earned run averages for nineteenth-century pitchers give Young a figure of 3.47, the second lowest on the Spider staff. Perhaps the most important consideration for the club owners in renewing Young's contract was the improvement in the team's play after Young joined them. Through August 5 the Spiders had won only 25 games and lost 61, for a percentage of .291. With Cyclone Young on the team they improved dramatically and, buoyed by a 10-game winning steak in September, managed to go 19 and 27 for the rest of the season, a pace of .413. They still finished in seventh place, a dismal 43½ games behind the pennant-winning Brooklyn Bridegrooms. But in the final stages of the season they were outdrawing their Players League rivals; Frank Robison might now believe that the Spiders could win in the competition for the Cleveland market.

Still, the season was hardly outstanding. Cyclone Young's road record was a disheartening 1–6. His earned run average, impressive for a member of the Spider staff, loses some of its luster when compared to the broader universe of all National League pitchers, who in aggregate managed an average of 3.56. While in the Tri-State League Young's strikeouts had exceeded his walks by eight to one, in the National League he struck out only 39 and walked 30. (I attribute the decline in this conventional index of control to the greater ability of major league batters to lay off fast pitches out of the strike zone.) Even his fielding was faulty. Though one newspaper commended him for his ability to cover first base on ground balls wide of the bag, his reported fielding average was a risible .796.[13] In sum, the dilution of talent in the major leagues in 1890 had afforded Young an early chance to test his ability at the highest level of competition, and his performance had earned him the right to return to the majors; but little so far had stamped him as a future star.

A word about the Spiders is now in order, for in 1891 the outstanding team that the club would be putting in the field on a daily basis—barring injuries—for much of the remaining decade began to take recognizable shape. Two of its members were already in harness when Cy Young arrived—Chief Zimmer and the powerful shortstop Ed McKean.[14] The dissolution of the Players League over the winter of 1890–91 not only eliminated intracity competition that had cost both clubs $60,000 in 1890, but allowed Frank Robison to acquire two players who had been popular with the now-defunct Cleveland entry in that circuit: the fleet Jimmy McAleer, thought by some to be the greatest defensive outfielder of his generation, and the foul-mouthed Patsy Tebeau, who had managed the Spiders' rivals during part of the 1890 season. To bolster the infield the Spiders pursued the American Association batting star Cupid Childs and then won a court fight over their rights to the pudgy second baseman's services.[15] In August of 1891 they added a final offensive cog by acquiring the contract of Jesse Burkett; it took Burkett three years to hit his stride, but he then became the greatest of the Spider hitters. Robison, meanwhile, expected a great deal from the coming 1891 season; he was opening a new home ballpark a bit further out along his trolley line, and he was counting on his team of able players to attract crowds to the new sports palace. And while there was still good reason to doubt that Frank Robison's money had assembled a team capable of winning the National League pennant, many observers believed that he had at least created a team that was— to quote a New York newspaper—"both dangerous and uncertain."[16]

The Spiders traveled to Jacksonville, Florida for spring training in 1891. The practice of sending a team south to limber up muscles and refine skills was far from universal in this era. But ever since Cap Anson had begun experimenting with Southern spring training many deemed it advantageous. For Cyclone Young a trip south was a new adventure, and especially useful since he was recovering from the effects of "a severe attack of fever," later identified as typhoid fever, contracted during the off-season.[17] The Cleveland team looked good in Florida, winning six of nine games with Pittsburgh.[18] Having enjoyed his first spring-training trip, Cyclone Young participated for the first time in major league season-opening ceremonies. All of it was new to him—the uniformed procession by horse-drawn coach from hotel to ballpark, the speeches from political notables, the persistent blare of local bands. Cleveland happened to be opening its season in Cincinnati, and so it is descriptions of the Cincinnati opening that I draw on, but similar festivities marked the return of baseball to cities around the league and the association. Young has left no record of his reactions to these events, but he was likely to have been delighted by the rituals that marked the annual revival of baseball.

Cyclone Young began the official season well. Pitching the season opener on April 22, he rewarded manager Bob Leadley with a 6–3 victory over the Reds. Pitching Cleveland's home opener on May 1—the game that inaugurated action in Frank Robison's new League Park and drew a crowd of eighty-three hundred people—he again took the measure of Cincinnati, this time by a score of 8–3. Only one of the Reds' runs was earned. "I wouldn't have lost that game for $100," Young was soon quoted as saying.[19] On June 1, in defeating Boston and Kid Nichols by a score of 6–1, he pitched his finest game of the year and the fourth consecutive game in which he allowed only a single earned run. There were, of course, bumps. He had an occasional bad outing, and on May 9 he was, for the first time in his major league career, lifted from a game. Sometimes he was ill-served by his teammates; on May 11, for example, the Spiders committed 10 errors and a month later they bobbled 11 chances. Still, by the end of June, ordinarily pitching with three days of rest between each start, he had won 12 games and lost 9. During July Young improved even on this record, winning 7 while losing only 2 and scoring his nineteenth victory on July 30. Meanwhile, on July 14 he defeated the first-place New York Giants 10–2, and on July 17, facing the Reds' Tony Mullane, he hit his first major league home run—an inside-the-park blow that aided his 12–8 victory over Cincinnati. With speed, endurance, composure, and intelligence, Cyclone Young was winning a reputation as one of the National League's best hurlers, and the press reported that the Spider management, in recognition of his good work, was extending him "extra compensation for every game he pitches out of his regular turn."[20]

August, however, was another story. While players' slumps are always mysterious, I am inclined to associate Young's faltering with a change in managers that Frank Robison engineered the second week in July. A few weeks before Cyclone Young had arrived in Cleveland in 1890 Bob Leadley had assumed direction of the floundering Spiders. The subsequent improvement in the team's record, which owed much to Young's success, also reflected well on Leadley and he was rehired for the 1891 season. But after a good start in the new season, the team sputtered. Frank Robison had reacquired Patsy Tebeau in anticipation of such a downturn, and when at midseason the Spiders found themselves unable to climb up from the middle of the standings, Robison replaced Leadley with Tebeau. But whatever difficulties Leadley may have been having with certain players, players, he had had none with Cyclone Young, who gave him a quality start every fourth day. I am guessing that Young appreciated the confidence and reciprocated the respect.

Initially, Young pitched well for Tebeau, too. But with his first start in August a dry spell began. When Young had lost four in a row—and even though the last of those four was a well-pitched 3–2 defeat—Tebeau took him out of the starting rotation, assigning him instead to relief duties. For three straight appearances, over the course of eleven calendar days, Young was called upon only to complete games that others had started. Whatever Tebeau may have intended, Cyclone Young could only interpret the move as a sign that his manager no longer had confidence in him. After all, in this era no hurlers were groomed as relief specialists. For over six weeks Young struggled. Though he finally picked up his twentieth win on August 19 and a twenty-first on September 1, at the middle of September his once-shining record had fallen to a disheartening 21–22. By now Young was going public with his discontent, complaining that he was "being used to pitch out the fag end of losing games," declaring that his salary was "far too small" (this complaint may reflect bonus opportunities lost when Tebeau didn't start him), and speculating whether he might not be happier playing for some other team.[21]

But that's not all. I suspect that Young's disenchantment may have an additional explanation. Tebeau urged a confrontational style of play upon the Spiders. A scrapper himself, he sought to infuse in each player a fierce sense of enmity toward all opponents, and under his direction the Spiders raised rowdiness to an art form. To Tebeau a game was a battle; he expressed this attitude in his pronouncement that "a milk and water, goody-goody player can't ever wear a Cleveland uniform," and in his challenge, "Show me a team of fighters, and I'll show you a team that has a chance."[22] One of his primary weapons was vituperation, and the Spiders under his tutelage became famous as the foulest-mouthed team in baseball. To Tebeau, being occasionally expelled from a game for "kicking"—the term of the day—was a badge of honor.

On August 17 at Cincinnati, in the fourth of Young's consecutive losses, a vicious fight broke out between the Spiders and the Reds. Fists and even bats were used as weapons. It was necessary for the Spiders' treasurer to join the civilian peacemakers on the field before the fray was ended. Press accounts of the fight mention Jimmy McAleer, Cupid Childs, Ed McKean, Lee Viau (from the bench), and even the mild-tempered Chief Zimmer as participants in the brawl. But not Cyclone Young. Even though he was the pitcher, Young apparently did not join the fight. This is not surprising, since his aversion to uncivil behavior was already a matter of record. *Sporting Life* had reported in June that he would "rather lose ten ball games than do an ungentlemanly act on the ball field."[23] It seems plausible that Tebeau sent Young to the bullpen after this game not because it was Young's fourth consecutive loss but because he wanted the pitcher to reflect upon his calm response to frustration. Tebeau was acting not simply on a want of confidence in his hurler but also on a hope of reeducating him.

If Tebeau was fighting for control of Young's conscience and sense of prudence, he lost the contest. To be sure, Young was a fighter—intense, driven, relentless, his language could be as colorful as anyone else's. But he fought through his pitching, not his punching. He did not hold to the notion that, either in baseball or in life, violence was an appropriate response to disappointment. It took Tebeau several months to accept this truth about Young. In 1891 he came close to losing him for the team. But ultimately the manager accepted Young's way, and never again in his decade-long tenure as Young's manager did he use the pitcher in three consecutive relief appearances. It was this reconcilation between a strong-willed manager and a resolute pitcher that, more than any other factor, made Cleveland a strong team for the next six years.

The reconcilation occurred during the final two and a half weeks of the season. For all of his energy, Tebeau was not getting better ball playing from the Spiders. In fact, under Tebeau's direction the team slipped below the .500 benchmark that had been Leadley's legacy. But just as mysteriously as it had descended, Cyclone Young's slump lifted. The resurgence began on September 17 as Cleveland was completing an eastern swing. First Brooklyn and then Pittsburgh fell before his fastball. After the Spiders returned home Young's success continued—against Cincinnati, Chicago (twice), and Pittsburgh. He won all of his final six starts, never yielded more than 5 runs in a game, and finished the year with 27 wins, the highest total posted by any pitcher representing a Cleveland major league team since Jim McCormick won 28 in 1883. We will probably never know what exchanges occurred between Tebeau and Young during Young's six weeks of misery, nor whether Robison intervened. But from mid-September of 1891 onward, for the rest of Patsy Tebeau's tenure as manager of the Spiders, Cyclone Young was Tebeau's money pitcher. And on September 24, with the grievances of August now put to rest, Young signed a contract for 1892 raising his salary by almost $600, to $2,000, and allaying rumors that he might join a new Chicago team in the American Association the following year.

There is a story within the story of the preceding paragraph. As the 1891 pennant chase moved into its final three weeks, the race had been reduced to a two-team battle. The Chicago Colts held the lead, and the Boston Beaneaters were challenging. Historical attention has usually focused on the events surrounding Boston's remarkable charge, as the club reeled off 18 straight victories and stormed past the Colts to take the flag. Many observers smelled a fix: too many of Boston's foes seemed to be obligingly rolling over for the Beaneaters—especially the New York Giants, who conveniently benched their two star pitchers, butchered easy plays in the field, ran the bases as if drunk, and handed the Beaneaters four straight apparently undeserved victories. Concurrent with Boston's surge, however, was Chicago's tumble. And no one pushed the Colts harder than Cyclone Young. On September 28 he outpitched Bill Hutchison 4–2. Two days later he defeated Ad Gumbert 12–5. "Old Cy Young," Leonard Washburne commented, "messed up Anson's pennant plans."[24] Whatever shenanigans may have been going on in the East, the teams were playing it straight in the West. And Cyclone Young was demonstrating that he was back on his game.

When Young returned to Tuscarawas County for the off-season, to help on his father's farm, play ball with friends and neighbors, and resume his courting of the barely twenty-year-old Robba Miller, he had ample reason to feel pleased with his work. Among Spider hurlers he had been by far the best. Ed Beatin had been released before the season ended, Henry Gruber had struggled, and Lee Viau, at 18–17, was the only other Cleveland pitcher who had managed to compile a winning record. Therefore, to evaluate Young's achievement, a wider field of comparison is necessary. Only four pitchers in the National League—Hutchison with 44, John Clarkson and Amos Rusie with 33, and Kid Nichols with 30—had posted more victories than Young's 27. Only two pitchers—Hutchison and Rusie—had appeared in more games than Young's 55. Only two pitchers—again Hutchison and Rusie—had been responsible for a higher proportion of their teams' victories than Young's 42 percent. Young's earned run average of 2.85 was seventh best in the league. Despite the greater concentration of National League batting talent following the demise of the Players League, Cyclone Young had demonstrated a remarkable durability and performed at a level that almost justified Cleveland sportswriter Charles Mears's preseason prediction that Young would be "the star of the League too."[25]

Still, it had not been a truly grand year. First, there was the disappointing Spiders' performance. Though their capture of fifth place represented the second-best finish ever achieved by a Cleveland major league team, the Spiders had once again finished below .500. Second, there was Cy Young's dreadful late-season slump. Of Young's 13 decisions between August 1 and September 15 only 2 were wins. Since he had not yet learned that all athletes endure arid spells, we can assume that it bothered him deeply. Third, there was the continuing problem with his control. With 140 walks on his record Young was not exactly a wild pitcher. Amos Rusie, for example, a genuinely erratic hurler, had walked 262 batters. But by way of contrast, Kid Nichols had provided a model of what Young might aspire to, allowing only 103 bases on balls in almost the same number of innings. Young knew that since he did not have the sharp curve that Rusie used to complement his fastball, he would need to refine his control to keep his pitches away from batters' strengths.

In saying this, I admit to a bit of guessing. Young left no account of his thoughts at this time. But one of the remarkable trends that leaps out from the printed form of Cy Young's year-by-year statistical record is the downward movement in his annual bases on balls totals. Never again would he even approach 140, within three years he would be below triple digits, and by the end of the decade he would be celebrated as baseball's foremost control pitcher. This trend was not the result of accident. Nor, in an era when pitching coaches were unheard of was it the product of skilled guidance. Rather, it was the outcome of determined hard work. Throughout his career Cy Young was constantly applying his intelligence to improving his mound work. The decision to focus upon control difficulties after 1891 is an early example of that application of intelligence to problems.

A note on names is now in order. By the end of the 1891 season baseball writers were beginning to use "Cy" as the nickname for Dent Young. "Cyclone Young" would still make occasional appearances, even into 1892, but the shorter version was now dominant. In later life Cy Young always explained that the nickname was an abbreviated form of "Cyclone," and it is easy to trace the terminological transformation in the baseball press of 1891. But why did "Cyclone," a colorful, pointed, and suggestive nickname yield to a shorter form? I suspect—matters of convenience aside—that the move to "Cy" was rooted in that name's bucolic echoes. Dent Young came into professional baseball straight from the farm; he dressed like a farmer; Cap Anson had mocked him as a farmer; the press occasionally reported that, like a rube, he chased fire engines or revealed an unfamiliarity with the more sophisticated ways of urban life.[26] When baseball writers didn't call him "Cyclone Young," they more often than not employed "Farmer Young." Baseball in the 1890s was still very much an urban sport, so that a giant player from the agricultural hinterlands was something of an anomaly. "Cy" at this time was a common nickname for a hayseed. Thus, it is my guess that the consensual acceptance of "Cy" represents both a typographic abbreviation of "Cyclone" and a conceptual conflation of stormy speed and rustic roots.

Over the fall and winter before the 1892 season, major league baseball underwent another shake-out. The wobbly American Association, relegated by and large to midwestern and midsouthern urban areas ignored by the National League, finally collapsed, bequeathing four of its eight teams—those in St. Louis, Baltimore, Louisville, and Washington—to an enlarged National League. The demise of the association meant that in the course of just two years the number of major league teams had fallen from twenty-four in three circuits to twelve in one. This development had two important consequences. First, it meant that the number of places available at the top level for aspiring baseball players had been cut in half. On the assumption that the less talented players were weeded out, we may conclude that the quality of play at the major league level in 1892 was significantly better than it had been just two years earlier. Second, the amalgamation of all major league clubs into one circuit, all of whose members employed contracts with reserve clauses, meant that teams no longer needed to outbid rivals for the best players.[27] After several years in which players had dominated wage negotiations, the leverage now shifted back to the owners, who wanted in future contracts to lower their players' wages and return their clubs to greater profitability. The hope to make more money also led them to increase the length of the season from 140 to 154 games. And, fearful that a twelve-team pennant chase might leave too many clubs out of the running—and too many cities unable to sustain adequate fan interest throughout the season—the owners decided to adopt a split season. There would be a "Spring Series" pennant race, ending in July, and a "Fall Series" race, ending in October. If, as everyone hoped, this schedule produced two different winners, the two clubs would meet in a postseason playoff analogous to the World Series that had pitted National League and American Association winners against each other for several years in the 1880s.

When Cy Young reported to Hot Springs, Arkansas, for spring practice in mid-March of 1892, there was an important new face in camp—Nig Cuppy's. Having earned a shot at the majors on the basis of a baffling set of slow pitches and an irritating inclination to take his time between deliveries, Cuppy promptly became the complement to Young that Cleveland needed in order to be truly competitive. Before Cuppy's arm soured late in the decade, he and Young would establish themselves as the winningest pitching duo of the 1890s.[28] Meanwhile, despite snow in Arkansas, the Spiders rounded impressively into shape, leading the *Cleveland Plain Dealer* to declare that the 1892 club was the "best team Cleveland has had in many seasons."[29] Young predicted he would play a major role. "The old arm," he explained, "is as good as ever now."[30]

Cy Young opened his third season with a bang, holding Cincinnati scoreless on April 15. This shutout—his first after 36 major league victories—was also the first of his 76 career whitewashes. It provoked comment, largely because the *Reach Guide* had recently speculated that an absence of shutouts so deep into a successful career was "probably the only case of its kind on record."[31] Success followed on success. He won his first four decisions, extending a two-season winning streak to ten games. On April 25 he defeated Chicago in a twelve-inning game and drove in four of the Spider runs. On May 6 he pitched another shutout, this one against Baltimore. On May 17 he held Louisville to two hits in a 9–0 ballgame. On May 21 he was involved in a bizarre "doubleheader." When the St. Louis Browns failed to arrive at the ballpark on time, the umpire signaled Young to throw a pitch and, when the pitcher had complied, declared the game forfeit to Cleveland. (In accordance with the scoring rules of the day, this game does not count in Young's victory record.) But the Browns arrived shortly thereafter, and in order to avoid refunding the gate, the two clubs agreed to play another game. Young yielded 4 runs in the first inning and lost 4–1, his second defeat of the year. Still, by the evening of May 27 he had won 10 games, 4 of them shutouts (he was making up for lost time), and had lost only 2. Ordinarily it was his "great speed" that carried him to victory, but even when velocity was missing he won with a "dinky" curve.[32] Cy Young was close to unbeatable, and almost singlehandedly he was keeping a Cleveland team that was 8 and 12 in games he did not start respectably in the chase.

At that point a slump set in. As Cleveland circled through the east, Boston, Washington (twice), and Brooklyn handed Young defeats. The first of these was a tough loss. Dueling with John Clarkson he held Boston scoreless through nine innings, but weakened in the tenth inning and lost 4–0. (As was often the case in the 1890s, the home team chose to bat first.) The other three losses were deserved; Washington rapped him for 15 hits and Brooklyn for 14. "Old Cy," declared the *Plain Dealer*, "is breaking a great many hearts."[33] But as Young faltered, Cuppy hit his stride, and so the Spiders' hopes for a 'Spring Series' pennant remained alive. And despite the four-game slide, when the *Sporting News* first published its calculation of "Av earned runs per game by Opp" in mid-June, Young stood second in the league, behind Jack Stivetts.[34]

Late in June the Spiders arrived in St. Louis hoping to improve their record in a series against one of the league's more inept teams. But in Ted Breitenstein the Browns had a very fine pitcher, and on the afternoon of the 24th, Young hooked up with this wily lefthander. As early as April, Young had voiced his respect for the southpaw: "No one," he opined, "is going to hit young Breitenstein of St. Louis very hard. He hasn't much speed, but he's got a quick and wide curve difficult to find"[35] The one thousand spectators saw a memorable game. St. Louis scored single runs in the second and fourth innings; Cleveland came back with single runs in the fourth and ninth. Knotted at 2–2, the game went into extra innings. For five additional innings both pitchers labored as if invincible. Finally, in the top of the fifteenth inning the Browns broke through to take a 3–2 lead. But in the bottom of the fifteenth Cleveland tied the game again and was prevented from winning only by a spectacular running catch of a long fly off the bat of Jesse Burkett with Cy Young on second base. The two hurlers then resumed their mastery, posting goose eggs in the sixteenth inning. At that point, daylight failing and Young having allowed only five hits, umpire Tim Hurst called the magnificent duel to a close. In later years Young sometimes included this outing on a short list of his greatest games.[36]

When the Spring Series pennant race ended on July 13, the Boston Beaneaters claimed the crown. Even though the Spiders had performed creditably, winning 40 games and losing 33 for a percentage of .548, they had finished 11½ games off Boston's torrid pace and isolated in fifth place in a twelve-team league. Though Young had lost three of his last four decisions, he had finished the first half of the season with a fine record of 15 victories and 9 defeats. With 13 wins and 7 losses, Nig Cuppy had performed almost as well. That's why Frank Robison decided to spend money to acquire a third strong pitcher for the second half of the season—someone who could give Cleveland a consistently strong three-man rotation and make the Spiders competitive with the Beaneaters. Here Robison got lucky. The club owners had been waiting for their opportunity to pare back payrolls. During the July break between the pennant races Boston chose to drop John Clarkson, who, though pulling in a high salary, had managed only an 8–6 record for the high-flying Beaneaters. Frank Robison promptly snatched him up, hoping that, as Cleveland's third starter, he could recover some of the craftiness that had already earned him 287 career victories since his major league debut in 1882. The dope on Clarkson was that he had a tender ego and wilted when deprived of praise; Robison and Tebeau were prepared to lavish commendation upon the hurler if that's what it took to restore the Clarkson magic of old.

From the opening of the Fall Series, the Spiders were in the hunt. A victory by Cy Young on August 1 secured sole possession of first place for them. After dropping back into a tie with Boston, they slipped in front again on August 9 with another Young victory. Thereafter the Spiders began to pull away. During August they won 20 of 25 games. By September 6, cruising along with 33 victories and 11 defeats, Cleveland held a

7-game lead over Boston. Thereafter, their pace eased somewhat and the Beaneaters made a powerful run, winning 14 of their last 16 games. But when the curtain fell on the Fall Series pennant race, the Cleveland Spiders, with a record of 53 wins and 23 losses, sat atop the National League, claiming the flag for the first time in the major league history of a Forest City club. They had prevailed despite a scheduling quirk that gave Cleveland only 36 home games during the second season and Boston 42. Boston's late drive had left the Beaneaters 3 games off the pace, with the Brooklyn Bridegrooms, at 9½ games out, a nonchallenging third. Frank Robison's ambition to bring championship baseball to Cleveland had been fulfilled.

A team that plays at a .697 clip must have more than one good pitcher. But even though Cuppy (at 15 and 6) and Clarkson (at 17 and 10) performed well, vindicating Robison's confidence in them both, it was Cy Young who dazzled. During the course of the Fall Series pennant race Young triumphed 21 times and lost only 3 times. Between August 23 and October 8 he won 13 straight decisions. In none of his last 16 starts did he yield more than 2 earned runs. During the course of the second season he defeated every team in the league except New York and Washington; in the process he bested some of the league's finest hurlers—Bill Hutchison, Kid Nichols, Tim Keefe, Ed Stein, Sadie McMahon, Red Ehret, Jack Stivetts, and Ted Breitenstein. On August 4, by defeating Louisville, he won his 20th victory. On September 19, defeating Pittsburgh, he reached the 30-victory mark for the first time. He prevailed under all sorts of conditions. On July 24, for example, he defeated Philadelphia even though his defense committed 6 errors. On August 12 he defeated Chicago even though his offense provided him with only two runs. On August 23 he defeated Philadelphia when his outfielders accepted $5 fine for stalling in order to let him recover his wind after he tried to score on a close play at the plate. On September 5 he defeated Philadelphia despite a game delay occasioned by a cushion-throwing frenzy among the spectators. On October 5 he defeated Cincinnati in weather so cold that only 100 fans paid to see the game. When the 1892 season was over, he had recorded 36 wins and only 12 defeats. Most of the year he was, as the *Plain Dealer* so eloquently put it, "a sealed mystery to the . . . batters."[37] There were occasional periods during Cy Young's career when he became transcendentally good. The fall season of 1892 marks the first of these occasions.

According to plans laid before the season began, Cleveland's victory triggered a postseason championship competition between the winners of the Spring Series and the Fall Series. Initially the Boston club management was reluctant to play, fearing that by accepting the Cleveland challenge they would fortify the rumor that the outcomes of baseball games were rigged. This concern arose from the allegation made during the second season that the Beaneaters were deliberately losing games—"hippodroming," in the colorful language of the day—in order to assure themselves of a postseason engagement and the income from such a championship series. With memories of the club's tainted triumph of 1891 in mind, Boston's directors were inclined to forgo a championship series. Three influential groups drove the directors to change their mind. First, there were their own players, incredulous that they were to be denied the opportunity to make some extra money. Second, there were the nation's baseball fans (or at least the sportswriters who spoke on their behalf), who could only interpret the Beaneaters' reluctance as a sign of fear. Finally, there were the other league owners, and especially Frank Robison, who wanted to see a season of financial retrenchment and waning fan interest end on a high note rather than mired in another controversy. So, bowing to league pressure (and probably glad to do so), the Boston directors permitted the championship series to go forward, the winner to be the first team to take five games.

The Beaneaters were a strong club. Managed by future Hall of Famer Frank Selee, they had come into 1892 as the defending league champion, and four of their players—Hugh Duffy, King Kelly, Tommy McCarthy, and Kid Nichols—later also made the Hall of Fame. Their impressive three-man rotation featured two 35-game winners in Kid Nichols and Jack Stivetts and a 22-game winner in Harry Staley. If Nichols had the lowest earned run average on the team, Stivetts could boast of a no-hitter pitched against Brooklyn in August. The Beaneaters were not a hard-hitting team, but they played solid ball and had no obvious weaknesses. Despite the Spiders' remarkable second season, most observers—moved perhaps by Boston's late-season charge and the suspicion that Nichols-Staley-Stivetts were better than Clarkson-Cuppy-Young—thought the Beaneaters the stronger team. Tebeau may have agreed. "We are not claiming to be equal to the big task of beating the Bostons," he declared, "but we will do our best."[38]

The "World's Series" (the term first used in the 1880s for postseason championship play) opened at midafternoon on October 11 before 6,000 fans in Cleveland, with Cy Young facing Jack Stivetts.[39] Just before Stivetts delivered the opening pitch (note that the home team batted first), King Kelly declaimed: "Let the dance go on."[40] When that dance ended two hours later, virtually everyone interested in baseball agreed that it had been one of the greatest games of all time. Defense was outstanding on both sides, with Hermann Long robbing Cupid Childs, and Jim Mc-Aleer robbing Hugh Duffy. Chief Zimmer picked one runner off first and threw two others out trying to steal second. Meanwhile, both pitchers were magnificent. Boston threatened in the fourth inning when Duffy reached third base with two outs. But Young then struck out Kelly. An inning later Bobby Lowe reached third base in similar circumstances, but Young retired Joe Quinn on a ground ball. For their part, the Spiders failed to push a runner past second until the ninth. Then, with one out, Jesse Burkett beat out a bunt and advanced to second on a single by George Davis. When McKean grounded into a close force play at second, inspiring an altercation at the bag, Burkett crept off third and then dashed toward home, hoping to take advantage of the distracted Quinn. But an accurate throw to Kelly nailed Burkett and ended the inning. In the bottom of the ninth Kelly again became the center of attention, calling out "instructions" from the Boston bench in an effort to confuse the Spiders' field play on a pop-up. His widely condemned prank failed to induce an error, and so the game went into extra frames. In October, however, the hours of daylight were not as ample as at midseason, and after two more darkening and pitcher-dominated innings, umpire Bob Emslie called the game. Stivetts and Young had opened the series with an 11-inning 0–0 tie. Young had allowed 5 hits, struck out 6, and walked none. Stivetts had allowed 4 hits, struck out 7, and walked 4. (In some accounts of this wonderful and exhausting contest Kid Nichols is identified as the Boston pitcher. There would, I suppose, be a poetic aptness to having Nichols as Young's foe; they were, after all, great rivals of the 1890s. But the honor belongs to Stivetts.) Over eleven years later, a few months before pitching his perfect game, Young said of his duel with Stivetts, "all things considered that was my greatest game."[41]

From there on out, however, the World's Series was a disaster for the Spiders. In the second game Harry Staley, aided by a base-running mistake by McAleer, defeated John Clarkson, 5–4. In the third game Young and Stivetts again faced off. The rematch was another close game, but with a critical double, Stivetts positioned himself to score the winning run in a 3–2 victory. With Cleveland down by two games the teams took a day off to travel to Boston for the next three contests. On October 21 Kid Nichols shut Cleveland down completely, besting Nig Cuppy 4–0. The next day John Clarkson blew a 6–0 lead to hand Stivetts a 12–7 victory. That left matters up to Young. But bothered by tenderness in his throwing arm, Young was not optimistic, remarking matter-of-factly before the game that he'd either win or spend the winter "splitting rails by the hundreds."[42] The latter option quickly became the operative one, as Young struggled in the cold weather before a paltry crowd and, unable to hold a 3–0 lead, lost to Nichols 8–3. The Series belonged to Boston. It is true that it turned into a rout only after George Davis was driven from the Spider line-up by an injury and after Cleveland had the ill luck of being unable to turn even one of the first three well-played games into a victory. Still, by sweeping five straight contests the Beaneaters had left no doubt that the champions of 1891 were still baseball's strongest team in 1892.[43] A disappointed Frank Robison was reduced to warning the Beaneaters: "Never mind, boys, we'll go at you harder in 1893."[44]

The World's Series notwithstanding, Cy Young was baseball's big story in 1892. In fact, 1892 may have been the greatest season of his career. (I will make a similarly qualified statement for four other seasons.) Cy Young stood first among league pitchers in five important categories—victories (36—a title he shared with Bill Hutchison),[45] winning percentage (.750), earned run average (1.93), shutouts pitched (9), and the on-base percentage of opposing batters (.266). The first four of these figures represented categories understood in Young's day, and so, though the numbers were sometimes improperly calculated and presented, the impact of his achievement was recognized. Young's 13-game winning streak was to be the longest of his career, and when one adds in the games prior to his last loss before the streak began, it turns out that between July 30 and October 8 he won 19 games and lost only 1. His total of 36 victories was—though no one of course could know this at the time—the highest seasonal figure he would ever reach. Cy Young had been a good pitcher in 1891, but he was a great one in 1892.

  It is possible to highlight the area in which Young's improvement lay. During the 1891 season Young had given up 9.17 hits for every nine innings he pitched. In 1892 he improved that figure significantly, yielding only 7.21 hits per nine innings pitched. The same improvement can be seen in bases on balls allowed. In 1891 Young had granted 2.98 walks every nine innings; in 1892 he improved that figure to 2.34 walks per nine innings. Putting the two improvements together, we can see that

Young was allowing almost two and two-thirds fewer base runners per game in 1892. That's a significant reduction in potential run-scorers.

One might assume that coaching from veteran John Clarkson accounted for the difference between Young's Spring Series record of 15–9 and his Fall Series record of 21–3. But the rate at which he issued walks shrank only slightly in the second season while the rate at which he allowed hits actually increased by a small amount. Statistically, these changes are insignificant. This is not to say that Young learned nothing from Clarkson. On the contrary, Clarkson showed Young how to improve his curve ball, advised him on ways to sharpen control, and prodded him to think about pitching strategy. Many years later Young declared unequivocally that Clarkson had helped him become a better pitcher. But the evidence clearly shows that Cy Young in 1892 was, from his opening shutout in April to his October record of allowing only 2 earned runs in 28 innings of pitching, a dominant hurler. The difference between his first-half record and his second-half record is probably best attributed to fortune—an occasional turn of bad luck in the Spring Series, an occasional turn of good luck in the Fall Series. He was helped by Patsy Tebeau's willingness to use three main starters supplemented by a fourth starter when games piled up. With Nig Cuppy performing solidly throughout the year (Cuppy ended the season with a 28–13 record) and John Clarkson pitching consistently during the second season, Tebeau could allow Young adequate time for recuperation between starts. On 22 occasions the manager gave Young three intervening days of rest between appearances, on 18 other occasions he sent him to the box with two intervening days, and never did he ask Young to start games on successive days. Perhaps this is why several baseball writers concurred with the *Plain Dealer* that "Cy Young has more speed this season than ever."[46] When Cy Young's mustachioed likeness graced the front page of the *Sporting News* on December 10, 1892, it was a confirmation of his newfound prominence among the elite of baseball.

By the time that sketch appeared, Cy Young's personal life had changed in an important way. On November 8, 1892, after several years of courtship, he married Robba Miller. According to an account he gave fifty-five years later, the couple had waited until he had put enough money away in the bank; returning to Ohio after the 1892 season with $1,000 in his pocket, a vast amount for the Tuscarawas hills, he was finally ready to marry "the girl on the farm next door."[47] Robba had recently turned twenty-one. Small in stature, she was a tomboy, an avid hunter, and a crack shot. After launching their marriage with a honeymoon in the East, the newlyweds returned to Gilmore, probably living with Cy Young's parents on the Young farm. All the evidence suggests that this was a firm and sustaining union, and that throughout their lives Cy and Robba Young enjoyed each other's company.

꒰꒱

CHAPTER THREE

The Birth of the Modern
Pitching Regime

DURING THE OFF-SEASON between 1892 and 1893 the major league owners approved a change in playing rules that created the modern pitching regime. In brief, the change moved the pitcher five feet farther from the batter, establishing the dimensions of the modern baseball diamond. But this rule change was far more than that cursory explanation suggests. To understand the impact of the new rule, we need to look abstractly at the game of baseball from the viewpoint of generic competition.

Baseball is a point game; that is to say, the side that scores the most points wins. In this respect it differs from competitions like racing, where the task is to cover a specified distance faster than your opponent, or chess, where victory goes to the competitor who manages to capture a specific board piece of the opponent. Unlike most point games, however—and here the contrast with sports like basketball, football, and soccer is dramatic—the ball with which baseball is played does not itself tally the points. Indeed, the ball is usually nowhere near the player who makes a point.

Baseball is also a station-to-station game, in which the side on the offense tries to advance its players through four successive stations, earning a point only when it successfully pushes a player to the fourth station. Each offensive player begins his attempt to make a circuit of the stations by using a wooden club to try to hit balls thrown by one member of the defensive side. There are specified ways in which a hitter can be successful in trying to reach the first station (and thereby become a runner); and there are specified ways in which a runner can advance. When three offensive players have failed to meet these requirements, the side that has been hitting exchanges positions with the side that has been defending.

As this stylized description makes clear, the person who throws the ball to the hitter plays the central role in this game. (It is a mark of that truth that only for the thrower is a separate set of statistical records considered essential.) In the dawning moments of the game his task may actually have been to *enable* the hitter—that is, to be a player who, though standing on the field (like a member of the defense), has the responsibility of allowing the hitter to put the ball in play. Whether that speculation (which is not original with me) is accurate or not, the thrower's role vis-à-vis the hitter quickly became adversarial and has been so ever since. Every offensive player's chance to reach the first station begins with a confrontation between the thrower and the hitter. The thrower is charged with preventing hitters from reaching stations and, if they nevertheless succeed in gaining a station, with preventing them (as runners) from making a circuit of all four stations. The rules governing the relationship between the hitter and the thrower therefore require careful calibration, for if they tilt too heavily in favor of the thrower, games are devoid of offense and lack excitement. Likewise, if they favor the hitter too heavily, games are overly offensive and again lack excitement.

By the time Cy Young appeared on the baseball scene, most of the basic conventions of the game had been in effect for long enough to seem fixed. As early as the 1850s the rules specified: (1) that the stations ("bases") were 90 feet apart, located at the corners of an imaginary square, with the fourth station ("home plate") also serving as the starting point for the hitters ("batters"); (2) that each side consisted of nine players; (3) that batters could be retired if the ball they hit was caught on the fly; (4) that runners could be retired by being tagged with the ball while not in contact with a base they were entitled to or by failing to reach a base they were forced to occupy before a defensive player holding the ball got there; (5) that three offensive failures ("outs") compelled a team to relinquish its offensive opportunity to its opponent; and (6) that each team would have nine such scoring opportunities ("innings"), if needed. In short, baseball as played on the eve of the Civil War was already recognizably like baseball today.

The task, however, of finding the equilibrium point of maximal entertainment in the confrontation between pitcher and batter remained unresolved when Cy Young reached the majors. The matter was proving difficult not only because players, owners, fans, and commentators each came to rule-making deliberations with slightly different interests, but also because the conditions under which the game was played, the skills of the players involved, and even the tastes of spectators kept shifting. The previous quarter century had been marked by extensive experimentation. Sometimes the rules had tilted toward the pitchers, sometimes toward the batters. In one early year the National League batters had hit as poorly as .239, in another as robustly as .271; in one early year individual teams had averaged only 4½ runs per game, in another over 6. About all that might have been said about the matter in Cy Young's rookie year was that over the previous two-and-a-half decades the game's rulesmakers, in trying to discover the proper equilibrium, had left a bewildering pattern of apparently inconsistent changes in the legislation that defined the pitcher-batter confrontation.

Some of the changes in rules had tended to help the pitcher by liberating him. Certain rules, for example, defined what counted as a legal delivery. In 1868 pitchers were first permitted to take a step before releasing the ball, in 1872 they were first allowed to put spin on the ball (i.e., to curve it), and in 1884 they were first allowed to make their deliveries overhand. (It is a mark of baseball's conservative terminology that the thrower is called a "pitcher" even though the obligation to make underhand deliveries disappeared over a century ago.) Other rules described the strike zone. In 1887 batters lost the right to request "high" or "low" pitches and were forced instead to deal with an expansive strike zone that stretched across the full seventeen-inch width of the plate and extended from the bottom of their knees to the top of their shoulders.

But other changes tended to hurt the pitcher by confining him. Consider, for example, those designed to limit his ability to practice deception, obliging him instead (in 1879) to face the batter head-on when preparing to make a delivery, ruling out (in 1885) almost any hesitation or jerkiness not found in his regular delivery motion, and requiring him (in 1889) to hold the ball visibly in front of himself prior to pitching. Or consider the change that narrowed the width of the pitcher's box (from six feet to four feet in 1879), confining the pitcher's opportunity to take an angle on the batter. Or finally, consider those changes that steadily shrank the number of pitches outside of the strike zone (from nine in 1875 to four in 1889) that authorized a batter to take a base on balls. Because these changes—and others relating to where the batter should stand at the plate, what kind of bat he might use, and what constituted a foul ball—interacted with each other in complex ways from year to year, it would be inaccurate to suppose that the rules-makers were working systematically either to advantage or to disadvantage the pitcher. The effect instead was one of uncertainty.

The simplest and most important dimension of the confrontation between pitcher and batter was, of course, the sheer physical distance that separated them. At close quarters a pitcher throwing to intimidate a batter is virtually unhittable. At distant quarters a pitcher is a tepid lobbing machine. When the National League launched play in 1876, the pitcher was allowed to make his deliveries from a distance of 45 feet from the batter. Under this circumstance pitchers thrived and hitters languished, and so in 1881, after the league batting average had fallen 26 points in three years, that minimal distance was increased to 50 feet, and offense briefly surged. But thereafter the National League batting average tended again to move downward. By the end of the 1892 season the men who ran the game, noting that the steady decline in offense over the past four years had been accompanied by a decline in attendance and profits, were ready to believe that baseball needed another offensive kick.[1] A possible solution lay close at hand: push the pitcher still farther back.

And, with Frank Robison's full enthusiasm, that is what the owners did.[2] Several proposals for increasing the distance between the pitcher and the batter were considered over the winter of 1892–93, and the magnates chose one of the less radical ones. In effect, it moved the pitcher 5 feet farther away from the batter. Sources still sometimes assert that the distance was increased by 10½ feet, but that claim rests on a misunderstanding. Under the old rule the pitcher was required to begin his motion with a foot on the back line of a "box" that was 5½ feet deep. The rules stated that the front line of the box was to be 50 feet from home plate, and that figure stuck in people's minds. But the back line was, of course, 55 feet, 6 inches from home plate. Under the new rule the "box" disappeared, and the starting point for the pitcher, which today we call a "rubber" but which at the time was called a "plate," was located at a distance of 60 feet, 6 inches from home plate. The effect, therefore, was that the "pivot distance" had been increased by 5 feet.[3] And there was a second important change. As noted, the new rule dispensed with the "box" (although we still use that term), replacing its rear line with a foot-long "plate" embedded in the ground. The short length of the plate had the effect of virtually eliminating the pitcher's opportunity to deliver a pitch from an angle. Thus, not only was the pitcher now farther from the hitter, he was also directly in front of his opponent.[4] John Clarkson, a knowledgeable veteran, predicted that "the new rule will revolutionize the base ball world."[5] He was right—at least in the short run. But the longer-term impact of the decision was that it resolved once and for all the basic question of pitcher-batter equilibrium. There would be further fiddling at the margins of that relationship in later decades, especially with the banning of the spitball and the redefining of the strike zone. But on the central issue—how far apart the batter and the pitcher should be—the rules-makers of 1893 have found their judgment ratified by history.

The rule change had the desired effect on the offensive dimension of the game. The National League batting average jumped 35 points in 1893 and another 29 points—to the all time record figure of .309—the following year. Whereas in 1892 teams averaged 5.1 runs per game, by 1894 they averaged 7.4 runs per game. And while one out of every ten games produced a shutout in 1892, only one in forty produced a shutout in 1894. Historians of the game have long puzzled over why the fullest effect of the rule change was not felt until the second year of the new regime. One theory is that pitchers, in exploring how to adjust to the new circumstances, exhausted their arms in 1893 by trying to sustain the customary pitching loads of the past; they then found themselves in 1894 not only struggling with the greater distance but also toiling with throwing arms made lame by the overwork of the previous year.[6] Another possible explanation is that all pitchers had to relearn their trade in 1893, causing a scarcity of pitching that was most dramatically felt in 1894.[7] Both lines of argument may have merit.

What is certainly true is that the new rule brought some fine careers to an end. The two players who most dramatically proved unable to adjust were Will Hutchison and Silver King. Hutchison, who had won at least 36 games each year from 1890 to 1892, never again topped 16; King, who had won 23 in 1892, won only 10 in 1893 and did not pitch in the National League in 1894. But the pattern of declining effectiveness was widespread. Ed Stein fell from 27 victories in 1892 to 19 in 1893. Mark Baldwin fell from 26 to 16. John Clarkson fell from 25 to 16, Scott Stratton from 21 to 12, Tim Keefe from 19 to 10, Adonis Terry from 18 to 12.[8] In some of these instances increasing age may have been the chief factor. But whatever the cause, many of the mound stars of 1890–92 visibly faltered at the new distance.

Under the new regime pitchers faced two separate problems. First, they had to develop pitches that worked at the longer distance. Fastballs that were overpowering at 55½ feet sometimes became batting practice deliveries when batters had the extra split second to size them up; curves which seemed to explode at the shorter distance just hung at the longer one; and even some of the pitchers who could still put the requisite speed or twist on their deliveries found they could not reliably locate them. "Curves," Clark Griffith said two years later, "are supposed to be the stock of every pitcher, and every pitcher had to revise his whole stock when the new rules went into effect."[9] Second, pitchers had to learn how to pace themselves to throw longer pitches. The greater distance stressed the arms of most pitchers, and those who could not learn how to protect their arms from overwork—or whose managers were too slow to understand that they needed larger pitching staffs—soon left the game. "At the old distance," Kid Gleason remarked many years later, "a fellow could pitch every other day, if he was tough. . . . The reason the hurler can't work so often now is because of the increased pitching distance."[10] The 1892 season was the last major league campaign in which any pitcher—both Will Hutchison and Frank Killen did it—won at least half of his team's victories. It was also the last season in which any pitcher recorded more than 500 innings pitched.[11] By 1895 most managers assumed they needed to be rotating at least three different starting pitchers in order to give each adequate rest.

Only three pitchers seemed unaffected by the change: Amos Rusie, Kid Nichols, and Cy Young. (I'm being a bit arbitrary in saying that. A few others—including Nig Cuppy, Brickyard Kennedy, Frank Killen, and Sadie McMahon—managed to enjoy some significant successes on both sides of the change. But only Rusie, Nichols, and Young were consistently dominating both before and after the dawn of the modern pitching regime.) It was sometimes later claimed that the rule change had been legislated to neutralize Rusie's (or Young's) speed, but that notion is nonsense. Nichols declared that a modest revision—precisely the sort of change that was instituted—would not bother him, and he was right.[12] Young, who tended to oppose all changes in the rules, said of the new prescription that "base ball legislation is tending to put the game back to the old three-old-cat game, when old women and babies could play as well as men, and when 80 or 90 runs were made in a game," and his lobbying on behalf of pitchers may in fact have lain behind the decision in 1894 to double the length of the pitcher's plate.[13] But whether the rubber was a foot or two feet in length, Young remained an outstanding hurler. It is not known what Rusie thought of the change, but his speed allowed him to replace Will Hutchison as the league's strikeout leader in

1893, and he retained that dominance through 1895. Two years after the rule change, the great batter Dan Brouthers opined that, while hurting most hurlers, the longer distance had "made the [pitching] stars more than ever conspicuous," and his future fellow Hall of Famer Buck Ewing concluded that the factor that saved that handful of stars was their speed.[14] He may have been right, for these three great survivors were all celebrated for their fastballs. Comparing the last two years of the old regime against the first two years of the new, we see that Young moved from an average of 31.5 victories per year to an average of 30 victories, Rusie moved from 32 to 34.5, and Nichols moved from 32.5 to 33.[15] No one else even came close to these totals. Moreover, these three chalked up these numbers even though the season was shortened in 1893. Rusie, Nichols, and Young showed that the change in rules was not a death warrant for pitchers.

In his fascinating extended essay on pitching entitled *Strikeout*, William Curran suggests that it was in the 1893 season that pitchers first began to go through a wind-up motion that resembled the movements of the hurlers of today.[16] The speculation is plausible, for several developments occurred between the mid-1880s and early 1890s to make possible the emergence of the modern pitcher. First, in 1884 came the lifting of the prohibition against overhand throwing. Then, in 1887 came the establishment of a prohibition against taking more than one stride in delivering a pitch. Finally, in 1893 came the institution of the pitching rubber and the requirement for a pitcher to be in contact with it when beginning his windup. About the same time, the site from which the pitcher made his deliveries became elevated, and catchers began giving signals to their pitchers.

And so we are probably not far wrong if we visualize Cy Young in 1893, from his station in the middle of the diamond, going through a sequence of movements that is entirely recognizable to a modern-day fan. First, with his rear (right) foot barely in contact with the rubber, he looked in to pick up any information that Chief Zimmer might be sending. Then he straightened up and, briefly hiding the ball in his right (throwing) hand with his other hand, pivoted slightly away from the batter on his right leg, again concealing the ball. Next, striding forward with his raised left leg, he swept his arm from behind his head and past his right ear to hurl the ball plateward. Finally, his weight now shifted to his left leg and his right arm flung across his chest, he positioned himself to field a ball batted in his direction. This reconstruction is, of course, speculative. But with the confluence of rule changes that arose after 1887, and especially the lengthening of the distance from the pivot point to the plate, we can confidently date the beginning of the modern pitching regime. It is not a long stretch to believe that pitchers of yesterday started looking like pitchers of today almost as soon as the modern dimensions and rules of the diamond were in place.

CHAPTER FOUR

1893–1895:
Success at Sixty and Six

WHEN CY YOUNG arrived in Cleveland in mid-March 1893 to begin earning his handsome $2,300 salary, he won praise from Patsy Tebeau as one of only two Spiders—the other was Chief Zimmer—who "were in prime condition."[1] Self-respect, hard work, and good habits explain Young's fitness, but in 1893 being ready to play was more important than ever to the twenty-six-year-old, for he returned that spring in a different role. I'm not referring here to the redefined role of pitchers in general, even though we know that the new pitching rules weighed on Young's mind. (When asked if the longer distance might lead him to quit pitching, he had cautiously replied that he'd "try and stand it, if the rest [of the pitchers] did." I suspect that he began smiling at that point in the interview, however, for he added by way of explanation—and remember: he's almost the biggest man in baseball—"I've got a little strength left yet.")[2] Rather, the new role I'm alluding to involved his growing fame in the baseball world. No longer merely a pitcher of promise, Young was now an authentic baseball celebrity. In pronouncing his 1892 performance the finest of any major league pitcher in five seasons—the writer was probably thinking of his winning percentage of .750—the *Sporting News* had drawn the attention of baseball fans across the country to his extraordinary prowess.[3] Consequently, the 1893 season marks the first point in Young's career when he was forced to deal with the pressures of fame.

The Cleveland team to which he reported was now solely the property of Frank Robison, for during the off-season the majority owner had bought out the minority shares of Davis Hawley and George Howe.[4] Robison soon acquired a reputation as a baseball leader; he supported his players, he insisted on well-kept grounds, and he ran an exemplary base-ball organization. "Baseball, after all," he said later, "is like the show business. Give the public a decent attraction, and they will turn out to see you."[5] Robison believed he owned a fast-running and hard-hitting team. He thought Cy Young, Nig Cuppy, and John Clarkson the best three-man rotation in baseball, and he expected the Spiders to reclaim the pennant that they had won in the 1892 fall season. To Robison's way of thinking only one matter needed to be addressed: the low gate that the Spiders' home games regularly earned. To remedy that problem he set about trying to hire a player whose presence in the Cleveland lineup would pull in more fans. When efforts to swap Jake Virtue for Ed Delahanty failed— and what a team that would have been: Cy Young, Ed Delahanty, and Jesse Burkett—he negotiated a trade with the New York Giants, giving up the youth and promise of the versatile George Davis to acquire the experience and fame of the over-the-hill Buck Ewing. It was not, as some have said, the worst trade of the 1890s. But it stands very high on that list. Ewing arrived in Cleveland with a dead arm and gave the Spiders only one year of solid batting before fading into uselessness; Davis blossomed into stardom in New York and gave the Giants nine years of steady batting and outstanding defense. I see in this ill-fated trade a fit symbol of a season that, before it was over, would break many hearts in the Forest City.

Rather than use one location as base for spring training, the 1893 Spiders traveled through the Southeast in March, playing games in Atlanta, Savannah, Charleston, and Chattanooga before heading north in April for a week of rain in Cincinnati and a game in Columbus. For the club, these games were money-making opportunities. For Cy Young (and all other serious pitchers) they were opportunities to test their arms against the implications of the new rules. The reports that drifted north about Young's performances varied in tone and content. One account declared that he was "troubled with a sore arm;" another stated that he was "well nigh invincible."[6] I attribute some of the difficulty observers had in assessing Young's preseason work to his unfamiliarity with the longer distance between the mound and homeplate.

When the season began, however, Cy Young quickly reasserted his claim to dominance. Pitching Cleveland's season opener at Pittsburgh on a cool but sunny day, he defeated the highly regarded Pirates (who would finish the season in second place) 7–2. He must have been especially happy at this outcome, because before the game he had laconically described himself as having "no speed, no curves, no control."[7] Five days later, in Cincinnati, he took the measure of the Reds by a score of 3–2, showing "surprising speed."[8] On May 4 he lost Cleveland's home opener to Chicago, but in succeeding weeks he continued to win more often than lose. In a laugher on May 18 the Spiders crushed Cincinnati 21–4, and Young enjoyed one of the most successful offensive games of his career, stroking out 4 hits, scoring 4 runs, and even stealing a base. By the end of May, although Cleveland was no higher than fourth place, Young had posted 6 victories against only 3 losses.

June—much of it spent in the East—was Young's toughest month. After getting raked for 10 hits in a 9–6 loss to Boston on June 3, he was shifted to the bullpen for two brief and undistinguished appearances. On three other occasions later in the month Tebeau again used him in relief. When given the chance to start, he sometimes faltered; on June 21, abetted by sloppy relief work from Cuppy, he let a 5–1 lead against the Pirates slip away in the ninth inning. Perhaps his arm was giving him trouble during these weeks, though I find no references to lameness in the baseball press of the time. In any case, after the loss on June 21 his record stood at 9 and 9.

At that point Young's fortunes began to turn. I choose these words deliberately because, even though he won six of his next eight decisions, he continued to be hit hard. On July 3, for example he defeated Brooklyn while giving up no fewer than 18 hits; on July 11 he defeated Boston and Kid Nichols while yielding 12 hits. Meanwhile, playing in Washington on June 26, he blasted a 3-run home run over the fence in center field that some observers declared to be the longest home run ever hit in Boundary Field. "As Young's pitching deteriorates," one writer remarked, "his batting improves, so it's about a standoff."[9] By July 21, Young's record stood at 18 and 11 even though he had yielded hits in double-digit quantities in eight of his last nine starts. This phenomenon of the hard-hit winner attracted considerable attention. Opponents, one writer noted, "have made hits and hits plenty when [Young] pitched, but when a hit counted Young was an entirely different man."[10] This and similar comments mark the beginning of Cy Young's reputation—not really deserved, as statistical comparisons show—as a pitcher who yielded an uncommonly high quota of hits but who more often than not turned back the opponents' efforts to convert the hits into runs. Young's triumphs in 1893 also show that the Spiders themselves were pounding the ball. By the middle of the season, baseball writers were readily recognizing that the owners' intent in changing the pitching rules was being fulfilled: all across the league, offense was soaring and pitchers were hurting. And amid this league-wide offensive barrage the Spiders were doing well, for, having fallen as low as seventh place (in a twelve-team league), they were by July 17 back in third place.

The remarkable game played in Cincinnati on July 25 points up some striking differences between major league baseball today and major league baseball in the late nineteenth century. When the scheduled umpire failed to appear for the game, each team followed the common practice of the day by designating one nonplayer on the opposing team to serve as part of a two-man umpiring staff. The Spiders chose the Reds' pitcher, Frank Dwyer; the Reds chose the Spiders' injured outfielder, Jimmy McAleer. In the top of the ninth inning, with the score tied 3–3 and the Spiders at bat, McAleer made a blatantly pro-Spider call. Cleveland failed to score, however, and so the only consequence of McAleer's partisanship was to inspire Dwyer to retaliate spectacularly. In the bottom of the ninth, umpiring from behind the catcher, he called every single pitch that Young delivered to the first three batters a ball. Accordingly, twelve pitches filled the bases with no one out. For some reason the next batter, Piggy Ward, chose to swing at one of Young's offerings, allowing Cleveland to force a runner at the plate. But that "mistake" was quickly rectified—and the game ended—when Arlie Latham, who followed Ward in the order, stepped onto the plate and allowed a Young delivery to hit him. Thus did Cy Young lose his twelfth game of the season.

Just as he had been in 1892, Cy Young was almost unbeatable from midseason on. After the strange affair in Cincinnati on July 25, he went 16 and 4 for the rest of the year. On August 1 he shut Chicago down with three hits to win his 20th game of the season. On August 9 he held Louisville to four hits, a feat he duplicated against Boston on August 28 and then against Brooklyn on September 2. The victory over Louisville was his second against that club in as many days. The victory at Brooklyn was his first (and only) shutout of the year. So strikingly did his pitching improve that in only five of his last twenty-two starts of the season did he yield more than nine hits. Even when he lost, he was usually effective; the four losses came in successive appearances, scattered among nine consecutive team losses in August, and yet in three of those appearances he pitched well enough to win, Cincinnati beating him 4–1, New York (and Amos Rusie) edging him 2–0, and Boston prevailing 5–3.

Young won his thirtieth game on September 16 in another bizarre contest. A darkening sky at Cleveland led the visiting Baltimore Orioles to ask umpire Tim Hurst to call the game off in the eighth inning. When Hurst refused, the Orioles dramatized their indignation by lighting illuminatory fires in the dugout. When Hurst remained unmoved, the Orioles escalated their campaign by refusing to play balls that the Spiders hit. This technique succeeded, though perhaps not in the fashion that the Orioles planned, for after they allowed both Patsy Tebeau and Jack O'Connor to turn batted balls into home runs by neglecting to handle them, Hurst declared the contest forfeit to the Spiders. Since at least five innings had been played, the records of the players were official; since Cleveland led 16–11 when Hurst acted, Cy Young was credited with a victory.[11] Thirteen days later, having secured third place for Cleveland with a 10–3 triumph over Philadelphia, Cy Young wound up his season. By winning 25 of his final 32 decisions he had posted a season record of 34 wins and 16 losses.[12]

Though third place was clearly a good finish, it was 12½ games off Boston's pennant-winning pace. So why were Frank Robison's pennant hopes unrealized? Offense was not the problem. The team batted .300, second highest in the league; it scored 976 runs, third highest in the league. Defense was less successful: Jesse Burkett led the league in outfield errors, and Buck Ewing, relegated to right field in order to keep his bat in the lineup, was pitiful when obliged to throw the ball back to the infield. A glance at pitching records, however, tells the saddest story of all. Nig Cuppy was the only hurler on the staff aside from Cy Young who finished the year with a winning record, and his 17 victories fell 11 short of his 1892 total. John Clarkson finished the year with 16 wins and dropped below the .500 mark for the first time since his major league rookie season twelve years earlier. Only two other pitchers won any games at all. The Spiders in 1893 were essentially a one-pitcher club.

They were also hurt by injuries. The information to make comparisons among teams is not available, but the loss of Chief Zimmer, Jimmy Mc-Aleer, Patsy Tebeau, Jack O'Connor, and Buck Ewing for significant parts of the season was clearly a heavy burden for a pennant-ambitious team to bear. Shortly before going down with a broken collarbone in July, Zimmer had shown just how important he was to the squad by throwing out all four Pirates who tried to steal second base on him. At one point shortly after Tebeau sustained his injury the Spiders tried out four different third basemen in almost as many days. (Meanwhile, as the Spiders must have known, George Davis was playing almost daily at third for the Giants and hitting at a pace that allowed him to finish the year with a .355 batting average.) At another point the Spiders were so desperate for a catcher that they installed Pete Allen, fresh out of Amherst College, into the lineup for his sole major league appearance. "No team in the league," Tebeau lamented in late July, "has had as much bad luck to contend with as we have had."[13]

Finally, the Spiders made matters worse for themselves by yielding to factionalism. Though both Cupid Childs (with an on-base percentage of .463) and Jesse Burkett (with a batting average of .348) had fine years, they hated each other and allegedly wanted to duke it out. A widespread resentment of John Clarkson, grounded in the belief that he had betrayed his mates in 1890 by not honoring a pledge to join the Players League, erupted into some deliberately negligent defensive work behind him when he was on the mound. Even the hiring of Buck Ewing prompted dissension, for many observers believed that Frank Robison was grooming the aging star to succeed Patsy Tebeau as manager—a fear shared by Tebeau himself, even after Ewing denied all ambition in that direction.[14]

Once again, as in 1892, Cy Young had managed to avoid being caught up in the competing tensions among the players. And impressive as 1892 had been, there are two good reasons for believing that 1893 may have been even better. First, although the new season was shorter by three weeks, Young's figure of 53 appearances equaled his figure for 1892; thus, on average he worked with shorter rests between outings in 1893. Second, with the season shorter by 24 games, Young's 34 victories constituted 47 percent of Cleveland's 73 triumphs, the highest percentage figure of his career. Year-to-year comparisons between 1892 and 1893 may initially suggest a deterioration of performance, but that's not a surprise. The lengthened pitching distance led to increases of 35 points in the league batting average and 1.38 earned runs in the league earned run average. What is important is that Cy Young again stood among pitching leaders in many categories: third (behind New York's Amos Rusie and Boston's Kid Nichols) in both complete games and innings pitched, second (behind Pittsburgh's Frank Killen) in wins, second (behind St. Louis's Ted Breitenstein) in earned run average, and first in opponents' on-base percentage. The last-mentioned statistic reflects the impressive sharpening of Young's control; in 1893 he claimed the first of his twelve lifetime titles as league leader in allowing the fewest bases on balls per game.

On September 9, Cy Young reached a milestone (though it was unrecognized at the time): his one hundredth lifetime victory. He was at that moment in the midst of the ten-game winning streak with which he closed his grand season. This streak is important not simply as a mark of his skill but as proof that he had mastered the new distance. When in December the Giants sounded out Frank Robison on the possibility of buying Cy Young's contract, the Cleveland owner was uninterested: "The New York Club can have Cy Young for one-half of its capital stock."[15]

As soon as the season was over, Cy and Robba Young traveled to Chicago to visit the World's Fair. They then settled back into the daily chores of farm life—punctuated by an occasional baseball exhibition—in Gilmore, Ohio. Young did not even stick around Cleveland long enough to participate in a postseason series with the Cincinnati Reds, a match-up designed as much to make a little pocket money for the players as to identify the championship team of Ohio.[16] In January he traveled to Washington, D.C., staying there for over a month. The occasion for this unusually long trip is not known; it may have been related to the fact that a frustrated Frank Robison, stung that the third best team in the league had compiled the second worst home attendance record, was spending the winter trying to sell his franchise. At one point, when he threatened to take the National League to court for impeding his efforts, there was talk of having the club pass into a receivership directed by the circuit. Only when he had been rebuffed at every turn did Robison conclude that he should once again direct his ingenuity to the task of turning a profit with the Spiders. Since he already offered spectators a competitive, scrappy team and one of the three best pitchers in baseball, he saw no ready way to increase the attractiveness of his product. So he focused on ways to cut costs and announced over the winter that he would have fewer players under contract in 1894, that he was virtually dispensing with the distribution of complimentary tickets, and—the big cost-saver—that the Spiders would conduct their preseason training at the Cleveland Athletic Club. As the new season approached, Frank Robison's love-hate relationship with the city of Cleveland was on public display.

In the history of baseball the season of 1894 stands out for its unexampled offensive rage.[17] Counter to expectation, the surge in batting statistics triggered by rule changes in 1893 did not recede as players adjusted to them, but acquired new fury during the rules' second year in force. For Cy Young the season of 1894 marks the first year in which he clearly failed to match the achievements of his previous year. It is tempting to see the two developments as related—to attribute Young's faltering to his having to face hitters who were enjoying the most startling batting successes that batters have ever known. But the matter is more complicated. Like much else about 1894, the easy explanation may be the wrong one.

Cy Young reported to the Cleveland Athletic Club after most of the other players and in what we may readily suspect to have been ill spirits. Through inadvertence, the club's 1893 salary schedule had fallen into public hands, and Young was unhappy to learn that, contrary to assurances from a member of the Spider organization, John Clarkson had received a slightly higher salary than he—$2,500 ($100 over the league's cap) to Young's $2,300. Young disliked being lied to. Although willing to join in the workouts at the Athletic Club, he refused to sign a contract until he was assured of salary parity with Clarkson. (Hardly unreasonable, when 34 victories are pitted against 16.) He was also hurt that Patsy Tebeau, the manager who needed Young's right arm if the Spiders were to enjoy any success in 1894, took management's side in the salary dispute. "Zimmer [who also sought more money] and Young are good players," he said, "but they have no kick coming." [18] Before March was out, Robison reached a settlement with his hold-outs, Young and Clarkson both signing for $2,400. Astonishingly, however, instead of letting bygones fade away, Tebeau was still tossing barbs months later. "Neither Young, Clarkson, or Cuppy," he declared, "did himself proud last year." [19] Inasmuch as Young won almost half the Spiders' victories and more games than Clarkson and Cuppy combined, that statement was preposterous. It was an uncharacteristically mean-spirited remark from a man who was obviously feeling beleaguered.

When the season opened in late April, Cleveland bolted from the gate. After 24 games the club had posted 18 wins against only 6 losses. And oddly, although each of the Spiders' big three had earned 6 victories, Cy Young, with 5 of the 6 losses on his ledger, seemed to be the hurler least responsible for the club's success. In truth, Young was in large measure a victim of the club's offensive failings when he was on the mound; the team was averaging only 4 runs per game when Young started while it was offering 6 runs of support when Clarkson started and a crushing 10 runs of support when Cuppy started. After mid-May the team's fortunes turned. Both Cuppy and Clarkson went down with injuries, and when the schedule and inclement weather gave Cleveland a set of intermittent interruptions in their almost daily playing routine, Cy Young found himself called upon to pitch three consecutive games—though over the course of six days. By the time June began, with Clarkson in a nose dive and Cuppy still ailing, Young was the team's only dependable hurler. "Farmer Young," Charles Mears reported, "is doing wonderful work with his speed and curves."[20]

That dependability evidenced itself in many ways. On April 24 he shut out Cincinnati. On May 7 he held Chicago to one run. On May 10 he checked Pittsburgh in the same fashion, besting Frank Killen 2–1. In mid-June he pitched on three consecutive days, once as a starter and twice in relief; and then, with a single day for recuperation, he started yet again. Sometimes being sharp was not enough: on May 21 he lost to Cincinnati 2–1, and on May 29 he lost to New York (and Jouett Meekin) 2–0. Other times he simply was not sharp: in 6 of 7 outings between June 22 and July 13 he allowed the opposing team hits totaling in the double-digits—including a horrendous 22-hit game against Boston on July 7.[21] But still he won 3 of these miserable outings. In fact, through June and July Cy Young was just about the only Spider pitcher able to win games. Clarkson did so poorly, slipping from a 7–1 record to an 8–9 record, that he disappeared from the Cleveland scene in the middle of July, shipped off to Baltimore in exchange for Tony Mullane; Cuppy, meanwhile, couldn't shake a soreness in his leg. But Young gained a second wind, reeling off 6 straight victories at one point and almost always keeping the Spiders in the game. On July 31, pitching in relief, he registered his twentieth victory of the year. And he kept improving; on August 10 he beat Chicago and Bill Hutchison 2–1, scoring the winning run after doubling in the tenth inning, and four days later, in another ten-inning game, he registered his second shutout of the year, besting Washington 1–0. With that triumph, having won 17 of his last 23 decisions, he boasted a record of 23–12, almost exactly the same mark he had reached at mid-August a year earlier when he was launching himself into his blazing final weeks.

But at this point in 1894 everything abruptly went wrong. Between August 16 and September 5, Cy Young went to the mound as a starter 7 times and lost as many games. Not only was this losing streak the longest he had thus far endured in his career, it would be—over a career that still had 17 years to run—the longest (twice later equaled) he would ever know. And the losses were not squeakers. Boston, for example, pounded out 16 hits in a 12–10 triumph. Philadelphia pummeled him for 22 hits in a 16–1 rout—a game that inspired a headline writer to declare that "A Cyclone Struck Cy Young."[22] And before a vast Baltimore crowd of 25,000 on Labor Day, in what would turn out to be the worst game not just of the season but of his entire career, Young yielded 22 hits and 16 runs in just 6 innings to an Oriole club that was sweeping in upon the pennant; Joe Kelley set a record that still stands by stroking out four consecutive doubles during the game.[23] On September 13, after finally breaking his losing streak two days earlier, Cy Young became a 20-game loser for the second time in his career. (He would reach that mark only once again—in 1906.) And while the worst was by then over, he still managed to win only 3 of his final 6 starts. In this year of offense his last game stood out as a batting extravaganza. It was a remarkable 26–4 clobbering of Philadelphia, the most lopsided victory of his career.[24] Young wound up his roller-coaster season with a record of 26 victories and 21 losses. But how divided the season was: Young was 23–12 through the first three-quarters of the year, 3–9 through the last quarter.

There appears to be no obvious explanation for this calamitous conclusion to a season that had earlier held the promise of magnificence. If Cy Young ever mentioned what was troubling him, the press does not seem to have thought his explanation worth printing. And he may, of course, have said nothing at all; he was, at the best of times, a man of few words. Still, statistical evidence hints at answers. His speed may have slipped. Whereas he struck out 2½ batters per game in the first three-quarters of the year, he struck out only 2 batters per game in the last quarter. And that figure for the closing quarter is inflated somewhat by his best strike-out game of the year—a 9-whiff effort on September 21. It is true that his control seems to have held steady; he actually walked fractionally fewer batters per game in the last quarter of the season. But maybe the marginal fall-off in bases on balls can be accounted for by a heightened readiness among batters to swing at his offerings, for one thing is sure: he was easier to get hits off of. In the last quarter of the year he yielded 3½ more hits per nine innings than in the first three quarters.

Some historians have suggested that Cy Young, having pitched 1,299⅓ innings over the previous three years, finally grew arm weary.[25] That's possible, of course; excessive work lamed or ended the careers of Bill Hutchison, Frank Killen, and Gus Weyhing at about this time. But it's worth noting that Kid Nichols, having pitched 1,305⅓ innings over the same period of time (plus some winter ball in California), registered a 32–13 record in 1894 and that Amos Rusie, with an even more remarkable 1,514 innings under his belt, bettered even Nichols, with 36 and 13. Regularly pitching over 400 innings a year was therefore not invariably destructive.

And so we must conclude that the reasons for Cy Young's bad patch at the end of the 1894 season are simply unknowable. This string of losses presaged the occasional dry spells that would mock him at irregular intervals throughout the next seventeen years. Any inexplicable power outage must be frightening to a man whose living depends on the force of his delivery; and we can speculate that Cy Young returned to Gilmore after the 1894 season a chastened and worried man. After all, whatever he had accomplished in his cyclonic past, he cannot have appreciated being referred to in his home-state press as "Cyrus, the former king."[26]

Because the royal crown slipped only in the final seven weeks of the season, Cy Young actually finished this year of offensive thunder with some impressive statistics. His total of 26 victories was fifth highest in the league. His earned run average of 3.94 wound up fourth best. His 44 complete games was third highest. He retained his title as the National League pitcher who allowed the fewest walks per game. And even though Nig Cuppy closed the year with a dash, garnering 24 victories (8 in relief) for the season, he could not challenge Young as team leader in any important respect; his earned run average, for example, was over half a run higher than Young's. Clearly, if Cy Young had spread out his wins and losses—if he had pretty consistently won 5 of every 9 games throughout the year—contemporaries would have been prompter to recognize the strength of his record. But because he soared until mid-August and plummeted thereafter, judgments were darker. In a sense, both views are fair. His seasonal record kept him among the elite of National League pitchers; his final quarter raised deep doubts about his future.

Cleveland finished the season in sixth place, at the bottom of the first division. It's not clear why the Spiders did not do somewhat better. Though the team's batting average, at .303, was below the league average of .309, the team's earned run average was second best in the league. Ed McKean, Jesse Burkett, and Cupid Childs all batted in the .350s, and Childs staked out a posthumous claim to be the most valuable second baseman of the decade by getting on base—as we now know—almost 48 percent of the times he came to bat. Perhaps all that can be said is that four clubs were bunched fairly tightly in the middle region of the standings, and that with slightly better luck the Spiders might have finished as high as fourth.[27] But if the reasons for Cleveland's relatively undistinguished performance are uncertain, the explanation for Baltimore's success seems clear: alone among National League clubs Baltimore had spent the spring in the South. The Orioles had been a test case, and the lesson to be drawn struck observers as unmistakable: to forgo spring training in warmer climes was to be penny-wise and pound-foolish.

Frank Robison was paying attention, and the Spiders left Cleveland in March of 1895 to swing across the mid-South before angling back into Ohio through Indiana. Though Cy Young, as usual, left no record of his thoughts from this period, we may reasonably infer from his well-attested professional pride an eagerness to prove wrong those who dismissed him as "the former king." Manager Patsy Tebeau was a Young booster. He announced before the team headed south that "I'm mighty sweet on Cleveland's chances this year"; two weeks later he noted that "Young is in good shape."[28] In fact, however, the spring was troubling. Wild against Memphis and a loser against Nashville, Young was clearly struggling. When he failed to start for Cleveland in the season opener in Cincinnati on April 18, the fact that he was ailing could no longer be disguised. Word later came out that he was suffering from "tonsilitis" compounded by "grip and muscular rheumatism," and in the judgment of Charles Mears he was "almost dangerously sick."[29] Whatever disease these vague medical terms pointed to, they signaled an inauspicious beginning for a season that, in the estimation of famous baseball writer, Henry Chadwick, should be seeing the Spiders reign as the finest team in the West.

Ravaged by an array of illnesses and injuries, the Spiders lost their first four games.[30] They had come north with a mascot—a thirteen-year-old black boy picked up in Little Rock—and since he quickly disappeared from press coverage, it is likely that he was abandoned where the team's fortune's plummeted.[31] But almost as quickly as the club dropped, it suddenly revived. Led by Nig Cuppy, the Spiders won 19 of their next 28 games and at the end of May sat in third place. Even though he did not pitch his first game until April 27 or gain his second victory until May 15, Young contributed to the Spiders' spurt, ending the month with a 6–1 record. By that point, his health fully restored and with victories over Jack Stivetts and Amos Rusie under his belt, Young was moving back into his customary role as the club's bellwether pitcher. Still, by one crude reckoning of the day, he was only the 33rd best pitcher in the National League as June opened.[32]

The month of June—much of it played away from Cleveland—saw Young move from triumph to triumph. He started 8 games and recorded 7 victories. On June 11, Young's "flukey kind of hit" drove in the winning run against Philadelphia,[33] on the June 14 his sharp pitching defeated Dad

Clarke and the Giants 1–0. Elmer Bates, who had covered the Spiders for several seasons, declared that "Cy's work in the East this trip has been as good as he has ever done in his life."[34] His work in July surpassed even the achievement of June. He made 10 appearances, 8 of them starts, and only once allowed more than 2 earned runs. On July 16 he matched pitches with Baltimore's Duke Esper, scored Cleveland's only run on a wild dash from second base, and, backed by extraordinary defense, became the first pitcher of the year to shut out the mighty Orioles.[35] (With four victories over the Orioles in two days the Spiders regained third place at this time.) Four days later he held Brooklyn to one run and pitched the Spiders into first place. A win in relief on July 22 gave Young his 150th career victory. Three days later, with a 6–4 win over Boston's Kid Nichols, Young won his 20th game of the year. Only on July 27, in his fifth appearance in eight days, did he finally stumble. But still, by the end of the month he had a 20–6 record, and the Spiders led the National League.

It would be nice to know what Young's midsummer magic was based on, but the sports press was typically imprecise in its coverage. Elmer Bates confined himself to declaring that Young was "pitching this year in his old-time form," adding later that, according to Chief Zimmer, he was faster than ever.[36] Charles Mears simply restored his crown: he was "the Tuscarawas king."[37] My guess is that he was using high heat, an occasional curve, and outstanding control to keep hitters in their places.

During August, as the Spiders dueled the Orioles for the lead, Cy Young continued to shine. Of Cleveland's 19 victories he registered 8. On August 5 he held Louisville to 2 runs, and on August 17 he shut out Cincinnati with only 4 hits. Even when not sharp he usually won, yielding 11 hits to both Washington and Boston in two victories later that month. Led by Young's pitching and Jesse Burkett's phenomenal batting, the hard-driving Spiders compiled the league's second-best record during August. Unfortunately for them, however, the Orioles did even better, and before August was out Baltimore had narrowly reclaimed first place. When league president Nick Young declared in his customarily fussy fashion that "the race for the pennant this season comes before any other in point of glorious uncertainty," he echoed a view that, in terser formulations, graced many sport pages in September.[38]

The lively chase pointed out Young's remarkable durability, for, as he expressed it himself many years later, in the Spiders' final drive "they put it squarely up to Cuppy and me."[39] Some accounts go so far as to declare that through much of September Young and Cuppy pitched on alternate days. The reality, while not quite that dramatic, is impressive enough. Of September's 20 games, Cuppy started 8, Young started 7. During the crunch of 10 games between the September 13 and September 21, Young started 3 times and relieved twice while Cuppy started 4 times and relieved once. With a victory over St. Louis on September 13 Young secured his 30th victory of the year. For the month Young was 7–2 and Cuppy was 4–3. It was almost as if Cleveland had a two-man staff.

The pennant race also gave rise to one of the most famous anecdotes in Young's career. From at least his second year as a Spider Cy Young had insisted that his contract contain a clause excusing him from any obligation to pitch on Sundays. Presumably arising from Young's desire to respect the Sabbath, the clause had not worked an excessive hardship on the Spiders because, owing to Ohio legislation, they could not play Sunday home games in any case. When the rare Sunday road game had arisen, Tebeau called upon another of his hurlers. On September 15, with the Spiders facing the strain of a Sunday doubleheader in the midst of the tight race, Young informed the manager that, if needed, he would accept a relief assignment. Sure enough, in the second game Phil Knell faltered, and Young made his first Sunday appearance. Though not exactly sharp, he managed to win. The appearance caught press attention, and in later years Young's own account of the day became one of his favorite anecdotes. The Bible, he liked to note, stated that rescuing your neighbor's ass from the pit on the Sabbath was not a sin. "Well, boys," he said—and I can readily imagine the smile spreading across his face—"I'll be durned if I know any bigger ass than Tebeau anywhere, and he certainly was in an awful hole. So I helped him out"—here I imagine a pause—"and that's the whole story."[40]

The story of the pennant race itself, however, was less happy. Strong as the Spiders' charge was (they won 10 of their last 12 games), the Orioles' charge was stronger, and Cleveland finished three games off the pace. Cleveland's winning percentage of .646 was the highest in the short history of major league baseball in the Forest City, but Baltimore finished the year at a still loftier .669.[41] It had turned out to be disastrous—a matter of four games in the standings—that the Spiders had lost their only two September engagements with the Orioles. Fortunately for Cleveland there was still a road to possible redemption. It was called the Temple Cup competition.

Initiated at the prompting of Pittsburgh businessman William C. Temple, the competition pitted the team that finished first in the league against the team that finished second in a best-of-seven match-up. The competition had arisen in 1894 as a response to the baseball world's desire to devise, in a one-league era, some sort of postseason competition that could generate the interest that the World Series matches had been designed to foster in the two-league era of the 1880s.[42] The first Temple Cup series in 1894 had, in fact, been a disappointment—some even used the word "scandal."[43] The pennant-winning Baltimore Orioles did not take it seriously—they had, after all, already won the flag—and so they had been swept by the runner-up New York Giants. Puzzlement about their poor performance yielded to cynicism among fans when rumors circulated that the players on the two teams had agreed in advance to forgo the proposed 65-35 percent split of the gate in favor of a 50-50 division. But if 1894 had proven the scheme flawed, it had not proven it inherently unworkable. And so, after rejecting the absurd claim that the Giants, as holders of the cup (and despite their ninth-place finish in 1895), should defend it against the Orioles, baseball officials authorized a postseason series for the Orioles and the Spiders.

The competition promised to be as interesting as the pennant race. Led by manager Ned Hanlon, Baltimore unquestionably had a strong squad, finishing the year with league's highest team batting average and lowest earned run average. But Cleveland's credentials were far from shoddy, featuring the league's third highest batting average and its second lowest earned run average. Perhaps more to the point, the Spiders had actually taken the season series from the Orioles, 6 games to 5. Moreover, the Spiders boasted the league batting leader in Jesse Burkett, at .409;[44] the league's victory leader in Cy Young, with 35; and several players who were completing unusually fine seasons, including Chief Zimmer with a batting average of .340, Ed McKean with 283 total bases, Cupid Childs with 90 runs batted in, and Nig Cuppy with 26 victories. Both teams were ferociously effective when playing on their home grounds, and so, if after three games in each city the series should be tied, the decisive seventh game was to be played at a neutral site. John McGraw later called the Orioles of the mid-1890s "the greatest ball team of my knowledge," but according to the *Sporting News* on the eve of the series, many observers thought the Spiders should be favored.[45]

The Temple Cup competition opened in Cleveland on October 2 before a remarkably large crowd (for Cleveland) of 7,000. To no one's surprise, Cy Young pitched for the Spiders. The starting choice for the Orioles, however, occasioned some comment, as Hanlon bypassed rookie Bill Hoffer and his remarkable 31–6 record in favor of the veteran Sadie McMahon. Injured for much of the season, McMahon had compiled only a 10–4 record. But of those 10 victories four—a league-leading total he shared with Cy Young and others—had been shutouts, and all the shutouts had been recorded since the opening of August. Clearly McMahon was hot. The game was exciting to the end, and going into the ninth inning the score stood knotted at 3–3. In the top of that inning John McGraw drove in Wilbert Robinson to give the visitors a 1-run lead. But in the bottom of the ninth Cleveland quickly retied the game on a double by Burkett and a single by McKean. And the Spiders did not stop there. Further singles loaded the bases with one out, and when the lumbering Zimmer managed to beat a relay to first, foiling a double play effort by the Orioles, Cupid Childs scored the winning run. By holding Baltimore to half of its annual average of 8 runs per game, Cy Young had given the Spiders a 1-game lead in the Temple Cup competition.

The next day Nig Cuppy defeated Bill Hoffer, 7–2, before a still larger crowd of 10,000 Spider faithful. By scoring 3 runs in the first inning, Cleveland seized a lead it never thereafter relinquished. Famous for his slow pitch and his slow pitching, Cuppy mesmerized Baltimore, holding the Orioles to 5 hits. Cleveland led the series 2 games to none.

After an off-day, the two clubs—and Cy Young and Sadie McMahon—reengaged on October 5. To the delight of the 12,000 fans who spilled over onto the outskirts of the outfield, Young was in command throughout the contest. Given a three-run cushion in the first inning and additional support later on, he coasted to his second victory in the competition, this time by a score of 7–1. Not until the eighth inning did the Orioles hit a ball that reached the outfield. The Spiders meanwhile rapped out 13 hits, including 4 doubles, on the way to pounding in their 7 runs. The Temple Cup competition was turning into a mismatch, and perhaps for this reason the Cleveland fans, who had hurled vegetables, bottles, garbage, potatoes, seat cushions, and at least one firecracker at the visitors after the first two contests, deported themselves more civilly after this third game. Patsy Tebeau told his players to pack only one shirt for the trip to Baltimore; they wouldn't, he declared, be sticking around for long.[46]

Baltimore was not, however, a friendly town. Reports of how the unruly Cleveland fans had abused the Orioles had appeared in the Baltimore press, and some of the Oriole faithful decided to reciprocate. When the

Spiders left their Baltimore hotel on October 7 to proceed by bus to Union Park, they were forced to make their way through a reception of eggs, fruits, peanuts, and an occasional rock. The game was no happier. Benefitting perhaps from playing at home, the Orioles reached Nig Cuppy for 5 runs. Meanwhile, the curve-balling Duke Esper held the Spiders scoreless. Jesse Burkett, who had batted his way on base 7 times during the 3 games in Cleveland, failed in 4 at bats to touch the crafty southpaw for a hit. After 7 postseason games Baltimore had finally contrived to win one.

The triumph apparently had an incendiary effect on the rowdy element in the crowd, for the propensity to pelt that had been a nuisance prior to the game became life-threatening in its aftermath. Although the Spiders used a different door to leave the ball field and reach their bus, the unruly fans were not long fooled and rushed to pursue them with a rain of sticks and stones. The ten-man police unit assigned to crowd control quickly found itself outmanned and for ten minutes the crowd ruled the situation. Some in the mob held the horses while others struggled to detach the bus. A stone struck Cupid Childs in the head. The Cleveland players fell to the floor of the bus to avoid being visible targets for the mob and tried to protect themselves with their gloves and clothing bags. A not entirely reliable source quotes Cy Young as later reporting that "the regulars were on the bottom, the substitutes, writers and fans stacked on top for protection."[47] Even when the players had dropped from sight, the crowd continued to lob a storm of dangerous missiles into the conveyance. Only when enhanced police protection appeared was the volley suspended and a path cleared to allow the frightened horses to draw the bus away. Later, in the safety of the hotel, several Spiders displayed some of the debris that had fallen into the bus—stones, bottles, and pieces of iron. The episode reminds us that baseball enthusiasm is not entirely independent of a spirit of riot.

If the Oriole fans thought that Esper's victory portended a trio of Baltimore home triumphs, they were disabused of that hope the next day. On October 8, before a much smaller crowd (the fans may have feared a replay of the previous day's hooliganism) and with a more visible police presence, Cy Young faced Bill Hoffer. For six scoreless innings the two hurlers—either of them arguably the best in the league in 1895— matched masteries, the Spiders having 3 hits and the Orioles having 5. Cy Young led off the top of the seventh with a double; he later scored the first of the 3 runs the Spiders finally pushed across the plate during the inning (aided, it should be noted, by some Baltimore sloppiness). In the bottom of the inning Baltimore got one of the runs back. A fight loomed in the same half-inning when Hoffer, believing that Tebeau had deliberately tripped him, threw the Spider manager to the ground. But Tebeau chose not to retaliate, and the matter passed. In the eighth the Spiders raised their lead to 5–1 when, again aided by errant Baltimore fielding, they pushed across 2 more runs. And that's where the score stood until two were out in the bottom of the ninth.

But then Young suddenly lost his control, walking John McGraw and Willie Keeler and hitting Hughie Jennings with a pitch. Solely on his own Young had loaded the bases. In today's world the closer would surely now appear, if he had not already been summoned. But thinking was different in the 1890s; Cy Young was the Spiders' best pitcher, and a team went with its best. Joe Kelley promptly made Young pay for his carelessness by driving in McGraw with a sharp hit that McKean could only knock down. Then, with the crowd cheering desperately for the rally to continue, Steve Brodie tapped a pitch back to Young and was thrown out at first base. The game was over, Cy Young had a 5–2 victory over the Orioles, and Cleveland had won the Temple Cup four games to one.[48] For the first time since 1887 a team not representing the East Coast could lay claim to being the best in baseball.

The players left Baltimore that evening to return in glory to Cleveland, the Temple Cup in hand. Back home, they were greeted by some of their most devoted fans, fifteen hundred of whom had squeezed into the Cleveland Music Hall to watch a "bulletin board" that featured figured re-creations of the distant games, with the play-by-play information arriving via the telegraph machine. A party at the Elks Club extended the welcoming festivities, and over 300 fans, including Frank Robison and the mayor of the city, joined in the celebration. William Temple sent congratulations. The lead table was graced with a bizarre floral decoration that, by depicting spiders gobbling up a hapless oyster (a reference to the Chesapeake Bay), re-told the tale of the series. The Spider players had already voted to divide the winning club's financial pot equally among all team members, whether they had played in the match or not, and this mark of cameraderie, not the universal practice for postseason play (indeed, Baltimore had not observed it in 1894), intensified the sense of bonding that the evening fostered. A nonplaying and grateful Jack O'Connor probably spoke a shared sentiment when he remarked on receiving his equal share of $528, "I tell you this is a club of goodfellowship [*sic*]"[49] Some party-goers drank home-brewed beer. But according to one participant's account from several years later, a steady flow of champagne produced ever higher levels of boisterousness until, shortly before the revelries ended, the celebrants began playing drop-kick with the Temple Cup.[50] We know Cy Young was present; we don't know whether he was one of the drunken revelers. But whatever his state that evening, he was soon again the sober Tuscarawan, who, with a contract for the 1896 season in his pocket, had returned to Gilmore to resume his off-season routine of wood-chopping, running, and hunting, interrupted by an occasional baseball game to earn a little extra cash.[51] It must have seemed a very different life from the exuberance of big-city celebrating.

Shortly after the Temple Cup series ended, the *Sporting News* ran a large picture of Cy Young on its front page. The short article beneath the likeness identified him as "the premier pitcher of the Cleveland Club, of the National League."[52] That's like calling the pope the most important Catholic in Rome—true, but hardly adequate. Cy Young was now the premier pitcher in baseball, having completed yet another season that baseball historians regard as the best of his career. With 35 victories, he was the winningest pitcher in 1895.[53] With 95 victories, he was the winningest pitcher over the past three years.[54] He was the first (and last) pitcher to win 3 games in a Temple Cup series. Three considerations explain his success in 1895. The first was his ever-improving control. He walked only 75 batters in 369⅔ innings pitched, and over the final six appearances of the regular season (43 innings) he walked only one opposing hitter. It is useful to recall that the deepest significance of this statistic is not so much that batters had to earn their way on base when facing Young, but that most of the time Young could pitch a ball pretty much wherever he wanted to. The second consideration is that he conserved his strength in 1895. For the first time since his abbreviated season of 1890 he pitched fewer than 400 innings, and fully 7 of his victories resulted from relief rather than starting appearances. If, as seems possible, his disappointing close in 1894 had been a consequence of weariness, his powerful close in 1895 was a consequence of a determination, shared with his manager, to avoid overtaxing the arm. The third consideration is his consistency. He was truly a slump-stopper; only once in the entire season did he lose as many as two games in a row. Moreover, his month-by-month record, after he recovered from his season-opening illness, has an almost metronomic regularity: 5–1 in May, 7–2 in June, 7–3 in July, 8–2 in August, and 7–2 in September. Here was a man who could be counted on at every point in the season. And so, at the age of twenty-eight and with six major league seasons under his belt, the giant from Tuscarawas had emerged as "the king of pitchers."[55] I'm inclined to think that Young, a rustic republican, got a kick out of the press's continuing resort to royal imagery.

CHAPTER FIVE

ॐ҉ॐ

1896–1898:
A Durable Man

I N MOST human activities, when you reach the top there's only one way to go—and that's down. In the three years following the Temple Cup triumph of 1895 both Cy Young and the Spiders experienced the disappointments of falling short. They remained good, it's true. But as age corroded the core of the once-splendid Cleveland club, the team slowly lost its capacity to compete with the National League's best. And as Kid Nichols pulled away from the small pack of leading hurlers in the National League to establish himself as an unrivaled superstar, Young had to accommodate himself to continued membership in that group of reliable, dependable, strong, but only occasionally overwhelming pitchers. Meanwhile, as an ominous backdrop to all that happened on the ball field, there was a steady erosion of fan support for the Spiders in Cleveland. A businessman to the bone, Frank Robison was not slow to wonder whether he would be better off trying to hawk his diamond entertainment in another city. Still, in the early months of 1896 these difficulties were not yet discernible.

For preseason practice the Spiders returned to Hot Springs, site of their training prior to the successful 1892 season. Before leaving for the spa Cy Young declared his optimism about the coming season. "I am in fine shape," he said "and if the other Spiders are in as good shape as I am, no team in the league will be in it with Cleveland this season."[1] This widely shared confidence was based on the belief that the returning Spider players would be as good as ever and that several new pitchers—Icebox Chamberlain, Zeke Wilson, and Cy Swaim—would fortify the team's already formidable hurling staff. The springtime work of the squad did nothing to undermine the hopes of its fans. In fact, by winning a majority of a series of games with the Pirates, who also chose Hot Springs for preseason preparations, the Spiders reinforced the view that they would march to the pennant. When they headed north to begin the regular season, the team and many of its fans fully expected a flag and another Temple Cup victory.

Instead, however, the 1896 season became known as the year of the "riotous" Spiders.[2] The term doesn't refer to the team's play, which, though not as dominating as its devotees had hoped, still managed to secure second place and a return to Temple Cup competition for the club. Nor does the adjective refer, except indirectly, to the team's continuing reputation—with a few notable exceptions, including Cy Young—as a gang of diamond rowdies who slashed, insulted, and cheated their way to success. Rather, the term *riotous* arises from the participation of several prominent Spiders (again, not Young) in the so-called Louisville riot.

The trouble, which had been simmering throughout the contest of June 26, broke out in the bottom of the tenth inning when umpire Stump Weidman cited darkness to call the game and perhaps deprive the Spiders of a victory. (The "perhaps" is important. When Weidman ended the game, the Colonels had the bases loaded, and so it is far from certain that the Spiders could have retained the one-run lead they had secured in the top of the inning.) Several Spiders rushed Weidman. Hundreds of Louisville fans swept onto the field to confront the angry Cleveland players. When profane exchanges failed to dissipate the fury of the moment, punches were thrown and a bloody melee ensued. It finally took armed authority to pry the combatants apart, and the Spiders left the playing field and later the ballpark under police protection, lying face down on the floor of the wagon that bore them to safety. But the cessation of fighting did not end the matter, for later that day the enraged Louisville owner swore out assault warrants against the Spiders. This action, by transforming a baseball brawl into a judicial contest, assured that the storm would not quickly blow over.

The Spiders' problems were just beginning; the very next day police arrived at the ballpark to arrest the team and bring them before a special Saturday session of police court. It was deemed a particularly humiliating turn that they were not even given the opportunity to change from their uniforms into civilian clothes before being hauled off to the courthouse. After hearing much conflicting testimony, the judge imposed fines of $50 to $100 on four Spiders—Patsy Tebeau, Jim McAleer, Ed McKean, and Jack O'Connor. Further problems followed. Several clubs around the National League announced that they would insist on special police protection when the Spiders were in town. The baseball press lit into the Cleveland team, with Henry Chadwick denouncing the "blackguardism by the roughs of Cleveland" and *Sporting Life* declaring that the legal confrontation pitted the "law, order and decency" of the National League against "forces [in Cleveland] that are lawless, demoralizing and damaging to the national sport."[3] Raucous crowds in hostile cities felt free to threaten the Spiders. Finally, the league itself, hoping to make an example of the Spiders' intolerable behavior and thereby rein in the diamond rowdiness of the era, imposed an additional fine of $200 on Patsy Tebeau.

Frank Robison was enraged at the way his team was being singled out for punishment. And so, instead of trying to iron out the disputes, he raised the stakes by declaring the league's action in imposing a second fine on Tebeau illegal. He then won an injunction from an Ohio court prohibiting the collection of any of the fines, and directed the four players not to pay them. "It is war," the club president announced, "and I like nothing better."[4] The team members appreciated Robison's prompt and vigorous support. But the overall effect of the ensuing turmoil—a police presence wherever they played, hotels reluctant to house them, umpires disinclined to be fair to players who had slugged one of their own—hurt the team's play. And lurking behind all of these difficulties was a far more ominous problem: if Robison did not finally prevail in his showdown with the National League, the league might declare all of the games that the noncomplying players participated in to be forfeit, thereby depriving the Spiders of the opportunity to compete a second time for the Temple Cup. Much of the remainder of the 1896 season was played under the shadow of uncertainty generated by the riot, and Patsy Tebeau later blamed "this infernal piece of business" with breaking "the hearts and backbone" of a team that stood in first place on the day of the riot.[5]

Cy Young was not pitching on that tumultuous day in Louisville, and no newspaper account lists him among the players who swarmed from the bench into the fight. Nevertheless, many years later the tale of the conflict entered his repertory of standard reminiscences, acquiring in the process at least two fictive elements. First, he gave Stump Weidman a colorful motive for arbitrarily calling the game; according to Young, three gun-toting gamblers threatened to shoot the umpire if he failed to comply with their wishes. Second, he claimed that the sun, far from sinking from view, still sat high in the sky when Weidman invoked darkness to call the game.[6] The elderly Cy Young liked to revisit his past; these tales remind us that he was neither the first nor the last yarn-spinner to believe that good stories invite embellishment.

As for Young's pitching in the 1896 season, it began wretchedly. He lost his first start and was knocked from the box in the second. In his first 25 innings he gave up 41 hits. Though the season began in mid-April, he was still without a victory at the end of the month. *Sporting Life* posed the question that many in the baseball world may have begun puzzling over: "Was ist los mit Cy Young?"[7] Then, however, he moved into recognizable form, winning 14 of his next 18 decisions and "banging the ball over with his old-time speed."[8] On May 22 he bested Boston's Kid Nichols, 4–1, even though Nichols had been sent ahead to Cleveland to be rested for the match-up.

But the game that most clearly stands out in this string of midsummer victories—a 2–0 triumph over Philadelphia on July 23—was a contest that deserves inclusion among Cy Young's finest career achievements. Before a friendly home crowd Young cruised through inning after inning without yielding a hit. It was not until two were out in the ninth that he finally slipped, allowing the fearsome Ed Delahanty to stroke a clean single to the outfield. He retired the next batter and settled for a one-hitter. This effort was one of only three one-hitters thrown in the National League during the season (there were no no-hitters), and because Young issued but one walk, this game was adjudged the league's finest mound performance of the year. After the game he stated that he knew from the moment of his first delivery that "I would pitch good ball," adding "I played to shut the Phillies out without a hit." Though unsuccessful in that goal, Young was prideful of his "speed and curves." It is easy to imagine him pronouncing his final judgment with quiet self-assurance: "I don't think any team could have hit me, the way I was working Thursday."[9]

On August 4, Cy Young became a 20-game winner for the sixth straight season. And by that time he had already passed another career milestone, for on June 8, by posting his one-hundred-seventy-fifth major league victory, he had become the winningest pitcher in Cleveland baseball history, surpassing the total accumulated by Jim McCormick in the 1880s.[10] Even some of his losses were memorable. On July 26, for example, while enduring a pasting by the Reds, he stood on the mound as hundreds of incensed Cincinnati fans chased after Cupid Childs, who had just ignited their anger by grappling a Reds base runner to the ground. Two days later Young was the pitcher of record in a still more bizarre game that saw an angry Patsy Tebeau so completely lose command of his senses that he switched positions with Young—this is Tebeau's only major league mound appearance—and deliberately yielded the game-winning hit to the astonished (and doubtless grateful) Reds.

There are three other aspects of Cy Young's 1896 season that merit comment. The first involves equipment. Hard as it is to believe, Young had worked without a glove thus far into his major league pitching career. His barehandedness was not unusual. Unlike position players, pitchers had in general been slow to seek the protection of a glove. But Nig Cuppy had been hurling with a glove since 1894, and more recently Kid Nichols had adopted the practice. At some point during the summer of 1896 Cy Young joined their company. The leather device he used was skimpy by modern-day standards, but it afforded a significant measure of protection against sharply hit balls.[11] The second point worth commenting on was Young's midseason decision to make himself regularly available for Sunday mound duty, despite his preseason protestations that his Sabbath appearance of the previous September would not be replicated. I know too little about Cy Young's religious beliefs or behavior to speculate on the reasons for this shift. But from 1896 on, as the Spiders sought out opportunities for money-making Sunday games away from their home grounds, Cy Young no longer stood among the small number of Sabbatarians on major league rosters. The third point about 1896 is that it affords a glimpse of Young's emerging reputation as an honest man. In mid-June, when Chicago and Cleveland were without an umpire, in accord with the common practice of allowing each team to choose an opposing player to officiate, the Colts chose Young to assume the Cleveland side of the officiating task. This appears to be the first time Young was designated for such service; it was not the last.

When the 1896 season ended, the Spiders found themselves where they had been the previous year—in second place, behind the Baltimore Orioles. But while the 1895 pennant race had been tight, with Cleveland trailing by only 3 games at the end, the 1896 race saw the Orioles finally soar away from the rest of the league, leaving the Spiders 9½ games out. As a consequence, Cleveland home attendance, which had surged (as Robison had doubtless intended) when Cleveland's stand against the fines had seized the fans' attention, returned to its customary feeble levels in the final weeks of the season; only 800, for example, attended the game that clinched second place for the club. Eager for a lucrative series, the Orioles did not disguise their unhappiness that the Temple Cup competition would again match them against a team that drew so poorly at home.

Cleveland owed much of its success in 1896 to a pitching staff that recorded the lowest earned run average in the league (3.46). Cy Young won 28 games, Nig Cuppy registered another 25 (and a slightly lower earned run average—3.12 to Young's 3.24), and Zeke Wilson, though finishing at only 17–9, had started the season strong and thereby provided mound power when Young was still struggling.[12] The Spiders' hitting was sufficient to give the club, at .301, the league's second highest batting mark. Jesse Burkett stroked out a .410 average to win his second consecutive batting crown, and Cupid Childs, rebounding from a disappointing 1895 performance, turned in the best season of his career, batting .355 and reaching base better than 9 out of every 20 plate appearances.[13] Meanwhile, the furor over the Louisville riot had subsided when National League authorities, recognizing that rancors had softened over time, retreated from confrontation over the various disputed fines and acknowledged the legitimacy of the games that the accused players had participated in.[14] Although troubled by some late injuries, the Spiders recalled that they had again taken the season series from the Orioles and entered the postseason matches confident that they could retain their claim to the Temple Cup.

Instead, the Spiders ran into disaster after disaster. Rainy weather prevented them from playing during the last week of the season; thus, while Baltimore kept sharp, the only thing the Spiders could do was try to keep dry. On the way to Maryland, their train had an accident, and they spent twenty uncomfortable hours on a backup rail car before reaching Baltimore on the evening before the first game. Then Baltimore's manager exercised his peculiar privilege and denied the Spiders a chance to use the field for warm-up practice on the morning of the game. Finally, in the first game Patsy Tebeau wrenched his back and had to leave the contest and the series. But even had none of these mishaps occurred, the Spiders would still have been in trouble because, unfortunately for them, they were taking on one of the most versatile offensive teams ever to play professional baseball—one that had recorded a team batting average of .328 and stolen a mind-boggling 441 bases in 122 games. Hughie Jennings had batted .401, Willie Keeler .386, Joe Kelley .364, Wilbert Robinson .347. This was a team, moreover, that smarted from the humiliation of losing the cup matches in 1895. And so, in four straight, brisk games, none of them even close, the Orioles dispatched the Spiders. Cy Young pitched only once, losing the opening game to Bill Hoffer, 7–2. The very first batter Young faced, John McGraw, smashed a ball back off his pitching wrist. During the course of the game Young gave up 14 hits, struck out only one batter, and by his own admission lacked his customary speed. No wonder. The postgame swelling in his wrist and fingers was testimony to the force of McGraw's blow. Nothing was broken, but Young could not pitch again in the series. "When Cleveland lost the opening game with Young in the box," one writer opined, invoking the wonderfully vague theory of momentum, "the series was over."[15] Nig Cuppy, despite an injured finger, wound up bearing most of the Spiders' mound responsibilities in the series. When the one-sided competition ended, the Spiders divided their losing shares fourteen ways, the meagerness of the crowds in both Baltimore and Cleveland obliging them to settle for only $117 each. The four games had provided a decisive demonstration of the Orioles' diamond preeminence. They also showed that the Temple Cup series was becoming a bore.[16]

Several months after the series Tim Murnane, a widely read Boston baseball writer, declared Cy Young to be "on the decline." It was a provocative judgment, by some measures scarcely credible. After all, Young had won 29 games (corrected by latter-day historians to a marginally lower 28), the third best total in the league. He stood second in games pitched (51), games completed (42), and innings pitched (414⅓)—all important measures of quality in his era. He led the league in shutouts with 5, in strikeouts with 140, and in fewest bases on balls allowed per nine innings with 1.35.[17] He blazed through September, winning 6 of 7 decisions.

Still, Murnane was on to something. At the opening of the 1896 season Frank Robison and Patsy Tebeau had quarreled over whether Tebeau had overworked Young in 1895. Tebeau had won the argument, and Young had gone on to pitch 40 more innings in 1896 than the 1895 total of 369⅔ that Robison had feared was already too high. A pace as intense and relentless as this takes a toll, and even with the statistical uncertainties of the age Murnane may have seen signs of overwork. In 44⅔ additional innings, for example, Young gave up fully 114 additional hits. While the league's earned run average (as later calculated, of course) was falling by almost half a run, Young's earned run average stood virtually unchanged. Most intriguingly, Cy Young himself declared that in order to spare his arm the stress of delivering a constant barrage of fastballs, he was relying increasingly on a change-up.[18] In one way or another Murnane was aware of these points. He also knew that Young would turn thirty before the next season began, which gave further support to his assertion. After all, history afforded no example of a pitcher who had improved in his fourth decade of life, and only two examples—Pud Galvin and Charley Rad-bourn—of pitchers who had continued to enjoy significant success past thirty.

Sadly for Cy Young, the 1897 season seemed to bear out Murnane's observation. By a variety of indices it was his worst since he became an established star. His won-lost record was (by modern reckoning) a disap-pointing 21–19.[19] (Kid Nichols, by comparison was the league's best, at 31–11.) Young's victory total represented only 30 percent of his team's wins, the lowest such figure he had posted since becoming a regular. Be-tween August 25 and September 10 he lost seven decisions in a row. His earned run average rose by more than half a run (to 3.78) even as the league's earned run average slipped slightly downward. His opponents' on-base percentage reached .318, a figure exceeded during his career only in the offensively unique season of 1894. Barring the 1893 season, when all pitchers were struggling to cope with the new pitching distance, he recorded the lowest number of strikeouts per nine innings of pitching for any season of his regular career. Perspective on all of this is, of course, necessary. During the year Young passed Silver King and Jack Stivetts on the all-time victory list, and on May 24 he won his two hundredth career game; he again led the league in issuing the fewest walks per game; he tied for the league lead in pitching appearances; his opponents' on-base percentage, though elevated for him, was nevertheless, at fourth best in the league, pretty good. Still, Cy Young was not accustomed to being just pretty good.

Young did not know what to make of his difficulties; in the words of the only writer who interviewed (and paraphrased) Young on the matter, the pitcher was "at a loss to account for his spell of losses."[20] I think we can do better. First of all, Young was probably feeling the strain of pitching 784 innings during the previous two seasons. This was a pace that few pitchers could bear year after year even in this early era. News-paper accounts often note that his deliveries in 1897 lacked the zip and bite of old; that sounds like a description of an arm suffering from over-work. Second, Young's pitching was probably impaired by Frank Robi-son's decision to save money by requiring the club to stay in Cleveland for the bulk of its spring practice. A long patch of cold weather prevented the squad from enjoying the benefits of outdoor work, and just as the ill-conditioned team stumbled from the starting block, losing its first five games in 1897, so the ill-conditioned pitcher launched his year haltingly, not winning his third game until the season was almost a month old and still standing below .500 on July 1. Third, Young experienced spells of poor health in 1897. In the April chill of Cleveland he caught cold, in May he was described as "not in the best of health," and in early June, with the Spiders on the road, he returned briefly to Cleveland to recuperate from an unspecified arm problem.[21] It's likely that Cy Young was finding the year confusing, and we can perhaps ascribe occasional press accounts of an unwonted prickliness in his demeanor to his frustration at what must have struck him as a puzzling season.[22]

Despite its problems, the 1897 season offered Cy Young one moment of supreme glory. On September 18, pitching briskly in Cleveland against Cincinnati, he required only an hour and 35 minutes to record a 6–0 no-hitter. It was the league's first no-hitter in over four years and just the second at the new pitching distance. Young struck out 3 and walked 1 while facing only 29 batters. His fastball was quick and sharp. Cleveland committed three errors, however, and two of them—both by Bobby Wallace—aroused comment. In the fourth inning the Spider third baseman made a remarkable grab of a sharp ground ball off the bat of Bugs Holliday but then threw errantly to first. In the seventh inning Wallace allowed a slow roller, again from Holliday's bat, to elude him. "The ball came straight at me," he explained, "but in some way got through me."[23] In at least one of these instances, and perhaps in both (the accounts are inconsistent), the scorer initially gave Holliday a base hit. But Wallace, aware that Cy Young was otherwise untouched, prevailed upon the scorer to change his judgments from hits to errors. "I have never forgotten the little fellow for that," Young said later.[24] The scorer may have acted out of hometown favoritism; Holliday and the Cincinnati writers certainly thought so. But other observers, perhaps more impartial, thought the plays genuinely ambiguous—authentic and difficult judgment calls.

Cy Young, of course, was very happy at his achievement.[25] At the distance of a century we may suspect that he was the beneficiary of the judgments of a sympathetic scorer. But since virtually every no-hitter that involves an error by the pitcher's team—and a majority do—also involves an exercise of the scorer's judgment, we ought not deprecate an achievement just because some interested parties disliked the judgment. It is clear from all the available evidence that the accomplishment was widely applauded within the world of baseball. For example, when O. P. Caylor of the *Sporting News* summed up the year, he called the no-hitter one of the two most remarkable feats of the 1897 season and explained his satisfaction by noting that Cy Young was "honest, deserving, [and] popular."[26] The adjectives are telling; if Young got the benefit of a dubious decision, the outcome reflected at least in part his growing reputation for untempered probity and quiet dignity in a profession full of reprobates, hoodlums, and scallawags.

The Spiders' performance in 1897 mirrored Cy Young's struggle. Highly touted before the season began, the club limped home in fifth place, their 69–62 record situating them a full 23½ games behind the pennant-winning Boston Beaneaters. Cy Young's work was not the only individual disappointment of the year. Nig Cuppy, after three straight seasons with victory totals in the 20s, was out of action for almost three months with arm trouble and won only 10 games. Jesse Burkett, after two straight batting championships, slipped below .400 and yielded primacy to Willie Keeler. Cupid Childs's batting average was off by 17 points, Ed McKean's by a monumental 65 points. As a team, the Spiders scored 70 fewer runs in 1897 and slipped from best to fourth best in team earned run average. There were, to be sure, some bright spots: Lou Criger's emergence as the talented successor to Chief Zimmer behind the plate; Bobby Wallace's shift from satisfactory work as an occasional pitcher to outstanding work as a daily third baseman; Jack Powell's arrival as a hurler of promise. The team even managed to win twelve consecutive games in September. But no one could hide the sense of disappointment when the season ended. For all of Patsy Tebeau's brave talk before the season opened ("Cleveland will take the pennant"), the Spiders had never been in contention.[27]

Oddly (and, Cy Young might have added, thankfully), all of the foregoing considerations were overshadowed in the public's view by two other long-running dramas. The first featured the most celebrated major league rookie in many years, Louis Sockalexis, a Penobscot Indian inevitably called "Chief." Sockalexis was the original Cleveland Indian and (most probably) the circuitous inspiration for the nickname of the current American League franchise. A man of immense talent with an equally large capacity for self-destruction, Sockalexis burst upon America's baseball imagination during spring training, showed flashes of great ability in the opening months of the season, and then immolated himself in drinking binges at midseason. His subsequent life—a short existence crippled by an inability to escape the blight of raging alcoholism—became a morality tale for the age and a reinforcement of racialist thinking in the sports-focused sector of American society.

The other long-running drama turned on Frank Robison's determination to increase his gate receipts by staging professional baseball games on Sundays in Cleveland. By state law such games were illegal, but Robison was heartened by the fact that the law was regularly ignored in Cincinnati and Toledo; moreover, a Cleveland city ordinance exempted baseball from the strictures of the law. Dreaming of selling tickets to factory hands who could attend games only on Sunday, Robison spoke with customary directness to city leaders: "I have been quoted as saying that if we could not play Sunday ball at home we would take the team where it would not be interfered with. That is exactly what will occur."[28] To force his point he scheduled eleven Sunday games in Cleveland and decided to violate the law ostentatiously, confident that the prohibition would be ruled unconstitutional. He faced opposition, of course, chiefly in the form of an unlikely alliance between Protestant clergy and saloon keepers, each of whom hoped to prevent the legitimization of a Sabbath recreation that would compete with Sunday activities that they themselves sponsored. The test game, against Washington, was played on May 16 before 9,500 fans, and after the first inning, in an act of friendly theater, the police arrested all participants on both teams.[29] (Cy Young was not on the mound that Sunday and thus escaped arrest.) The immediate trial upheld the law but, with appeal succeeding appeal, the matter was in litigation throughout the season. And as long as the matter remained unresolved, Sunday games were permitted. Attendance at these contests—15,000 patrons in one instance—justified Robison's beliefs. In fact, thanks to these Sunday games the Spiders contrived to turn a small profit in 1897, despite having the league's lowest home attendance figure.[30] But with the outcome of the litigation still uncertain when the season ended, the possibility that the success of 1897 could not be repeated in 1898 loomed large in the owner's mind.

Frank Robison had another worry: during the 1897 season he had seen the great Cleveland club he had constructed early in the decade show clear signs of deterioration. The magnificent tandem of Cy Young and Nig Cuppy had managed only 31 victories. Slowness of foot was damaging the work of Ed McKean both at bat and in the field. Chief Zimmer's legendary durability was a thing of the past. Jimmy McAleer was so short of enthusiasm that he decided to retire not long after the season opened.[31] Meanwhile, quarreling and factionalism were taking a toll on morale. Jesse Burkett, whose well-earned nickname was "Crab," poured racist scorn upon Louis Sockalexis, and Ed McKean and Cupid Childs, who together constituted one of the most successful keystone combinations in baseball history, spoke to each other only to exchange recriminations. In August, Childs expressed his disgust at what was happening to the team: "We are no longer the Spiders or the Indians. We are the Quitters."[32] And by the end of the season the clubhouse environment had become so poisoned by these rancors that, according to one press account, fully seven players—McKean, Childs, Burkett, Zimmer, Nig Cuppy, Jack O'Connor, and Harry Blake—were hoping to be traded away.[33] A shrewd judge of baseball players, Frank Robison surely recognized these signs of dissolution. One can speculate that he felt both bitter and sad. After all, he had given Cleveland the third best team of the decade—a team that had three times qualified for postseason competition and once won the Temple Cup—and his reward had been empty seats in League Park and a cranky set of employees. If he now had to start rebuilding, he might well prefer to test his luck in a city that would be willing to tolerate Sunday baseball.

True to form, Cy Young stood apart from the fracases. He was never identified as a troublemaker, never marked as a member of the unhappy set. But his disappointing record in 1897 meant that he too was now an object of speculation. Frank Selee, for example, who just a year earlier had declared Young to be worth $10,000, now rated him at under $7,000. Young's defenders were prompt to issue rebuttals. "Young," Patsy Tebeau said, "is the equal of any pitcher in the League." Charles Mears added, "To think that he has seen his best day is outlandish." And Davis Hawley predicted, "If Cy Young is sold or traded to a good club, I'll bet $100 he'll beat us two out of three games he pitches against us next year."[34] No doubt Cy Young followed these press reports with interest after his return to Tuscarawas County. But we have no evidence of his thoughts during the off-season; in fact, his only postseason public appearance occurred in mid-October when he joined his neighbor Cy Swaim to play in a pickup baseball game in Dennison, Ohio. Still, testimony about his attitude the succeeding spring suggests that this proud man spent the winter counting the days until he could demonstrate that he was still a master of the mound.

For when the cold of a mid-Ohio winter finally broke, Cy Young was ready to show his stuff. He had already signed a contract for the coming season, agreeing to the ostensible league maximum of $2,400. It was the same salary he had received in 1897, and in both years it was probably augmented by several hundred more dollars. Young was pleased that the team was training in Hot Springs, for he found the conditions at the spa salubrious. He journeyed to Arkansas in mid-February, unusually early for the era, and clear evidence that he had resolved to be in good condition when the season began. Robba Young accompanied him. (It is possible that she had traveled with her husband on earlier spring jaunts, but this is the first time for which I have evidence of her presence. She must have liked the experience, for from this season on, until responsibilities at home became too demanding, she accompanied her husband on his spring training trips.) For several weeks Cy Young submitted to a daily regimen of baths, sweats, massages, and runs—the "weakening process," as it was called.[35] A notoriously early riser, he often spent his prebreakfast hours tramping about the forested hills surrounding the spa. He had brought his dog and rifle with him, and on at least one occasion he shared a wild turkey he had bagged with his teammates.[36] Once daily play began, he quickly demonstrated that he would be "a hard man for any club to beat."[37] When the club finally left Hot Springs on April 1, Patsy Tebeau professed to be a happy man. "This is our season," he predicted, "and no mistake."[38]

Back in Ohio, however, waiting for the return of his club, Frank Robison was far less happy. For even as the baseball season was getting launched, the Ohio Supreme Court handed down the judgment about Sunday play that he had feared. The court held that the state law prohibiting ball playing on the Sabbath was constitutional and that local authorities might therefore enforce it. The decision left Robison with only one option. If he wanted both to make money and to keep his franchise in Cleveland (and he did), he had to find a municipality just outside the city limits where Sunday contests would be tolerated. To this end he sought to lease a field somewhere—in Cedar Point perhaps, or in Euclid Beach, or in Collinwood Park; he even talked of building a grounds for the purpose of playing Sunday games (and offering horse racing on weekdays). Since attendance was sinking nationally in 1898, a consequence some attributed to the nation's fascination with the war with Spain, such ambitions were genuinely heady. As late as mid-June Robison declared that "our interests are here [in Cleveland], and here the club will stay."[39]

But on June 19, 1898, Frank Robison's patience finally snapped. He had scheduled a Sunday game that day in Collinwood Park, which lay just outside the city, to evade the prohibition in Cleveland proper. But an assiduous clergyman swore out warrants against the Cleveland players, and when the eighth inning was over the marshall executed the warrants. (Not pitching that day, Cy Young was not arrested.) For Robison this was the final proof that the local clergy, not content with hounding his team out of the city of Cleveland on Sundays, were conspiring to prevent the club from playing anywhere at all in northern Ohio on the Sabbath. "I am not in the baseball business for fun nor for patriotism for my own city," Robison had declared a year earlier, "and I do not propose to have a few people in Cleveland"—he had the ministers chiefly in mind—"run my team to my disadvantage when I can see good money in it elsewhere."[40] The city had not heeded four years of warnings. From this point on Robison bent his energies to moving his team to another locale.

Several other sites seemed attractive. Buffalo, Detroit, Indianapolis, and Milwaukee figured in press speculation during the late summer. There was talk too of some sort of merging of Cleveland with the Brooklyn team. But for several years Robison and his brother Stanley had spoken favorably of the baseball environment in St. Louis, where the quixotic Browns owner, Chris von der Ahe, was caught up in an apparently hopeless struggle to retain command of his floundering team. The Robisons reckoned that if they could purchase the St. Louis franchise, they could shift their stable of talent westward and sell tickets to the baseball-savvy fans of the Gateway City. And so the Robisons' chief negotiations focused on St. Louis as the summer advanced.

Meanwhile, in an extraordinary gesture of anger and contempt for Cleveland, Frank Robison acted early in July to transfer as many as possible of the club's remaining home games away from the Forest City. This might at first seem a self-destructive decision, but Robison had calculated that even with the additional transportation and housing costs he might stand to gain, since his club was the third best attraction in the National League when on the road. If the choice was between 1,000 fans in Cleveland and 6,000 in Cincinnati, Robison knew where the advantage lay. Besides, now that he was burning bridges, he saw no reason to forswear settling other scores. Engaged in a bitter legal dispute with Mark Hanna, with whose trolley company Robison had merged his own in 1893, Robison decided to deny the company (and Hanna) the custom that would come from riders traveling out to League Park.[41] The rescheduling was not easy; the club wound up playing major league games in such places as Rochester, New York, and Weehawken, New Jersey. But Robison was remarkably successful in this final act of spite, and of the club's final 74 playing dates, 70 saw games on the road. To no one's surprise, Cleveland in 1898 once again drew the smallest number of fans to home games.[42]

For Cy Young and his teammates these were trying times. At the beginning of the season there was press discussion about whether the club was more aptly tagged as Spiders or Indians; after midseason the choice of terms became derisive, with Wanderers, Vagabonds, Tramps, Pothunters, and Nomads looming large in headlines.[43] For a while the team did well. As late as August 8 the Wandering Willies were in second place and ahead of Boston. But a late-August slide combined with the Bean-eaters' rush to the finish line left Cleveland 21 games out when the season ended. Initially the players had hoped to demonstrate their professionalism by shrugging off the inconvenience of homelessness, but the absence of supportive crowds, the constant confrontation with home-team umpiring, and the lack of familiarity with playing grounds finally took a toll on morale. Their offensive power dissolved, and the team finished ninth in team batting averages; the once dazzling Jesse Burkett fell to .341.[44] Pitching held up better, and Jack Powell in particular, with a 23–15 season, stepped forward to replace the sore-armed Nig Cuppy as Cy Young's chief partner. But the obstacles to success were simply too large. Although the team won two of every three games played at home in 1898, it failed to win even half of the many more games played on the road. Cy Young probably spoke for many when he was later quoted as saying that as late as June "I had great hopes that the long-coveted pennant would be ours this year. I still think we could have won it by playing all our home games at home, and I regret exceedingly that a situation should have arisen making it necessary to transfer our games."[45]

Cy Young remained strong throughout the season, improving in almost every important respect on his previous year's performance. His won-lost record moved from 21–19 to 25–13.[46] He was consistent, going 13–6 through the Fourth of July and 12–7 thereafter. He was significantly better at home than away, but even so his 14–11 record on the road marked him as the club's only reliable hurler once the wanderings had begun. At one point he pitched 9 straight games without ever yielding more than 2 runs in a game. It is interesting to note that even as early as the 1890s baseball had a sense of its history and was sometimes aware of milestones. Thus, as Young added to his lifetime victory list, the press began to mark how he was passing the career totals of some celebrated forerunners. Bob Caruthers's 218 lifetime victories were exceeded on April 29, Will White's 229 were passed on July 9, and Charlie Buffinton's 233 were eclipsed on July 23. Meanwhile, Young completed all but one of his 41 starts. He reduced his yielding of base hits by more than one per game. His earned run average plummeted—from the embarrassing

3.78 the previous year to 2.53. Even though the season witnessed a general recession in earned run averages as starting corps expanded and as pitchers who had known only the new pitching distance began to arrive in large numbers in the league, the drop in Young's average was as impressive as anyone's.

The press, however, focused on yet another aspect of his improvement: although pitching 42 more innings in 1898, he walked 8 fewer batters. He had, in the sportspeak hyperbole of the day, "cut bases on balls out of his repertoire."[47] In every year from 1892 on Young had led the league in fewest walks per game. This was, however, not a statistic gathered in his own day. It was only in 1898 that observers began widely to comment on Young's command of the ball. In 13 of his complete games he issued no walks at all. He never issued more than 3 in a game. At one point he went 4 straight games without yielding a pass. All of this seemed impressive. And latter-day statisticians have ratified the judgment that contemporaries were drawing: in 1898 Cy Young became the first major league pitcher working at the new pitching distance to yield less than one base on balls per game.

When the season ended, Cy Young had reclaimed his title as one of the National League's preeminent hurlers. And while the dominant pitching star of the three-year period of 1896–98 was clearly Kid Nichols, who posted 92 victories over the span, Cy Young during that period recorded a very creditable 74 wins—a total sufficient to put him in second place behind the Boston ace and to make him, with Nichols and Clark Griffith, one of only three pitchers to win 20 or more games in each of the three seasons. He was nevertheless troubled when the season ended. Although most observers believed that St. Louis would be the new home of the Spiders, the matter remained unresolved as the team members dispersed for the winter. According to some press speculation, Young was sufficiently disenchanted with the prospect of relocating to St. Louis that he had declared he would likely abandon baseball entirely and resume the life of a farmer. His only published comment sounds more like a wish than a prediction: "I expect to see ... the Cleveland team in the forest city. I have no proofs for this. It is only my opinion."[48] He decided that his best protection against a hazy future was to remain uncommitted, and like all but one of his teammates he went into the winter without having signed a contract.

CHAPTER SIX

꿰

1899–1900:

St. Louis Blues

T HE PLAYERS' situation became clearer early in 1899 when Frank Robison and his brother Stanley, acting with the support of the National League, effectively secured the rights to the St. Louis franchise. The brothers now controlled two ball clubs—one in Cleveland and one in St. Louis—and were free to distribute players between the two as they wished. Such multiple control was called "syndicate baseball." It is now impermissible, largely because it allows the person who controls the two clubs to cluster his talent in one of them and reduce the other to a joke—a path that the Robisons almost immediately embarked upon. St. Louis was famously a good baseball town, unencumbered by any law banning Sunday games. In the 1880s its team had won four consecutive American Association pennants and one World Series. Of late, however, under the direction of Chris von der Ahe, the St. Louis club had become a laughingstock, and its record of 68 wins and 213 losses over the course of the 1897 and 1898 seasons remains even today the poorest two-year performance for any club in the history of the major leagues.[1] With little to cheer about, St. Louis fans had been staying away from games. But informed observers said that interest remained high among St. Louisians, who were ready to respond to any team that could contend. To the Robisons, stung by their inability to draw a crowd with their fine stable of players in Sabbatarian Cleveland, the laxer atmosphere of St. Louis seemed a fit alternative. To maximize their chance of winning the hearts of St. Louis fans they shifted virtually every Spider, including, of course, their greatest star and drawing card, Cy Young, to the new franchise. And to make the move more palatable to Young, they increased the sub rosa portion of his salary to allow him to earn more than $2,750—and perhaps as much as $3,000—for his work.

Cy and Robba Young traveled to Hot Springs in January of 1899. The pitcher was readying himself for his tenth season in the major leagues, but he apparently had gained a few pounds over the winter, causing writers to comment on his weight. When we summon up images of Young today, we are inclined to see the hefty hurler of the early twentieth century. Throughout his Spider years, however, Young had been strapping rather than simply large. The press comments from 1899 hint that he was taking on the broader silhouette with which we are familiar. And Young seemed to confess as much a year later: "Training is not a picnic for a man of my build. . . . No one knows what I went through with last spring to get in condition."[2] Throughout the preseason St. Louis sportswriters introduced their readers to the new players. The scribes devoted much ink to Patsy Tebeau and Jack O'Connor, two sons of St. Louis, and to the dapper Cupid Childs. Generally speaking, the colorless Cy Young gave them much less to write about, though his strength and his height— he was still about as tall as any player in the league—aroused comment. Concerning the prospects for the coming season, the reporters were optimistic. Patsy Tebeau delivered a new version of his annual springtime pep talk: "With the support we expect to receive from the St. Louis enthusiasts we will surely be winners."[3] And in one account Cy Young was heralded as the "elongated twirler" who, with "a few bushels of speed to spare" and control that was "all that could be desired," would lead the charge.[4] Though overwrought to our ears, the prose bespoke an authentic excitement among the St. Louis baseball fans.

Cy Young pitched St. Louis's home opener on April 15, a 10–1 laugher against—as fate would have it—the ragtag bunch of former St. Louisians who now made Cleveland their "home."[5] It was a game pitting the Robisons' A-team against their B-team. Over 15,000 fans thronged into the ballpark, a structure still scarred from a great fire in 1898. They constituted the largest hometown crowd Young and his teammates had ever played before, and armed with cowbells and bugles, they may also have been the noisiest. Before the game began various local luminaries, including the mayor, made enthusiastic remarks to the crowd. The euphoria generated by this opening-day triumph did not immediately dissolve. The club played well through the first month of competition, hanging on to first place until the fourth week in May. Young reeled off victories in his first five starts, never yielding more than 6 hits in a game and winning praise as "the premier pitcher of the year."[6]

When he led his team into Cleveland, the local fans cheered for St. Louis rather than the Spiders, and a poem hailed his arrival with the wonderfully obscure lines:

> Well, well, well. Old One Lung!
> Me and Betsey. Big Cy Young.[7]

As if to underscore the marked difference between the Robisons' team and von der Ahe's team, St. Louis fans abandoned the old team nickname of "Browns," in favor of the "Perfectos," a name which offered, in the term "Pat's Perfectos," the attraction of alliteration to baseball writers.[8] Only when the team finally ran into stiff competition in late May—facing first the 1898 pennant-winning Boston team and then the 1899 pennant-winning Brooklyn team—did it slip from first place. Its descent thereafter was steady, however, and by June 28 the Perfectos were in sixth place. Meanwhile, Young, suddenly "receiving his medicine ... with the rest," fell from 5–0 to 11–8.[9] The nadir came on June 16 when he lost an extra-inning game to Louisville 13–12, giving up 19 hits to the winners.

Two things seem to have gone wrong. First, as a team of veterans, the Perfectos showed the continuing impact of advancing age that had become visible the year before. Only Jesse Burkett regained the brilliance of the mid-1890s, while Cupid Childs and Ed McKean sank to mediocrity. The second problem was not unrelated to the first: as the team's record declined, its interpersonal acrimonies flared. Press accounts afford revealing glimpses of these quarrels. There's Burkett sulking. There's Tebeau publicly berating Childs. There's Burkett and Ossee Schreckengost exchanging fierce blows. There's McKean quarreling—and then retiring from baseball. Finally, there's the ever-cantankerous Burkett again—remember, he's the "Crab"—leaping into the Negro section of the outfield stands in St. Louis to pummel a black spectator who had presumed to criticize his play. For much of June and well into July the Perfectos were out of control, riven by conflicting prides and untempered frustrations and taking their irritation out on beleaguered umpires.

Though laboring throughout much of the early summer, Cy Young was not one of the whiners, scrappers, or loners. Indeed, there is evidence of something quite different occurring—we might call it the emergence of Cy Young as a role model. One press account referred to Young, Lave Cross, and Nig Cuppy as the only gentlemen on the St. Louis team. Another commended him for his self-effacing avoidance of the spotlight. Tales of his honest self-command circulated. In one mid-August game, for example, he thought umpire Hank O'Day had made an errant call. After the game, as the story ran, he approached the umpire to say, "Mr. O'Day, I think that was a strike." "I don't," was the arbiter's terse reply. "Alright, Mr. O'Day," Young softly countered, "but in my opinion it was undoubtedly a strike."[10] No fight. No quarrel. End of story. The picture slowly coming into focus in the final years of the nineteenth century was one of a baseball statesman, and the baseball press occasionally spoke of Young as the "G.O.M.," an abbreviation ordinarily associated with the late and respected Grand Old Man of British politics, William Ewart Gladstone. But the firmest evidence that the baseball world admired Young was that wherever the Perfectos went during the summer of 1899, the fans applauded "the mighty Young."[11] He was beginning to transcend traditional notions of partisanship and rivalry.

Young recovered from his early summer slump to win 10 of 13 decisions between July 14 and August 31. And toward the end of that period he managed to seize the full attention of the baseball world. On August 18 he shut out the Phillies in Philadelphia. Three days later he shut out the Colts in St. Louis, coincidentally recording his twentieth victory. Three days after that he again shut out the Phillies. The final whitewash was a three-hitter, his finest pitching effort of the season. Before he was finally scored upon he posted 31 consecutive frames of pitching. He was equally stingy with bases on balls, not yielding a single walk in any of the three shutout games. Umpire Ed Swartwood, who officiated the game against Chicago, declared: "You should see Cy Young pitch ball. . . . He is faster now than he has been in two years. His speed is something terrific."[12] When Young himself was asked after the third shutout about his achievement, he replied with characteristic self-effacement. "I am not so much to blame for it as the other fellows [the Phillies]. They were not batting at their usual gait today."[13] In a sense, he was right: both Larry Lajoie and Elmer Flick were injured and out of the lineup. But to put the matter in perspective, it is useful to recall that the Phillies, victims in two of the three shutouts, wound up leading the National League in 1899 in batting, slugging, and runs scored. The shutout inning streak was the outstanding pitching performance of the year and proved that when Cy Young was in his groove, there was not a team in the league that could do much against him.

Unfortunately for the Perfectos, team success in baseball requires more than a few outstanding individual performances. And so, even though Cy Young finished with a splendid 26–16 record and Jesse Burkett hit .396 to finish second in the batting chase, the St. Louis club finished only in fifth place in the National League, 18½ games off the pace. The reason? Burkett was a one-man offensive operation; only two other batters hit above .300. And while Jack Powell matched Young for a while and ended up with 23 victories, his earned run average was almost a run higher than Young's. Fifth place was, of course, not a disaster; for the first time since joining the National League in 1892 a St. Louis club had finished in the first division. But the influx of talent had promised even fuller success. Still, while the Robisons had not secured the sought-after flag, they had certainly succeeded financially, the franchise turning a profit of $40,000 on the season. Moreover, the club was such a strong draw that in addition to attracting 100,000 more home fans in 1899 alone than the Browns had drawn in the previous two seasons together, it emerged as the league's most popular road team and wound up, home and road combined, playing before a league-leading total of almost 600,000 fans.[14] No player contributed more to the Perfectos' popularity than Cy Young.

For once again Young had been magnificent. The baseball press hailed him as the season's winningest pitcher—27 victories said the *Sporting News*, 29 said *Sporting Life*.[15] (An aside is necessary. It is startling to a late-twentieth-century observer that tasks seemingly as elementary as the summing up of victories were matters of disagreement a century ago.[16] When later historians examined the records from 1899, they not only reduced Young's victory total to 26, they dislodged him as victory champion, bestowing the joint title instead on Baltimore's sensational, submarine-delivery rookie, Joe McGinnity, and Brooklyn's outstanding sophomore, Jim Hughes, each with 28.) Young led the league with the most complete games (40) and the lowest opponents' on-base percentage (.285). He was second in shutouts (4) and in earned run average (2.58). He was third in innings pitched (369⅓). He was also a slump breaker, never losing more than two games in a row. He even had the satisfaction of winning a bet from teammate Jack Powell that he would end the year with the higher batting average. (Young's was .216, Powell's .201.)[17] In trying to account for these successes, we should consider that for the first time in his career he pitched an entire season without ever having fewer than two full days of rest between starts.

In a late-season analysis of his pitching success, one writer stated that Young's "speed was never better and his command is wonderful. The corners are so easy for him that it is a rare thing for him to use a curve, but just to show that he has something more than speedy straight ones on [*sic*] his repertoire, he will occasionally bend one over or shoot in an underhanded ball which is very effective."[18] At about the same time Patsy Tebeau offered a complementary judgment: "You will notice that Cy seldom uses a slow ball but depends on control and the knack of his quick-breaking shoot. He is constantly whizzing them over at top bursts of speed."[19] A New York writer trying to capture the frustrations of hitters who stepped in against Young wrote, "the batting of Mauser bullets would have been just as easy a proposition."[20] With Amos Rusie no longer pitching, Cy Young may have been the fastest hurler in the league.

But not all went well in 1899. Cy Young found the Missouri weather oppressive. In one interview he ascribed the team's difficulties to the "hot, humid and malarial" climate of St. Louis. He said, "I attribute many of our defeats in the home grounds to the change in climate."[21] The claim is somewhat odd, since neither the team's record nor Young's record bears it out. Young was actually better at home than away, posting a 15–7 record in St. Louis and an 11–9 record on the road. He was also at his best when the heat was highest, recording 11 wins against only 4 defeats in July and August. As for the Perfectos as a team, they played .600 ball at home and .500 ball on the road. But Young was not a complainer by nature, and his remarks about the St. Louis climate may be subjectively true even if objectively unverifiable. Something was clearly troubling him. In press reports about a game in early September Young was singled out for the totally uncharacteristic behavior of deliberately bumping an umpire. It's possible that he was simply reflecting his wife's unhappiness with St. Louis, for Robba had found summer life in Missouri far less comfortable than in Ohio. Whatever the explanation, however, it appears that even as the Tuscarawan farmer added more achievements to his career record in 1899—his two hundred and fiftieth victory on June 2 and the passing of Jim McCormick on the career victory list on September 16— he was, for the first time in his life, finding the responsibility of regular baseball toil somewhat irksome. It is a point the reader needs now to bear in mind.

Over the following winter, in an effort to improve the umpire's view of pitches, the owners changed the shape of home base, giving the game its modern plate. Through the 1899 season home plate, though embedded in the ground, had nevertheless been shaped like any other base. That is, it was a square, with sides 12 inches in length and hence a diagonal width of just about 17 inches; one of its four corners had been lodged where the baselines met and the opposite corner had pointed at the pitcher. In this configuration, the outside corners of the plate—and notice that they really were "corners"—were just tiny spots. The new plate was a pentagon, still only 17 inches wide but now covering 216 square inches rather than 144 and therefore replacing the tiny spots that had previously marked its widest point with more visible straight edges. There was much speculation about what effect this reshaping of the plate would have. Cy Young was among those who expected a significant change in major league pitching. "There will be fewer bases on balls given this year than in any previous season," he predicted, adding by way of explanation that "with the plate square in front of you you have a bigger target to throw at and consequently you have more confidence."[22] Interestingly, as far as I know, there was no speculation about the consequences of increasing the size (rather than just the visibility) of the plate, even though this expansion offered a larger target to any able curveballer, who, in order to pitch a strike, needed only to catch a small portion of the three-dimensional batting zone defined by the plate and the batter.

During the same winter the owners negotiated a far more important change—nothing less than surgery on the National League. The twelve-team circuit created in 1892 had increasingly proved dysfunctional. The root of the problem was the wide range of wealth among the owners. Some clubs lacked the funds necessary to field strong squads. Only a few clubs—and generally the same ones, year after year—were competitive. The resulting imbalances in talent assured that pennant races were unexciting for most fans. Without excitement, gates were small (especially in the cities represented by floundering franchises), making it impossible for many of the owners to turn a profit. The owners had hitherto been hesitant to drop teams because such an action would entail the considerable short-term expense of buying out their expelled colleagues. But after the financial disappointments of the 1899 season, drastic action seemed necessary, even at the cost of buy-out expenses. Moreover, the fact that there were now two instances of syndicate baseball in the league— the Cleveland–St. Louis connection and the Baltimore–Brooklyn connection—made the task somewhat more manageable. And so, just weeks before the 1900 season was to be launched, the owners announced that Baltimore, Cleveland, Louisville, and Washington would no longer have National League franchises.[23] The announcement was not a surprise, for rumors of a reduction had been circulating for months. But until the final decision was made, much else remained in suspension. Only at this point, for example, could the schedule for the coming season be published. And only at this point did it become publicly known which players might now be looking for new employers.

Cy Young, who had signed his 1900 contract shortly after the end of the previous season, was in Hot Springs when the news about the reduction broke. It did not affect him in any direct way, though it meant that talent in the league in the forthcoming season would be more concentrated than in the recent past. That did not bother him. In exhibition contests he was already showing his famous speed, while in an interview he declined to offer predictions for the upcoming season as long as the number of teams in the league remained uncertain.[24]

Frank Robison, meanwhile, anticipating the decision to drop four franchises, spent much of the winter seeking reinforcements for his St. Louis squad among the ranks of the soon-to-be uprooted, and although he failed in efforts to gain the contracts of Joe McGinnity (from Baltimore), Bill Dinneen (from Washington), or Honus Wagner, Fred Clarke, or Deacon Phillippe (from Louisville), he secured the rights to three Baltimore stars—middle infielder Bill Keister, catcher Wilbert Robinson, and third baseman John McGraw. Since McGraw was known to harbor managerial ambitions, Patsy Tebeau did not disguise his uneasiness with Frank Robison's move. "Kid," he told a reporter, "they're trying to give me the double-cross."[25] But St. Louis fans were delighted. In the judgment of one writer, "not since the days of Comiskey's four-time winners"—a reference to the great Browns' teams of the 1880s—"has St. Louis had such a formidable array of baseball talent."[26] That judgment was sound; the acquisitions meant that on days when Cy Young pitched, the St. Louis club could field a line-up of five future Hall-of-Famers.[27] But it was the feisty, outspoken, hard-playing, and savvy McGraw who grabbed the spotlight. Though not yet in camp—in fact, he held out until May and came on board only after winning the most lucrative contract in baseball—he was featured almost daily in the St. Louis baseball press.[28] It was his prospective presence on the field that made a pennant seem achievable.

What followed was a debacle. Though the Perfectos broke quickly from the gate, Cy Young winning the opening-day game with a 3–0 shut-out of the powerful Pirates, the team soon crashed. By June 19 it was in the league cellar. In the words of one commentator, the Perfectos were "the biggest disappointment in the League so far."[29] What happened? For starters, the club suffered a raft of injuries and illnesses. Jesse Burkett, John McGraw, Wilbert Robinson, Bobby Wallace, Emmett Heidrick, Lou Criger, Mike Donlin, Jack Powell, and Cy Young all went down for significant periods of time. Cy Young's problem—a bruised rib incurred when he collided with Ed Doheny of the New York Giants—was the first major injury he had ever sustained and kept him out of play for twenty days in June, the longest period of enforced inactivity in his career.[30] Still, health difficulties are not sufficient to explain the team's collapse. The Perfectos batted .291 in 1900, second highest in the league. They were second in slugging and in stolen bases. They were fourth in earned run average and, with that ranking, better than the pennant-winning Brooklyn team. In short, the usual indices of performance suggest that the St. Louis team was playing at a level that ought to have made them pennant contenders. A comparison of hits to runs, however, points to a problem; despite all their offensive power, the Perfectos needed almost 2 hits to generate 1 run whereas all the teams ahead of them in the standings clustered around the more efficient ratio of 1.75-to-1.

Inefficiency on the field—and here lies the real problem—was a re-flection of dissipation off the field, for in 1900 a team that had been show-ing symptoms of discord for several years finally lurched into self-destruction. "There is no use trying to duck it," an unidentified player said late in the season. "Booze is the cause of our being where we are."[31] Mike Donlin was a case in point; the injury that kept him from playing was a knife wound sustained in a bar fight. In fact, however, booze was not alone in exacting the toll. Gambling and womanizing also seared the team. John McGraw's appearance in May brought the club's divisions into the open, for he preferred wagering on horse races to playing ball even while criticizing Patsy Tebeau for the manager's inability to control his players or think strategically. Speculation in the press that McGraw and Wilbert Robinson were being paid almost $9,000 between them in salaries alone did not endear them to the veterans on the squad. In retro-spect we can see McGraw's first appearance in a St. Louis uniform on May 12 as a foreshadowing of his impact on the team: he got on base four times but committed the error in the ninth inning that allowed Brooklyn to defeat Cy Young 5–4.

Tebeau wilted under criticism from McGraw and the press and in August resigned the managerial position he had held for Frank Robison since 1891. The owner then offered the job to McGraw, but the third baseman, who had already declared his determination not to play for St. Louis in 1901, declined to lead the demoralized squad. An odd arrangement was finally patched together. Louis Heilbroner, a businessman with no playing experience, agreed to serve as nominal manager and to assume responsibility for getting the bar-hopping Perfectos into bed on time. John McGraw, though not formally manager, agreed to be what had once been called a team captain to make on-the-field decisions. In fact, it scarcely mattered what was done. A team that had played 42-and-50 ball under Tebeau completed its season with a 23-and-25 record under Heilbroner and McGraw. I'll give the last (and self-serving) word on the 1900 Perfectos to McGraw. When asked after the season what had gone wrong, he replied: "management, that's all. There was no discipline, and I may add, no intelligent direction."[32]

Amid the turmoil of off-the-field shenanigans and on-the-field acrimonies Cy Young was his usual sturdy self. He led the league in shutouts (4), was third in opponents' on-base percentage, and—despite missing three weeks—fourth in innings pitched. He accounted for 29 percent of his club's victories; only Joe McGinnity and Bill Dinneen did better by the teams they served. Despite the new shape of home plate, neither he nor the league posted a dramatic change in the frequency of bases on balls.[33] But he recorded a higher rate of strikeouts per game than in any previous season. He opened particularly well, recording nine of these strikeouts in his first appearance, a total that no other pitcher matched all year. And he closed well too when, with his two-hundred-eighty-fifth lifetime triumph on September 24, he surpassed the career total of Tony Mullane. Meanwhile—it's a mark of his durability and versatility (though it was unnoticed at the time)—the number of occasions across his career that he had served as a reliever rose to fifty-nine, establishing Young as the major league career leader in relief appearances. In coming years he would slowly add to that total, relinquishing his lead only in 1911.

One reason for his satisfaction with the season was the installation of the young Lou Criger as the catcher he would ordinarily work with. As early as 1898 Criger had established himself as a worthy replacement for the aging Chief Zimmer—as shrewd in his judgment and as accurate and quick with his throws. But he was more fragile than the resilient Zimmer, and in 1899 Jack O'Connor had served Young as frequently as Criger.

In 1900, however, the soon-to-be-famous duo of Young and Criger was effectively born. The 1900 season provided a foretaste of excitement to come in another respect. Twice during the year—on April 19 and September 24—Cy Young dueled against the gifted Rube Waddell, pitching for Pittsburgh, Young winning by scores of 3–0 and 1–0. Young-Waddell match-ups would become celebrated in later years, and the 1900 editions were portents of future pitching excitement.

Still, though much went well, Young was not entirely untouched by the confusions swirling about him. During the heart of the season he suffered some real poundings; one batter ascribed his difficulties to an uncharacteristic inability to keep his pitches away from the middle of the plate. Then on August 20, reflecting his mounting sense of frustration, he climbed into the stands to confront a fan who called him a quitter. The matter ended peacefully enough when the fan withdrew the charge, and Young later said, by way of (lame) explanation that, while he didn't mind honest criticism, he wouldn't tolerate abuse.[34] Whatever one makes of the incident, it was, for a man whose temperament was famously placid, unusual behavior. Finally, because he had lost three weeks to his injury, his victory total was lower than any he had posted since his rookie season. As calculated by the *Sporting News* and most sources, that record stood at 20 victories and 18 losses; the *Spalding Guide* modified the figures slightly, putting the record at 20 and 16.[35]

And here we run into what counts for us, though not for Cy Young, as the oddest disappointment of the season—a disappointment not even widely recognized until after Young's death. As latter-day baseball historians recovered information about the 1900 season and sought to regularize the application of scoring rules, it was determined that Cy Young had been credited with a victory he did not deserve. How this happened is still unclear.[36] But the correction is of more than minor importance. It was long believed that Cy Young had won twenty or more games in fourteen consecutive seasons, an accomplishment unparalleled in baseball history. By slipping below the threshold in 1900, however, Young lost his claim to that record. And what makes the incident even more vexing in retrospect is that at the end of the season he was unwittingly deprived of two chances to secure what could have been his twentieth victory. The first occurred on October 7, his final appearance of the season. He lost that day to Pittsburgh, 3–2, but the tight game was inexplicably ended after seven innings when umpire Bob Emslie called it on account of darkness even though the sun was shining brightly. Had it been thought that

Young had 19 wins rather than 20, Emslie might have let the game go ahead. As it was, the umpire needed a police escort to avoid the wrath of the crowd. The second occurred exactly a week later, when, for unknown reasons and contrary to press predictions, Young did not pitch the final game of the season. We may again speculate that, had it been known he had only 19 victories, he would likely have started.

If fractiousness among teammates provided one backdrop to Cy Young's season, league wide turbulence between players and owners afforded another. One issue was the players' often expressed dislike for the reserve clause. To the players it was a form of "bondage."[37] The players also disliked the owners' freedom to buy and sell contracts without the consent of the player involved and resisted the owners' power to move players around between major and minor league teams. None of these, however, was a new grievance. What brought these long-standing tensions to a boil in 1900 was the owners' avowed determination to cut salaries. Ever since 1892 a maximum individual salary cap of $2,400 had been in place, and only the greatest of the players had been allowed to exceed the limit. Cy Young, for example, recognized as one of the league's stars, had been receiving an annual salary of between $2,750 and $3,000 for at least two years. To our ears today these salaries are laughable. But to the owners at the turn of the century they were too high.

Hoping to forestall any action by the owners that might diminish their own wage-earning capacity, the players formed a labor union. A summons to all interested major leaguers was drafted in April, the various teams chose their delegations in the spring, and on June 11, while the western teams were in the East, the delegations met at Sturtevant House in New York City to create the Players Protective Association. Cy Young, nursing his side injury, was one of three Perfectos at the meeting.[38] There is no information about how the delegation was chosen, but since the other two members were Jesse Burkett and Emmett Heidrick, it is likely that the team decided to send players of eminence, two of whom were also veterans.[39] The Association met twice more during the season, defining itself as a body that represented the interests of the players, declining to affiliate with the American Federation of Labor, and professing no desire to seek a quarrel with the National League (for it remembered the outcome of the Brotherhood dispute of 1890 all too well). Despite these conciliatory statements, however, it denounced the language of the standard contract as "unfair, illegal, and too one-sided," and it undertook to propose a text with more equitable wording.[40] It also formed a grievance committee, with power to hear complaints from players against their employers. We may infer that Cy Young was keenly interested in the work of the Players Protective Association since he was the only St. Louis player to attend all three of its sessions. But since he was not elected to an office in the organization, we may also conclude that he was not seen by his colleagues as leadership material. That was probably his own judgment as well. He had done his duty by his teammates, and he hoped that ownership would attend to the statements of complaint issued by the Protective Association.

He could not foresee—nor could anyone else—the bizarre circumstance that gave rise to a new St. Louis grievance almost as soon as the season came to a close. On October 16 Frank Robison mailed out extraordinary letters to his players. In these documents the normally cheerful owner vented his anger at the disappointing season that had just ended. He accused the players of indifference, drunkenness, gambling, and what the press gently termed "kindred vices."[41] He explained that the last installment of their pay for 1900 was being withheld, and he told them to prepare for lower salaries in 1901. What was even more astonishing than the tone of the broadside was the identity of the four players specifically exempted from the criticism: John McGraw, Wilbert Robinson, Jesse Burkett, and Patsy Donovan. This categorization defied belief. McGraw, Robinson, and Donovan were high-livers; Burkett was a malcontent. To exempt them while indicting "the reliable Wallace, the steady Criger and the veteran Young"—press accounts might have added the astonished Heidrick and the indignant Cowboy Jones—was to turn reality inside out.[42] Several players complained to Cy Young, "just as if," he later smiled, "I was in the position to help them out of their troubles."[43] Young declared himself "surprised beyond anything I had ever imagined."[44]

Confronted by outrage from his players and incomprehension in the baseball press, Robison quickly backtracked. He acknowledged that the letter might have been directed to some persons who did not deserve the rebuke. He added Cy Young to the list of players who were to receive their final paycheck immediately. But the damage had been done. Through one stroke of ill-considered anger Frank Robison had sacrificed the goodwill that years of being his players' advocate (think of his defense of Tebeau in 1896 or his words of encouragement for the Players Protective Association) had won him.

More unhappily for him, he could not have chosen a worse time to lose his temper.[45] For even as National League owners were talking openly of reducing salaries, they were in great danger of losing their chief point of leverage in dealing with their players—namely, their monopoly control of major league playing opportunities. As has often been the case in the history of the game, the owners proceeded with a short-sightedness that was astonishing. By insisting on the inviolability of the reserve clause, they assured that there would be player discontent. By abandoning several traditional cities as they reduced the size of the league, they assured that there would be important urban areas eager to respond to new organizations. By snubbing ambitious businessmen who wanted to cooperate with the existing baseball structure while underwriting the widening of the game, they assured that all efforts at expansion would occur independently of input and guidance from the National League. The owners should not be accused of greed in all of this; only three of them had turned baseball profits in 1900, and they needed to find a way to transform their franchises into money-earners. But their peculiar status as almost autonomous feudal lords left them, despite their purported alliance through the National League, ill-equipped to cooperate when their realms were challenged.

Two such efforts were well under way as the 1900 season ended. One involved such luminaries of the baseball scene as Cap Anson, Francis Richter, and Alfred H. Spink. These men were promoting the creation of a second major league that would be called the National Association (or, occasionally, the American Association). The other involved an ambitious minor league that, having risen to a position of domination in midwestern baseball, proposed to challenge the National League for national preeminence. Known through the 1890s as the Western League, this organization had signaled its wider vision by adopting a new name—though not yet a new status—in 1900. The new name was the American League. The circuit's president was Ban Johnson, and to protect his league against traitorous actions by hard-pressed club owners, he insisted on holding 51 percent of every club's stock. The great miscalculation of the National League owners in the face of these maneuvers was not that they allowed a rival league to be born. Given the circumstances of the day, that outcome was probably unavoidable. Rather, their error was that, through their obstinacy, they lost the opportunity to help shape the emerging new baseball order. In November they refused to talk with Ban Johnson about the peaceful elevation of his circuit to major league status; in December they refused to talk seriously with representatives of the Players Protective Association about language for a new standard contract. Faced with these rebuffs, Ban Johnson and representatives of the Players Protective Association then met to discuss the possibility of cooperation against the National League. Once the leaders of the players union were persuaded that the American League would accept the bulk of the union's suggestions, they gave their blessing to Johnson's enterprise, triggering what the press happily called the "baseball war."[46]

In January of 1901 the American League carried through its plan to designate itself a major league and to plant teams in such eastern cities as Boston, Washington, Baltimore, and Philadelphia. To enhance the strength of its rosters it also developed a raiding plan, assigning to each of its eight franchises the names of three or four National League players whom those franchises should pursue. These lists of stars were secret. But men on the lists were not the only ones to benefit. Almost all major league players now had a choice of employer, for unless they had already signed their contract for 1901—and only a few had—they could probably draw their old National League club and one of the new American League franchises into a bidding war.[47] The circle of beneficiaries extended even wider, for with a doubling of the number of major league teams, many talented minor leaguers could hope to gain major league berths. On the surface the Players Protective Association did not want to play favorites between the two circuits. But by insisting that only those few players who had already signed contracts for 1901 were not free to choose between the leagues—that is, by effectively denying that any player was bound by the reserve clause in his 1900 contract—the Protective Association sanctioned league-jumping and hence earned the wrath of the National League.

The American League decision to move into Boston was a late one, made in an effort to forestall efforts by the faltering National Association to plant itself in the heart of New England. It was also a chancy decision, for the Boston franchise in the National League was one of the older circuit's most successful clubs, the winner of five pennants in the 1890s alone. A major element in American League strategy in every city where it was challenging a National League club directly was to win over players from the intracity rival. In Boston this meant going after the great Beaneater stars, and the new team scored a triumph toward the end of February when Jimmy Collins, widely regarded as the older circuit's best third baseman, accepted a contract with the Boston Americans. It was in fact a double triumph, for not only did the new Boston team get a star, it got a leader—a point made clear when Collins was named manager. Collins immediately set out to persuade other Beaneaters to take the risk of signing on with the new league. (It's important to recall that there was a significant element of risk in these decisions. At the distance of a century we know that the American League succeeded. Contemporaries did not have that knowledge, and their caution is understandable; to sign on with the American League and then to see it fail in the manner of the Union Association or Players League would be to lose a lucrative employment opportunity at least for the short term and perhaps forever.) At his first news conference after becoming manager Jimmy Collins sketched out his hopes. Among them was the ambition to create a formidable pitching staff by luring four fine National League hurlers to his squad: Bill Dinneen and Vic Willis of Boston, Bill Bernhard of Philadelphia—and Cy Young of St. Louis. The declaration was public confirmation that Young was on Boston's list.

It is not clear when Cy Young first received a proposal from the new Boston American League team. But he knew that the fluidity of the situation might offer him an opportunity to make more money, and when asked late in 1900 to comment on the upcoming season, he was very cautious: "it is useless to discuss 1901 until the magnates meet and lay their plans for the next race."[48] When the Players Protective Association assembled in Cleveland in early February 1901, Young represented St. Louis. The site of the meeting made Young an obvious choice for St. Louis's delegate, but even if that was his reason for attending, the gathering was an occasion for swapping thoughts with other leading players—including Jimmy Collins. The meeting voted to boycott the National League, on the grounds that the older circuit did not recognize the contract language proposed by the Protective Association. Though the National League was still able to sign many of its stars, it is surely significant that of the fifteen National League delegates present in Cleveland, eight started the 1901 season in the American League. Another influence on Young's thinking may have been his old Cleveland contacts. The Forest City was returning to the majors through the new league, and while the Cleveland club apparently made no effort to secure Young's services (he was, after all, on Boston's list), Jimmy McAleer, the man who would manage the new Cleveland entry, urged Young to switch leagues. Beyond that, much of the money behind the new Boston franchise was being supplied by Cleveland magnate Charles Somers; if he found an opportunity to share views with Young, we can assume that he also recommended a switch.

Still, Cy Young was a careful man: "a methodical, conservative fellow, with a good farm and a nice bank roll. . . . He will hesitate."[49] Four considerations finally inclined him to accept the offer from the new American League team. The first was his anger with Frank Robison for what Young called the "malingering" letter. "After getting that letter," he later declared, "I swore that I would never pitch another game for Mr. Robison."[50] Had that statement been strictly true, the matter would have been resolved. But it is more likely an example of post facto hyperbole, providing a simple explanation for a complicated choice. The second consideration was actuarial. Young had declared the previous spring that he believed he would retire after the 1901 season.[51] If he planned to retire soon anyway, he had no reason to be troubled by the prospect that an American League collapse in the longer term would deprive him of an employment opportunity. The third consideration was the decision of Lou Criger to accept the Boston offer. He and Young were in communication and shared views about the prospects for the new league. Criger's action weighed heavily with Young, for the pitcher thought Criger an intelligent younger man, and he valued his battery-mate's skills as a backstop.[52]

The fourth consideration, of course, was the money. "I'm in the game for Cy's wife and babies," he said late in the winter (though he had no children), "and will go where the most money is obtainable."[53] He was in Hot Springs at the time, shedding pounds and waiting to see how high Boston and St. Louis were willing to bid for his services. In the end Frank Robison came very close to meeting Boston's offer for 1901; in dollar terms Robison may actually have topped Boston's offer. But the Boston management finally trumped Robison by proposing a three-year contract to the hurler. Frank Robison would not go beyond a one-year commitment, and Stanley Robison explained the club's reasoning: Young was in decline and would probably not last more than one more year in the National League. And so in the third week of March 1901, Cy Young chose the new Boston team, signing his first American League contract for a salary of about $3,500.

It is easy for us to laugh at Frank Robison's poor judgment. But in fact he had much actuarial experience on his side. Cy Young celebrated his thirty-fourth birthday about the time he signed the contract. How well had pitchers past their thirty-fourth birthday done over the past quarter century? Charley Radbourn had done best—58 wins and 36 losses from the age of 34 on. A few others had continued to be effective enough to hang on in the majors—Pud Galvin with 36 wins, Tim Keefe with 34,

Tony Mullane with 25, and Bobby Mathews with 16. But that's about it. Such legends as Charlie Buffinton, John Clarkson, Silver King, Jim McCormick, Jack Stivetts, Mickey Welch, and Will White had hung up their gloves by the time they were 34. Thus, Robison had history on his side in declining to extend Young a lucrative, multi-year contract. Why then was Boston willing to take the risk? In part, I suspect, because Criger assured his new manager and owner that Young was still a fine pitcher. In part too because the inaccurate records for 1900 credited Young with 20 victories, a figure that (assuming it was accurate) tied him with several other hurlers for second place in total wins. In part again because over the past two seasons Cy Young had been the second winningest pitcher (though well behind Joe McGinnity) in baseball. And finally in part because he was a famous star, a symbol of endurance and probity, likely to draw crowds into the new ball field that the Boston ownership was building. We who know what followed can only say: rarely has so much been secured for so little.

CHAPTER SEVEN

❧❦

Snapshot of a Private Man

S OME PROFESSIONAL athletes glory in fame. They seek opportunities to bring their names before the public. They embrace
requests for interviews and public appearances. They pursue media
discussion, revel in attention, and need constant adulation. Cy Young was
not this sort of athlete. It was not that he was shy, or timid, or arrogant,
or ungrateful, or ashamed. Rather, his indifference to acclaim was rooted
in his own centeredness: he lived within himself, confident that he knew
the difference between right and wrong, satisfied in the company of family and authentic friends, and ready to let the world judge him by his
deeds. One cannot say about Cy Young that the private man was an ex-
tension of the public persona. Instead, one must conclude that the private
man provided the foundation—the undergirding—for the public man.

The central person in Young's life was his wife, Robba Miller Young.[1]
Four years younger than her husband, the daughter of Robert and Sue
(McAbee) Miller, she had lived in Peoli, Ohio, from birth, but she had
spent much of her childhood on an uncle's farm adjacent to the farm in
nearby Gilmore owned by McKinzie Young Jr., Cy Young's father. I suspect that Cy and Robba were related, perhaps second cousins, for McKinzie's wife (hence, Cy's mother) had been Nancy Miller before her marriage. Robba and Cy had often played together as children, and since Cy
later said that Robba had been his only girlfriend, it is likely that one
reason he returned from Nebraska in 1888 was to resume his courtship
with her. They were married on November 8, 1892, and made a wedding
trip to the East. A photograph taken a year later during a postseason
visit to the Chicago World's Fair shows the handsome couple in their
early years of marriage. Although a printed description of her calls her a
"stylish blonde,"[2] her few photos suggest that her hair was actually darker

· 93 ·

than that. Small of stature (and hence affording a marked contrast to her towering husband), Robba had been a tomboy and enjoyed the outdoors all her life. Her skills at riding and marksmanship won countywide acclaim. She readily expanded her athletic interests to include baseball, keeping scrapbooks that celebrated her husband's career (these are now at Cooperstown) and becoming an informed commentator on the game. In St. Louis and Boston Robba attended ballgames almost daily, and she often accompanied Cy on spring-training trips to Hot Springs. The desire to be together was mutual; throughout his career, and especially when he was playing in nearby Cleveland, Cy regularly sought out opportunities to get home to Robba. Cy's nicknames for his wife were "Bob," "Rob," and "Bobby." He also called her "the brains of the Young family," and almost all the relevant evidence—though admittedly there isn't much of it—confirms that judgment.[3]

For the first decade after their marriage, Cy and Robba Young resided in Gilmore, either with McKinzie and Nancy Young or with one of the nearby Millers. During the 1890s Cy spent the summers with the Spiders and the winters in Tuscarawas County, helping his father by chopping timber on the Young farm. He was also saving money during these years, and in 1904 he used the Miller connection to purchase 160 acres near Peoli. At that time the farm belonged to the estate of the recently deceased Joseph Miller. It is not clear who this Joseph was or what his precise connection to the Miller clan had been. But in earlier days the farm had been the home of Robba's grandfather David Miller, and the executor who disposed of the estate in 1904 was Robba's father Robert Miller.[4] The purchase price was $7,000, a figure that seems high for the time and area, and Cy paid cash.[5] Cy and Robba then moved to Peoli and began enlarging the farmhouse that sat on this new property. When finished, the Youngs' home was described as one of the finest residences in the county, a handsome vine-covered, two-story, brown-framed structure consisting of twelve rooms and a large front porch.[6] Though not electrified until several decades later, it was served by a telephone as early as 1906.[7]

Because Peoli lay only about four miles from Gilmore, the move did not significantly disrupt the opportunities for the Youngs, the Millers, and their local friends to get together, though it meant that Cy and Robba, hitherto neighbors (or perhaps guests) of Cy's parents, were now neighbors of Robba's father, Robert. Robba's mother died in 1903, and since the 1903 baseball season marked the last summer that Robba spent with Cy in the city, we may conclude that thereafter she felt the need to stay in Peoli to assist her aging father. By 1910, Robert Miller had actually moved in with his daughter and famous son-in-law, and the two contiguous farms were handled as a single unit, with Robba as the administrator of farm activities. Cy Young was very happy with life in Peoli. He regularly declined postseason barnstorming trips, preferring a prompt return to Ohio to the opportunity of making a little extra money and seeing some of the country.[8] After the 1908 season ended, he declined an offer from a New York City newspaper to attend the World Series and lend his byline to the paper's coverage of the event. And when he was swapped to Cleveland before the 1909 season, he cited the possibility of Sunday visits to his farm as one of the reasons for his pleasure with the trade. When commentators, publicists, and cartoonists cast Cy Young as a farmer, they spoke accurately.

Cy Young was able to purchase the Peoli property with cash and then build a commodious house on it because by 1904 he had become, by Tuscarawas County standards, a relatively rich man. One press account from 1905 grouped him with baseball's "millionaires."[9] That, of course, was sportspeak hyperbole, but it reflects a general impression that Young was a man of independent means. His wealth was estimated at $20,000 in 1899 and at close to $100,000 in 1908.[10] Some of it derived from the gift of stock he had received near the beginning of his Cleveland career, but most of it came from the foresighted use of his salary. During the 1890s (and perhaps beyond) Cy Young invested regularly in Cleveland real estate in anticipation of road construction projects. Although anecdotes about Young's shrewdness as a real-estate investor were a common filler in the sporting press of the 1890s, Cy Young himself lacked the expertise (or inside information) to make a string of profitable investment decisions. In all likelihood he was guided in his choices by Frank Robison, who prided himself on helping his ball players grow rich, or by Davis Hawley, who, although severing his connection with the Spiders during the 1890s, remained a friend of Cy's even past the pitcher's retirement from baseball. The fact that Young invested so heavily was understood as testimony to his prudence, even to his frugality. From very early on he had the reputation for being tight with money. One tale had him talking the price of a bicycle down by $50 before purchasing it; another declared him a meager tipper; yet another told how he had confined nonessential spending to $25 over the course of an entire winter.[11] It's true that in 1910 he splurged on an automobile. But in general Young was happy to live as he had always lived, putting money away for a rainy day. "As Young's habits are exemplary and his tastes are simple," one writer summarily declared, "he will never know poverty."[12]

As an adult Cy Young was a strapping man. At six feet, two inches, he was taller than almost all ball players of his day. The velocity of his pitches was attributed to his broad shoulders, oaken legs (Patsy Tebeau once spoke of "Cy's spectacular props"), and barrel chest.[13] There was an awkwardness to the way in which he carried his body: even at the opening of his career, long before he put on pounds, one observer remarked that "he possesses the grace and agility of an 'ice wagon.'"[14] But in almost all he did he exuded strength, and even the forcefulness of his handclasp aroused comment. His eyes were blue, his hair sandy. In most photos he parted it in the center or just to the left of center. Like many other major leaguers, he sported a mustache in the early 1890s, but unlike most of his colleagues, he stuck with the fashion past the middle of the decade. Though he was often expressionless when on the mound, he could, when off duty, flash a smile wide enough to warm hearts. He was deemed handsome, and according to one report from the late 1890s, when Cy Young was scheduled to pitch, women flocked to the ballpark.

That may surprise some readers. After all, the most widely known photographs of Cy Young feature a hurler of marked heftiness. They date, however, from the later portion of his career and mislead about his appearance in his early years. When he joined the Spiders in 1890 he weighed only 170 pounds.[15] Within two years he had added ten pounds; within another two years, ten more. By 1896 he was reported to weigh 206 pounds; by 1897, 210 pounds. In 1900 he may have reached his peak weight, for one writer logs him in at 230 pounds; but we must treat this appraisal cautiously, since another suggests the far less startling figure of 205.[16] If the figure of 230 in 1900 is inaccurate, he was probably at his heaviest in 1903, when he weighed in at 218 pounds.[17] Thereafter he receded a bit, beginning most subsequent seasons at about 210 pounds. But portliness and a double chin marked him throughout the final decade of his career.

The transformation in Cy Young's silhouette did not pass unnoticed, his weight being the most widely discussed aspect of his appearance during the second half of his career. Because the figures in the previous paragraph may not be accurate, and because a person's weight often changes with exertion (Young is reported to have lost eight pounds during the

1903 World Series),[18] I report these numbers not so much as fact but to convey a trend which aroused bemused comment. Though a description of him as "beefy" from as early as 1893 is unusual, by 1901 allusions to his swelling were commonplace in the baseball press.[19] "This fat, old codger," one writer declared in that year, is "altitudinous and girthsome"; he is, another alliterated, "the fat fossil from the Ohio valley."[20] A cartoon from about 1903 depicts a Boston-based Young as so weighed down by his own bulk and by his pitching records that continental North America is tilting into the Atlantic Ocean.[21] Perhaps what we are seeing in his transformation from lithe lion to hefty honcho is a foretaste of the Babe Ruth syndrome. The general point, however, may be taken as demonstrated: well before Cy Young approached middle age, svelteness was yielding to pudginess.

Like many persons favored with physical strength, Cy Young enjoyed activities that kept him moving. The most famous of these was rail-splitting. Young loved to wield an ax, by many accounts he spent several hours almost every day during the off-season hewing logs, and he often delighted baseball writers with some version of the declaration that "my way of getting into shape is to take my ax and get out in the timber."[22] As an alternative to chopping wood, he sometimes spent hours digging coal for the kitchen stove, for a seam ran through the Gilmore-Peoli countryside. He enjoyed other rural pastimes as well. Like Robba, he took pleasure in shooting, and it became a yearly ritual for them to spend part of November on a hunting trip in Michigan, Indiana, or Wisconsin. Over the years, both far afield and on his own land, he bagged all sorts of game—squirrels, rabbits, raccoons, quail, even deer. He also occasionally participated in formalized fox hunts, which provided suitable venues for displaying both his horsemanship and his marksmanship. Sometimes he simply jogged—mile after mile through the Tuscarawas hill country, building up his legs and his endurance. There were quieter activities as well. Young bred hunting dogs for profit, though he sometimes presented them as gifts to friends. He constructed and sold large trunks, fashioned to meet the needs of traveling ballplayers and widely used in the major leagues. Finally, he tended his sheep, chickens, and corn, the major revenue-earners for the Young farm.[23] It was because Cy Young was at core an agriculturalist, raised in the rhythms of farming, that his hours seemed so peculiar to most of his ballplaying friends. Whatever the season, whether in the big city or Peoli, he rose early ("I find it hard work to stay in bed after 5 o'clock") and consequently retired early.[24] This was one of the reasons that Cy Young never got lured into the bar-hopping habit that ensnared so many of his major league colleagues.

Not that Cy Young disapproved of alcoholic beverages. Although the press occasionally tried to include teetotaling among his virtues, he in fact enjoyed beer, whiskey, and hard cider. Sportswriter Jimmy Isaminger quoted him as saying, in response to a query about whether Kentucky bourbon and mineral water damaged one's health, "well, it never seemed to be fatal for me."[25] Young also liked tobacco, though not in the form of cigarettes, about which he spoke stridently: "I hate 'em. I wish the tax on 'em was a dollar apiece and then we would never see the things again."[26] He ingested his nicotine in other forms, by chewing wads, smoking cigars, and puffing pipes. In his old age the ubiquitous pipe became his trademark. For quiet relaxation Cy Young enjoyed gabbing with friends. When at ease, he could be a spinner of tales. He was not, however, a reader. The few letters and cards of his that I have seen reflect his discomfort with the written word. And even though Boston sportswriter Jacob Morse commends Young's taste for the works of writers like Charles Dickens and William Makepeace Thackeray, the fact is that Cy listened while Robba read the works aloud.[27] None of this, of course, is surprising; Cy Young's formal education ended with sixth grade. He was an intelligent man, but it is useful to keep in mind that he was only marginally literate.[28]

He was also a man who respected morality. At the core of his moral understanding was a commitment to moderation. "Common sense," he once said, "is all a man needs."[29] By way of elaboration, Young added that he didn't eat foods that gave him indigestion, didn't smoke more than he should, didn't stay up late, didn't lose his temper, and didn't meddle in the affairs of others. In our more open age, Young might have included other habits in the litany. He didn't carouse, he didn't abuse alcohol, and he didn't womanize. It is relevant that, so far as I can tell, the press never placed Young in the middle of a brawl, never suggested that he was feeling the effects of overindulgence, and never declared that he suffered from "malaria."

But for Young "common sense" entailed more than simply avoiding self-destructive behaviors. It meant, most centrally, being honest. A revealing story, dating from a visit to New York in 1896, tells how Young discovered a wallet containing $190 in the folds of a chair in a hotel lobby. By working with clerks at the hotel and the postal service, he identified the owner of the wallet as G. B. Slemaker of Sistersville, West Virginia, and he promptly returned it.[30] In light of tales of this sort it is not surprising that he quickly acquired a reputation among ball players for being straight with people.

That is why he became so indignant when accused of easing up on an opposing team simply because he enjoyed a big lead. "When you see me let any club make runs off my pitching on purpose," he declared, "come around and I'll give you a brand new hundred dollar bill."[31] To ease up, except when exhausted, "puts the game on the level with lawn tennis, tiddle-de-winks, or some other school girl frivolity," he was once quoted as saying.[32] Schooled in the habits of morality, the adult Cy Young made his ethical decisions prereflectively. An upbringing in the woodlands of rural Ohio had taught him right from wrong and this was the moral lodestone of his life.

Common sense also involved a readiness to work hard, and Young was celebrated for his industriousness and focus. "No one," Cleveland sportswriter Elmer Bates opined, "can ever accuse Cy Young of losing a game through lack of earnestness."[33] Linked to this honesty and diligence was a determination to fulfill obligations. "My word is just as good as my signature to a paper," he once stated.[34] He prided himself on being a loyal employee, fully prepared to repay his employer for the trust implicit in having had a job opportunity extended to him. "It has always been my notion," he said late in his career, "that, having signed a contract with a club, it was my duty to work for that club to the best of my ability."[35] He liked the colloquial truism about life: "If you give it a 'yare deal it will give you a square deal."[36] That's why, until Frank Robison unleashed his ill-considered denunciation of Young and several other players at the end of the 1900 season, Young was a loyal employee of Robison's. To Young, Robison's accusations were both patently false and rankly ungrateful; the owner had violated the assumption of mutuality that underlay Young's view of obligation.

The press provides occasional glimpses of Young being moved by the silent virtues of gratitude and generosity. (And remember: this was in an era before press agents were around to remind players about the utility of making socially responsible gestures.) After almost every season he spent lots of time with the youngsters of Tuscarawas County, giving them pointers about sound baseball play. In the aftermath of Boston's Cy Young Day celebration of 1908 he conveyed his appreciation to those who had mounted the event not only by feting his teammates with a grand complimentary dinner at Putnam's Hotel, but also by personally writing thank-you notes to each of the several hundred fans who had contributed to his loving cup, and by sending boxes of cigars to each of the sportswriters who had lent their support to the occasion. In 1908 and 1909, in the midst of fall celebrations to welcome him back to Tuscarawas County, he joined some major leaguers he had recruited to pitch in charity ball games to raise money for the Union Hospital near New Philadelphia. In addition to the profits earned by the games, Young made a contribution to outfit the premier room in the hospital. Finally, Young engaged in community service through his membership in the Masons, Shriners, and Knights of Pythias.

Like many private persons, Cy Young was a quiet man. This trait was famously evident in his aversion to interviews. Billy Hamilton asserted unequivocally that Young "won't be interviewed," and the blunt claim was virtually true.[37] It was also evident in his reluctance to talk about himself. That's why, from a baseball writer's point of view, Cy Young was not good copy. That's also why, when he traveled, he signed hotel registers as "D. T. Young."[38] He preferred anonymity. With friends, however, he could be more at ease. When sharing gossip with Tuscarawas neighbors, or when relaxing in the comfortable all-male environment of a baseball clubhouse or practice field, he revealed the fun-loving heart of a man who had the good fortune to be paid for playing a child's game. And a quiet love of fun marked his baseball career. In a spring training contest, for example, he once found himself hung up in a run-down between second and third. According to the press account, he bellowed and twisted his way out of the pickle, at one point sitting down on third base and ultimately capping the bizarre sequence of blunders with a stylish slide back into second. His reaction was to roll in laughter. We also have stories of him doffing his hat to a cheering crowd after hitting a home run and trying to sneak trolley car rides back to a spring training hotel to avoid the prescribed jog. By the twilight of his career, when he had returned to the city he had started with and was known to one and all as "Cyrus," Young's smile and "his hearty laughter" made him "one of the most frolicsome men on the Cleveland team, a regular cut-up in fact."[39] While we don't ordinarily envision Cy Young as a cutup, it is important to recall that he was more than an efficient pitching machine.

Basically, although a shy man, Cy Young liked people. A Boston elevator boy in the summer of 1902 shared daily impressions of the sports pages with him whenever the Boston team was playing at home.[40] And if

Young was somewhat cautious about interactions with older players in his early days, he happily assumed the role of helpful mentor for younger players in his own later days. Mike Fitzgerald, told how Young, old enough to be his father and not even a teammate, bought him cigars as a friendly gesture when the Yankees dismissed him to the minors. The Young Larry Gardner credited a 40-year-old Young with taking time to extend him much-needed encouragement over whiskeys. And Tris Speaker, speaking of himself when he had been 20, attributed his ability to break quickly on fly balls to a 41-year-old Young's willingness to spend hours hitting fungoes to him.[41]

Young disliked brawling. On one occasion, he broke up a barroom fight between two illustrious Boston rivals, Kid Nichols and Buck Freeman. As far as I can tell, he never traded punches with another player, either off the field or on. Nor did he ever criticize a fellow player to a baseball writer. He could, it is true, speak bluntly during a game; he once threatened Billy Hamilton with a beaning if he did not stop fouling off pitches, and he taunted Ty Cobb by lamenting that General Sherman had left so many corncobs in Georgia.[42] Verbal assault was part of baseball, and Young overcame his early discomfort with it to become, by the mid-1890s, a man who, with authentically colorful and crude invective, could give as good as he got. But even when forced to pause and regather himself, he almost never lost his self-command. And that's why—and this is an astonishing fact, since he pitched over 7,000 innings in over 900 games and endured countless bad calls by umpires, bad plays by teammates, bad behaviors by opponents, and bad performances by himself—he was never thrown out of a game. Young's self-control was as impressive as his mound control.

Which brings me to my final point. Cy Young valued his good name. He was clear in his own mind about how an honorable man should behave, and he tried to conform to that standard. On one occasion he suggested five rules for living well in baseball, and essentially they are rules of honor: (1) be moderate in all things; (2) don't abuse yourself; (3) don't bait umpires; (4) play hard; and (5) render faithful service to your employer.[43] His sense of betrayal at Frank Robison's outburst lay in his belief that the owner's accusation had "cast a cloud over my reputation, which is and always has been above reproach."[44] It is not surprising that within two years of appearing in a Spider uniform Cy Young was sometimes dubbed "Old Cy Young." The term referred to neither his age nor his appearance, but to his moral presence. Even though he was barely twenty-five, teammates and baseball writers perceived him as a mature, self-contained, faithful, and reliable man. Toward the end of his career the same image prevailed; he was, it was suggested, "one quite above his fellows."[45] Cy Young was no saint. But he was an honorable man, he treated people fairly and considerately, and he thus merited the confidence that his colleagues placed in him. All this was possible because his identity was grounded not in a need for fame but in his commitment to what one admirer called "the whole science of right living."[46] Amid the shifting sands of baseball excesses Cy Young was a rock.

CHAPTER EIGHT

━━━━━━━━━

☙❧

1901–1902:

The Toast of Boston

BY ENTERING the Boston baseball market in 1901, the new American League was—in the accepted metaphor of the day—declaring war on the Boston Beaneaters. During the previous quarter century the National League team had garnered an unrivaled eight pennants and earned the enthusiastic support of Boston's fans. In light of such intensity of feeling among partisans, many suspected that a transfer of fan loyalty to the new franchise was unlikely and predicted that the new American League entry would be laughed out of town. Ban Johnson could not let that happen, of course, and that is why he paid so much attention to his Boston commitment, developing with Charles Somers, the chief owner of the new team, a strategic plan to penetrate the local baseball market. The first step was to build a new ballpark. Snow was still on the ground when construction began at the end of a trolley line on Huntington Avenue. With seating for over 9,000 fans and an expansive outfield (530 feet in center field), the Huntington Avenue Grounds would be Boston's best ballpark. Another marketing step involved underpricing the competition—specifically, offering bleacher seats for a quarter when the Beaneaters sold no seats for less than half a dollar. A third step aimed at providing new conveniences for the paying customer, the most discussed of which was the introduction of an announcer with a megaphone who informed the fans about batteries and personnel changes. Still, in the last analysis a business can't succeed if it doesn't provide a quality product. And so the fourth and most important element in the new club's marketing plan was to use Somers's money to purchase a strong and popular team.

The easiest way to achieve that goal was to fish for stars who had played in 1900 for the Boston National League squad. Each catch would bring Somers a player already known to Boston fans and simultaneously weaken the rival club's roster. The acquisition of Jimmy Collins had been a triumph, and the new manager bluntly explained his defection to his teammates and fans by saying that "I like to play baseball, but this is a business with me. I can't be governed by sentiment."[1] Once Collins, a leader on the Beaneaters, had shown himself willing to cast his lot with the new circuit, four teammates followed: Chick Stahl, one of the National League's best outfielders; Buck Freeman, one of the older circuit's heaviest hitters; Ted Lewis, one of the club's strong pitchers; and Nig Cuppy, looking for another chance to reclaim glory. For a while it appeared that Bill Dinneen, an even finer pitcher than Lewis or Cuppy, would join them in jumping, but after considering a Somers offer well into April he decided, for $4,000, to stay with the National League.

Another tactic Somers used in his effort to build a team that fans would support was to hire minor leaguers with ties to New England. Freddy Parent, a native of Maine, arrived to play shortstop, and Hobe Ferris, a native of Rhode Island, was assigned to second base. Together they would soon establish themselves as the League's best keystone combination. Fred Mitchell, a resident of nearby Cambridge, signed on as a pitching prospect. Somers even gave a chance to the dubious Larry McLean, a Canadian by birth but well known in Boston by virtue of his love of parties and an ostensible resemblance to the still popular Boston Strongboy, John L. Sullivan.

But try as he might, Somers could not build a team solely with New Englanders and former Beaneaters, and so he made contact with stars from other National League clubs. It is probably no coincidence that Somers, a Clevelander himself and friend of Davis Hawley, succeeded chiefly with former Spiders (sometimes in their alter egos of disillusioned Perfectos) when the bidding war began. Jesse Burkett eluded his bait, preferring the cautious course of staying with the National League. But outfielder Charlie Hemphill and catcher Ossee Schreckengost, both of whom had played with St. Louis in 1899 and in the minor league version of the American League in 1900, joined up. And so too, as we know, did two former Spider stars—prime catches for the new franchise—the famous battery of Lou Criger and Cy Young.

Throughout his career Cy Young had consistently worked hard to improve his skills. It was this character trait that Charles Somers was banking on, calculating that an intracity competition for success against the exploits of such Beaneater pitching stars as Kid Nichols, Bill Dinneen, and Vic Willis would ignite an additional flame under his new hurler. But Young had a reason beyond pride for wanting to do well by his new employer. It lay in his anger at the graceless behavior of the Robison brothers, who, having lost the rights to his services, tried to discredit his reputation. According to one account, quickly (and accurately) denied by Young, the pitcher had snubbed Frank Robison when the two men were briefly in St. Louis together.[2] Then there was Stanley Robison's insultingly blunt explanation for why St. Louis had not countered more vigorously in the bidding for the pitcher's services: "Young is through. In the new bush league he may last another year, but we couldn't have used him."[3] These actions help account for the starkness of Young's assertion that he would not work for Frank Robison again even if offered $10,000.[4] It is revealing that in the scrapbooks that Robba Young kept, the only nonplaying episode of her husband's career that she retained clippings of was the decision to jump to the new league. They represent his wife's effort to underscore the justness of Young's behavior.[5] And just as the Robisons now represented monopoly, Ban Johnson stood for opportunity. Without Johnson's work, Young declared, the salary cap might well have declined from $2,400 to $2,000 for the coming season.[6] The pitcher was therefore eager to demonstrate that the support that Somers and Johnson had shown him was warranted.

Moving to a newly formed team, Cy Young was largely unfamiliar with many of his new teammates, but that did not trouble him. He had always been independent—if not a loner, then at least a man who was untroubled if his own sense of the appropriate or ethical was out of step with the inclinations of his colleagues. He was, of course, pleased at the prospect of rejoining Nig Cuppy. But he took even greater pleasure knowing that Lou Criger would be his catcher. The professional respect shared by the two men ran deep. Indeed, had Criger not decided to commit his career to the viability of the new league, it is unlikely that Young would have accepted the same risk. Criger knew Young as no other player did, and Young valued Criger as he did no other player. Criger was smart and called good games; his powerful arm made him a useful ally against opposing base runners. Thus, though dogged with poor health—a legacy perhaps of work in a lead plant in his youth—and therefore lacking the durability of Chief Zimmer, Criger was already being hailed as one of baseball's finest backstops.[7] (It is interesting that the man whom the National League apparently deputed to try to lure Young back to the senior circuit was none other than Zimmer. In a very real sense during the spring of 1901, Young's two most celebrated battery associates were struggling for control of his professional soul.)

Two other people helped to make Boston a pleasant home in the summer of 1901. One was Jimmy Collins, whose managing style was casual—"He did not rule his men with a rod of iron," Young later recalled approvingly[8]—and who made the shrewd spring-training decision to allow the pitcher to work himself into shape in Hot Springs rather than join the rest of the squad in Charlottesville, Virginia. The other was Robba Young, whose distaste for the heat of St. Louis had been a spur to her husband's decision to jump and who, after spending part of the summer of 1901 in Boston, came to enjoy the seaside city. Given their affection for each other, it is likely that her presence helped to spare Young the loneliness that had been his greatest dissatisfaction with the lengthy baseball season.

Unhappily for Cy Young, he was sick when the season began, unfit to pitch the historically significant opening game in the new club's opening season. When he went to the mound for the second game, on April 27, he proved just how ill he was by throwing what would turn out to be his worst game of the year—a debacle in Baltimore in which he yielded 10 runs in 5⅓ innings, walked 5 (his season high), and wound up the loser by a score of 12–6. But then matters began to go better. On April 30, after Boston had suffered losses in its first three games, Young became the pitcher of record in the first victory ever chalked up by the Boston American League franchise, whipping the Athletics of Philadelphia 8–6 in ten innings. He was saved from his second loss when Buck Freeman hit the club's first-ever home run in the ninth. On May 8 the Boston club finally played its first game in the new Huntington Avenue Grounds. After an hour of rousing band music to set the stage, 11,000 happy fans saw Cy Young pitch the literally hungry home team—the men were playing without lunch because their train from New York had been late—to a 12–4 victory over Bill Bernhard and the Athletics.[9] He contributed a triple, a single, and a stolen base to the club effort. On May 17, with 10 strikeouts against Baltimore, he reached the double-digit level in a major league game for the first time in his career. By the end of the month Young had chalked up 5 victories and was batting well over .300. "Cy Young," *Sporting Life* reported, "is now in his best form, and can be counted on to bring home the tough games."[10]

But if Cy Young had righted himself when May ended, the club had not. "We are too anxious," Jimmy Collins hypothesized. "I know that we have a better ball team than we have shown so far."[11] It turned out that what was needed was home cooking. Reeling off 23 victories in 26 games in Boston, the club climbed from sixth place on June 3 to first place on July 8. At the heart of the charge stood the redoubtable Cy Young. Between June 2 and July 16, on a schedule that allowed him at least two days of rest between starts, he won 12 consecutive games, bringing his season's record to 17 wins and 3 defeats. In only one game during the streak did he allow more than 4 runs. He made four straight appearances without yielding a base on balls. It is true that on one occasion during the streak he was simply lucky; called in to relieve in a lost game against Detroit, he was the beneficiary of a nine-run eighth-inning rally by his team. But much more often he was truly dominant, allowing, for example, only five runs during one span of four consecutive complete games. On July 6 Washington became the victim of his first American League shutout. Even when the string finally ended on July 19, he pitched magnificently, losing in the tenth inning at Cleveland by a 2–1 score.

In carrying the team to the top Young was also winning the hearts of Boston's fans. As the summer advanced, Bostonians increasingly frequented the American League grounds, where a competitive team was fighting for a pennant, instead of the National League park, where an offensively inept team could not climb out of the second division. Because Cy Young was leading the Boston Americans' charge, the fans quickly took to the rustic from Ohio. " 'Farmer Cy' Young," the *Boston Globe* declared, "harvested his crop with the skill of an expert."[12] The aging hurler basked in his celebrity. "I guess there is a little pitch in me yet," he declared at the height of the streak.[13] (I imagine a puckish look on his face as he delivers the judgment.) Jacob Morse became a believer. Young, he wrote, was providing "phenomenal pitching for the club. . . . All the visiting clubs have paid the highest tribute to his work." Young himself reported "that he never felt more fit in all of his life."[14] That's easily credible. After two years of frustration in St. Louis and four seasons playing for an also-ran, Cy Young was again pitching with grand success and involved in a tight pennant race.

Boston's chief rival was the Chicago club, flying high on the pitching of Clark Griffith and Roy Patterson. From the middle of July through much of August the two teams were in close contention, Boston winning most of its games from Chicago, but Chicago doing better against the rest of the league and clinging to first place. Cy Young remained brilliant, compiling a 1.26 earned run average from July 19 through the end of the season.

But even without the modern statistical analysis, Young's contemporaries knew that his achievements were noteworthy. On July 29 he defeated Roy Patterson and Chicago, 4–1. On August 16 he again defeated Chicago, with Nixey Callahan pitching, 6–2. On August 20, with a curious Christy Mathewson seated among the fans, he shut out Milwaukee, 6–0. On August 27, by extricating himself from a bases-loaded, no-out situation in the fourteenth inning, he won a fifteen-inning game from Detroit, 2–1. On September 11 he pitched his first American League three-hitter. Over the course of fifteen consecutive starts he never allowed more than one base on balls in a game. Meanwhile, on August 2 he won his twentieth game; on September 14, his thirtieth. And the career milestones continued to pile up, as he passed Bobby Mathews' lifetime victory total on June 25, Mickey Welch's on August 16, and Charley Radbourn's on August 23. Along the way, on July 3, he became the seventh pitcher in major league history to win at least 300 games in a career.[15] What one writer said of his performance on August 5 applied equally to his entire summer-long effort: he "had everything—speed, curves and control."[16]

The season came down to a series in Chicago in the second week of September, when the home team's superior pitching depth—they had Roy Patterson to support Clark Griffith whereas Boston had no one to support Cy Young—contributed to a four-game sweep of the visitors.[17] Young pitched in the contest of September 8, before a crowd estimated at fifteen to twenty thousand (the largest of the year in the American League), losing to Patterson 4–3 in the bottom of the ninth inning when he gave up a two-run single to Dummy Hoy. The wipeout in Chicago left the club too far off the pace to be able to challenge again, and so even though Boston won 13 of its last 18 games, it still finished 4 games behind Chicago.[18] But even if the pennant had eluded Jimmy Collins's squad, there was still much to stir satisfaction in Charles Somers's office. His team had outdrawn the rival National League club by more than 2 to 1 in the Boston baseball market; in fact, the home attendance figure of 289,000 was the second highest in the league and fourth highest in the majors. Moreover, Boston's celebrated "Royal Rooters," an organization of noisy and intense fans of Irish ancestry, had transferred their allegiance during the summer from the city's National League club to its new American League squad. This shift was wonderful publicity. Fans did not yet know what to call the team—the name "Red Sox" came later—but whether they styled the club the Puritans, the Pilgrims, the Plymouth Rocks, the Somersets (a bit of a pun), or just the Bostons or Boston

Americans, they liked what it was doing. And there was no doubt who the fans' favorite players were. Pete Kelley (a sportswriter using the odd pseudonym "HiHi") declared, "To Young and Collins must the success of the Somersites be attributed."[19] Jimmy Collins and Cy Young were the toasts of Boston.[20]

How good was Cy Young in 1901? Consider these points for starters. He was the only major league pitcher to record more than 30 victories and the first to reach that mark in three years. (We now credit him with 33. At the time he was ordinarily given 31.)[21] His 12-game winning streak was the longest of the season. He led the league in strikeouts (158). He tied (with Clark Griffith) for the league lead in shutouts (5). In 18 of his complete games he yielded not a single base on balls, leading *Sporting Life* to remark that he had "been in a class by himself this season as regards accuracy."[22] Latter-day historians have devised other measurements, and they tell the same story. Young led the league in fewest hits allowed per game, in fewest walks allowed per game, in lowest opponents' batting average, and in lowest opponents' on-base average. He was the pitcher of record in 42 percent of his team's victories, a figure he exceeded only in 1893. His earned run average was an astonishing 1.62, almost a full run lower than the figure of his nearest American League rival and more than two runs lower than the league figure of 3.66.[23] This earned run average represented .44 of the league's earned run average, the lowest figure he posted in his entire career. And his enthusiasm was unflagging—"as hard working and conscientious [a] player as I ever saw in my life," wrote Jacob Morse.[24] Cy Young was the pitching story of baseball in 1901; indeed, the year is another candidate—along with 1892, 1893, and 1895 (and, as we'll see, 1904)—for the best season of his career. And remember: at 34 years of age he was the oldest regular starter in either league.[25]

What accounted for this dominance? How did a pretty good but perhaps fading hurler of 1900 become the world-beater of 1901? A similar phenomenon arose among batters, where Larry Lajoie, who had hit only .337 in the National League in 1900, soared to a still-standing American League record of .426 in 1901. There is a ready explanation for these pumped-up figures: the expansion of the major leagues from twelve teams throughout much of the 1890s (and only eight teams in 1900) to sixteen teams in 1901 inevitably entailed a dilution of talent, which in turn allowed players who were already stars to shine even more brightly. This effect was more sharply felt in the American League, since the bulk of baseball's finest batters—including Jake Beckley, Jesse Burkett, Fred

Clarke, Sam Crawford, Ed Delahanty, Elmer Flick, Willie Keeler, and Honus Wagner—remained in the senior circuit in the first year of the new league's existence. Just as the American Association of 1882 and the Union Association of 1884 claimed major league status with somewhat suspect credentials, so too did the American League of 1901 advance its claim with players who were, on balance, inferior to the roster of the National League. It may not have been, in Stanley Robison's phrase, a "bush league." But it was not genuinely competitive with the National League in 1901.

But the dilution of major league talent does not fully explain Young's triumphant years. After all, other former National League pitchers besides Cy Young jumped to the American League, and yet none approached the quality of his work. Joe McGinnity, for example, after two consecutive 28-victory seasons in the senior circuit, fell to 26 in the American League.[26] Win Mercer also slipped, as did Nig Cuppy, Jack Dunn, and Gus Weyhing. Clearly the offense in the new league was not so feeble that by itself it could rejuvenate fading careers. The pitching of Clark Griffith, Nixey Callahan, and Chick Fraser makes the same point, though less starkly; all improved in the new league, but not as much as Young did. In sum, Cy Young's performance in 1901 considerably exceeded the margin of improvement that one might have anticipated from the modest decline in the quality of batters he was facing.

And that leads to a second point. Cy Young did not pitch in 1901 armed only with the weapons of previous years. As he joined a new league, he began to incorporate into his armory a new pitch he had been struggling to master. Up until this point in his career Young had relied chiefly on his fastball, a delivery marked both by speed and by movement. He had sometimes complemented this "shoot" with a curve, but his bread-and-butter pitch had always been a well-located fastball. For his shift to the American League he added a change of pace—a "slow ball," in the lingo of the day—to his fastball and his occasional curve. We can even date his first significant use of the pitch. It occurred on May 17, when, confronted with a Baltimore club that was hitting his fastball without trouble, he tested (and now I quote from a report of the game published in 1902) "a slow one, delivered partially underhanded. It just lobbed up lazily, and then all of a sudden it dropped from the batter's shoulder almost down to his knees." Not surprisingly, Young noticed what was happening. In succeeding weeks he learned how to deliver the pitch from his standard overhand motion. "Before the season was old he had [the pitch] down pat."[27]

This might seem to be one of those all too-typical baseball yarns, an apocryphal story of a pitcher discovering a new delivery. However, the statistics from the game—10 hits but only 2 runs allowed and a season-high 10 strikeouts recorded—are consistent with the account. And other evidence suggests that something important happened in the game with Baltimore. The appearance was Young's sixth start of the season. Though he wound up winning 4 of these 6, he yielded 10 or more hits in half of them—and that tally does not include his dreadful first game, from which he was lifted after giving up 9 hits. In his remaining 35 starts, however, he yielded 10 or more hits only 6 times—that is, only about once every 6 games. Moreover, his strikeout pace quickened after May 17, from 3.16 to 3.91 per 9 innings. In light of his entire record in 1901—a record that calls for something more than a simple dilution of talent by way of explanation—the story seems plausible. It is fair to say that Cy Young became the toast of Boston in 1901 by adding a change of pace.

Cy Young's rediscovery of the joy of playing baseball put an end to all thoughts of retiring after the 1901 season. Although his three-year contract with Boston carried through 1903, at some point near the end of the 1901 season it was renegotiated. Under the new agreement, he would receive a splendid raise for 1902, to about $5,000 for the season. Charles Somers was doubtless grateful for Young's outstanding work, but he was also protecting his greatest asset, for in an era of interleague war Young was a very desirable acquisition and might well decide to return to the National League if the Boston Americans seemed unappreciative. Once signed, Young lent his presence to a brief postseason barnstorming tour to several New England towns which gave fans outside of the city a chance to see such regional heroes as Cy Young and Jimmy Collins in action. In Greenville, New Hampshire, Young and Lou Criger served as the battery for the local nine. The takings from the tour were spare— perhaps $50 per player—but Young's teammates were grateful that the pitcher, an authentic attraction, had been willing to defer his return to Ohio for a short time. After the tour he headed for the privacy of Gilmore. Having spent some of the summer with her husband, Robba Young had come to enjoy the home of Young's new team. "I just love Boston," she was soon quoted as saying.[28] But for a truly quiet and restorative life, Tuscarawas County could not be beat, and characteristically, Cy Young's only documented break from farming and woodchopping over the entire off-season was a three-week hunting and fishing trip.

During the off-season the baseball war intensified. The American

League moved its Milwaukee franchise to St. Louis, challenging yet another National League club head-to-head. Thanks in part to Cy Young's marvelous season, the American League had gained credibility, and National League players who had earlier been hesitant about jumping decided that the salary offers coming from the new league deserved fuller attention. Among those who signed on with the junior circuit before the 1902 season began were Ed Delahanty, the 1899 National League batting champion; Jesse Burkett, the 1901 batting champion; Elmer Flick, who had batted .333 for Philadelphia in 1901; Bobby Wallace, one of the finest shortstops in the game; and George Davis and Joe Kelley, both of whom had hit over .300 for nine consecutive seasons. All would later wind up in the Hall of Fame. Some fine pitchers also switched leagues, among them Jack Harper, Red Donahue, Al Orth, and Jack Powell. Of central importance for Young was Bill Dinneen's decision to jump from the National League's Beaneaters to the new Boston American League team. His arrival meant that Jimmy Collins's team would have more than one strong pitcher to rely on in 1902. More generally, the continued drift of talent from the National League to the American League meant that the two circuits would be virtually equal in ability as the new season got under way.

Cy Young returned to Boston in late February of 1902 not to link up with his teammates but to serve as pitching coach at Harvard University. He was accompanied by Robba, who spent the summer with him in Boston. It was not unusual at this time for universities to hire major league players to assist in the training of their baseball squads; in fact, Young's counterpart as batting coach for the Crimson was two-time National League batting champion Willie Keeler. But the press had much fun with the notion that Young, whose schooling had ended with sixth grade, would be teaching Harvard students. The pitcher enjoyed the assignment and got on well with the Harvard players.[29] Moreover, because the indoor training facilities offered him a chance to exercise his arm even as he helped the university's pitching corps, he was able to ready himself for the coming season.

While Young worked himself into shape in a Cambridge gymnasium, the rest of the Boston squad traveled to Augusta, Georgia, for spring training. The most notable newcomer in camp, Bill Dinneen aside, was Candy LaChance, acquired from Cleveland to shore up defense at first base by allowing the ham-handed Buck Freeman to shift to a less-exposed slot in right field. At the opening of April, his duties at Harvard fulfilled,

Young traveled to Georgia to join the club. He was optimistic about the coming season, pronouncing Jimmy Collins, Freddy Parent, and Hobe Ferris to be "the best infield in the American League" and predicting that Boston would be "in the running [for the pennant] from the very start."[30] Willie Keeler's judgment on Young provided additional grounds for optimism: "Cy Young is in fine fettle and he has that old-time speed of his."[31]

Cy Young won Boston's season opener on Patriots' Day, April 19, by a score of 7–6, yielding five doubles but striking out nine Orioles. In the best beginning of his entire career he won his first three starts, experienced an awful one-inning outing against Baltimore, and then won ten straight games. Almost every appearance offered something special. He caught the fans' attention on April 24 when he threw 13 consecutive strikes. He threw three four-hitters in five games. During his streak he bested Eddie Plank, Clark Griffith, and Addie Joss. On May 10, in the fastest complete game of his career, he needed only 65 minutes to defeat Washington. By June 8 his record stood at 13 wins and 1 loss. Jimmy Ryan, a recent jumper from the National League, stated that "he never saw such speed in his life"; Lou Criger said that "Cy Young is pitching better ball than ever"; and Pete Kelley declared that Cy Young had become as popular with Boston fans as the legendary King Kelly had been.[32] In the process of compiling his remarkable record he defeated every team in the league at least once, he allowed only one base on balls over the course of five consecutive complete games, and for a full month (seven games) he never allowed more than 2 earned runs per game. During this period of almost total success he even had the satisfaction of blasting what turned out to be the most enjoyable home run of his career, a smash at Cleveland on June 5 over the head of Piano Legs Hickman. When the outfielder caught up with the ball at the wall, he found it tightly wedged into a gap under the scoreboard. Before he could pry it loose, a chortling Cy Young—"I almost laughed myself out of a home run"—had lumbered around the bases for an inside-the-park four-bagger.[33]

Because career records were imperfectly marked at this time, fans were unaware of two other major achievements of Cy Young chalked up during this streak. On May 27, with his three hundred and twenty-ninth lifetime triumph, he surpassed the victory total of his old teammate and mentor John Clarkson. Then in his next outing, a five-hit shutout of Detroit on May 30 that gave him his three hundred and thirtieth lifetime win, he moved past Kid Nichols. (Nichols had left the Boston Beaneaters after 1901 to manage and pitch for Kansas City in the Western League. His "retirement" left Young as the winningest active pitcher in major league baseball. In fact, Nichols, would return to the majors from 1904 to 1906 to add another 32 wins to his career record. But by then he would be chasing Young, not vice versa.) "The veteran Young," *Sporting Life* observed, "is like wine—he grows better with age."[34] Indeed. Cy Young was now the most effective thirty-five-year-old pitcher in baseball history.

Unhappily for Boston's fans, the rest of the team was not keeping pace. It was a measure of the pitching weakness of the team that when Young won his fourth game of the season on May 3, it was only the fifth win for Boston. Feeble hitting also hurt, as preseason efforts to secure Honus Wagner—wouldn't *that* have been a catch—failed, and Hobe Ferris, Freddy Parent, and Buck Freeman all performed below their 1901 levels. As of May 11 the team was no higher than fourth place. But then, owing to the faltering performances of its foes, the club began slowly to rise, and by the fourth week in June it had secured second place. Through midseason it appeared that the defending champion Chicago White Sox would be the team to beat. But thereafter the Philadelphia Athletics surged, powered in part by the remarkable pitching of Rube Waddell, the famously flaky hurler who returned to the majors from the West Coast and did not even appear in an American League game until June 26.[35] The Athletics took over first place in the middle of August and were never thereafter headed, although as late as September 7 Boston was only a game and a half back.

Cy Young remained the heart and soul of Boston's effectiveness throughout the second half of the season. On June 21 he pitched a fifteen-inning victory against Detroit, his second such triumph over the Tigers in as many years. On July 4 he defeated Baltimore in twelve innings. On July 19 he never allowed a Chicago player to reach second base. On July 22 he chalked up his twentieth win; on September 6, his thirtieth. In both cases the date marked the earliest point in his career at which he had reached those milestones. His victory on August 8 aroused no special comment at the time, but we now mark it as his three hundred and forty-third lifetime victory, a total that allowed him to pass Tim Keefe in career triumphs and left only the legendary Pud Galvin ahead of him. The luster of the year was modestly tarnished in September when he prevailed in only one of in three head-to-head engagements with the brash Waddell. His success came on September 12, when he stroked out a double in his 5–4 victory over his rival. But three days later he weakened late in a tight game, yielding 6 runs in the ninth inning in a 9–2 loss. And four days after that he lost again, this time by a 6–4 score when he gave up the winning runs in the bottom of the eighth. By mid-September the Athletics, energized by the most successful home record ever achieved by an American League club, were pulling away from the league, and when the season ended they led St. Louis by five games. But Cy Young was not to blame; even when contending against the champion Athletics in 1902 he won more often than he lost.

There was no disguising the sense of disappointment among Boston players and fans at the final standings. Despite establishing the best road record in the league—astonishingly, the Bostons were the only American League team to finish above .500 away from home—the club had wound up in third place, 6½ games behind the Athletics. And it was not difficult to lay blame for the disappointment. Take pitching. First off, Bill Dinneen had failed to fulfill expectations. He had, it is true, overcome a disastrous start to win 21 games, but he had also recorded a league-leading 21 losses. Dinneen's work was symptomatic of a wider hurling problem. Although Boston is now credited with the lowest team earned run average in the league, Cy Young accounted for almost one-third of the innings recorded in that calculation. For the second year in a row the club lost more games than it won in contests begun without Young on the mound. Injuries were also a factor. All teams endure them, of course, but the Boston club was peculiarly afflicted, as Jimmy Collins, Chick Stahl, Lou Criger, and hard-hitting rookie Patsy Dougherty all stepped out of the lineup at various times to recuperate. It did not help the already strained pitching staff that George Winter went down with appendicitis. A final element contributing to Boston's slippage was Charles Somers's decision to permit three men—pitchers, no less—to go to Philadelphia early in the season when a Pennsylvania court decision stripped the Athletics of several players who had jumped from the National League. Somers took the action to help keep the American League internally competitive. But one of those hurlers, Bert Husting, proceeded to win 14 games as his new team charged to the pennant.

Although he regretted losing two matches in five days to Rube Waddell, Cy Young enjoyed another glorious season in 1902. Once again he was the only pitcher in the major leagues to post over thirty triumphs. Contemporary sources agreed that Young's victory total came to 32 (a figure that historians accept), though they disagreed about his losses (we now calculate the total to be 11). He thus won 65 games during his first two years in the American League, a figure that constitutes the second highest two-year total in the league's history.[36] His durability was extraordinary. He missed only one start (with a sore throat) and he led the league in appearances (45), in complete games 41, and in innings pitched (384⅔). His reliability was also remarkable, as he never lost more than two games in succession. His ten-game winning streak was the second longest of the season.[37] For the first time since 1892 his ratio of bases on balls to games was insufficient to lead the league, but it was still second best—an impressive 1.24.[38] He was also second in strikeouts, with 160, thus far his highest figure at the longer pitching distance. It is a sign of how misleading a won-lost record (or perhaps an earned run average) can be that even though his record after June 8 was merely 19 and 10 whereas it had been 13 and 1 through that date, his earned run average was actually marginally lower—2.13 to 2.21—in the second period. Had not Waddell exploded on the scene in late June, winning 23 games and striking out 50 more batters than Young even though pitching more than a hundred fewer innings, we could safely say that Young was once again his league's best hurler. But even if he was only second best on the season, he was still a wonder. As Jacob Morse asked, after reflecting on Young's work since joining the American League: "Is it any wonder that Bostonians are so fond of the clever veteran?"[39] Not surprisingly as the season came to a close, newspapers hinted at rumors that the Cincinnati and Boston clubs in the National League were dangling large offers before him.

The war between the National and American Leagues, however, was almost over. The 1902 campaign proved ultimately decisive. Though the interleague contention stayed bitter throughout the season—with John McGraw and several of the Baltimore stars jumping back to the National League and the American League planting at least one agent on a National League team with the responsibility of encouraging defections— it was in ticket sales that the matter was settled. More than 2.2 million fans paid to see American League games; somewhat fewer than 1.7 million paid for the same privilege at National League parks.[40] In each city in which the junior circuit had challenged the senior circuit directly, the new entry won the attendance battle. In Boston, for example, the American League franchise outdrew its National League rival by a ratio of 3 to 1—almost 350,000 to less than 117,000—even though it raised the price of some of its tickets.[41] The Boston Americans were so popular that their home attendance figure was the second highest in the majors in 1902. In city after city the fans were showing that they preferred the junior circuit's product.

There were several reasons for the success of the new league: good players, good umpiring, good press, and good games figure prominently among them. The role of Larry Lajoie and Cy Young in giving credibility to the new league cannot be ignored. But the advantage of good leadership was the decisive consideration, for the American League had the visionary Ban Johnson while the National League effectively had no one. Thus, whereas the National League magnates defended their monopolistic claims like eight independent feudal lords, each trapped in self-serving behavior, the American League conferred wide powers on Johnson to devise a strategy for the common interest. This meant that, whereas the National League owners, despite much talk, could not agree to establish a "war chest" to try to buy back lost stars, the American League owners, led by Johnson, were able to devise a plan to deal with the Pennsylvania Supreme Court decision that threatened to deprive the junior circuit of the services of Larry Lajoie. In accordance with the plan, Johnson simply dispatched the batting star from Philadelphia to Cleveland, at once strengthening a struggling franchise, placing the batting champion beyond Pennsylvania's jurisdiction, and retaining the great drawing card for the new league. Because this kind of maneuver was precisely the sort of swift action that the leaderless National League could not manage to pull off, the National League owners, one by one, were reluctantly resolving that they needed to sue for peace and end the costly bidding war for talent.

Such a peace was what some of the players feared. They reasoned that if the two leagues came to terms, and in particular if they agreed to insert reserve clauses in all contracts and to honor each other's contracts, then salaries would recede, perhaps to pre-war levels. This is why a few players struggled to keep the Players Protective Association alive. But as a product of the penurious atmosphere of 1900, the Association seemed irrelevant in the heady bidding wars of 1901 and 1902. Meanwhile, its integrity was undermined by its inability to punish contract breakers and by its insensitivity to conflict-of-interest complications for some of its officers.[42] Through the 1901 season Cy Young represented the Boston club in association meetings, and he retained his own membership in the association at least into the early months of 1902. But as a player whose salary had more than doubled in just two years, and a member of the franchise with the second highest payroll in baseball,[43] he no longer felt the prod of under-compensation and was among the large majority of players who, through inattention, allowed the union effectively to wither away during 1902. It was a short-sighted negligence on the part of the players. By forming the association in 1900 and winning American League endorsement for its model contract for 1901, they had allowed the junior circuit to inaugurate and then win the baseball war. By failing to support the association in 1902, they left themselves unarmed when the end of the interleague war, which seemed imminent as the winter approached, proved to be a prelude to a renewed conflict between owners and employees.

One sign that the two leagues were approaching a peace was the willingness among some owners in both leagues to allow an interleague post-season competition. The plan did not pit the two league champions against each other; hence it was not a World Series. But it did allow the National League champion Pittsburgh Pirates, a great team that had won the pennant by an extraordinary 27½ games over the second-place club, to play four games against an American League all-star team. Pittsburgh won the series, taking two games while the "All-Stars" (also called the "All-Americans") won one (with one game ending in a tie). Cy Young pitched two of the games, losing the series opener to Sam Leever in Pittsburgh, 4–3, and defeating Deacon Phillippe, 1–0, in Cleveland.[44] To call the American League squad the "All-Stars" was a bit of a misnomer. Ed Delahanty, Rube Waddell, Socks Seybold, Piano Legs Hickman, and Jimmy Collins were not interested in participating, and Larry Lajoie, still unable to play in Pennsylvania, had to avoid the two games in Pittsburgh. As a money-maker the series was also a disappointment, and Pirate owner Barney Dreyfuss was unhappy that the American League used the series to try to lure some of his outstanding players into defecting.[45] But at least it was an ice-breaker, presaging the serious discussions that all major league owners entered into over the winter. These discussions ended the war, as the National League owners, grim realists in the face of American League successes, chose finally to acknowledge that if they could not destroy their rival they had no option but to tolerate it. And so, well before the opening of the 1903 season, peace was restored to the world of major league baseball and the modern era of bifederal baseball was launched.

CHAPTER NINE

❦

The Triumph of
Bifederal Baseball

I T MIGHT SEEM appropriate to attribute the settlement of the baseball war in early 1903 to the vision of the club owners. After all, the final agreement marked the triumph of bifederalism. That is, it established the successful arrangement that now exists in professional sports, with two circuits offering simultaneous competitions followed by a capstone event featuring a match between the winners from each circuit. Professional basketball has two conferences and the final round of the playoffs, professional hockey has two conferences and the Stanley Cup finals, and professional football has two conferences and the Super Bowl. The paradigm for them all was baseball, with its two leagues and a World Series. It seems simple and natural. Weren't the owners foresightful?

The trouble with this story is that it reads history backwards—from outcomes to purposes. The fact is, the settlement of the baseball war was grounded not in the logic or implications of bifederalism or in any notion that a season-ending contest between champions would engender fan interest. (Indeed, many National League owners initially hoped merely to re-expand the league). Rather, the settlement was a product of the owners' desire to eliminate the two chief dangers that experience had taught them could be financially crippling.

One of those dangers was the threat of an unrestrained bidding war for talented players. The reserve clause had been created and refined precisely to deal with this danger. But the reserve clause worked only if all clubs agreed to honor it, and the reason the struggle launched by the American League in 1901 was denominated a "war" is that the new circuit, by not including reserve clauses in its own contracts and not accepting the validity of reserve clauses in the contracts of National League players, was willing, at least temporarily, to forgo the use of baseball's most controversial tool of salary suppression. As Jimmy Collins appositely remarked: "Everything is fair in love, war and baseball."[1]

The other danger was the threat to profitability posed by including too many members in a league. Since every club drew some of its revenues from playing in the home parks of other clubs, it behooved the owners to create a structure of competitive balance that allowed most clubs a real chance for success. Otherwise fan interest might drop precipitously in cities where clubs had fallen from contention. An inability to be competitive explains why the National League had purged four perennially unsuccessful squads in 1900.[2] But the aftermath of this proved the solution to be worse than the problem, for in light of America's expanding urban population and a widespread interest in watching good baseball, the cities in disfavor, once given an option, supported new clubs and a new league. After all, with sixteen cities in the United States boasting populations of at least 250,000, it was not possible for a single eight-club league to satisfy the nation's appetite for high-quality baseball.[3]

Initially the National League owners had hoped—and even expected—that the American League would fade as promptly as the upstart Union Association of 1884 and the Players League of 1890. But by early 1903, with the new league proving itself resilient and popular, National League owners had a powerful inducement to sue for peace, especially since they had good reason to suspect that the American League owners, wanting nothing more than to share in the pie, would be amenable to terms that would restore profitability to all the clubs in major league baseball. All that was needed was for a majority of National League owners to look beyond the personal animosities that two years of internal bickering and external warfare had fueled and to accept that recognizing the new circuit was a small price to pay for reopening a route to riches. By January of 1903 that majority existed.

Because the terms of settlement rested upon a National League recognition of the American League (that's what suing for peace meant), the American League must be adjudged the winner of the war. But at this point the military imagery begins to mislead, for ownership on both sides of the struggle profited from the resumption of business as usual. By acknowledging the major league status of the American League, the National League clubs were in effect recognizing the coequal status of the eight constituent clubs of the new league—clubs that it had previously treated as minor league or outlaw franchises. This acknowledgment meant that each league would honor the contracts (and the restored reserve clauses) of the other league and that neither league would claim the right to draft players from the other. And this honoring of contracts meant in turn that club owners were now free to try to ratchet salaries downward without fear of losing a player's services in a bidding war.

The settlement offered the owners in both leagues other protections as well, the most significant being the assurance that each individual major league franchise owner could be confident that no future interlopers would be tolerated. This agreement on territorial exclusivity rested on a compromise: the American League's recent entry into New York City would stand, but in return the American League would abandon plans to locate a club in Pittsburgh. With this arrangement, major league baseball ended a four-year period of franchise instability, inaugurating instead what turned out to be its palmiest era of territorial fixedness. For the next half century the majors operated with three teams in metropolitan New York City; two in Boston, Chicago, Philadelphia, and St. Louis; and one each in Cincinnati, Cleveland, Detroit, Pittsburgh, and Washington. To protect themselves from indiscreet or selfish actions by fellow magnates in the future, the owners banned interlocking ownerships and agreed that any future franchise shift would require the approval of a majority of the owners in each league. With these arrangements, clubs could plan for their own futures with the reasonable expectation that most of their opponents would be competitive and without the worry of being poached upon by a rival.

Because any agreement delimiting the actions of sixteen self-interested ownership groups was vulnerable to disputation, the owners created a three-member body called the National Commission to oversee major league baseball and to adjudicate all quarrels. Each league president—Ban Johnson from the American League and the newly elected Harry Pulliam from the National League—sat on the commission, which was chaired by Garry Herrmann, president of the Cincinnati Reds. The mathematics of the situation suggested a National League triumph: the commission, after all, consisted of two representatives from the senior circuit and only one from the junior. In fact, however, the choice of Herrmann bespoke Johnson's tactical skills. Johnson, who knew from long friendship that Herrmann was a tractable man, was soon able to assert his domination over the new body, playing a more prominent role in charting the course for the major leagues during the next decade and a half than any other person. Early evidence of his influence was the outcome of the prompt adjudication of the few contracts which remained in legitimate dispute. Nine of the sixteen players in limbo, including all who were headliners (Sam Crawford, Ed Delahanty, Willie Keeler, and Larry Lajoie), were awarded to American League clubs.

Having secured satisfactory resolutions to all of the fundamental points, Ban Johnson could afford to be generous on relatively minor matters. That meant that Johnson, for the sake of uniformity, was willing to yield to National League practice on the one major discrepancy between the playing rules in the two leagues. In 1901 the National League had introduced what was called the "foul strike rule." The aim of the rule was to shorten the time required to complete a game. Prior to the installation of this rule, all balls that were batted (but not bunted) foul were deemed inconsequential—that is, counted neither as balls nor as strikes. After the rule went into force, the first two foul balls were registered as strikes. (The reader will recognize this as the modern practice.) The American League, however, had chosen to launch its claims to major league status by sticking with the older procedure. Thus for two years the leagues dealt differently with many foul balls, and observers, in a manner that anticipated later discussion of the designated hitter rule, vigorously debated the merits of the foul strike rule. In 1902 there had even been an effort to negotiate a compromise that both leagues would accept, but it collapsed, in part because it was too complicated but also because the two leagues, engaged in war, were disinclined to compromise.[4] One thing, however, was clear to everyone: the new rule aided the pitcher and presumably helped to account for the better pitching statistics in the National League. In the older circuit, for example, strikeouts outnumbered walks by a 3-to-2 ratio during the two years of rule difference; in the junior circuit the two measures of pitching ability were virtually equal. More tellingly, American League games featured about 1½ more runs per game than National League matches. In accepting the foul strike rule Ban Johnson was agreeing to a modest diminution of offense.

As a pitcher, Cy Young was interested in the implications of Ban Johnson's decision. Like no other American League hurler he had thrived under the old rule. Thus he did not support the new rule, even though he acknowledged that "the foul-strike rule is certainly a good thing for the pitcher."[5] The two newspaper accounts that describe his opposition to the change attribute it to the peculiar notion that the foul strike rule would make games too short, especially in hot weather, and to the still more peculiar concern that offense would be further weakened.[6] Needless to say, this is a puzzling reaction for a pitcher. Maybe all that can be said is that throughout his career Young consistently displayed a temperamental aversion to the adoption of new rules even as he manifested an almost inexhaustible capacity to adjust to them. With the introduction of the foul strike rule into the American League we can see those traits once again conjoined; Young may have disapproved of the change, but he thrived under its regime, enjoying in the next three seasons the best strikeout years of his career. Already formidable, Young achieved still wider mastery when aided by the foul strike rule.

The foul strike rule was not the only development to hamper offense in the opening decade of the twentieth century. The trend toward "inside baseball"—a style of play that was "up-to-date, progressive, and fast"— meant that managers in both leagues were willing as never before to trade outs for advances on the base paths.[7] Teams played for a single run rather than the big inning. Managers regularly turned to the sacrifice bunt, instructed batters to choke up on the bat, and commended bat control over bat power. It was all deemed very "scientific"—a revealing term used by exponents of the new systematization—and it certainly promoted lower-scoring games.[8] Complementing the strategic devaluation of big innings was the addition of the "spitball" to the armory of weapons available to pitchers. The term was generic, encompassing a variety of pitches which had, as their common element, the application of some liquid substance—spit, soap, oil, tar, tobacco juice, whatever—to a portion of the ball before it was delivered. Appearing in 1903 or 1904, the spitball quickly eclipsed even the foul strike rule as a source of controversy in the baseball press. Writers argued over its fairness, its purported tendency to damage pitchers' arms, even its hygiene. But what no one could deny was its effectiveness, especially when used by masters such as Jack Chesbro and Ed Walsh.

It might be claimed that these last two offense-deflating developments emerged quite independently of the settlement of the baseball war in 1903. In a sense, that's true. But in another sense, though they arose for reasons unrelated to the war, they were allowed to persist unchecked because they served the interest of the postwar owners. The reasoning goes like this. It was an article of faith with the magnates that, other things being equal, fans preferred high-scoring to low-scoring games. That was, for example, the conviction that lay behind the rule change of 1893 which moved the pitcher back five feet. Thus, when the primary task confronting the owners was the need to increase attendance, they were likely to take steps to increase offense. But in the opening decade of the twentieth century attendance was rising from its 1899 low without any special priming, even in an environment of falling scores. In those circumstances, the need that the owners regarded as primary—especially after the war was over—was not so much to attract fans to the ballpark as to cut payroll expenses. And at this point low-scoring games played into the owners' hands. Why? Low scores were a product of reduced offensive productivity; reduced productivity was reflected in lower batting averages; and a lowering of batting averages led to a reduction in the ability of offensive players to demand higher salaries. When Honus Wagner won the National League batting championship in 1906 by hitting a mere .339, or when Elmer Flick copped the American League title a year earlier with a stunningly low .308, it was difficult for them or any of the players who performed even less well to argue that they merited salary increases. The postwar owners thus were lucky in the trends they inherited, and they had enough wisdom not to foul up their good fortune.

The best indication, however, that the owners were looking at the past, not the future, in shaping the settlement of 1903 was their complete incapacity to plan for the emergence of the World Series. In retrospect, the sheer reasonableness of having the two league champions engage in a postseason contest is overwhelming; it brings the season to artistic closure, and it satisfies fan curiosity about which pennant-winning team is better. But the peace settlement of 1903 was silent about postseason play. In part this silence reflected the sense that intracity entrepreneurship offered the promise of local and exciting postseason competitions.[9] In part it reflected the fact that postseason championship matches, whether the contests between the National League and the American Association in the 1880s or the Temple Cup contests of the 1890s, had in general not drawn large crowds. In part it reflected the power of the rancor that continued among the owners. Still, however one accounts for it, the omission is striking. Almost everything that the owners crafted in 1903— governance by commission, stability grounded in sixteen clubs, renewed recognition of the reserve clause, uniformity of rules between the two leagues—has been superseded by later practices. Bifederalism aside, the only important enduring product of 1903 is the World Series. And the peace settlement did not create it (though, once it proved successful, the National Commission moved quickly to assume control of it). As I said at the beginning of this chapter, while the owners in 1903 may have had good business sense, they did not have vision.

CHAPTER TEN

\~\~\~

1903–1904:

The King of Pitchers

WHEN CY YOUNG reemerged into the public light from the winter recesses of Tuscarawas County in February 1903, he was in Macon, Georgia, coaching the Mercer University baseball team. According to Mercer lore, he used his stint as coach to introduce the pitchout to southeastern college baseball.[1] Meanwhile, the town ball field was also serving as a dusty spring training facility for Young's Boston club. Young was now generally regarded as the most remarkable pitcher in baseball history. With his 65 victories since joining the American League, he had amassed more triumphs than any major league hurler had won in any two-year period since 1893 and 1894, when Amos Rusie had won 69 and Kid Nichols had won 66. In addition to his talent, there was his unexampled durability. Only three men who had shared the field with him in his first game back in 1890 still played in the majors. An equal number were under the ground. He had launched his American League career at the age of 34. Now, at 36, he was as old as that most resilient of his great predecessors, Charley Radbourn, had been when he had stopped running in fast company. Young was, in short, close to moving into uncharted actuarial territory; and yet he could still plausibly claim to be at the top of his game.

In only one respect was Cy Young disappointed with his work over the past two years; despite his efforts and ambitions, the Boston Americans had still not captured a pennant. What about the coming year? The objective observer might have seen little chance for improvement. After all, the club was entering the new season with virtually the same roster that had fallen short in 1902. An optimist could hope that Bill Dinneen, having struggled during his first year in the junior circuit, would recover the skills that had earned him success in the National League. But what Boston needed even more than reliable pitching was greater offensive power, and yet the club had stood pat over the winter trading season. Nothing, in short, portended the success that lay just ahead. Or am I missing something? For it seems to me that Cy Young's pronouncement about the coming season rang with more confidence than his usual spring-time cheerleading. "We want the pennant in Boston, this year," he said, "and we are going after it."[2] Manager Jimmy Collins was even more forth-right. He liked Boston's pitching, and professed assuredness "that we will have a club in Boston far stronger than that of 1902."[3] Still, one wonders if these two men had even an inkling of just how foresighted their decla-rations would prove to be.

The end of the baseball war over the winter brought three changes to the team's world. First, it meant that Boston would henceforth be play-ing games in New York City, for as part of the peace settlement the Amer-ican League had transferred the Baltimore franchise to New York where Ban Johnson would finally be challenging the baseball dominance of his two fiercest opponents, John Brush and John McGraw of the Giants. Sec-ond, it meant that the era of salary escalation was at an end. Because most major league players had signed their 1903 contracts before peace was concluded, the retrenchment could not begin immediately. In fact, the migration of talent to the American League was continuing, as Jack Chesbro, Jesse Tannehill, and Willie Keeler joined the new New York club (soon styled the "Highlanders"), while Sam Crawford added power to the feeble Detroit offense.[4] But the settlement reestablished the reserve clause, and by all predictions the 1903 season would be the final summer of roses for the players. Finally, the end of the baseball war allowed Charles Somers, the Boston Americans' principal bankroller during their first two years of existence, to sell his shares of the club and concentrate upon his various Cleveland interests. The team's new owner was Henry Killilea, who, as a Milwaukee lawyer, was another carpetbagger from the Midwest. But since his ambition was to own a pennant-winner, he was happy to defer talk of salary-cutting until another day.

The Americans began their season slowly. They split an opening-day doubleheader with the Athletics, Cy Young faltering in the afternoon game and blowing a 6–0 lead in a contest that Boston finally lost (though Young was not the pitcher of record). After two weeks of play they stood in sixth place. But then lightning struck, and through the rest of the season the club played almost .700 ball. An 11-game winning streak propelled them into first place before May was over. Through the beginning of August the defending champion Athletics were able to keep the race close, but then Boston began to pull away from the pack. By the middle of August the club had an 8-game lead. It closed the season by winning its final 18 home games. During one scorching week in September, the club scored 64 runs in 49 innings. When the season was over the team had recorded 91 wins and only 47 losses (for a percentage of .659) and led second-place Philadelphia by 14½ games. The American League now had its third different champion in as many years, and it was not a coincidence that all three represented the only cities that, from the birth of the circuit, hosted National League franchises as well. Ban Johnson had known that he needed to be successful in the head-to-head rivalries, and he had shrewdly channeled talent to Chicago, Philadelphia, and Boston.

A statistical summary of the team's work underscores Boston's dominance in 1903. The club led the American League in both batting, with .272, and earned run average, with 2.57. (The reader may be surprised by that apparently low team batting average. To put it in context, the league batting average, presumably affected by the new foul strike rule, plummeted from .275 in 1902 to .255 in 1903. The end of the baseball war had introduced the era of the pitcher.) The team also led the league in slugging average, in runs scored, and in home runs. And its roster contained several individual leaders, notably (on the offensive side) Patsy Dougherty, who topped the league in hits, and Buck Freeman, who amassed the most home runs and runs batted in (the latter not yet an official statistic). Not surprisingly for a team that won frequently, three of its pitchers—Cy Young, Bill Dinneen, and Tom Hughes—reached the important 20-victory milestone. "When a team has pitching such as I have," Jimmy Collins noted, "it is bound to win a lot of games."[5]

But if these figures show that the 1903 Boston club was strong, it is interseasonal comparisons that demonstrate that it may deserve inclusion in even loftier company. Not until 1923 would the winner's margin of 14½ games over the second-place club be exceeded in the American League. On only nine other occasions in American League history has a team won the pennant while leading the circuit in both batting and pitching. If we leave the various Yankee juggernauts out of consideration, only the 1948 Indians and the 1971 Orioles have shown such dominance. Finally, only the 1927 Yankees managed to lead the league in both hitting and pitching *and* win the pennant by a wider margin. This is not to suggest that the 1903 Boston Americans could have held their own against the 1927 Yankees; there are reasons to regard the 1903 season as a fluke. But I do believe that no powerhouse of the twentieth century has been as overlooked as Jimmy Collins's 1903 team. It had everything: a reliable offense, a strong defense, and effective pitching. With the 1903 season the American League had come of age.

At the heart of the Boston machine stood Cy Young. Once again he was magnificent. Because he finally had a sound supporting cast in Bill Dinneen and Tom Hughes, Young saw somewhat less action in 1903 than in previous American League years; Jimmy Collins asked him to start 8 fewer games than in 1902, and over the course of the season called on him for 43 fewer innings. Nevertheless, Young's thirty-six-year-old arm pitched more innings than any other American League hurler. His usual strengths were evident. He did not walk a single batter until his fourth game. From May 24 through July 25—during which time Boston took over first place—he reeled off 13 wins and 2 saves (the latter not yet a recognized statistic) while losing only 1 game. From August 10 through September 3 he won another 7 games in a row. We now assign him a record of 28 wins and 9 losses, although the *Spalding Guide*, perhaps through a misprint, registered him at 29–8.[6] He led the American League in victories, shutouts (7), innings pitched (341⅔), and fewest bases on balls per game (.97), and tied for the lead in complete games (34). Both his opponents' on-base percentage (.259) and his earned run average (2.08) were second lowest in the circuit. Without a doubt, Cy Young compiled the strongest record of any hurler in the American League.

Was Cy Young helped by the foul strike rule? At least one observer, Patsy Tebeau, his old manager from Spider days, certainly thought so, remarking: "Cy should thank his stars for the foul-strike rule."[7] Tebeau's argument—and I admit I'm fleshing it out from somewhat fragmentary remarks—was that Young was a fastball pitcher who relied heavily on control, locating his deliveries on or just beyond the outside corner. Because hitters had trouble getting around on Young's speed, they often fouled these outside pitches off. Prior to 1903 such fouls were inconsequential for the hitter; from 1903 on, the first two fouls for each batter were recorded as strikes. As a result, Young was able more frequently to stay ahead in the count and able more frequently—with only one overpowering pitch rather than three—to strike a batter out. Does the statistical evidence bear out Tebeau's claim? Actually not. In a year that saw improvements in all measures of pitching skills in the American League, Young's improvements in such categories as strikeouts per game, walks per game, and hits allowed per game failed to match, when taken as a percentage, the improvements of the league's pitchers in aggregate. His strikeout total, for example, increased by only 10 percent and his strike-out pace (taking innings pitched into account) increased by only 13 percent.[8] One could reasonably argue that Young was already so good that additional enhancements to his record could only be marginal at best. But the question of whether Young was helped by the foul strike rule must, Tebeau's declaration notwithstanding, be left unresolved.

Within this splendid year Cy Young enjoyed some singularly memorable stretches. On June 13, pitching in Boston, he held St. Louis to 4 hits and no runs and fielded his position with distinction while his teammates scored 7 times. It was already his third shutout of the year. The team then headed west, and Young missed two starts while attending the funeral of Robba's mother in Ohio. He returned to the mound in Detroit on June 23 and won 1–0, hurling a 7-hitter and initiating a difficult 1-2-3 double play. Five days later he pitched a 6-hitter against St. Louis, again winning 1–0. The Browns put runners on first and third to open the ninth inning but could not push the tying run across. On July 1 he pitched a ten-inning game in Chicago, throwing a 5-hitter. Not only did he win again by that familiar 1–0 score, but he did so by smashing a double past third base in the tenth inning to drive in the only run of the game.[9] In sum, Young threw 37 consecutive scoreless innings and 4 consecutive shutouts. What makes the feat particularly remarkable is that the final three contests were won 1–0. No other pitcher in major league history has won three straight 1–0 games.

Another achievement, entirely different in character, is best treated a curiosity. On September 15 the heavy-set Cy Young stole two bases in one game. "When huge Cyrus made the second steal," a writer for the *Chicago Journal* opined, "the earth must have quaked and the sun must have blinked bewildered."[10] It was that kind of year.

Young's season was notable for one other reason. Not only was he the best throwing pitcher in the league, he was also, for the only time in his career, the best hitting pitcher, at least among men who appeared in a regular rotation. His ambition to be a good batter was of long standing.[11] But since he had never previously hit higher than .289 (an average achieved in the far more batter-friendly environment of 1896) and since his career batting average would finally come in at a paltry .210, the .321 figure he posted for 1903 can only be regarded as an aberration. Twice he made three hits in a game, he batted his way on base in 31 of his 40 games, he drove in 14 runs, and in his only pinch-hitting appearance of the season he singled. He is one of only a handful of ten-year veterans who managed a higher batting average in 1903 than in the bonanza year of 1894. His "stick work this season," commented *Sporting Life*, "is remarkable."[12]

Not all of Young's appearances were glorious, however, and one disaster merits mention as possibly the worst game of his American League career. It is not clear why Jimmy Collins chose to leave him on the mound against New York on July 29—maybe, because the game was close, Collins thought Young would right himself—but whatever the manager's reasons, Young stayed in the game, yielding 18 hits and 15 runs (8 of them earned) and finally losing 15–14. With Jack Chesbro starting for the Highlanders, it was an embarrassing day—with a score reminiscent of 1894—for two of the finest hurlers in the league. But for Chesbro, at least, there was the cover of an exit after five innings. Young, on the other hand, labored on to the humiliating end.

Still, by any reckoning the season was a triumph. And there is a final achievement that merits comment. Throughout this book I have made a point of charting Cy Young's climb through the ranks of career victory totals. With his win over St. Louis on June 13 he reached the top of the heap, passing Pud Galvin's lifetime total of 360 victories to become the winningest pitcher of all time. He was, of course, not finished; his total of 361 would rise to 511. But it was on June 13, 1903, that he claimed first place, a distinction he has now held for over ninety years and will probably never be compelled to relinquish. Other apparently unchallengeable lifetime claims to fame—4,191 base hits, 714 home runs, 2,130 consecutive games—have come and gone. Not Young's. And while his accomplishment in 1903 did not (so far as I can judge) arouse comment at the time, within two years, as baseball historians launched the struggle to pin down statistical information about the greatest winner in the game's history, the dimensions of the achievement would begin to receive attention. I cannot think of any player who has held the leadership position in an important cumulative baseball statistic for as long as Cy Young has enjoyed the claim to being the game's winningest pitcher.[13]

As the 1903 season moved into the heat of August, people who followed baseball began to speak of their hope of seeing a postseason match-up between the winners of the two pennant races. In retrospect, of course, such a series seems a natural conclusion to a summer of baseball. Peace had returned to the major leagues; the memory of postseason competition in the 1880s had not been effaced; those earlier championship engagements had even generated a name for such a match—the "World's Series" (notice the spelling). Still, the baseball world was forced to wait upon events. Happily for the fans, Barney Dreyfuss's Pittsburgh Pirates held off the challenge of John Brush's New York Giants to win the National League pennant. Brush contemned the American League. Dreyfuss, however, grateful that he had been spared American League competition in Pittsburgh, was inclined to seek amity among owners. So in August he issued a challenge for postseason play to Henry Killilea. The Boston owner conferred with Ban Johnson, who, having received an assurance from Killilea that the Boston Americans could defeat the Pirates, urged acceptance. Then, just when it appeared that the season of peace would be crowned with a best-of-nine World Series, a dispute over money threatened to upset the plans. The two owners had agreed to split the gate for the series evenly between the two clubs. Dreyfuss decided to give his players the entire Pittsburgh portion of that gate, though he kept the decision a secret until well into the series. The Boston players wanted profitable financial arrangements for themselves. When Killilea insisted that he should receive 50 percent of Boston's take, the players threatened a strike and agreed to play only after Ban Johnson intervened to negotiate a compromise settlement. It involved obliging Killilea to pay his players for two weeks of play in October (their contracts ran only through September 30) and then to claim only 25 percent of Boston's gate as his own. No evidence suggests what role, if any, Cy Young played in this contretemps.

The Pirates were a powerful team, winners for the third straight season of the National League pennant. In the infield they boasted the magnificent Honus Wagner, the National League batting champion and Larry Lajoie's only rival for the mythical title of the best player in the world. In the outfield they featured both Ginger Beaumont, the batting champion of the previous year, and Fred Clarke, who in addition to managing the Pirates, was runner-up for the batting title in 1903. Their pitching staff, built upon Sam Leever, Deacon Phillippe, and Ed Doheny, had done good work throughout the season, even managing during a magical week in June to hurl 56 consecutive scoreless innings, still, almost a century later, the major league team record. But the 1903 Pirates were not as strong as the awesome squad of 1902, chiefly because two fine pitchers from the 1902 squad, Jack Chesbro and Jesse Tannehill, had jumped to the American League for 1903. Perhaps for this reason Jimmy Collins felt emboldened to say that "the Pittsburgs do not look so strong to me. They show up strong because they are in a poorer league than the American."[14] At the time Collins spoke those words, they smacked of bluster. But then in the final weeks of the season the Pirates suffered further blows. Wagner was slowed by a leg injury, Leever had a sore shoulder, and in the saddest development of all, Doheny had a severe mental breakdown.[15] So calamitous were these developments that there was briefly talk of calling the series off. But even when lame, the Pirates felt confident that they could prevail, asserting that Cy Young, Bill Dinneen, and Tom Hughes had not done well against Pittsburgh in their National League days. Moreover, everyone stood to profit from the revenues that a series would generate. And so the talk of cancellation faded, and the professional gambling community, which acts on an objective reading of the available evidence, installed the Boston club as modest favorites.

The first game of the first modern World Series was played in Boston on Thursday, October 1, pitting Cy Young (28–9) against Deacon Phillippe (25–9); each manager went with his best.[16] Over 16,000 fans—with many men in long-tailed coats and many women in ankle-length skirts—swarmed into the seats and roped-off outfield margins of the Huntington Avenue Grounds. A letter carriers' band entertained the crowd with a medley of popular tunes. The first pitch of that first game—here's a good piece of baseball trivia—was thrown by Cy Young. But when the top of the first was finally over, Young found himself four runs in the hole, stung by four Pirate hits, embarrassed by three Pirate stolen bases, and victimized by three Boston errors (two by the usually reliable Lou Criger).[17] We can speculate that Young was nervous in the first inning; certainly he pitched fairly well thereafter, giving up only single runs in the third, the fourth, and the seventh innings. The last of those tallies was a consequence of a home run by Jimmy Sebring, the first round-tripper in World Series history. Young also yielded the first single (to Honus Wagner), the first triple (to Tommy Leach), and the first base on balls (to Claude Ritchey). The Pirates, however, had no need of any runs after the first inning. Phillippe held Boston scoreless until the seventh, and the American League club managed only three tallies during the game. Thus among other "firsts" recorded by Cy Young on October 1, 1903, was being the pitcher of record for the first World Series loss.[18]

The next day, October 2, Bill Dinneen faced the ailing Sam Leever. After yielding a home run, a double, a single, and a walk in the first inning, Leever retired from the game, and while his replacement, Bucky

Veil, pitched very well, giving up only one additional run during the rest of the contest, once again a first inning rally had sufficed to secure a victory—this time for Boston and Dinneen, by a score of 3–0. "Dinneen," Cy Young recalled many years later, "had a real good day."[19]

Jimmy Collins believed that pitching depth was Boston's key advantage in the series, and for the third home game, played on October 3, he turned to his third 20-game winner, Tom Hughes. Fred Clarke, on the other hand, his options confined by injuries to his staff, looked again to Deacon Phillippe. Because the day was Saturday, the Boston railroads promoted an afternoon at the game, and over 18,000 fans—the largest crowd of the series—bought tickets. Before game time perhaps another 7,000 crowded into the outskirts of the outfield. Packing so many people into such a small space led to much angry behavior, and when the players and police could not control the fighting, a call went out for police reinforcements and fire hoses. Only after 100 additional police had arrived was the ball field made playable. Pittsburgh opened the scoring with a single run in the second inning, and when the first three Pirate batters got on base in the third inning, Collins concluded that Hughes was not the man to stop the Pirate assault that day and sent for Cy Young. The manager engineered a delay at this point, for Young, not expecting to pitch until the series resumed in Pittsburgh, had begun the inning attired in civilian clothes and helping to count gate receipts in the club office.[20] Young dressed quickly and, after hitting the first batter he faced (Honus Wagner) with a pitch, found his groove. Had Parent not mishandled a grounder, no inherited runner would have scored. From the fourth through the eighth inning Young retired thirteen straight batters. At that point he briefly weakened, as the formidable Wagner doubled and later scored. This final run was, however, supererogatory. Phillippe was even sharper than he had been two days earlier, giving up only 4 base hits. The final score of the Pirate victory was 4–2. Of the Pirates' 7 hits, 3 were ground-rule doubles that, had a crowd not ringed the outfield, might have been catchable.

Fortunately for the shocked Boston Americans, trailing two games to one, the schedule now decreed that the clubs would suspend play for a Sunday train ride to Pittsburgh and the next four contests. Rain on Monday then extended the suspension of play for an extra day. Both teams played better at home than on the road, but what Jimmy Collins needed even more than friendly fans and a familiar playing field was a chance for his squad to regroup. Eight runs in three games was a sorry performance for an offense that had averaged five runs per game throughout the season; sixteen innings from Cy Young without a victory to show for the effort was a manifest disappointment. Moreover, if friendly fans were important to a team, the Boston players knew that about 125 noisy Royal Rooters would accompany them to western Pennsylvania. (Even during the regular season it was not unusual for the Royal Rooters to accompany their heroes into foreign ballparks.) "Tessie" was a well-known tune of the day, adopted by the Rooters as their theme song. In an effort to rattle Honus Wagner, who had gotten on base in almost half of his plate appearances in Boston, the Rooters changed the first line of the song from "Tessie, you know I love you madly" to "Honus, why do you hit so badly."[21] Rowdy support might help. Besides—and more to the point—two days off meant that Collins would have a rested Bill Dinneen to send to the mound in game four.

It did not work out as the Boston manager planned. On Tuesday, October 6, in the first game at Exposition Park, the remarkable Deacon Phillippe came back for his third start and won his third game, providing the earliest of the great stories of individual achievement in the World Series. Sharp into the ninth inning, he survived a 3-run Boston rally in the final frame to put Pittsburgh fairly comfortably in the series lead, 3 games to 1.

Boston could not afford to lose the fifth game. That's why Cy Young was Jimmy Collins's only reasonable choice for pitcher. Pittsburgh, on the other hand, needed to give its strained staff a break. That's why Fred Clarke turned to the veteran Brickyard Kennedy, who was celebrating his thirty-sixth birthday that very day and who had won only 9 games for the Pirates during the year. Clarke hoped that Kennedy's wiles might eke out a victory, but even if he failed, Pittsburgh would still have the series lead, a more rested pitching corps, and two additional opportunities in Pittsburgh to take the championship. Over 12,000 fans paid to see the match-up; their presence around the margins of the outfield meant that unusual ground rules would be in effect. Boston threatened immediately, loading the bases in the top of the first. But the Americans failed to push a run across, and the game remained scoreless through five innings. In the sixth, however, Pittsburgh's strong defense, which had committed only 6 errors thus far in the series, lost its moorings. Three miscues (two by Honus Wagner) and 2 triples (one by Cy Young—the throng on the outskirts of play created 5 ground-rule triples during the game) helped Boston to score 6 runs. In the seventh the club added 4 more. Brickyard Kennedy was lifted before the eighth inning began; he never again pitched a major league game. From that point on Young could coast, and he wound up victorious by a score of 11–2; neither of Pittsburgh's runs was earned. Altogether, it was a grand day for the hurler. He collected 2 base hits, drove in 3 runs, and struck out 4 while walking none. Robba Young was in attendance (she may have attended other games as well), and as the pitcher commented to a writer after the contest, with his wife in the stands, "How could I lose?"[22] The laconic Young did not often supply remarks for writers, but many years later he ventured another comment about his feelings that day of the fifth game, suggesting that he still savored his success: "The Pittsburgh players and fans became just a little too cocky."[23] Cy Young stopped the Boston slide.

On October 8, Jimmy Collins sent Bill Dinneen back to the mound. Fred Clarke responded with Sam Leever. Dinneen held the Pirates scoreless until the Americans had secured a 6-run lead off the ailing Leever, and when the game ended Boston had tied the series at 3 games apiece with a 6–3 victory.

The next game was scheduled for Friday, October 9, but Barney Dreyfuss used the excuse of cold weather to put it off for a day. Observers cited a number of likelier explanations for his decision: the need to give Deacon Phillippe another day of rest; a reluctance to allow his team to face Cy Young's speed on a dark day; the hope that a Saturday crowd would be larger than a Friday crowd. The last hope at least was fulfilled, as over 17,000 people ignored the continuing cold snap to see the game. Even with the delay, however, Young bested Phillippe by a score of 7–3. Young entered the game breathing confidence. "I'll win if I can," he declared, adding that "it should not be so hard."[24] And it wasn't. Boston scored 2 runs (again with the help of tainted triples) in the top of the first inning and led 4–0 before the Pirates managed to push a run across. Young had secured his second victory; Phillippe had failed in his effort to secure his fourth. But in fact the two hurlers had turned in very similar complete-game performances, Young giving up 10 hits and 3 earned runs, Phillippe yielding 11 hits and 4 earned runs. The heart of the story, however, lay in the consequences of the game for the series. Once behind 3 games to 1, Boston now, by virtue of three straight victories in Pittsburgh (two credited to Young), led 4 games to 3 and was only one victory away from claiming the title. It is easy to believe that the Boston players were feeling high as they trekked to the train station after the game, accompanied by a double file of Royal Rooters and wished well by a surprisingly large crowd of 500 Pittsburghers and a local band that played, of all songs, "Tessie."

The eighth and final game of the World Series was played in Boston on Tuesday, October 13. Bad weather had given Deacon Phillippe an extra day to rest his tired arm, and further bad weather then helped explain the disappointingly small crowd of about seventy-five hundred that witnessed the game. But they were happy and noisy fans, for they saw Boston win, 3–0. The stars were Bill Dinneen, who pitched the 4-hit shutout, and Lou Criger, who first (in the fourth inning) thwarted Tommy Leach's effort to score a run on a delayed double steal with a sharp 2-5-2 play and then (in the sixth inning) picked Phillippe off at first base. By winning the final 4 games of the first World Series, the Boston Americans laid authentic claim to be the world champions, and when the game ended the jubilant crowd thronged onto the playing field to carry their heroes on their shoulders.[25]

As in most World Series ever since, pitching dominated the first. Boston batted .252, Pittsburgh .237. Among regulars, only Chick Stahl of Boston and Jimmy Sebring of Pittsburgh batted over .300. Jimmy Collins batted a feeble .250, Honus Wagner a feebler .222. The pitching stars were Bill Dinneen, who had won 3 games (including 2 shutouts); Cy Young, who had won 2 while posting the lowest earned run average of the series (1.85); and Deacon Phillippe, who had pitched over half of the innings of the 8-game series while winning 3 and losing 2. Although several other pitchers have won 3 games in a single series, only in 1903 did two different hurlers reach that level. Many years later Young commented on Phillippe. "He was one of the greatest pitchers of his time."[26] A final note is in order: with his appearance in this postseason match, Young became the only pitcher in baseball history to hurl in both a Temple Cup competition and a World Series.[27]

Although the Pirates tended to be gracious in defeat, Phillippe spoke for many when he declared that "had Sam [Leever] and Ed [Doheny] been in shape, there would have been nothing to it. We could have beaten them beyond a shadow of doubt."[28] There may be merit in that claim.[29] Leever, who was the National League's earned run average leader in 1903, flopped in both of his series appearances. Doheny was not even available. And so, after Phillippe, Fred Clarke was obliged to rely on journeymen who collectively in 1903 had recorded 16 wins and 9 losses. It would have been tough to fashion a championship out of that material, especially when facing Boston's twin speedballers, Dinneen and Young. Phillippe was a skilled performer, but even he could not handle the burden of pitching five complete games in less than two weeks. And this point has a further implication for the first decade of twentieth-century baseball. Virtually everyone admits that in 1906 the Chicago Cubs were a stronger team than the Chicago White Sox team that beat them. If the National League entry was really the better club in 1903 too, then the junior circuit, which lost every other World Series until 1910, might very well have been swept in all of its first six series appearances. That would have been a disaster for the reputation of Ban Johnson's circuit. So one important outcome of the 1903 engagement was that Boston's triumph gave the American League a credibility that it might not have deserved.

Finally, there is a story within this story—perhaps the most important tale coming out of the first World Series, even though it did not become public until two decades later. On the eve of the 1924 World Series, Ban Johnson, still the American League president and still looking for ways to skewer John McGraw, released an affidavit from Lou Criger that told of an effort by gamblers to buy the outcome of the 1903 World Series.[30] According to the catcher's testimony, he had been approached in the lobby of the Monongahela Hotel in Pittsburgh and offered $12,000 to throw the remaining games. By accepting the money, he was assured, he could "feather [his] nest for life." When Criger asked why he had been singled out for the offer, the gambler replied, "Because you are the only one capable of turning the trick."[31] Criger refused the money, and promptly related the incident to Young. Little interest was shown in this tale until almost another quarter of a century passed. Then Cy Young told a reporter that while he had been standing on the field in Pittsburgh prior to the fourth game of the series, two men approached him and, introducing themselves as representatives of some gamblers, offered him $20,000 if he wouldn't "bear down" the next day, when he was scheduled to pitch. By Young's account he rejected the offer and added that "if you put any value at all on your money, you'd better bet it on me to win."[32] Fourteen years in the ethically ambiguous world of major league baseball had not compromised Young's understanding of right and wrong.

Historians have been uncertain what to make of these accounts; many have chosen to ignore them. Criger drafted his affidavit in 1923; Young's tale did not become public until 1947. Both men had had ample opportunity to speak out before they finally broke their silences—if not at the time, then certainly in 1920, when the Black Sox scandal in the 1919

World Series rocked the baseball world. The passage of so many years and the discrepancies between the stories inevitably led to speculation that both men were wrong, or that Young misremembered, or even that Young deliberately concocted the tale to enhance his own reputation. That's why I think it's useful to begin any analysis of the accounts by highlighting three elements consistent in both stories. First, both claim that there was an effort in Pittsburgh to buy the outcome of at least one game of the series. Second, both accounts affirm that Cy Young knew of the offers—Criger's, because he says he mentioned it to Young and to no one else, and Young's, because his relation of the story purports to be a firsthand account. Third, both state that the offers were spurned.

Both stories are likely true in their central claim. The series certainly invited a surge of gambling; indeed, owners and players themselves wagered on the outcome of games.[33] We know that in the much less important 1903 postseason exhibitions between the two Chicago teams, pitcher Jack Taylor deliberately lost some games to the White Sox.[34] With so much money at stake in the championship series, and in the relatively relaxed ethical atmosphere of professional baseball at the time, it's very likely that some gambling interests sought to purchase the loyalty of players. In fact, it was claimed in some quarters that the reason for the low attendance at game eight was the widely held belief that the players, to maximize their take from the series, would contrive to effect a Pittsburgh victory and thereby assure a ninth game.[35]

I am not disturbed that Cy Young's and Lou Criger's stories don't coincide. Rather, it seems to me likely that they describe two separate events: one an effort to buy Young's involvement directly and the other an effort to approach the pitcher through his most trusted friend, his batterymate—and perhaps not in that sequence. The latter interpretation allows us to put a reading on the gambler's otherwise puzzling remark to Criger that he was "the only one capable of turning the trick." On its face, that statement was errant nonsense. By himself, Criger offered very little: he was a poor hitter and, while a good receiver, not really able to get his pitchers to perform poorly. But if Criger was seen as a door to Young, then the situation changed dramatically. For if Young was deemed likely to be almost incorruptible, then the only chance to snare him would be through the teammate he relied on most. And the argument that might convince Young was the lure of security: with the money, Criger (and Young) could feather their nests in their (presumably imminent) retirements. It is also suggestive—though here I am speculating—that Jimmy Collins never used Tom Hughes after his two innings of wretched work in game three and in fact promptly traded him away for a pitcher who was four years older and had an inferior record in 1903. Could the gamblers have gotten to Hughes, and might Collins have suspected as much? Pete Kelley may have been hinting at that when he offered this oblique explanation of the manager's readiness to get rid of Hughes: "He made bad breaks at the time of the world's series. He didn't behave himself and lost his popularity."[36]

If Young's and Criger's stories are true, why then did the two players remain silent about the bribe effort for so long? I don't know. But in the case of Lou Criger, we can be confident that he did not wait for two full decades to elapse before telling at least one other person—namely Ban Johnson—of the bribe effort. Rather, at some earlier point, and perhaps almost immediately, he informed the American League president that he had been approached. What brought the story before the public only in 1924 was not Criger's sudden recall of the event, but rather Johnson's belief that by revealing an old story in the wake of a new scandal, he would help to prove that John McGraw had colluded with gamblers for many years. Moreover, Criger thought (incorrectly as it turned out) that he was dying when he made his declaration; he may not have wanted his evidence to die with him. It is suggestive, as Lee Allen has noted, that after Criger's left leg was amputated, Johnson decided to pay him an annual pension;[37] the American League president may have wanted to thank Criger for being an honest man in 1903.

Cy Young apparently kept quiet for many more years. We do not know when he learned of Criger's affidavit. We do not even know that he ever learned of it. But it is easy to believe that when he finally went public with his story, he thought it essentially inconsequential—an oddity of the game from a half century earlier. It is also possible that, in his old age and speaking to a generation that knew of his glory only through history books, he wanted to give a good impression of himself. But I suspect the reason he kept the secret for so long was precisely that he did not need to blow his own horn. And in any case, we do not need Young's version to confirm that he made the right decision in 1903. For we know from Criger's tale that Young knew of the bribe effort. And if he had wanted to cash in, he had ample opportunity to make his own arrangements with the gamblers. It's because Cy Young looks good in Criger's version that we can credit at least the core point of Young's own version. And we should then assume that the stories refer to separate approaches. After all, any assiduous gambler would not take one refusal as the last word.

Does all of this matter? I don't know for sure. But I think that had Cy Young decided to accept the money—a sum of $20,000 was, after all, over three times his salary in 1903—and had it then leaked out that gambling interests had bought the outcome of the most important athletic competition in the country, the history of the World Series and of twentieth-century baseball would have been very different. That's why I think that anyone interested in the welfare of the game should be grateful that Cy Young's moral compass was sound.

In the aftermath of the World Series the Boston ball players went off to their respective homes. City leaders were late in implementing plans for a post-series dinner to honor the players at Faneuil Hall, and when Jimmy Collins said that he would not ask his men to linger in Boston while the plans were being completed, hopes for a celebration dissolved. Each player returned home richer by $1,182, the share voted to each of the seventeen men after Henry Killilea took his portion of about $6,700. (Because Barney Dreyfuss took nothing from the Pittsburgh portion, the losing Pirates actually had larger individual shares—$1,316.) Although the nation beyond Boston and Pittsburgh had not paid much attention to the competition, nevertheless, because over 100,000 fans had paid to see the eight games of the series, observers adjudged the experiment a grand success. "I should not be surprised," Jimmy Collins predicted, "to see post-season games each fall as long as there are two big leagues."[38] Even before he left Boston to return to Peoli, Cy Young received many telegrams congratulating him for his work, some of which Robba Young pasted into a scrapbook now held at the National Baseball Library in Cooperstown. One of the telegrams from Newcomerstown, Ohio, promised a parade for the local hero when he returned to Tuscarawas County. It would be nice if there was a contemporaneous quotation from the hurler describing his reaction to the club's triumph, but he seems to have exercised his characteristic taciturnity. I suspect, however, that the view he expressed in one undated clipping from about this time captures at least some of his feeling: "I am very glad, indeed, to be with the American League."[39]

For early preseason training the next year Cy Young secured permission to exercise himself into shape in Hot Springs, resuming his happy relationship with the Arkansas spa that had been interrupted by springs spent in cold Massachusetts and dusty Georgia. Meanwhile, most of the defending champions returned to Macon, though resistance to Henry Killilea's efforts to reduce the salaries of some of his players led several stars, including Bill Dinneen and Buck Freeman, briefly to protest the club's offers and to train with Young in Arkansas.[40] Young hooked up with his teammates in Montgomery, Alabama, as they worked their way back to the Northeast. The club had made only one important personnel change—the trading of right-handed Tom Hughes to the Highlanders for the former Pirate southpaw star, Jesse Tannehill. (After the season started Boston would make one other major change, sending Patsy Dougherty to New York for Bob Unglaub.) Jimmy Collins was upbeat about the coming season. While acknowledging that the talent in Philadelphia, New York, and Cleveland made another romp unlikely, he saw no reason to believe Boston could not retain the pennant. "We are ready," he declared, "for any team that they can line up against us."[41]

The Americans opened their title defense in New York on April 14 with Cap Anson in attendance; Cy Young yielded four runs in the very first inning of the new season and lost to Jack Chesbro, 8–2. (Losing to Chesbro was to become common place as the summer proceeded; the Highlander hurler would end the season with 41 victories, the highest total in league history and the twentieth-century major league record.) Four days later, just before the Boston team launched its home campaign, news broke that ownership of the club had passed from Henry Killilea to John Taylor, son of the owner of the *Boston Globe*. Taylor had a reputation as a bit of a playboy, but in general the move was applauded in New England because it finally brought ownership of the franchise into local hands. Since Cy Young was suffering from a sore throat, Collins sent Jesse Tannehill to the mound for the team's home opener on April 18. Young appeared the next day to complete a drizzly doubleheader sweep of Washington by a score of 3–2. "So far, so good," the new owner smiled. Young's record now stood at 1 win and 1 loss. Unexciting. Perhaps the only portent of what was about to come was his success at striking out four of the final eight Senators he faced.

What followed was the most remarkable episode of concentrated pitching dominance in Cy Young's entire career. He had always been a very good and unusually consistent pitcher, occasionally accomplishing extraordinary feats such as his 13-game winning streak in 1892, his no-hitter in 1897, and his four consecutive shutouts in 1903. But what he achieved in five appearances between April 25, 1904, and May 17, 1904, eclipsed even these master strokes. First, he pitched 45 straight scoreless innings. Second, within that string of 45 innings he pitched 24 straight hitless innings. Third, in the middle of that streak of hitless innings he threw a perfect game. Scarcely any major league hurler has ever controlled opposing batters over five consecutive appearances with such mastery as Young showed during these games.

Let's look first at the scoreless inning streak. It began in Philadelphia on April 25, when Young faced the Athletics and Rube Waddell. Both pitchers threw 6-hitters that day, but Philadelphia scored 2 runs in the first inning—one of them earned—and Waddell shut out Boston, winning 2–0. So Young lost. But he completed the game, holding the Athletics scoreless in their last 7 at bats. On April 30 in Washington, Young entered the game in relief of George Winter in the third inning (with 1 run in, 2 men on, and no one out), retired 3 straight batters without allowing a run to score, and pitched shutout ball over the remaining 6 innings in a 4–1 Boston victory. He now had 14 consecutive scoreless innings. On May 5 he pitched a perfect game against Philadelphia, 9 innings, bringing his total to 23 consecutive scoreless innings. On May 11 in Boston he hooked up in a dazzling pitching duel with Detroit's Ed Killian, winning 1–0 in the bottom of the fifteenth inning, with umpire Tommy Connolly about to suspend the game as darkness engulfed the field.[42] His streak now stood at 38 innings. Finally, on May 17 in Boston he held the powerful Cleveland club scoreless through 7⅔ innings, before yielding the winning runs in the eighth in a 3–1 loss. The streak thus ended after reaching 45 innings, establishing the major league record for consecutive scoreless innings pitched by one hurler. Since Young's day his mark has been eclipsed only by Doc White, Jack Coombs, Walter Johnson, Carl Hubbell, Don Drysdale, and—the current record-holder, with 59 innings—Orel Hershiser. And yet, outstanding as Young's streak may be, it is the least impressive of his accomplishments during his five games of wizardry.

Now let's look at a single game—the gem that lies almost exactly in the middle of the scoreless streak—Cy Young's perfect game. Because events of an almost-once-in-a-decade rarity cannot be predicted, perfect games rarely attract large crowds (Don Larsen's World Series performance in 1956 being the great exception to the rule). But when word went out that Cy Young and Rube Waddell would match skills on May 5 and the day then dawned warm and quiet, over 10,000 fans appeared at the Huntington Avenue Grounds. Young was always an attraction, but on this afternoon the eccentric Waddell was the real magnet. Ten days earlier, as noted above, he had beaten Young, 2–0. Just three days earlier he had again faced the Americans and bested Jesse Tannehill with a spectacular one-hitter. Justifiably cocky after defeating Boston's two star hurlers, Waddell took to baiting Young: "I'll give you the same what I give Tannehill."[43] The taunts provided wonderful fodder for the press on the eve of the game.

Once begun, however, the game became a stage for Cy Young. While Waddell labored, giving up at least one hit to every Boston batter except Young himself, the Boston hurler handled the Athletic batting order with dispatch. Inning succeeded inning, and not an Athletic reached base. Buck Freeman made a fine catch of a fly ball in shallow right. Chick Stahl raced to grab a Texas Leaguer to center. Patsy Dougherty grazed the wall bagging a foul ball to left. Freddy Parent and Hobe Ferriss handled sharp grounders around the keystone sack. Lou Criger almost stumbled on the Boston bench while nabbing a pop foul. But by and large, the plays were unexceptional; Young got most batters to hit lazy flies or easy grounders. Along about the sixth inning his teammates began to leave him alone with his thoughts when he returned to the bench, respectful of the traditions of superstition that enveloped the game of baseball. When the ninth inning arrived, Boston led 3–0, and the crowd was roaring its encouragement. Monte Cross was the first Athletic to come to the plate, and became Young's eighth and final strikeout victim. Ossee Schreckengost followed and grounded out to Parent. Rube Waddell then stepped up to bat for himself. (He was not a notably good hitting pitcher; perhaps Philadelphia manager Connie Mack liked the agonistic drama inherent in seeing whether Young's great mound rival could do what no one else had done that day.) Waddell hit the ball well but not dangerously, and when Chick Stahl put it away ("Y'know. I thought that ball would never come down," Stahl said after the game)[44] the crowd burst onto the field to praise Young for his achievement. The game had lasted only an hour and twenty-three minutes. On his seventy-fifth birthday he said, "I think the hullaballoo that broke loose after that game was probably the biggest thrill I had in my career," and when he was about eighty-five he declared, "that [the perfect game] always has to be my biggest thrill."[45]

Among the first to reach the mound in the explosion of postgame joy was first baseman Candy LaChance, who remarked coyly that "nobody came down to see me today."[46] According to Cy Young's later account, only then did he realize what he had done. Though this may sound far-fetched, it is not entirely implausible. Young realized he was pitching well—he was later quoted as saying that he knew almost from his first pitch of the game that "I should be able to put the ball exactly where I wanted to"—but no scoreboard at the Huntington Avenue Grounds recorded base hits.[47] His teammates had no interest in raising the subject. Moreover, even if he understood that he had a no-hitter in hand, he may not have realized that his no-hitter was a very unusual one. After all, a baseball game in which not a single batter reached base was almost so unthinkable that it took the press half a day to uncover the tales of the last two perfect games in the majors, thrown in the same week back in 1880 by John Montgomery Ward and Lee Richmond. That date under-scored the immensity of Young's achievement: he was the first hurler since the setting of sixty and six to keep every opponent off base.

LaChance was only the first of Cy Young's teammates to swarm around the pitcher—the "big, brawny, good-natured, hustling 'Cy'," as one writer identified him the next day.[48] Philadelphia players joined the crowd of enthusiasts; Connie Mack offered congratulations. A happy fan pressed money into his hand. (He returned some of it.) He had a postgame barb or two for the loud-mouthed Waddell, by one account shouting "How did you like that one? you hayseed" at his mound foe.[49] Once showered and dressed, he settled back to enjoy the adulation of friends, fans, and the press. The *Boston Globe* dislodged the siege of Port Arthur from its pri-mary place on the front page to feature a cartoon of Young wearing a laurel crown and to acclaim him "King of Pitchers."[50] Out-of-town news-papers wired the Boston papers requesting special stories about Young's feat and his career. His Boston teammate Duke Farrell mocked those who had expected deteriorating work from a thirty-seven-year-old pitcher: "And they said Uncle 'Cy' was all in, did they? He fooled them, didn't he."[51] Jacob Morse declared that Young "has earned every cent of the big salary he has received."[52] The feat even aroused *Sporting Life*'s poetic muse:

"The innings went swiftly with never a hit,
  And the strike outs kept slamming in Criger's big mitt.
"'Tis my lifetime's great climax," quoth Cyrus, "oh, glee!
  I am slated today for a star jubilee."[53]

This game is the obvious choice for pride of place in the list of the great pitcher's greatest games (see appendix 2). Although others can equal the performance, nobody can surpass the excellence of a perfect game.[54]

But there was an even more impressive accomplishment during these

Cy Young at age 21, 1888.
National Baseball Hall of Fame
Library, Cooperstown, N.Y.

*Cy Young soon after joining
the Cleveland Spiders baseball club, ca. 1890.*
National Baseball Hall of Fame
Library, Cooperstown, N.Y.

Cy and Robba Young, 1893.
Newcomerstown Historical Society:
Temperance Tavern Museum.

Above: *The 1894 Cleveland Spiders. Cy Young is second from the left in the top row. His battery mate, Chief Zimmer, is second from right in the bottom row. Patsy Tebeau has pride of place in the middle. Future Hall of Famers John Clarkson, Buck Ewing, and Jesse Burkett are second, third, and fifth in the bottom row. Notice how small the teams were in the 1890s.* Transcendental Graphics.

Below: *The 1898 Cleveland Spiders. Young (top row, center) was winding up his Spider career as this late-season picture was taken. Nig Cuppy is on the left in the seated row.* Transcendental Graphics.

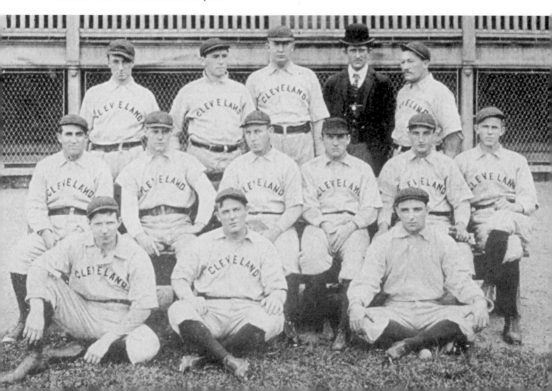

Cy Young as a member of the
St. Louis Perfectos, 1899.
Boston Public Library.

The Boston infield,
1901. Left to right:
Jimmy Collins, Freddy
Parent, Hobe Ferris,
and Buck Freeman.

The Boston club of the American League, 1901. Young is seated in the first row, second from the right. Lou Criger, arms folded, is in the first row, second from the left. Jimmy Collins, arms also folded, sits next to Young.

Boston and Pittsburgh teams pose for a commemorative portrait before the final game of the first World Series, October 13, 1903. Cy Young is fifth from the left among the long row of Boston uniforms. Pittsburgh's Honus Wagner stands on the far right.

Right: *Fans circle the infield to watch the players' pre-game practice. Once the game started, the infield would be cleared, but a swollen ring of outfield spectators would remain.*

Boston fans trying to get into the Huntington Avenue Grounds, October 13, 1903.

Top and bottom: *Boston's "Royal Rooters," complete with band accompaniment, prepare to cheer on their team.*

Boston dugout during the 1903 World Series. Cy Young is seated at far left.

Fans file out of the Huntington Avenue Grounds, October 13, 1903. Boston won the game, 3-0, and with it the first World Series, five games to three.

Boston raises its first World Series banner, April 1904.

The popular press pronounces Young "King of Pitchers"
following his perfect game, May 1904.
Boston Globe.

The Boston Americans pose after their pennant-clinching victory over New York, October 10, 1904. Cy Young looms tall at the far right.

John I. Taylor bought the Boston club in 1904. In 1908 he named the team the "Red Sox."

Young receiving loving cup on "Cy Young Day," 1908.
Boston Public Library.

Baseball Magazine *began publishing in 1908. This is the cover of the September issue, their "Cy Young number."*

Northeastern University,
World Series Room.

Cy Young reunited with Lou Criger, his longtime catcher with both the Cleveland Spiders and the Boston Americans. Sporting News offered this image as the second in their series of ballplayer photographs that fans could purchase.

National Baseball Hall of Fame Library, Cooperstown, N.Y.

The best-known photograph of Young, taken in 1909 by Charles Conlon, the great sports photographer.

National Baseball Hall of Fame Library, Cooperstown, N.Y.

*A weathered Young in
1909, near the end of
his career.*

National Baseball Hall of Fame
Library, Cooperstown, N.Y.

*This photograph may have been taken at spring training in 1912. It shows, from
left to right, Cy Young, Jake Stahl, Bill Carrigan, and "Nuf Ced" McGreevey, the
popular Boston tavern owner and head of the "Royal Rooters."*

A quartet of pitching excellence at the Old Timers' Day at Fenway Park in 1939: Smokey Joe Wood (then the Yale baseball coach), Cy Young, Lefty Grove, and Walter Johnson. All but Wood are in the Hall of Fame, and many believe Wood belongs.

Cy Young chats with veteran Red Sox pitcher Ray Scarborough, Fenway Park, 1951 or 1952. Behind Young, Ted Williams can be seen standing and leaning against the roof of the dugout.

An 87-year-old Cy Young stares out at batting practice in cavernous Municipal Stadium, Cleveland, in April 1954, almost two-thirds of a century after his first major league game.

Newcomerstown Historical Society: Temperance Tavern Museum.

Plaque commemorating Cy Young's career.

National Baseball Hall of Fame Library, Cooperstown, N.Y.

DENTON T. (CY) YOUNG
CLEVELAND (N) 1890-98
ST. LOUIS (N) 1899-1900
BOSTON (A) 1901-08
CLEVELAND (A) 1909-11
BOSTON (N) 1911
ONLY PITCHER IN FIRST HUNDRED
YEARS OF BASEBALL TO WIN 500 GAMES.
AMONG HIS 511 VICTORIES WERE 3
NO-HIT SHUTOUTS. PITCHED PERFECT
GAME MAY 5, 1904, NO OPPOSING
BATSMAN REACHING FIRST BASE.

five great games. For if the 45 straight scoreless innings that link the games constitute a feat that has occasionally been exceeded, and if his perfect game represents an achievement that has sometimes been equaled, there was a third record that emerged from these games that Cy Young—over 90 years later—still holds all by himself. Before he hurled his perfect game he had already pitched 9 straight hitless innings (2 against Philadelphia, 7 against Washington); in his first post-perfection start he reeled off another 6 hitless innings before Sam Crawford stroked a single to end the string. So Cy Young pitched 24 consecutive innings without yielding a base hit.[55] No one has ever equaled that mark. Even Johnny Vander Meer, aided by his back-to-back no-hitters in June of 1938, could manage no more than 22 straight hitless innings. And there is no reason to believe that Young was helped by friendly official scorers, for Boston made only one error in its game with Washington and none at all in its game with Detroit. In short, the revival of kingly imagery in reference to Young was eminently appropriate; if baseball had royalty by 1904, it was Cy Young who deserved the throne.

Led by Cy Young, who was amply assisted by Bill Dinneen and Jesse Tannehill, the Boston club led the league for the first three and a half months of the season. Young's contributions to this success included a six-game victory streak and a record of 15–8 when July ended. But then the club's lethargic stickwork finally exacted a toll. Often out of first place throughout August, the defending champions wrestled with New York, Chicago, Cleveland, and Philadelphia in a pennant race that was soon being celebrated as one of the most exciting in major league history.[56] Of Young's eight decisions of August, only three were victories. His "poor work" was said to be "worrying the talent."[57] But others stepped forward, including Jesse Tannehill, who on August 17 pitched a no-hitter against the White Sox. And so Boston stayed close. And as August passed into September three of the challengers—Chicago, Cleveland, and Philadelphia—bent before the pressure and slipped back. New York, however, led by Jack Chesbro and Willie Keeler, moved as if in lockstep with Boston. The schedule-makers had unwittingly crafted a season-closing masterpiece, studding the final four weeks of play with eleven games between Boston and New York, many of them in doubleheaders. We can be confident that Jimmy Collins was looking to Cy Young for help in the stretch, but he was disappointed on September 3, when Young recorded season-high figures in runs allowed (9), hits allowed (13), and earned runs allowed (7). He even heard some hometown jeers, as rumors that the old man was finally through gained force. Collins probably wondered about that, too. Meanwhile, he was left to reflect that at least he had been prescient: Boston was not going to win the 1904 race in a walk.

At this point Cy Young, whose record had slipped to 18–14, turned his and Boston's year around. After September 3 he lost only two more games all season. Even a brief illness did not deflect him. Starting on September 20 he took his thirty-seven-year-old arm to the mound each third day, like clockwork, for the rest of the season. Twice during this time he faced New York; twice he defeated them. When October arrived, his work got even sharper. On October 2 he shut out the Browns in St. Louis and pulled Boston back into first place; on October 5 he shut out the White Sox in Chicago to keep the Americans a single percentage point ahead of the Highlanders. But since New York was not cracking under the pressure, the season came down to the final five games of the year. On Friday, October 7, in New York, Jack Chesbro beat Boston, won his forty-first game, and nudged Young's team out of first place by half a game. Because a prior commitment tied up the New York ballpark on October 8, the two teams traveled quickly to Boston for a doubleheader in the Hub on Saturday. The New York manager Clark Griffith wanted to leave Chesbro in New York during the quick visit to Boston to assure that, if Chesbro's arm were needed for the season-closing doubleheader on Monday (Sunday baseball not being permitted in either city in 1904), it would be rested. But Chesbro insisted on making the trip to the Hub and even— where was the Old Fox's common sense?—on starting the first game. He was knocked from the box, and so when Cy Young took the mound for the second game of the twin-bill, he was in a position to give Boston a game-and-a-half lead.

That's exactly what he did, delivering his third straight October shutout and besting Jack Powell, 1–0, in a game called for darkness after 7 innings. The umpire was so eager to get the second game recorded before darkness came that he allowed no break between the two contests; indeed, since New York's leadoff batter Patsy Dougherty made the final out in the opening match, he simply stayed at the plate while Young replaced Bill Dinneen on the mound. Boston's one run came when Young hit a sacrifice fly to advance a runner to third and New York mishandled the play to allow the runner to score. As always, Young was glad to pitch with the benefit of twilight.[58]

Young was not involved in the game of October 10, once one of the most celebrated matches of all time but now little more than a footnote in baseball history. When Jack Chesbro allowed Boston's winning run to score on a wild pitch in the ninth inning of the first game of the day, he assured Boston of its second straight pennant. Young, ready to pitch the nightcap if Dinneen had lost the opener, stayed on the bench to celebrate. Five hundred Boston fans who had come to New York City for the games sang and played "Tessie."

Boston won the pennant in 1904 because it had the league's best pitching. As in 1903 it had three pitchers with at least twenty victories—Cy Young, Bill Dinneen, and (replacing Tom Hughes) Jesse Tannehill. Additionally, Norwood Gibson chipped in another 17. No pitching staff in American League history has pitched more complete games in a season (148), none has yielded fewer bases on balls (233). Boston posted the lowest earned run average in the league and gave up the fewest runs. Many years later Lou Criger, chief receiver for this magnificent staff, called Boston's pitching corps in 1903–1904 "the greatest pitching staff of all time."[59] This depth of talent allowed the club to survive both the decline of team batting power in the second half of the season and the arm-wrenching stress of a stretch drive laden with doubleheaders. But if pitching saved Boston, it is clear that Young was the strength of the club's pitching Corps. In the final four weeks of the season, the team posted a 7–1 record in games that Young started and a 10–10 record for other starting pitchers. Without Cy Young's contributions in September and October, the Boston Americans would have lost the pennant.

For Cy Young it was a season of spectacular spurts—the early and unexampled streak of hitless innings, the reeling off of six straight victories in July, the closing dash to the pennant. He had successfully added a slower curve to his repertory of deliveries, he had surmounted some difficult periods, and his final statistics for the year were good. His 26 victories tied him with Eddie Plank for second place in the American League. He posted 13–8 records both at home and on the road. He led the league in shutouts, with 10. Over the course of 380 innings he walked only 29 batters, figures that give rise to a career best of .69 walks per 9 innings. He was third in the league in complete games (40) and fifth in innings pitched; his 200 strikeouts, though only fifth highest in the league, marked a new career high for him. This strikeout success merits a few words. Although acclaimed for his fast ball, Young had led his league in strikeouts only twice in his career. But in 1904—as the foul strike rule helped in mystifying batters around the league—Young moved with many of the other pitchers in baseball to new strikeout levels. Early on in the season, in what we can see as a sign of what lay ahead, he was awarded a pair of shoes for being the Boston pitcher with the most strike-outs to his credit after fifty games. In a painful 13-inning, 1–0 loss to Eddie Plank and the Athletics on September 10 he recorded 12 strike-outs, a figure that he would tie but never exceed in later years. As these strikeout totals suggest, baseball was changing, and once again Cy Young was successfully adapting. On top of everything else, with his victory over the Athletics and Chief Bender on September 20 (and with old foe Billy Hamilton in attendance), Cy Young posted his 400th career victory. Still going strong, he was pulling away from the pack. For these reasons the 1904 season is the final candidate for Cy Young's greatest year.

Over in the National League the New York Giants rode to an easy pennant on the arms of Joe McGinnity, Christy Mathewson, and Dummy Taylor. Although almost everyone in baseball wanted to see another round of postseason championship play, with the Boston Americans de-fending their world title against the strong New York club, John Brush and John McGraw were still bent upon demeaning Ban Johnson's cre-ation, which Brush dismissed as a "league of minor fame." The Giant lead-ers therefore refused to engage the American League champions in a World Series in 1904, saying that by winning the National League pen-nant the Giants had already established themselves as world champions. Even pleas from the Giant players, who were after all losing out on an opportunity to make a tidy sum of money, counted for nothing. And when Brush's and McGraw's explanations sounded petty and self-serving (and what else was possible?), the virtually unanimous judgment of baseball fans was that, for some puzzling reason, the New Yorkers were afraid to play the Bostonians. As Chicago White Sox owner Charlie Comiskey said, "If the Giants do not want to play the champions of the American League, the followers of the game can draw their own conclusions."[60] John Taylor had little trouble drawing his own conclusion: if no one had dethroned his club, they would remain world champions throughout the 1905 season. As for the wonderful reference to the "league of minor fame," Herbert W. Joyce ridiculed it with a clever poem that devoted single verses to such American League stalwarts as Willie Keeler, Rube Waddell, Bill Donovan, Jack Chesbro, and Jimmy Collins, and two verses each to Larry Lajoie and Cy Young. The last three verses ran:

The name of Young recalls the scenes in mem'ry's golden frame
Of battles fought to victory in the league of minor fame!

In many contests nobly won his work received acclaim;
    He's better now than ever in the league of minor fame.

    Tho' Brush may think them minors, still we know they're
sportsmen game,
    And they have a few good players in the league of minor
fame.[61]

The mockery must have stung. By late October Brush was proposing that the two teams meet the following spring to settle the question of the championship. But that notion was laughable and rejected out of hand, and Brush had a long winter to reflect on the depth of his public relations miscalculation.

Before leaving for their various winter homes, the Boston players, perhaps recalling the neglect of the previous year, enjoyed two big parties. The first was held on the afternoon of October 13 at the Boston Theatre. The governor, the mayor, and various military figures were present to hail the champions, as were past Boston stars George Wright and Tommy McCarthy. The team itself sat across the stage, and Mike Regan, a celebrated Royal Rooter, introduced each member in turn. When Cy Young's moment came, Regan's words were lost in a swell of cheering that engulfed the hall. The afternoon festivities ended when the band played "Tessie." That evening a dinner party for the club and various writers followed, a more private occasion at Parker House, paid for by John Taylor. Each team member spoke. Jacob Morse gave the following account of Cy Young's remarks: "The veteran 'Cy' Young made one of the best speeches of the evening, paying a warm tribute to Boston as a base ball city, and asserting that it had been his desire if he ever left the West to come to Boston and play ball."[62] These were just the right things to say, a sign that Young either had learned to handle public situations well or took good advice. At 9:00 that evening Lou Criger and he, bent on catching a night train to the Midwest, were the first to leave the party. The two men had shared in two remarkable seasons. Neither man would ever again have as much reason to feel satisfied with work well done as he was entitled to feel that evening.

☞🕊☜

CHAPTER ELEVEN

The Foundations of Success

THE TIME HAS COME to look at Cy Young's pitching practices systematically. In the foregoing chapters I have had occasion to mention various kinds of pitches Young used, to allude to some of the strategies he employed, and to note several of the conventions he adopted on the mound. Now I want to aggregate and scrutinize these references, to try to explain—at least as far as analysis allows us to approach the mysteries of prodigious talent—his remarkable success as a pitcher.

We ought to begin our discussion with his mechanics, but here we immediately run into an obstacle. As far as I know, there are no publicly available moving pictures of Cy Young in his playing days delivering pitches to a batter, so we don't know what he looked like in action. I'm sure that somewhere such footage exists. After all, we have film of Christy Mathewson and Walter Johnson, whose careers overlapped Young's, and we know that motion pictures were made of ball playing in the opening decade of the twentieth century. But in this case, as in many others, Young's preference not to be a public figure may have reduced the likelihood that motion pictures were created or preserved. So we must rely on contemporary written accounts to draw our conclusions about what Cy Young looked like when he was pitching.

When Young came into the major leagues in 1890, the pitching rubber as we know it today did not exist. Instead, the pitcher made his delivery from within a marked-off rectangular box. The back line of the box was 55 feet, 6 inches in front of the plate, and rules required the pitcher to be in contact with this line as he began his delivery. Since the front line of the box was 50 feet from the plate, the pitcher had a legal space of 5 feet, 6 inches in which to stride forward as he hurled the ball toward the plate. The box was also 4 feet wide, thus allowing the pitcher a small element of discretion in choosing the angle at which he would deliver the pitch. The practice of providing the pitcher with a raised mound within the box had probably begun in the previous decade. But we do not know how extensive this practice was or how high mounds were, and it is virtually certain that the degree of elevation varied from park to park. These were the conditions under which the adult Cy Young learned the craft of pitching.

Like anyone who throws a ball, Young had long known that, as a right-hander, he could throw harder if he began his delivery motion when his left leg was in front of his right leg. As a pitcher, he had also long known that he could get more sheer speed on his deliveries if he strode forward with the left leg in such a way as to add his body weight to the propulsive force of his arm. He was still experimenting with motions when he joined the Spiders in 1890, and it appears that he may have been confusing jerkiness with effectiveness in his earliest years in the majors. A Cleveland writer compared his rookie-year motion to a "coffee mill."[1] In 1891 an amused baseball writer in Boston noted that "he winds up his arm, then his body, then his legs, bows profoundly to his great outfield, straightens up again, then lets her go. It is difficult to tell whether the ball comes from his hands or his feet."[2] A year later another Bostonian, struck by the gawkiness of Young's motion, wrote that he "goes into a convulsion, slaps his chest with his left knee and . . . [winds] those arms a few times around his body."[3] Chicago writers were similarly astonished; to one he "throws a ball like a man climbing a stake-and-rider fence," while to another he "looks like a corkscrew with an ecru handle."[4] These quotations underscore that, in his earliest years, Cy Young expended vast amounts of energy in launching a pitch.

All of this changed in 1893, when the box was replaced by a pitcher's rubber that, at 60 feet, 6 inches from home plate, required a pitcher to begin his motion from 5 feet farther back. Writers conventionally make much of the impact of the increase in the pitching distance. For Cy Young, however, the most important change was probably the introduction of the rubber. This new marker provided something that the box had lacked: a block that a pitcher might use to push off from. Today many pitchers are taught not to drive off the rubber. But when it first appeared, the pitcher's plate provided an additional tool for putting speed on a pitch. Presumably other considerations were also leading Young to reassess his tortuous pitching motion. Always a thoughtful student of his trade, he no doubt noted that Kid Nichols, who employed something like Don

Larsen's later no-windup windup, was enjoying success equal to his own and with a lot less effort. And so Young set about stripping away the inessential elements from his windup. As late as 1897 one writer still spoke of his "contortions."[5] And he never abandoned the practice of occasionally resorting to unusual motions in order to disconcert a batter. But by the time Christy Mathewson had occasion to see Young pitch in the next decade, the New York master declared that " 'Old Cy' Young has the absolutely perfect pitching motion."[6] Another hurler, Earl Moore, stated in 1911 that "Young is copied more than any other pitcher."[7]

What can we infer from contemporary accounts about Young's stylish windup in his prime? First off, he did not raise his left leg high; his stride was closer to a big step than a kick, and today we would probably call it a slide step. Second, when his left leg was raised, he briefly pivoted away from the plate on his right leg, turning some of his back toward the batter. This movement allowed him briefly to hide his ball and glove. Third, after releasing the ball he did not fling his right arm far across his body, preferring to get his raised right foot back down to the ground and so to plant himself to be able to deal with any batted ball. Finally—and this had been true from the beginning of his professional career—his basic delivery was released overhand, not from the shoulders or side arm. Many years later, and certainly by 1908, he sometimes pitched balls side-arm in order to alter his release point and give an unexpected axis of revolution to a pitch. And throughout his career—we should probably recall that the teenaged Young began to learn his craft when under-handed deliveries were the only lawful ones—he occasionally startled a batter with a submarine pitch.[8] But Young's bread-and-butter motion was a high overhand delivery, designed among other things to accentuate the advantage his height and the mound already gave him. By Cap Anson's testimony, when Young made a pitch, it seemed as if "the ball was shooting down from the hands of a giant."[9]

When Cy Young burst upon the baseball world in 1890 he was tagged very aptly as a fastball pitcher. And throughout much of his career the fastball remained his most important offering. As the pitch approached the plate it often appeared to rise slightly—"to jump," in the words of more than one observer.[10] Young, called this his "jump ball,"[11] and the future Hall of Famer Johnny Evers explained the trick by noting that "at the instant of releasing the ball [he] gripped it tightly with the finger tips and loosely with the thumb. The finger pressure increased the speed of the natural revolution of the ball"—clockwise when viewed from first base—"and caused it to jump more."[12] It is not surprising then that Young himself, at midcareer, told a writer that "whatever ability I may have as a pitcher comes almost entirely from my fast ball."[13] Despite his speed, however, Young was not a great strikeout pitcher. In part, that is because he did not seek high strikeout totals. In fact, it was not until the twentieth century, in an environment of diluted major league talent (supplemented from 1903 on by the foul strike rule), that Young managed a seasonal average of more than four strikeouts a game (peaking at 5.91 in 1905) or ever reach double figures for any single game. He preferred to keep his fastball high—in his day the strike zone really did extend up to shoulder level—and his jump ball at that height led to a lot of pop-ups. In the light of current debate about how pitchers should lay their fingers upon a baseball, it is interesting that Cy Young did not care whether he held the ball with or across the seams. "[I] just gripped it and let it fly," he explained.[14] Perhaps this is because most balls were already so scuffed that seams were unimportant.

So how did Young stack up against the fastest pitchers of his day? Were his "shoots"—to use an expression of the era—the speediest of them all? From the gauzy perspective of retirement he once compared himself to Amos Rusie and Walter Johnson. "I do not believe that either one was quite up to me in speed."[15] That was not the view of his contemporaries. One player from the 1880s and 1890s considered Amos Rusie, Jack Stivetts, and Jim Whitney the fastest pitchers of his day.[16] A writer in 1904 conferred that distinction on Jack Chesbro and Rube Waddell.[17] There were other similar judgments.[18] Strikeout titles point to the same conclusion. Amos Rusie garnered four in ten seasons; Rube Waddell won six in thirteen seasons. Cy Young, on the other hand, though he pitched for twenty-two years, won only two strikeout titles. We are left to conclude that while Cy Young, in his own words, "just reared back and flogged 'em through there," he was not the fastest flogger around.[19]

Many baseball historians have claimed that during the first decade of his career Cy Young relied only on a fastball. In the words of one of them, Young was "perhaps the greatest of all pitchers to learn the curve midway in his career."[20] This just isn't so. Most pitchers of the 1880s had curves of various sorts, and Young, who learned his craft in that decade and was blessed with long and strong fingers, certainly arrived in the majors with a breaking pitch. His very first game in Cleveland led the *Cleveland Plain Dealer* writer to declare that the rookie had "all the curves the law allows."[21] Three years later Young was credited with "meandering curves" and "zigzag curves."[22] Four years after that, the *Sporting News* spoke of his "shoots and curves."[23] We do not need to give any credence to the silly report from late in his career that Young had arrived in the majors with a "cobra curve"—so-called because he had patterned it on the movement of Tuscarawas rattlesnakes—to credit the well-substantiated view that Cy Young could make a ball bend from the first days of his Cleveland career.[24]

Though some of the foregoing comments suggest that Young commanded several types of curves in the opening stages of his career, he actually used only one in his earlier major league years—a delivery that was scarcely slower than his high-riding fast ball but that broke away from a right-handed batter, down and out of the strike zone. I first imagined that this pitch was what we today would call a slider, but, having consulted with Bob Feller as well as a man who as a lad had received backyard pitching instruction from Young fifty years ago, I am now inclined to think that it was a roundhouse curve delivered overhand.[25] Whatever its character, we can be confident that John Clarkson helped Young to refine this curve, for Clarkson possessed as full a repertory of deliveries as any pitcher of the 1880s, and years later, reflecting on their two seasons as teammates, Young said that Clarkson had given him "many pointers that since have stood me in good stead."[26] Improvement, it is true, was slow; as late as 1900, Wilbert Robinson could still dismiss Young's curve as harmless. But in 1902, speaking for most American League batters, Charley Hemphill called it impressive.[27]

Meanwhile, after arriving in the junior circuit and eager to improve his craftsmanship, Young began to experiment with a slower and wider curve, which he sometimes delivered with a sidearm motion. He slowly incorporated this pitch into his armory of deliveries, and so for much of the final decade of his career, Young commanded two curves. "When I threw overhand," he explained after his retirement, "my curve broke sharp and downward. If I cut loose sidearm my curve had more of a sweep."[28] Throughout his career, Young was sparing in his use of the pitch, saving it for special occasions. "A curveball is wearing on a pitcher's arm," he said as early as 1901, "and I use it only when it's necessary."[29] It was advice that he often repeated in later years.[30]

Fastballs succeed by arriving at the plate too quickly for a batter to catch up with them; curves succeed by arriving at a point where the batter does not expect them. The pitcher has a third possibility: a pitch that tricks a batter into committing himself too early, throwing him off stride.

We call this pitch a change of pace or change-up, but in Young's day it was more regularly called a slow ball, and it is effective only if delivered with a motion that is indistinguishable from the motion used for a fastball. Young did not have a change of pace when he reached the majors, and although he worked hard to add it to his repertory, he did not find it an easy delivery to master. Conversations with change-of-pace master Nig Cuppy failed to provide adequate guidance. Nor did reflection. "I have lain awake all night," he said in 1897, " . . . and have worried myself into a headache . . . trying to think how [Eddie Beatin] ever acquired his slow ball."[31] As late as 1900 Young remarked that "I have no slow ball."[32]

The latter assertion was, strictly speaking, an exaggeration, for in 1896 he had acknowledged turning to slow balls to protect his arm from wear.[33] Still, the real breakthrough in his efforts to capture the pitch came only in 1901 when, wearied one afternoon by heat and work, he experimented extensively with changes of pace and suddenly found them successful.[34] The trick, he concluded, was "to straighten out my fingers [while releasing the pitch] so that the ball left from the inside of my finger joints."[35] Delighted at his triumph, he used the rest of the season to gain command of the pitch by learning how to deliver it from his regular overhand motion. The next spring, while coaching at Harvard, he again applied himself to this task, earning the accolade from fellow coach Willie Keeler—who had spent 1901 in the National League, unacquainted with Young's new pitch—that he was "cultivating a slow ball that will fool them all."[36] Then, announcing that a change of pace would be necessary "with so many heavy hitters in the American League," he added his slow ball—effective not because it was truly slow but rather because it had less pace than his fastball—to his pitching armory.[37] Like his curves, he used his change of pace sparingly. But whenever he turned to the delivery, it was a humdinger—in the words of Addie Joss, "a peach."[38] By late in 1901 Young was noted for four different deliveries: "he would shoot the ball up . . . and the next one would loll over the plate. Then would come a high curve, and then a crinkling little drop."[39]

Finally there was the spitball. Reintroduced into the majors in 1903 or 1904, the pitch lifted hurlers like Jack Chesbro and Ed Walsh to levels of remarkable success. Young was impressed. Batters, he said, "simply can not hit the 'spit ball'. . . . Here is a delivery that will fool even the catchers, and if it fools them, how can the batsmen succeed in getting around on it."[40] But attractive though it was, it proved difficult to tame. "It hurt my arm," Young reported in the middle of the 1905 season, "and I have cut it altogether. An old pitcher like myself has no business using it at all."[41] That wasn't quite so. Crafty moundsman that he was, Young was not willing to forgo an advantage entirely, and throughout the rest of his career he occasionally employed the wet one—with real success, according to at least one observer.[42] Moreover, like many other pitchers, he learned that by appearing to moisten the ball he could get the batter to worry.

Before the opening of the 1908 season Jesse Tannehill reflected on the course of Cy Young's career: "He never has gone in for curves or slow balls much until recently. Now he has as many kinds of delivery as any pitcher."[43] Tannehill was right. Young began his major league career with two deliveries and ended it with five.[44] That was as full an array of pitches as any hurler of the day commanded. But the basic source of his success lay not in his palette of pitches but in his remarkable ability to control them. Batters are tamed when the pitcher can place pitches where the batters don't like them, and in the entire history of baseball no one has been as consistently successful at placement as Cy Young. The best measurement of a pitcher's ability to control is to look at the number of bases on balls he gives up per nine innings pitched. In every year between 1893 and 1906 (except 1902) Cy Young led his league in this statistic. In six of those years he averaged fewer than 1 walk per 9 innings. With adequate control at the beginning and end of his career and brilliant control through the long middle portion, Young—with a career figure of 1½ walks for each 9 innings pitched—stands sixth on the all-time list that compares masters of control.[45]

It is important to recall that a low bases on balls measures far more than simply a pitcher's capacity to avoid giving batters unnecessary admission to the base path. For Cy Young, the ability to put any of his pitches exactly where he wanted meant that he could place pitches where batters were known to have weaknesses, that he could work the corners and keep away from the middle of the plate, and that he could stay ahead in the count. Moreover, it meant that he was not confined to a single delivery even when faced with a tight situation. "I could throw anything with a count of three and two on the batter and be reasonably certain of pitching a strike."[46] Finally, it allowed him to keep his pitch count down and avoid wear and tear on his arm. "If a pitcher can get through a game throwing 125 balls," he said, ". . . and it takes some other pitcher 400,"— there's sportspeak hyperbole for you—"it stands to reason that the one who can get through with one-third the effort should last longer."[47] "Control is everything," he told one reporter after he retired. "Ability to get the ball over the plate, more than any other feature, kept me in the big leagues 22 years."[48]

The preceding quotations show that Young recognized that control—"command" was common synonym in his day—was the basis of his success. In each of his three ghostwritten primers on pitching, the centrality of control was stressed. One of the pieces tipped the lesson in its title: "First—Learn Control of Ball." In another the author declared that "command is indispensable." The third opened with the stipulation that "command of the ball is the first essential to success in pitching."[49] Young's prescription for acquiring control was unremitting pitching practice. The task was not to throw hard—that would hurt the arm—but to throw accurately. If possible, the practicing pitcher should avoid throwing at mere marks painted on a wall; a far better target was a catcher standing behind a plate—best of all, a plate protected by a batter. Only after gaining command should a pitcher try to enhance speed or develop a curve ball. As if to demonstrate his commitment to proper priorities, Young allowed himself to be identified with the judgment that "the curve is merely an accessory to control."[50] On another occasion he remarked that "in my day control was 99 percent of pitching."[51] Long before modern statistical analysis confirmed the point, Cy Young was recognized as the game's master of control.

A successful pitcher uses his head as well as his arm, and that's why it's notable that an observer of Young's very first major league game commended his good "judgment."[52] He maintained this reputation as a smart pitcher throughout his career, and by 1903 one experienced writer was calling him "the philosopher of the slab."[53] Still, much that Young wrote in his primers about pitching belabored the obvious. Know the batters' weaknesses and pitch to them. Change the speed of your deliveries to keep batters guessing. Take advantage of the full size of the strike zone. Work the corners. Rely on the seven men in the field behind you. Learn to field your position well.[54] We will not learn much about Young as a baseball thinker if we attend only to his words.

We can best go further by noting, above all, that Cy Young was a close student of the game of baseball. He watched players closely and studied their choices and actions. We know that he engaged in shoptalk with John Clarkson, Nig Cuppy, Bill Dinneen, Kid Nichols, Addie Joss, and Joe Wood, and we can assume that he shared opinions and experiences with many others. He had a good memory for what he had heard and seen. Cy Swaim, for example, told how in a conversation before he reached the majors he had informed Young of his own particular weakness as a batter and how Young had later used that information to retire him.[55] He watched how batters stood in the batter's box and adjusted to their plans. He moved his fielders about in accordance with his knowledge of batters' proclivities. He also learned the doctoring tricks of the trade—how to darken and deaden a ball and make it lumpy. "There were many ways to tamper with it," he once explained.[56] And he did not neglect other aspects of his position. When the balk rule changed in 1893, he spent hours mastering a new motion to first base and became known as a pitcher against whom it was difficult to steal.[57] He trained himself to be a good fielder, learning how to pounce on bunts, to cover first on grounders to the first baseman, and to back up the catcher on outfield throws to the plate. In an era when coaches as we know them today did not exist, much of what Young—or any good player—learned to do was self-taught.

And then there were the subtler things. Cy Young always appeared to be in command of the situation. He strode out to the mound with a steady gait, his eyes fixed on the ground, his face unsmiling, his fists clinched.[58] Once on the mound he allowed nothing to upset him—not bad calls, errant defense, or his own mistakes. He worked quickly, denying the batter any opportunity for reenergizing. Future Hall of Famer Billy Hamilton once said that "there never was a pitcher in the box that has the confidence that Cy has."[59] Young was a master of quiet intimidation. Before the institution of the foul strike rule, if he became impatient with persistent fouls he would warn batters to cease wasting his time and effort; and if the warning was unheeded, he would fortify it with a brush-back pitch. Similarly, he would not allow a batter to deprive him of the inside corner of the plate by crowding it. Ty Cobb remarked that, had he stood too close to the plate, Cy Young would have "blown me right out of the box."[60] In general, Young's demeanor toward his opponents, while neither fierce nor mean, was severe and cold; he was earning his livelihood and serving his employer, and in both of those roles he could only regard a batsman as an enemy.

On the other hand, Cy Young was benign in his dealings with umpires, even when he thought their calls bad. One tale actually has him defending umpire Jack Sheridan against the charge that Sheridan had inaccurately called one of his pitches out of the strike zone.[61] There was, of course, a reason for his civility: Young realized that a well-disposed umpire could be a pitcher's good friend. It is no coincidence that Young was never thrown out of a game in his entire career.

Another vital friend for a pitcher was his catcher, and no pitcher of his era was more publicly appreciative of the value of his battery mates than Cy Young. "Unless you have a first-class catcher back there to run the game," he remarked late in his career, "you'll never get within gunshot of a pennant."[62] Respect of that sort is one reason why Young was the pitcher in two of the most active batteries in the early years of baseball; Lou Criger caught him in 278 games, while Chief Zimmer caught him in 247 games.[63] He enlisted his catchers in a baseball variation of the good-cop-bad-cop routine, allowing them to berate the umpire for missed calls as he stood tranquil on the mound. It is not clear if Young took signs from Zimmer, since it was only in the 1890s that the practice of having the catcher call for pitches arose. But he certainly trusted Criger to choose his deliveries, and he later claimed that Criger and he understood each other so well that if they caught the opposing team picking up their signs they could proceed without them.[64]

In the year of his perfect game Cy Young said that he was still learning new points about baseball. Most great players have made similar remarks. Talent, after all, requires molding. Unchanneled by reflection, training, and self-control, talent will almost invariably prove inadequate for long-term success and will often self-destruct. As early as 1892, Cy Young was applauded for being able to "pull out of a big hole easier than any pitcher in the league today."[65] In 1899 he was called "one of the brainiest . . . pitchers in the National League."[66] In 1908 he was commended for his "wise head."[67] In assessing Young's career Christy Mathewson noted Young's intelligence. "Nothing pleased him more than to get the better of some star slugger in a battle of wits. Condition, nerve, and brains have made him a star."[68] John Thorn and John Holway divide hurlers into two groups—power pitchers and defensive pitchers.[69] It seems to me that Cy Young was remarkable because he was both; his speed allowed him to overawe batters, while his craftiness allowed him to fool them. When Young's ghostwriter declared "to my way of thinking, pitching is an art and a science combined,"[70] he was violating Young's manner of speech but capturing his judgment. Thoughtfulness and self-scrutiny transformed a capacity to throw hard into a gift for winning baseball games.

A final element contributed to Young's success: the remarkable physical durability that gave him twenty-two years of opportunity. In some measure, enduring health is simply a matter of good luck. Some careers are destroyed by accidents. Ask Herb Score. Others are undone by addictions. Ask Bugs Raymond. In some instances the body betrays the spirit.

Ask J. R. Richard. But luck aside, the well-maintained body will usually outlast the abused one. Cy Young was always preaching the importance of maintaining his health. He spent his winters away from the distractions of city life, building up his muscles by chopping wood, hunting, and jogging. Through his ghostwriter, he stated that a ballplayer "must take good care of himself. This is absolutely essential; a man's constitution is his stock in trade."[71] Young was, to be sure, not a health nut. He spent many springs in the second half of his career lamenting the need to take off pounds gained during the previous winter. But he avoided the kinds of overindulgence that might threaten his body. He cautioned against excessive use of alcohol or tobacco or coffee, and he recommended that ballplayers keep good hours, implicitly warning against womanizing. Young followed his own counsel and earned the reputation of a clean professional ballplayer.

Above all else, Cy Young cared for his right arm. A pitcher, he reportedly said, must nurse his arm "as artfully as the voice of a grand opera singer."[72] This did not mean submitting to the ministrations of a trainer. "I was never on a rubbing table in my life," he confessed. "I wouldn't let them monkey around with [my] old soupbone."[73] (In fact, there were not many trainers around in Young's day anyway.) Instead, Young applied liniment himself, as needed. He thought his straight overhand motion to be the natural and healthy way to throw, and he advised against other motions. "Underhand throwing," he declared in 1899, as Joe McGinnity's submarine offerings burst on the scene, "is contrary to nature and no man can last at it."[74] It was a determination not to overwork his arm that led Young to shift his pitching schedules as his career proceeded. After 1890 he never again started both ends of a doubleheader. In his early days he ordinarily went to the mound with two or three intervening days of rest. In midcareer he sought out three or four days of rest between appearances. By his final years his preferred schedule was once a week. This lengthening of his recuperation period was due not only to his aging but also to his acquisition of new and arm-wearying pitches. In light of what happened to overworked pitchers like Ed Walsh, Amos Rusie, Jack Chesbro, and even (for the majors) Joe McGinnity, Young was wise to insist on rest.

Young's desire to avoid overwork extended even into the game itself. He believed that an arm had a limited number of throws in it, and "there wasn't any use wasting them."[75] He limited his pregame warm-up to about a dozen tosses. When he returned to the mound each inning he rarely expended effort on warm-ups. He disliked throwing to first to hold a runner close. He bore down only when in trouble—admittedly an easier principle to follow in an era when home runs were rare. One reason he did not try to amass strikeouts was that it was less work to retire a batter with one pitch than with three. Young's goal was to win games while throwing as few pitches as possible. We do not have pitch counts for the era, but the recorded brevity of his games and the fact that he managed to hang around long enough to pitch 7,357 innings across his career suggest that he was extremely efficient in dealing with his opponents.

Securing longevity was not easy. "It takes hard and constant work to become a pitcher," Young was quoted as saying late in his career, "it is a plugging from the very first day."[76] But he was pleased with the results and proud of his achievements. He boasted, "I have never had a sore or lame arm in my life."[77] Strictly speaking, that was not so. But he never had a sore arm that lasted, and until late in his career he was never kept out of action for even a month by an injury or illness. Writing in 1905, the experienced baseball player and owner Tim Murnane linked Young with Kid Nichols and Amos Rusie as "the most perfect pitching machines" in baseball history.[78] Such surpassing skill emerged when outstanding natural throwing ability was combined with an intelligence that allowed adaptations to shifts in rules, to changes in distances, to advancements in knowledge, to expansions in sizes of rosters, and to the subtle effects of aging. It is no wonder that Cy Young became, in the words of Cleveland sportswriter Edward Bangs, "the cynosure of all eyes."[79]

CHAPTER TWELVE

─────────

❧

1905–1908:
Old Cy Young

OVER THE YEARS Cy Young had endured spells of bad luck and bad performance. But even in his worst hours and least glorious outings, the success that attended the bulk of what he did eased the pain of temporary failures. Still, aging is inevitable, and for the athlete it is invariably accompanied by a diminution of skills. It was in the campaigns of 1905 and 1906—seasons that saw Cy Young's victory totals dip below his loss totals—that the hurler first felt the force of that universal truth. What did he make of his disappointing work? There is no contemporary testimony from Young that gives voice to any worries. But it is hard to avoid speculation that two consecutive losing seasons, added to his impending fortieth birthday, took a toll on the pitcher's psychological resiliency. The fault was not all his. Some of the blame for the losses could be attached to a team that visibly faltered. But a pitcher stands alone in the middle of the diamond; that is why his work is measured by special statistics. Young could read those figures as well as anyone. He spent the two seasons on the mound every fifth or sixth day, and by October 1906, even if he dissented from the rumors, he surely understood why many observers of the game believed that time had finally overtaken the most durable pitcher in the history of baseball.

But the mood had been very different when, twenty months earlier, Young traveled to Arkansas in the late winter of 1905 to begin preparing for the coming season. Affectionately styled "Old Cy Young" in the press, he arrived in Hot Springs trimmer than he had been for several springs and hearing nothing but predictions for a third straight Boston pennant. The grounds for such confidence were clear. Already in possession of the strongest pitching staff in the American League, the club had moved to amplify its offense by swapping the youngster George Stone, with not a major league hit to his name, for the St. Louis veteran Jesse Burkett. Though no longer as gifted as when he had won three hitting crowns, Burkett was still regarded as a steady player who regularly got on base. "Our team," Jimmy Collins declared, "will be at least 15 per cent stronger than it was last season."[1]

Six months later that prediction was only a bad joke. The Boston Americans lost their first 6 games of the season. Even when they finally began to win, they failed to do so consistently. Jimmy Collins juggled his lineups, tried a variety of pitchers, and kept predicting imminent turn-arounds. But the team never rose much above the .500 level and when the year was over it stood at 78 and 74, in fourth place and 16 games behind the powerful Athletics. Statistical evidence suggests that a falling off in batting power was at the heart of the problem. As recently as 1903, Boston had led the league in batting, at .272; in 1905 the club figure of .234 came in below the league median. (A general recession of American League batting averages between 1903 and 1905 softens the precipitous-ness of this 38-point decline but does not explain away the slide from first to sixth place in the team batting ranks.) Pitching was no better. In 1903 and 1904 Boston had boasted the lowest team earned run average; in 1905 the earned run average rose to fifth best. In light of these declines in quality, Boston may have been lucky to finish as high in the standings as it did.

In seeking to explain the club's dismal performance, the press focused on the age of the players, pointing out that the manager, Jimmy Collins, had stood pat with the personnel from his championship years. The argument rings true. Boston's starting lineup in 1905 had the highest average age of any team in the league. Burkett was the league's second oldest regular, and could no longer beat out bunts; Collins was its fourth oldest, and overweight. The heralded preseason trade turned out to be a fizzle: the thirty-six-year-old Burkett hit .257 for Boston, while the twenty-seven-year-old Stone hit .296 for St. Louis. In pitching, another trade haunted Boston. Back in the middle of the 1903 season the club had sold Nick Altrock to Chicago for cash. For a year and a half it did not matter. But then in 1905 Altrock enjoyed his first 20-victory season—and he was younger than Jesse Tannehill, Bill Dinneen, or Cy Young. Boston ran out of gas in 1905 because its players suddenly became old men.

But not, it's important to note, Old Cy Young. Analysis gets a bit tricky at this point, for by the most conventional measure of a pitcher's ability—

namely, his win-loss record—Young had a mediocre year. In fact, for the first time in his career Young's winning percentage (18–19, for .486) was lower than his club's.[2] Also for the first time in his career (barring 1890) he was not the winningest pitcher on his team, since Jesse Tannehill recorded 22 victories. But other facts tell a different story. His earned run average of 1.82 was third best in the league and the lowest—though we must recall that he was now playing in a low-offense era—thus far of his career. Tannehill's by contrast stood at 2.48. Young led the league in fewest walks per game and lowest opponents' on-base percentage. He was tied for second in strikeouts, far behind Rube Waddell, but, with 210, at a personal career high. On three occasions during the year he struck out twelve batters in a game. He was third in the league in fewest hits allowed per game, and he yielded only 3 home runs all season despite standing sixth in the league in complete games, 4 games ahead of Tannehill. He made 5 relief appearances (including two occasions on which he relieved Tannehill in the first inning) and won them all. On May 30 he won both games of a doubleheader (one in relief), and three of his final four victories of the year were shutouts (two of them being two-hitters).

This is an impressive array of statistics, and I think in this instance, with the win-loss record pointing one way and so much else pointing the other, Cy Young may have simply suffered a streak of bad fortune in 1905. Of the fourteen games he appeared in that were settled by one-run margins, he won only four; of the six 2–1 games he appeared in, he won only one. Games like these led a writer in the *New York Globe* to opine after the season that Young's year had been almost as impressive as Christy Mathewson's—a stunning statement in light of Mathewson's 31–9 record and his domination of the World Series.[3]

In the middle of this good but disappointing season—on the Fourth of July in Boston—Young pitched one of the great games of his career. It was the afternoon game of a doubleheader, another memorable duel with Rube Waddell, the leader of the Athletics' splendid pitching corps. The game lasted 20 innings, with both starters going all the way. It was (to that point) the longest game in American League history and (again to that point) the longest game *played to a conclusion* in major league history. Waddell struck out 11, Young 9; Young did not yield a single base on balls. The game was knotted 2–2 at the end of 9 innings and stayed that way until the top of the twentieth, when 2 hits, 2 errors, and a hit batsman allowed Philadelphia to score twice. Accounts tell of Waddell celebrating his triumph by doing flip-flops from the mound to the bench and lighting up victory cigarettes. (In later years, to make some money, he sold off numerous baseballs, all of which he claimed to have been the winning ball from this game.) Young on the other hand was exhausted; he recalled that upon reaching the club house, "I all but keeled over . . . when I tried to take off my shoes I hardly had the strength to untie the laces."[4] Both pitchers gave up lots of hits but then shut the door whenever the opposing team threatened. Frederic P. O'Connor, covering the game for the *Boston Post*, said that Young never lost his speed but that, by the end of the contest, "Cy looked as though he had been put through a clothes wringer."[5] Young himself was typically sparing of words afterward: "I didn't walk anybody in twenty innings, and I still lost. Well, I'll be damned."[6]

Before leaving for Tuscarawas County after the season, Cy Young stayed in Boston long enough to participate in the first intracity series in the history of the Hub. With baseball peace at hand, the attractiveness of pitting interleague rivals against each other in a postseason exhibition series was financially compelling. In Boston there was an additional attraction to such an exhibition. In 1905 the National League squad boasted a fine rookie pitcher named Irving Young. He had won twenty games and been dubbed, probably inevitably, "Young Cy" or "Cy the Second [Cy II]." Fans looked forward to seeing Old Cy pitch against Young Cy. The match-up occurred in the second game of the series, on October 10, the same day on which, in New York City, the Athletics were winning their only 1905 World Series game. Young Cy pitched pretty well. But Old Cy was magnificent, striking out 15 and allowing only 2 hits. The American Leaguers won the game 3–1. And because they found their National League rivals so easy to handle, the Americans chalked up the necessary fourth victory after only 5 games, leaving no occasion for a return match between the Youngs. As soon as the series was over, after pocketing his share of the profits (it came to scarcely more than $100), Old Cy left for Ohio. Before departing, however, he let it be known that he was "good for another season."[7]

One wonders if, a year later, he was not regretting that decision. For if the 1905 season had been a disappointment, the 1906 season was a disaster. Cy Young signed his contract in January, accepting (in $4,000) the first salary cut of his career. The press declared that he wrote John Taylor to say, "I am pleased to be with the Boston Americans once more and hope to be in shape to do my full share of the work necessary to land another pennant for Boston."[8] He made his usual late-winter stay at Hot

Springs and then joined the team in Macon. But when the season began, nothing seemed to go right for Boston. The club quickly sank to the cellar of the American League. In May it plumbed new depths of ineptitude by losing 20 consecutive games. Meanwhile, disabilities piled up, the most significant injuries being sustained by Lou Criger, who spent most of the summer recuperating from a surgical searing of his spinal nerve, and Jimmy Collins, whose twisted knee refused to respond to rest. When the horrific season ended, Boston was in last place, 8 games behind the seventh-place Senators and 45½ games behind the pennant-winning White Sox. The descent from the triumph of 1904 had been swift, dramatic, and total.

The chief casualty of the year was Jimmy Collins. As Boston's slide picked up momentum, Collins sank into a depression. Ultimately, he literally deserted the team and, when summoned back from his consequent suspension, declined to insert himself into the lineup, pleading that his knee made competitive play impossible. A perplexed Ban Johnson, worried that one of his central franchises was self-destructing, made several trips to Boston during the summer to try to sort matters out. But in August Taylor finally grew weary of Collins's inexplicable behavior and dismissed him as manager, assigning his former responsibilities to the reliable outfielder Chick Stahl. Recognizing that Boston was hopeless with the lineup he had inherited, Stahl spent the rest of the season experimenting with younger players and preparing the club to be competitive in 1907.[9] It is not known what Cy Young made of this confusing situation, but on the eve of his retirement several years later he picked Jimmy Collins as the greatest manager he had ever encountered, commending Collins for standing with John McGraw and Hughie Jennings in preferring an aggressive style of baseball.[10] Most observers, even in Collins's glory years, could not reach that degree of enthusiasm for the Boston manager.

In assessing responsibility for the club's woes, it is impossible to ignore Cy Young's difficulties. In 1906, Young experienced what would be, far and away, his worst season as a mound regular. His record of 13 victories was his lowest figure since his rookie year and marked the fifth straight season in which his victory total had declined. His 21 defeats led the league. (Think of that: Cy Young leading the league in losses.) After he was driven from the box in the first inning on May 24, his record stood at 1–8, the worst start of his career. Five of Boston's 20 consecutive losses had been Young's, and his 7-game losing streak equaled his career record.[11] "Cy Young appears on his last legs," was the representative judg-

ment of Timothy Sharp.[12] Thereafter Young managed to improve somewhat, even winning 6 of his last 10 decisions. But hitters found him a
relatively easy mark throughout the year, as his earned average of 3.19—
a full half a run *above* the league figure—shows. Moreover, he never
threw a shutout, never won more than 3 games in succession. And only
once, on August 29, did he flash the brilliance of old, as he set down the
first twenty-three Cleveland batters to face him before Elmer Flick got
an infield hit. (Since this was Lou Criger's first full game of the season,
the performance was widely regarded as a measure of how valuable
Young's old battery-mate was to his work.) It is not clear why Young
sparkled that day. But a sore elbow that was inhibiting his ability to throw
his curve is probably as good an explanation as we are likely to get for
this summer of pummelings. In any case, the season of 1906 constitutes
the first season of his career in which Cy Young was indubitably not his
team's bellwether hurler. It may be significant, as a sign of his frustration,
that the only account of his deliberately beaning a batter (it was Dave
Altizer of Washington) dates from this year. In September he told one
baseball writer that, contrary to reports from his own mouth about an
imminent retirement, he would pitch for four or five more seasons; a
proud man, Young was serving notice that he was determined not to go
out a failure.[13]

It was not until the following January, after a face-to-face meeting
with John Taylor in Cleveland, that Cy Young signed a contract for 1907.
He had been resisting the club's effort to reduce his salary again and finally succeeded in persuading the owner to keep his salary at $4,000 de-
spite the disappointments of the previous season. Young then made his
regular February trip to Arkansas. This year he was soon joined by the
entire squad, for Taylor and Chick Stahl had decided that a change of
spring scenery—to Little Rock—might help the club to recover its bear-
ings. Most of the stars of 1904 were still on hand, even Jimmy Collins,
slimmer than the previous spring and pledging his support for the man
who had replaced him as manager. But the man the fans wanted to see
was the remarkable Cy Young, the oldest pitcher in the game. "Cy
Young," one press account ran, "is in his usual good shape."[14] He was also
a man other players looked up to, and whenever the squad divided into
regulars and "yannigans," Stahl asked Young to manage the squad of
youngsters. As the club left Arkansas to head north for the opening of
the season, plans were afoot to celebrate Young's fortieth birthday with
a grand party in Indiana on March 29.

But on March 28 Chick Stahl committed suicide.

It was not a quiet death. On the morning of the 28th Stahl suited up, drank a bottle of carbolic acid, staggered into Jimmy Collins's room, and died. According to Collins, before being convulsed by the poison, Stahl muttered, "I couldn't help it, I did it Jim. It was killing me and I couldn't stand it."[15] No one has ever conclusively established what drove the popular Stahl to take his life, though he seems to have contemplated the action for several weeks at least. Was it the pressure of managing? Rumors of sexual indiscretions before his marriage? Depression? All that is certain is that his teammates were stunned. It fell to Cy Young, as the club's elder statesman, to deal with the sense of loss, puzzlement, sadness, and fear that swept through the team. "It is mighty tough, boys," he told his quickly gathered teammates with tears in his eyes. "I never dreamed of such a thing. In fact, none of us could imagine Stahl doing away with himself. Players may come and go, but there are few 'Chick' Stahls."[16] With Stahl's death all plans for celebrating Young's birthday evaporated; the press was silent on the occasion, and we are left to imagine a subdued beginning of the hurler's fifth decade.

Two days elapsed before John Taylor wired his instructions to the team. His key decision was to ask Cy Young to succeed Stahl as manager. Young acceded—but only reluctantly and only on the understanding that his term would be brief. He had no interest in becoming the regular manager of the team. He had seen the price that the burden of responsibilities had exacted from Jimmy Collins and Chick Stahl. He suspected—for he had worked under Patsy Tebeau and (briefly) John McGraw—that his placid temperament would not be suitable for management.[17] He hoped that his spring mound work in Arkansas portended a return of pitching success. The message he delivered to Taylor captured all these points: "Judging from the way I have been going this spring I believe I will have my best year in base ball this year and I would rather not have anything to worry me. That's my main reason but I also believe that I have not the ability to manage the team. I feel highly honored at the offer. I also feel that I could not do justice to both positions."[18] His decision shows dignity and self-knowledge. There were those who argued that Young—by virtue of his common sense, his knowledge of the game, his resilience, and his popularity—would be a good choice for the permanent position.[19] Young was wise enough to see these remarks as the plausible but irrelevant arguments of artful flatterers. Besides, though he did not voice it at the time, Young had one additional reason for avoiding the duties of managing: by the end of March he knew that Robba Young was pregnant and that the baby, which would be the Youngs' first, was due about September 1.

Cy Young managed the Boston Americans for their final three exhibition games and the first six games of the season. Playing managers were not at all uncommon in these earlier years of baseball. In 1907, for example, Young joined the ranks of such stars as Frank Chance, Fred Clarke, Clark Griffith, Hughie Jennings, Fielder Jones, Larry Lajoie, Jimmy McAleer, and Fred Tenney.[20] It was rather more unusual for pitchers to assume managerial responsibilities, but Clark Griffith was currently successful as both hurler and manager, and Kid Nichols had recently tried his hand as manager. Perhaps Young was untroubled by his responsibilities because he knew they were temporary. In any case, he pitched well during his brief term, whipping Cincinnati in a preseason contest, winning the season opener in Philadelphia on April 11, and beating Washington in the Americans' home opener on April 16.[21] When his successor George Huff arrived, Young handed him a team that had split its first six games and occupied fourth place. Measured in terms of winning percentage, he would turn out to be Boston's most successful manager in 1907.

The season was another dreadful one for the team, its general mood of disquiet exacerbated by the lack of continuity in the manager's post. George Huff resigned after 8 games, Bob Unglaub led the team for 29 games, and Deacon McGuire assumed command in June for the final 112 games of the season. The team sank swiftly toward the bottom and finished in seventh place. The team batting average of .234 placed it dead last in hitting in the league. Meanwhile, the dismantling of the championship team of 1903 and 1904 was effected, as the club released Buck Freeman and traded Jimmy Collins and Bill Dinneen. McGuire saw his task as the assessment of younger players, and toward the end of the season he sometimes had so many players in uniform that a string of chairs had to be set up next to the bench to accommodate the overload. One of these youngsters was Tris Speaker, who would blossom into the star of the next Boston powerhouse. But that was several years away, and meanwhile nothing McGuire did lit a fire under the Americans. In September they even challenged their calamitous streak of early 1906 by losing 16 straight games. But the ever optimistic John Taylor could see light in even the darkest of tunnels: considering the improvement from eighth to seventh place, he said, "we are headed in the right direction."[22]

In the midst of this miserable season only Cy Young's work shone. He won 5 of his first 6 appearances, he was consistently reliable, and on September 2 he became a 20-game winner for the fourteenth time in his career. When Barney Dreyfuss sounded out John Taylor in midseason about purchasing Young's contract for the huge sum of $10,000 plus some ballplayers, the Boston owner rejected the offer. No wonder. As *Sporting Life* explained, "the superb box work of the veteran 'Cy' Young this season has given the fans all over the country something to talk about."[23] Two of his performances in particular caught the attention of the baseball world. On August 7 he handed the World Champion Chicago White Sox a 14-inning 2–1 defeat, giving up only 8 hits and outpitching both Nick Altrock and, in relief, Ed Walsh. His victory was one of four straight that the briefly resurgent Americans scored over the defending champions. Then on September 9 he asked to pitch a day early so that he could hook up again with Rube Waddell—it was their only meeting of the year—and when darkness ended the game less than two hours and 13 innings later, the score stood at 0–0. Young gave up 6 hits in the pitching duel, Waddell 4. Young struck out 8, Waddell 6. Neither pitcher yielded a base on balls.[24] Arthur Soden, one of the owners of the Boston National League franchise spoke for many when he said of Cy Young: "that boy must have taken awful good care of himself."[25]

The earliest public mention of Robba Young's pregnancy dates from the *Boston Globe* of August 10. It referred coyly to an "interesting event" that was anticipated in the Young family.[26] Boston became Robba's home at mid-summer. She was almost thirty-six as the time of her delivery approached, and both she and her husband were anxious. With the club's permission Cy Young remained behind with Robba when the team went west in mid-August; after nine days in Boston he traveled by train to Detroit, stayed with the team for a few days, sped home to Boston, rejoined the team in New York, then returned again to Boston. Fortunately the club played in Boston in early September. But when the Americans moved south in mid-September, he tarried behind, then joined them in Philadelphia just in time to pitch a game against the Athletics, and returned to the Hub two days later after pitching in Washington against the Senators. What was going on with all this "jumping about"?[27]

As the Youngs had feared, the pregnancy was difficult toward its end. Although much of the story is unknown, at some point around September 1 Robba Young gave birth to a baby girl who died a few hours later. The press said little about this tragedy; not even the baby's name was publicized. While we can only imagine what parental hopes and dreams might have sprung from an unexpected pregnancy in the fourteenth year of a marriage, the loss of her only child was a blow from which Robba Young never entirely recovered. Even for the stoic Cy Young, the daughter's death left an almost inexpungeable hole in his existence.

Cy Young did not win a regular game in 1907 after September 6. Although the tragedy might have played a part, it is also likely that Young's monumental effort against Rube Waddell on September 9 (proof, by the way, that his personal life was not invariably impinging upon his public life) left his arm exhausted. Commentators noticed that in his final games his fastball had lost its zip. Whether starting or relieving, he was generally ineffective. But even if the season tailed off in its final month, it was still a fine one. Most published works credited him with 22 victories, and though today we give him 21 instead (see appendix 3 for an explanation), he still ranked eighth in the league in wins. For his team he was a giant. He reached totals in games started, games completed, and innings pitched not seen since the triumphant season of 1904. He accounted for fully 36 percent of Boston's victories and only 17 percent of its losses, only one other pitcher on the team recorded as many as 10 victories. His 6 shutouts constituted the fourth highest seasonal total of his career and third highest in the league. He led the league in posting the lowest opponents' on-base percentage (.263) and was fifth in strikeouts (147) and earned run average (1.99).

The most likely explanation for Cy Young's recovery in 1907 from the diamond miseries of 1906 is the return of a healthy, strong arm. Throughout much of 1906 Young had labored with a sore elbow. In 1907 he regained his physical durability. Bunk Congalton, a skeptic about Young's talents when he played outfield for Cleveland, recanted his doubts after joining the Boston team during the 1907 season: "Play behind him a few weeks and you can see why he is so good. That old fast ball of his is about as effective as it ever was. He uses his head, too, and has the faculty of making men play behind him. . . . He has as much ability as anyone in the business."[28] There it is, a simple prescription. Just mix a fastball that has movement, the intelligence acquired by years of experience, and the knowledge of how to use the other players on a team, and you have a superb pitcher. The Grand Old Man was becoming a grand old fox.

When the regular season was over, the two Boston teams once again faced off for postseason play, in what some local wits—in recognition of the Beaneaters' ineptitude that marginally exceeded even the Americans' incompetence—called the "cellar championship."[29] The intracity series was scheduled for seven games, and it was pushed to its term even though the American League club removed all doubt about its outcome by winning the first four contests. Recovering his midseason form, Cy Young was dominant. He won the first game, 4–1, on October 7 and returned four days later to win the fourth game, 5–4, driving in the game- and series-winning run in the ninth inning with a clean single to right. Then, the matter of baseball superiority in Boston having been settled, he left immediately for Peoli. In his absence his teammates completed the drubbing of the National Leaguers by winning two and tying one of the three remaining contests.[30] Clearly, after the fourth game his teammates no longer needed Young. But the haste with which he departed town reflected his state of mind: after several months of pain, he and Robba needed to return to the solace of friends and family in Tuscarawas County. And perhaps it was the persistence of the pain that caused him in December to decline a request from the United States Military Academy at West Point that he coach the cadet baseball team the following spring.

When the new year arrived, the domestic tragedy of the Young family had disappeared from the press. Instead, writers were focusing attention on the astonishing durability of the hurler. The *Sporting News* led the way with its year-opening comment that Young "is a physical anomaly, for few pitchers last more than 10 seasons in the fast circuits." He has, it continued, "shown no signs of decline in the last few seasons"—well, *that* was a bit hyperbolic—and "he is today the best-liked character in the game, both at home and abroad."[31] All of this was to say that the remarkable Cy Young would be forty-one years old when the season opened. People took notice. Reporters sought him out at Hot Springs; Deacon McGuire, back for a second season at the helm, predicted that "Cy will take many a game"; and when his birthday rolled around, his teammates gave him a silver loving cup.[32]

But if the appearance of Cy Young in a Boston spring camp was a sign of baseball's continued vitality in the Hub, other cues pointed to a changing of the old order. First, there was the new uniform and the new name. Gone were the pale blue stockings that had been a mark of the team since its founding; instead the players donned red hose and accepted John Taylor's decision that they would henceforth be known as the Red Sox. Second, the old team was largely dispersed. With the trade of Hobe

Ferris and Freddy Parent over the off-season, Lou Criger and Cy Young were the only players still with the squad who had stepped out on the Huntington Avenue Grounds back in 1901. Third, there was even a change in the pattern of spring training. Rather than moving north as a unit, the club divided into two squads, one headed by Deacon McGuire and the other by Cy Young, and pursued two separate routes back to Boston. Young's group of yannigans wound its way through Ohio to maximize the opportunity for raising money by displaying the state's favorite diamond son.

Cy Young opened his nineteenth major league season like a thoroughbred. He won his first four starts, never yielding more than a run in a game. After stumbling during the first three weeks of May, he regained his season-opening form, and on May 30, pitching against Washington in Boston, he set the baseball world buzzing with a dazzling one-hit shutout.[33] Only Jerry Freeman's single prevented him from hurling the third no-hitter of his career. Pretty good for a forty-one-year-old whom Detroit owner Frank Navin had written off as a has-been before the season began. And Cy Young's surge was far from exhausted of his next six starts, he won four games, and saved one. The sole defeat came in Chicago by a 1–0 score against Chicago's extraordinary spitballer, Ed Walsh.

On June 30, exactly a month after the one-hitter, Young pitched in New York against the Highlanders. He walked Harry Niles to open the game. But Lou Criger soon caught Niles trying to steal second, and meanwhile Young retired the next twenty-six batters in a row. As if a no-hitter was not enough, he also had a memorable day at bat, driving in four of Boston's eight runs with two doubles and a single. "This gay old blade," sportswriter W. W. Aulick quipped, "was the life of the party."[34] Outstanding defense helped Young on his great day; shortstop Heinie Wagner made two sparkling off-balance throws to nab runners at first, center fielder Denny Sullivan twice snagged potential Texas leaguers, and left fielder Gavvy Cravath leaped to catch a fly at the fence in the ninth. But any pitcher who throws a no-hitter enjoys some lucky breaks, and Clark Griffith, the New York manager, was simply being ungracious in declaring the next winter that "with ordinary fielding Young would have been hit safely half a dozen times in that game."[35] Perhaps Griffith was annoyed that from the sixth inning on the New York crowd was audibly in the old man's camp. When Young recorded his final out, he ran over to the bench, beaming broadly, to receive the enthusiastic congratulations of his teammates. The game had been his third career no-hitter.[36]

Young's mound magic continued into July, and although a twisted ankle obliged him to miss two starts in the middle of the month, by August first he had a record of 14 victories and only 6 losses. Meanwhile, as his extraordinary lifetime achievements began to register with a wider public—*Sporting Life* reported, for example, that his no-hitter was his four hundred sixty-eighth lifetime victory—various people floated the idea that organized baseball should honor its Grand Old Man. John Taylor picked the proposal up, won Ban Johnson's approval for scheduling a celebration, and then met all costs involved in staging the event. August 13 was designated Cy Young Day in Boston. Brass bands were lined up, Robba Young came east from Ohio for the occasion, baseball celebrities and local politicians were invited, regular American League games were canceled, and as the centerpiece of the festivities a game was staged pitting a squad of American League all-stars against the Red Sox.[37] Before a crowd of almost 20,000 sweltering fans (with, according to some reports, another 10,000 left outside), Cy Young rode in a wagon around the Huntington Avenue Grounds diamond. To underscore the light-hearted side of the occasion, the Red Sox players wore fantastic costumes; Young himself was attired as—what else?—a farmer. But the deeper meaning of the hour was not ignored, as Young's teammates gave him a plaque, his American League colleagues gave him a loving cup,[38] Boston merchants gave him another loving cup (he got at least three in 1908), the National League Boston club gave him a floral horseshoe, the American League umpires gave him a travel bag, and the lieutenant governor of Massachusetts—after praising him for his "great ability, self control, and hard work"—gave him the key to the city of Boston.[39] The most extraordinary gesture of all was John Taylor's: he gave the entire gate of $7,500, a sum greater than Young's salary for the year, to his star hurler. A man with an unrivaled record had occasioned an unrivaled celebration—the "greatest testimonial ever given any ball player in this country."[40]

Cy Young's season ended virtually as it had begun. He started 6 games in September. In each of the first 5 he gave up only one run—though twice he lost by 1–0 scores—and the sixth game wound up as an extra-inning 2–2 tie. His final record of 21 victories and 11 losses made him a 20-game winner for the fifteenth time in his career. His career matchups with Rube Waddell were now over, but on August 31 he faced the young Walter Johnson for the first time.[41] Although his victory total paled in comparison to Ed Walsh's 40; it was still the fourth-highest total in the league. He was second in complete games (30) and in earned run average (1.26). This last figure was the lowest of his career—how's that for success at age forty-one?—and there are two ways to measure its significance. On the one hand, lots of American League pitchers were stingy in 1908; in fact, five other hurlers threw no-hitters, only three batters topped .300, and the league earned run average of 2.39 still stands as the lowest in the history of the junior circuit. On the other hand, even allowing for the remarkable dominance of pitching in 1908, Young compiled an earned run average that was only .53 of the league's—an astonishing figure that he bested for his own career only in the triumphant season of 1901.

Can we account for this astonishing success? There is much evidence that the Red Sox were taking measures to protect Cy Young's health and strength by 1908. He was asked to pitch only 299 innings, the lowest total (barring dismal 1906) of his full-season career thus far; and he was assigned Denny Sullivan as his roommate, a man who was training to be a physician and who kept Young fortified with pills. The lighter load certainly helped; the medications may have been useful. But the key to Young's success in 1908 was a wiliness learned from thoughtful experience. By 1908 Cy Young had become the complete pitcher, with a wide array of deliveries (including an occasional spitball) and masterful control of them all. Early in the season Lou Criger told a writer that Young "has cut out some of that fierce speed [this year] and crosses the batsmen with slows and benders."[42] But on this matter we can let the pitcher speak for himself. For when asked, after his no-hitter, how he had turned this wonder at his age, Young replied, "I just mixed things up. I'd throw a curve, then a fastball, then a change of pace. I guess knowledge of the batters helped too."[43] That is an explanation that covers not just the game but the season.

Once the season was over Cy Young hung around in Boston long enough to be a judge at a "barn party"—perhaps again playing the role of "Farmer Young"—before leaving in time to see the foliage of a Tuscarawas fall.[44] Less than two weeks after Cy Young Day he had signed a contract for 1909 for the same figure of $4,000 he had been paid in 1908. The Boston team was still changing: the midseason departures of Jesse Tannehill and George Winter left him and Lou Criger as the only holdovers from the world championship team of 1904, and the late season resignation of Deacon McGuire gave him, in the person of Fred Lake, yet another manager to work with. But he approved of John Taylor's willingness to spend money to secure talent, and he saw and supported the potential in such youngsters as Gavvy Cravath, Joe Wood, Tris Speaker, and Eddie Cicotte. The team's fifth-place finish seemed to vindicate the increasing reliance on youth. But even while recognizing that the club was in transition, he had no sense that he himself might be a valuable piece in the intricate bazaar of baseball personnel transfers. After all, as writers had been saying for years, Cy Young had a "life 'sit' " in Boston;[45] and John Taylor had been quoted to the same effect on several occasions.

But while management appreciated Young's strong work and his popularity with the fans, it also believed that he was playing on borrowed time and that if he could be exchanged for several promising youngsters before his arm gave out, the gain would be all Boston's. It is unclear at what point John Taylor and Fred Lake decided that Young might be dealt away. It is possible that the owner had reached this decision as early as midseason 1908—and that Cy Young Day was, among other things, a farewell bash for the pitcher—but in any case when Boston unexpectedly dealt Lou Criger to St. Louis in December (after Taylor had equally unexpectedly given the catcher a farewell gift of imported guns in October), the club's intentions became clear. While Criger was angry—publicly and blazingly so—at the trade, Young was stunned at the loss of his valuable battery-mate.[46] According to one report, he wept upon learning the news. For over a month thereafter the Red Sox organization proclaimed its intention to retain the hurler. But the pitcher's own public expressions of disillusionment with Boston—"I thought," he said to one reporter, "I had his [Taylor's] promise that we were never to be separated"[47]—gave the club an acceptable rationale for dealing him away. Rumors said he would follow Criger to the St. Louis Browns or wind up with one of the Chicago clubs. But in mid-February John Taylor traded the winningest pitcher in baseball history to the Cleveland club in return for $12,500 and Charlie Chech and Jack Ryan, two pitchers who between them had 27 major league victories to their credit. Taylor justified his action by declaring that Young's "pitching days are about over."[48] According to Joe Wood many years later, the Red Sox players "were really stunned . . . they couldn't believe it."[49] By the time the swap occurred, however, Young was ready for it. Ever since learning of Criger's fate, he had been mentioning that he would like to end his career in Cleveland, the city that had hosted his rise to stardom. The affection of Cleveland fans for the hero of the 1890s was unabated: on his first appearance there in 1908 he received a three-minute ovation. "I think," he said after the trade, "I will be of some service to the Naps."[50] Still, the trade was a surprising denouement to a surprising season. And the opportunity to prove yet another owner wrong gave Old Cy Young one additional reason to want to sparkle on his return to the Forest City.

CHAPTER THIRTEEN

True Nobility

CY YOUNG'S third no-hitter, the highlight of his 1908 season, triggered much commendation. But what is interesting about these tributes is that they focused less upon the accomplishment of the day than the achievement of the lifetime. One writer in *Sporting Life* called him a "physical marvel and moral wonder."[1] Another *Sporting Life* author styled him "the greatest pitcher the world has ever seen."[2] A biographical piece in the *New York Times* declared that "Young is the most remarkable ball player the game has yet produced when good work for a long period is considered."[3] The *Sporting News* stated its position in a headline: "Old Cy Young in a Class by Himself."[4]

Several writers chose to celebrate their hero in verse. In the concluding stanzas of "Good Old 'Cy' Young," a poem printed "by permission of A. Tennyson," the anonymous author placed these words in the pitcher's mouth.

> I wind them in, I wind them out,
>   I split the blooming platter
> Until I have my man struck out,
>   A sad, but wiser batter.
>
> To play the game the best I know
>   Is always my endeavor,
> For men may come, and men may go,
>   But I go on forever.[5]

George Whitefield D'Vys concluded his poem "Old 'Cy' Young" with this exhortation:

Now, then, up and shout for Cyrus who has certainly made good;
He is still the Bostons' mainstay, he has done all mortal could!
Year and year, though others vanished he has mastered yet his will,
And the Bostons keep a-winning just because of Old Cy's skill.

So, then, up and shout for Cyrus! Hard and strong now let us yell!
Let it ring out o'er the hilltops, let it echo thro' the dell!
Hence alone of Boston's vet'ran let the praises all be sung,
For there's never been the equal of the doughty old Cy Young![6]

The scheduling of Cy Young Day gave "Jac" Lowell an occasion for displaying his poetic talents:

So it's rah! Cy, rah! you're the best game's star
    And the eagle screams, "All hail, pal!"
        I will flaunt your name
        From the heights of fame,
    For you've helped my wings to sail, pal!"

Yes, it's rah! Cy, rah! from the wide world's heart!
    You're the pride of every fan, Cy!
        You are prince and peer
        Of the speeding sphere,
    And besides, a clean, square Man, Cy!

As you bow to-day to the thrilling throngs,
    And the honored friends address you,
        In the cup you hold
        Will be more than gold—
    Our love—and a grand "God bless you!"[7]

The press celebration of Cy Young reached its peak when the September 1908 issue of the newly founded *Baseball Magazine* appeared. It featured one article, purportedly by the hurler, entitled "How I Learned to Pitch," and another, by veteran Boston baseball writer Jacob Morse (well known for his admiration of Young), that told "The Story of 'Cy' Young."[8] The first piece stressed the importance of character traits—determination, hard work, and self-control. The second depicted the hurler as an immensely talented but nevertheless quiet, genial, loyal, neighborly, and commonsensical human being—a man who loved his pipe and hunting dogs, who happily passed the winter hours being read to by a devoted wife, and who thought farming the most rewarding of activities. Most ball players, Morse suggested, were unremarkable human beings. "But with Young," he continued, "it is entirely different. The answer to it all is—he is a man."[9]

And it was this image of talent combined with humanity that endured. He was both "a shining example" and "the real marvel of the game."[10] In 1909 the *Sporting News* began offering photographs of baseball stars to its readership; the second snapshot in the series was of the celebrated Young-Criger reunion early that season.[11] In 1910 Alfred Spink commended Young in *The National Game* for being unequaled "in long years of service and steady, faithful work." A year later a history of the game singled him out for "that quiet sweetness of disposition which has made him a favorite with all men all his life." And when *Baseball Magazine* editorialized late in 1911 about the likely imminence of Young's retirement, it offered this extraordinary accolade: "[Young] has achieved the highest renown that a human being may achieve in his special field of labor . . . there is nothing more for him to win. Like Alexander of old, he has no other worlds to conquer."[12]

While it was the third no-hitter that occasioned this effusive flow of praise, a subtle recasting of Cy Young's public image had been under way in the baseball press for several years. He was still the rustic, still plain-spoken, still the embodiment of integrity and hard work. But these traits were increasingly linked to a heroic past that would be understood by any reader as emblematically American. By 1907 the image of Young as an American hero was so widespread that he had become an almost universally applauded player, cheered whenever and wherever he appeared, "the best-liked character in the game, both at home and abroad."[13] Grantland Rice, the most gifted poetaster of the diamond, reflected this appreciation in a poem published over four months before the no-hitter. Titled "Tribute to Denton (Cy) Young," it drew on Victorian sentimentality in linking the pitcher to baseball's recent but mythic past.

> Fame may be fleeting and glory may fade—
>   Life at its best is a breath on the gale.
> One hero passes, another is made.
>   New stars arise as the old ones pale.
> So when a stalwart steps out from the throng,

On with the tribute, let garlands be flung—
Here's to the sturdy and here's to the strong—
Here's to the king of them all—Denton Young.[14]

In succeeding stanzas Rice moved through a catalogue of the game's greatest stars—Anson, Rusie, Ewing, Clarkson, Kelley, Ward, Meekin, Delahanty, Breitenstein, and others—always to return to the melancholy conclusion that only one warrior remained. The last stanza completed his argument:

Where is the mighty Dalrymple to-day?
   Miller and Denny and Cuppy the sly?
Show me their names in the line-up, I pray—
   Vainly I wait for an answering cry.
Few of us stand to the guns through the years;
   One at a time from the heights we are flung.
Heroes soon pass in the Valley of tears—
   But here's to the king of them all—Denton Young.

In the eyes of many baseball writers Cy Young had become the enduring symbol of the American game.

One reason America follows sports is that the world of athletic competition gives us many of our most revered heroes. Before Michael Jordan there was Babe Ruth. Before the Bambino there was John L. Sullivan. It is true that Cy Young never reached the lofty heights achieved by these national icons. But he managed, before his skills yielded to age, to stand tall as "this grand oak of base ball."[15] The virtues that the writers attached to him as his career neared its end were many: honesty, moderation, industry, self-reliance, dependability, generosity, self-control, modesty, laconicism, durability, loyalty. "He has no bad habits," one writer sweepingly declared.[16] But if, from among his many virtues, there was one that loomed largest, it was his readiness to tell it as it was—to speak the simple truth. Not surprisingly, umpires were among those holding the pitcher in highest regard, with Billy Evans, Silk O'Loughlin, and Tommy Connolly all citing him as one the easiest hurlers to call pitches for.[17] The sportswriter H. G. Merrill, summarizing the judgment of players, fans, and officials alike, voiced the appropriate generalization: Cy Young has "always deported himself like a true nobleman."[18]

In early-twentieth-century America the ascription of nobility made sense. For if the traditional American commitment to republicanism involved a repudiation of all notions of inherited nobility, it embraced the vision of natural nobility. That is, America still honored nobility, but America's was a nobility of character, not of birth. It was the nobility of honesty and hard work, a nobility bred by rural life. But with the dawning of a new century, the vision of natural nobility was increasingly under assault. Rural America, the Jeffersonian seedbed of the country's moral health, was slowly disappearing; urban America—an America of foreigners, crime, and corruption—portended a future of national moral decay. Or so many pundits feared. That is one reason why the national game of baseball, an activity that had taken its origins from the cities, was being metamorphosed by those who sought to control its image into a game rooted in bucolic conditions. Indeed, that is why the Mills Commission absurdly identified Cooperstown, not New York City, as the site of baseball's birth. For baseball to be the *national* pastime, it needed an appropriately rural pedigree.

At this moment of incipient division over competing views of national identity, Cy Young could be cast as the carrier of older virtues. He stood at the heart of the national pastime as the embodiment of American nobility. A republican (as well as a Republican), a "rail splitter,"[19] and a denizen of rural Tuscarawas County (a name that connoted a rough, hard, and wooded Indian country),[20] Cy Young was a hero who could be enlisted into service in the cultural struggles of the day. I don't want to press the point too far. Many fans admired Young simply because they respected his success and durability; many spoke fondly of him simply because he was a nice old guy. But it is significant that the headline provoked by his visit to California in 1910 spoke of his belief that the Japanese (and Cubans too) were too small ever to be a major factor in major league baseball. "That's the trouble with all foreigners," he was quoted as saying. "Base ball will always be an American game."[21] This sentiment—that baseball was a peculiarly apt emblem of American greatness—was common in the baseball press of the day and consistent with the broader attitudes toward foreign nations that undergirded much of the populism of the 1890s and the progressivism of the early 1900s. Cy Young's transformation into "the noblest Roman of them all"[22]—a doubly useful phrase, we should remember, since Brutus was a defender of republicanism—coincides so neatly with the needs of one side in the debate over national identity that it is hard to resist the conclusion that, for some writers at least, he was an iconic pawn.

Cy Young did not stand alone in that spotlight. Instead, he shared the role of true republican noble with Christy Mathewson, the other great symbol of idealized manhood that baseball offered to America in the first decade of the twentieth century.[23] But the two men personified different versions of American nobility. Matty was promoted as a role model for youth; Young—long since dubbed the "Grand Old Man of Base Ball"[24]— was promoted as a role model for adults. Mathewson was a product of the American gentry; he was tall, handsome, and well proportioned; he was educated and well spoken; the public associated him with gallantry. Young, on the other hand, had sprung from the American yeomanry and was plain in appearance; he had had little formal education; he was taciturn and somewhat shy; the public associated him with integrity. Each man was an authentic athletic hero; each represented the best that baseball and America could offer. But as they emerged from the sports pages of the day they were very different sorts of men, and they evoked different responses. The baseball press encouraged fans to feel distant admiration for the young National Leaguer and close affection for the elderly American Leaguer. It is perhaps even fair to say that Young represented virtue past while Mathewson represented virtue future. If so, we may then understand why Young's final fading, when it came, struck fans as a portentous passage. After all, as Grantland Rice had written in 1908:

> Where are the heroes saluted of old?
> Heroes to whom through the years we have clung.
> Have all deserted the Clan of the Bold?
> Not while the echoes are ringing for Young.

Should those echoes ever fade completely, the Clan of the Bold—the society, that is, that from ancient days had linked Greek heroes, Roman republicans, warriors on the battlements, defenders of the republic, and men of old-fashioned virtue—would be extinct. By Rice's reckoning, Cy Young was the last noble knight.

CHAPTER FOURTEEN

1909–1911:
Recessional

W HEN CY YOUNG returned to a Cleveland baseball club in
1909, he was joining a pennant contender. Which is precisely
why the Naps wanted him.[1] In 1908 Cleveland had finished just
half a game behind first-place Detroit. The club already had Addie Joss,
who had finished the 1908 season—his fourth in a row as a twenty-game
winner—by throwing the twentieth century's second perfect game. It
was easy for the Cleveland management to believe that if Cy Young had
been wearing a Nap uniform in 1908, Cleveland would have swept to the
flag. Manager Larry Lajoie, who had urged Charles Somers to go after
Young's contract, was delighted at the addition to his already strong staff.
"Cy Young," he declared, "will be one of our mainstays for several seasons. . . . The beauty about Cy is that he can work in any kind of weather."[2]

Rather than make his customary trip to Hot Springs, Young joined the
rest of the Nap squad in Mobile, as big as ever but in high spirits and
ready to trim himself into shape. Alabama fans swarmed into the ballpark
in March to see the three stars now playing for Cleveland—the brilliant
Joss, not yet thirty and presumably approaching his prime, and the veterans Lajoie and Young, whose activities eight years earlier had given cru-
cial credibility to Ban Johnson's experiment. When Young marked off his
forty-second birthday, his teammates threw a party.[3] Far from being a
merely local occasion, the celebration triggered a deluge of congratula-
tory messages from around the country. Most observers expected a Cleveland team fortified by Cy Young to appear in the World Series in 1909.

Things did not work out that way. But the season still provided Cy
Young with several memorable moments. The earliest came with Cleveland's opening series. Scheduled for St. Louis, it gave him and his former

battery-mate Lou Criger an occasion for getting together again, even if only briefly. Unimportant as this reunion might seem in light of current expectations of player mobility, the meeting of the old friends in 1909 attracted wide attention in the baseball community. (In the game itself the weak-hitting Criger proved that all those years as Young's receiver had been instructive as he stroked out two singles.) Another memorable moment came when the team reached Cleveland, for April 23 had been designated Cy Young Day. The celebration itself was something of a dud, as very cold weather held the crowd down to 5,000, and Young, though pitching well, lost 3–1. Still, the pitcher was pleased at being honored. On June 11, Young made his triumphal return to Boston. Former teammates rushed to greet him at the special pregame ceremony, a crowd of 11,000 roared its welcome to the hero from happier days, and Young wept quietly when the Boston mascot Jerry McCarthy ran out to hug him. But he quickly regained his composure and topped off a satisfying afternoon by holding the Red Sox to two hits. On July 19, Young was on the mound when Cleveland shortstop Neal Ball stunned a home crowd by executing major league baseball's first unassisted triple play.[+] Shortly thereafter he would have noticed—though characteristically he left no recorded reaction—that Boston had dispatched both Charlie Chech and Jack Ryan back to the minors, signaling its admission that the trade that had sent Young to Cleveland had not worked out. Finally—and this was an unanticipated personal triumph of the year—when the season ended Young was the winningest pitcher on the Cleveland club.

But in that fact lay the embracing disappointment of 1909. For the Cleveland club had been expected to waltz to a pennant, and while Young had done his part, injuries, slippage, and dissonance had shattered that ambition. Early in the season observers took to berating the club for poor fielding and inattentive base running, and as the summer progressed rumors of dissension reached the newspapers. In August a cranky Larry Lajoie, his club playing only .500 ball, resigned as manager, making way for Deacon McGuire, Cy Young's friend from Red Sox days, who had spent much of 1909 assisting Lajoie and scouting young players in California. McGuire's appointment, however, only exacerbated tensions, because several other players—though not Cy Young—believed that they had been promised the managerial job if Lajoie stepped aside. Disabilities further compromised the club's work. Among the key players who went down with injuries or illnesses were Lajoie himself, who nevertheless finished with the third highest batting average in the league; former league batting champion Elmer Flick, who hit only .255; and Addie Joss, who won a scant 14 games. When the season closed, Cleveland was in sixth place, a humbling 27½ games behind the position it had been expected to claim.

Though the club did poorly, Cy Young finished the year with fine statistical credentials. Although he fell short of the 20-victory level for only the fifth time in his career, part of the explanation for his near-miss lay in lost pitching opportunities in September. On September 10, with 19 victories under his belt, he was struck by a batted ball and minor surgery was required. Young pitched only twice after being injured. Even so, his victory total tied him with Eddie Plank for fourth highest in the league. For a man of 42 he was proving remarkably durable, finishing second among league hurlers in complete games (30) and fourth in innings pitched (295). His 109 strikeouts stood as the record for a forty-two-year-old pitcher until Nolan Ryan obliterated it eighty years later. During the course of three consecutive complete games in early July he yielded only one run; 2 of his 3 victories in the streak were over the league champion Detroit Tigers.

But Young's fine performance was marked by a troubling pattern. Between May 19 and July 24 he was like his old self, winning 12 and losing only 3—with 2 of his defeats recorded in games in which the Naps were shut out. Leaving aside that ten-week period, however, his record stood at a poor 7 wins and 12 losses. Here was evidence that his wonted consistency was fading. Also slipping was his legendary control: 59 walks during 1909 constituted his highest total since 1896, a year in which he had pitched over one-third again as many innings as in 1909. He admitted that he missed Criger behind the plate. On August 21 he became so frustrated at his work that, having uncorked a wild pitch that let one run in, he neglected to cover home and allowed a second runner to score. Wildness and self-destructive negligence—these were uncharacteristic of a pitcher who was ordinarily master of himself and the situation. The late-season injury masked another sign that age was exacting a toll. Early in his career Young's skill had never flagged as the months ground on—indeed, his best-ever month was the September of 1893, when he had posted 9 victories and no losses—but in the final seven years of his career Young won only 36 percent of his post-August games of record. There were, in short, for those who would see them, hints of the final decline. Still, when the season of 1909 was over, it was legitimate to keep Cy Young's name on the roster of baseball's best pitchers.

That Cy Young would return in 1910 was certain. He had finished the previous season with 497 lifetime wins. A countdown toward 500 was on in the press. Though talk of retirement trailed him everywhere, no reasonable person believed that the only pitcher in major league history to have won as many as 400 games would hang up his glove before becoming the first pitcher in major league history to win 500. Especially since he was still being paid about $4,000 per season. And so, after a visit to his brother Alonzo in California and a trimming spell in Hot Springs, he joined the club in Alexandria, Louisiana, finding himself, with forty-three years under his belt, twice the age of some of the men in camp. But spirits were high as the Naps won all but one of their exhibition games against major league clubs.

In the opening weeks of the season, Young's age loomed large. For while the team did well, the veteran lost his initial four decisions (although it was a marginal extenuation that the Naps were shut out in three of them). His first loss occurred on April 21, when, before 19,000 fans and a gathering of baseball luminaries, he pitched in the game that inaugurated Cleveland's dramatically renovated League Park, duplicating the dedicatory role he had played when the ball field had hosted its first game on May 1, 1891.[5] On May 4, though he finally pitched well, he was stuck with a fourteen-inning tie and only the brief presence of President Taft among the spectators as a consolation. Moreover, the extra inning game exacted a price, for he soon dropped out of the rotation with a sore shoulder and went back to Peoli, not returning to the mound until May 30. Commentators read the writing on the wall, but Young, like most great athletes in their final slide from excellence, seems to have blinded himself to the implications of his performances. After all, he could easily say to himself, I'm working just as hard as ever, and in the past, effort has always translated into success; besides, I've had slumps before.

Toward the end of June, Cy Young rediscovered his secrets. On the June 21 he registered his first victory of the season by defeating Chicago, 3–2, in twelve innings. The winning run scored when Larry Lajoie leaned across the plate to convert what was designed to be ball four of an intentional pass into a game-winning single. On June 30 he faced only 28 batters in shutting out St. Louis with 2 hits. The day was particularly notable because the lumbering Young actually tried to steal home—unsuccessfully. The victory was his four hundred ninety-ninth lifetime win. As mysteriously as they had returned, his secrets then left him, and his next three starts—all undistinguished—moved his season record to 2 and 7. But finally, on July 19, against the Washington club that over the years had been his readiest victim, Young won again, becoming the first and only pitcher ever to record 500 victories in a major league career. Though he allowed only one hit through the first eight innings, it was not an easy triumph. The game went eleven innings. In the ninth he let the Senators load the bases. In the eleventh he put the first batter on base. But ultimately he prevailed, and that was the story the baseball public was interested in. Cy Young, *Sporting Life* declared (in a breathlessly extended sentence), has "capped the most remarkable pitching career in base ball history by recording his 500th victory—a unique feat requiring 21 years of continuous effort, which has no parallel in baseball annals, and may never be repeated by any pitcher now before the public, with the possible exception of the illustrious Mathewson."[6] The Giant star had his own comment: "Young is the greatest pitcher that ever lived."[7] The five hundredth victory inaugurated a 5-game winning streak that by mid-August had given Young a 7–7 record. It is easy to imagine him feeling that, just when he was becoming worried that his skills had deserted him, they had returned.

But after that seventh victory Cy Young failed to win another game all season. In fact, except for those five victories in a three-week stretch in late July and early August his record in 1910 was 2–10. Casting back to the previous season we can see that beginning with July 24, 1909, he had been losing more often than winning. Baseball writers dropped caution in speculating about his future. Edward Bangs, for example, after praising the club for shedding players who no longer performed, added that the team still had some men who were "out of place as Naps" and noted finally that "a ball player can't go on forever."[8] Young was sensitive to the speculation. "Quit the game, well, I guess not," he told a Cleveland writer defensively. "I am better now than I have been in years"—this claim was lent brief plausibility by its timing: right after the 5-game winning streak—"I'd be awfully lonesome, and you know this is a healthy game. I'll not quit until I have to."[9] But it was surely an ominous sign that when another Cy Young Day was held on August 15, the expected crowd of fans from Tuscarawas County never showed up.

And necessity seemed to be closing in. In July Charles Somers bought out his partner to secure full control of the club and launched a movement that would bring the young players Joe Jackson, Roger Peckinpaugh, and Vean Gregg to the squad. Soon thereafter the owner declared that Larry Lajoie was his only untradeable player. Deacon McGuire remained a supporter of Young's, but the manager, probably at the owner's instructions, kept the old hurler on the bench after his embarrassing outing of September 6, when he yielded 5 hits and 3 runs in 2 innings. During the closing weeks of the 1910 season Cy Young was confined to coaching young pitchers, taking the mound only for exhibition games,[10] and watching while the Naps, though playing without him, finished with a surge and captured fifth place. Was Cy Young depressed by these developments? No one said as much, but early in the season he had admitted to no longer finding it fun simply to watch a baseball game, and for the first time in his career the pitcher allowed himself to put on weight even while a season was in progress. When Cy Young left for Peoli at the end of the season, one reporter commented that he "looked like a prosperous alderman."[11]

Still, Cy Young wanted to come back for another season, unconvinced that his arm had really lost its power. He knew that he remained popular with the Cleveland fans, and he had found in fellow Ohioan Addie Joss—a talented pitcher who had thrown his second no-hitter early in the 1910 season—his closest ball-playing friend since his separation from Lou Criger.[12] There was the question of salary, of course. Cleveland put pressure on the pitcher to sign by asking waivers on him in December 1910. Young was angry at the action, but he understood that he could no longer expect to earn $4,000 a season. We don't know the terms that he agreed to for 1911; I suspect that he signed for about $2,000. But since Young was, for a ball player, a wealthy man, he was not really playing for money at this point. And he surely enjoyed his fame. This much is clear: as the clubs moved south for spring training in 1911, fans across the country were opening their *Reach Guides* to ponder Francis Richter's judgment that "no greater, better or more remarkable ball player than pitcher Young ever lived or lives now."[13]

During the spring sessions in both Hot Springs and Alexandria Cy Young had to deal with daily queries about his plans. He tended to strike a stubborn pose, asserting, "I'll stay till they tear off my uniform!"[14] One account had him declaring his determination to last a quarter of a century in the majors. But occasionally he was more subdued, at least once even announcing his retirement. His forty-fourth birthday triggered a story that he was, as his twenty-second season opened, "in better physical condition now than he has been for two years."[15] But in fact Deacon McGuire and Charles Somers were annoyed that he remained stubbornly at 210 pounds. The club floated a story that he was not assured a place on Cleveland's staff in 1911. Young responded with tales of his new pitches, claiming on one occasion that he was ready to jump on the spitball wagon and on another occasion that he had developed the "hot-water ball," a delivery that he described as "a slow jump and wonder."[16] And whatever else might be said or thought about him, he remained one of America's most celebrated athletes, a point demonstrated when the Arkansas legislature adjourned its session so that members could attend a Nap game in Little Rock and show, as the resolution ran, their "respect and esteem for the venerable Cy Young."[17]

In much of this preseason maneuvering there was an element of play, but matters turned abruptly tragic at the opening of official competition. On April 14 word reached the club from Toledo that Addie Joss, who everyone thought was recuperating at home from a stubborn sickness, had died. The loss was a devastating blow to Cy Young. "My baseball experience has thrown me with practically every man in the league for more than twenty years," he said, "but I never met a fairer or squarer man than Addie."[18] The funeral was held in Toledo on April 17, and a special train was hired to bring the entire Cleveland squad from Detroit for the occasion. The club members had even threatened in effect to strike on that day if the schedule was not recast so they could attend. Young was one of two non–family members invited to accompany Joss's widow Lillian and her two children when they entered the church; he wept frequently throughout the service, the largest Masonic funeral Toledo had ever seen.

Soon thereafter Charles Somers suggested that to raise money for the Joss family an exhibition game featuring the Cleveland team and various American League stars might be arranged. The idea lacked steam, however, until Young and several of Joss's other friends pushed the proposal. With Ban Johnson's approval, the game was scheduled for July 24, and when it was held, nine future Hall of Famers took the field—Frank Baker, Ty Cobb, Eddie Collins, Sam Crawford, Walter Johnson, Larry Lajoie, Tris Speaker, Bobby Wallace, and Cy Young. Also in action were such stars as Hal Chase, Russ Ford, Joe Jackson, Gabby Street, and Joe Wood. Young pitched three frames for Cleveland, yielding first-inning singles to Speaker, Collins, and Cobb. The game was seen by over 15,000 fans and raised almost $13,000 for the Joss family.[19] Young was proud to have been associated so centrally with an event to honor the memory, and assist the family, of his friend.

By the time the Addie Joss game was played, however, Cy Young had other matters on his mind. As the team broke from spring training, he had come down with a chest ailment that turned into a severe case of bronchitis—pneumonia, by one account—and had traveled to Peoli to recuperate under Robba Young's care. He did not even make an appearance in a game in 1911 until June 9. By then Cleveland had a new manager, George Stovall. He was, to be sure, a friend of Young's, but he was replacing Deacon McGuire, the man who had been Young's firmest fan on the club. Stovall was considerate as he worked the veteran pitcher back into the rotation, but after Young won his first two games, his performance begin to deteriorate. On July 19 he experienced the mortification of lasting fewer than three innings against Boston while giving up 7 hits and 2 walks. Ten days later he pitched exactly three innings against Washington, yielding 6 hits and 5 runs. The legendary Cy Young was tossing batting practice balls up to the plate.

Management meanwhile had been trying to figure out how to do what now seemed the inevitable. The club probably asked waivers on Young in June, though it denied rumors to that effect. Then it waited for the Joss game to pass before acting. The first step was to remove Young from play, and the game of July 29 marks his final appearance in a Cleveland uniform. In the measured words of one long-time baseball writer, he had "outlived his usefulness in select society."[20] The second step followed on August 15 when the club gave him his unconditional release. The event was almost anticlimactic, but to anyone with a sense of baseball history it marked the end of an epoch. After almost exactly twenty-two years of work in the major leagues, the winningest pitcher in baseball history— and as of June 30 the losingest too—was without an employer.[21]

But not for long. Cy Young made clear to all who would listen that he had not given up on himself. "There is a lot of good pitching in me yet," he declared to one writer; "the public hasn't seen the last of me," he told another; "I will be a good pitcher for a number of years," he said to a third.[22] He needed only one club to agree with that judgment, and the feeble Boston Braves of the National League, under new ownership and desperate for fans, concluded that the risks involved in hiring him to complete the year—presumably coming to less than $1,000—were acceptable.[23] Everyone understood that a major element in Boston's calculations was the belief that Boston fans would turn out to see the celebrated veteran on his return to the Hub. The club wanted him, Tim Murnane wrote, "simply to draw the crowd."[24] That was good enough for Young, and on August 19, four days after being released by the Cleveland Americans, he signed on with the Boston Nationals.

This Boston coda allowed Cy Young to add a few more happy memories to his career. His first appearance in the Hub drew 8,000 fans. When the Braves reached Cincinnati, two old nineteenth-century buddies, Bid McPhee and Jake Stenzel, came to the park just to see him. More important, he won four games for his new team, two of them shutouts over the hard-hitting Pirates. In the second of these games, on September 22, he bested Pittsburgh's ace Babe Adams, 1–0, walked no one, and struck out Honus Wagner three times. Given his success that day, few would have thought that this win, number 511, would be the last of his career. Even one of his losses was memorable, for on September 7 he dueled with Philadelphia's sensational rookie Grover Cleveland Alexander, losing 1–0 as Alexander threw a one-hitter.[25] Since in his next appearance, an otherwise unmemorable loss, he drew Christy Mathewson as his mound opponent, Young faced within a single week the two pitchers who are tied for third place on the all-time victory list. (Indeed, 1911 is the only season that saw all of the top four career winners—for Walter Johnson holds second place—in simultaneous action.)[26] As the season wound down, Young lost his edge. His last three decisions were all defeats, and in his final appearance of the year—it was, in fact, the last game of his major league career—he was relieved in the seventh inning in Brooklyn after being pummeled for eight consecutive base hits. Nevertheless, his work for last-place Boston sparked commendation. His earned run average of 3.71 was more than 1⅓ runs lower than the team's, and his won-lost percentage of .444 was higher than any regular starters'. "Few pitchers in the country," Jacob Morse wrote, with an exaggeration that was tolerable under the circumstances, "had anything on the work Cy did since his connection with the Boston Nationals."[27]

When the 1911 campaign ended, Cy Young hoped to pitch for at least one additional season. He sent in his contract in February 1912, traveled promptly to Hot Springs to lose weight, and then joined Boston's spring camp in Augusta, Georgia, pointing to his notably trimmer shape as a demonstration of his determination. He pitched well enough in practice games in March and remained on the roster as the squad moved north to begin official play. "The old boy," *Sporting Life* wryly noted, "is said to look better than any previous season since 1663, considered by many to be his best year since the Summer of 1169."[28] But in fact his arm was sore, and despite the Braves' miserable start, he passed his time warming the bench. When Boston reached Pittsburgh the fourth week in May, it was announced that the veteran would finally make an appearance; on

May 23 he actually began warming up. But then, his arm still aching, he walked back to the bench, declaring (by one account), "It's no use. I'm not going on. These poor fellows have lost too many games already."[29]

Almost immediately he left for Peoli, turning down his teammates' offer to pay the fare to Ohio and apparently announcing his retirement. "It was a good old game," he said. "My best days were spent on the diamond. . . . I hate to leave the game."[30] But no sooner did he begin wandering about his home in Peoli than the old ambition flamed anew, and he decided to try out the ministrations of Akron's celebrated mender of baseball limbs, Bonesetter Reese. After examining his patient, Reese was reportedly optimistic: "You will be ready to work again in two weeks."[31] But when Young tried his hand against semipro opposition after Reese's therapy, he discovered that the touch of old was still gone. His problem was age, and when on August 2—apparently the last day on which he tried to pitch seriously—he found his deliveries so ineffective that even an amateur Ohio team could rip into them, he finally acknowledged the truth he had been trying to shun: "My arm will no longer do the work that was so easy."[32] A few days later, having traveled to Pittsburgh to forewarn the Braves' manager Johnny Kling, he announced yet again that he had played his last game. And this time the forty-five-year-old veteran with twenty-two years of major league play to his credit meant it.

Cy Young sometimes stated that he retired because he had gotten too big to field bunts. "The boys are taking unfair advantage of the old man," ran one version of the tale. "They know that this big stomach of mine makes it difficult for me to field bunts, so instead of swinging at my stuff they are laying the ball down. When the third baseman has to start doing my work, it's time for me to quit."[33] It made a good yarn but it was not accurate. It is true that opposing teams had sometimes tried to exploit the heavy veteran's clumsiness afield by laying the ball down, but when he had his stuff, bunting was not an adequate offensive weapon against Cy Young. The real reason for the retirement, as Young himself explained to some at the time, was his sore arm. "When I quit the Boston club in Pittsburgh," he told one writer, "it was because I was not in shape to pitch."[34] In later years he could be even more candid. "My arm went bad in 1912," he told Burton Hawkins in the 1940s, "when I was in spring training and I guess it was about time."[35]

In saying that, Young was confirming as well a point he had often made over the years: when his term in the major leagues was up, he would not return to the minors. Today such a career trajectory, except for rehabilitation, would be almost unthinkable. In Young's day, however, it was a common route for players who could no longer handle competition at the major league level—a route taken, for example, by Bill Hutchison, Joe McGinnity, and Rube Waddell. But Young did not need the money, and he was faithful—barring his one quasi-rehabilitative appearance in a Canton uniform—to his declaration of 1906: "if I can not earn my living in the big leagues, I will not impose on the backwaters."[36] And so retirement meant retirement.

There is something sad in the sight of a once great performer slipping from excellence, trying to resist the toll of age, and ultimately submitting to it. But the alternative is the sadder sight of a performer brought down while still in command of his skills—think of Dizzy Dean, Ed Delahanty, Lou Gehrig, and Roberto Clemente. There is no cheerful way for a great career to end. Cy Young negotiated the transition to retirement about as well as one might hope, aware that athletes, like politicians, rarely have the opportunity to end their careers on high notes. With money in the bank, he had prepared for the inevitable day. Besides, life in Peoli had never lost its power to comfort.

CHAPTER FIFTEEN

1912–1955:

Life after Glory

A S A SUBJECT for biography, an athlete offers a career of peculiar proportions: the achievements that draw the attention of the biographer occur relatively early in the subject's life, and the last half of that life—the period that for most biographical subjects sees the fulfillment of earlier effort or promise—is little more than a vast anticlimax. Except for a small number—Joe Cronin, for example, as a baseball executive, or John Montgomery Ward as an attorney, or Jim Bunning as a politician—most diamond greats cannot find post-diamond opportunities for distinction. The talent that brought them fame turns out to have no applicability beyond the ball park. When Cy Young retired at the age of forty-five, he had more than four decades of life still before him. To anticipate my judgment on those forty-three years: even though Young failed to establish a new career for himself, and even though he experienced some awkward bumps and disappointments, his pride and common sense allowed him to weather the vicissitudes of life after glory pretty well.

By the fall of 1912, Cy Young had returned to his farm in Peoli. Although it seems the natural step for him to have taken, he toyed with alternatives. A Boston sporting goods vendor had offered to install him as store manager. His brother Alonzo had encouraged him to move to an Oregon cattle ranch. Instead, he did what he had always said he would do; he tended his farm in Tuscarawas County. He had hunting and fishing to pass the time, and he briefly lent his approval to a project involving a ghostwritten "history of base ball in his times, told in autobiographical form."[1] Upon hearing reports that his land might sit atop an oil deposit, he invested in some unsuccessful drilling efforts, announcing that "I'm going to be John D. Rockefeller's hated rival."[2] But a hankering to get back on the baseball scene gnawed at him, and early in 1913 he confessed that "I would still like to be identified with the greatest game of all in some way."[3] That's why, despite having professed a lack of interest in managing in the past, he agreed to try his hand at it.

Of the three offers that came his way—one from Ohio University, one from the Portland club in the Pacific Coast League, and one from the Federal League Cleveland team—he chose the opportunity in the city that knew him well. In 1913 the newly formed six-team Federal League, operating independently of the world of organized baseball, was not yet claiming major league status, though that ambition was present in the minds of league organizers.[4] History knows this new Cleveland club as the Green Sox, but the press quickly dubbed it the "Youngsters" or the "Youngmen" or simply "Cy's Band." It played its games at the ball field at Luna Park, an amusement facility on the eastern outskirts of the city that was owned by M. F. Bramley, who was also chief owner of the Green Sox. The hiring of Young was part of a broader league strategy to draw fans by giving managerial authority to a hometown hero.[5] Young's team, like the other clubs in the league, featured former major leaguers, lifetime minor leaguers, and hopeful recruits from the semipro ranks. Its star was Red Kleinow, a veteran of eight major league seasons. On May 3 Cleveland and Covington played the league's inaugural game, and thereafter much went well for the Green Sox. Despite the presence of an American League franchise in the city, the local papers gave adequate coverage to Federal League activities, and the Green Sox, after a poor start, stayed in contention until mid-August. The club drew as many as 5,000 fans to some of its home games, and on "Cy Young Day" over 3,500 fans came out to Luna Park to help honor the manager, cheering lustily when he walked onto the field. The ownership may have hoped that Young would occasionally assign himself to the mound, but he abided by his declaration that his hurling career was finished and never entered a game. When the season was over, there was ample reason for him to be pleased with his work: after all, a second-place finish bespeaks success. Nevertheless, 1913 was Cy Young's last year in professional baseball.

It would be easy to explain his final retirement from the game by noting that the Cleveland club departed the Forest City after 1913. It left because, with the Federal League preparing to claim its destiny as a major leagues, all of its member clubs needed larger ball parks. Unable to lease or build an adequate facility closer to the heart of Cleveland, the Green

Sox were ejected from the circuit, and as a consequence Cleveland had no entry in the Federal League when it began its brief career as a major league.[6] In fact, however, Young's retirement from managing antedated the ownership's final desperate efforts to find a playing field in Cleveland. M. F. Bramley appreciated what Young had done with the team. The owners liked having a former star of his stature on the payroll. But when Young showed unwillingness to spend time and effort working to lure players away from teams in the American and National Leagues, and especially away from the intracity rival Cleveland Naps (Larry Lajoie was the chief target), his utility to the Green Sox was severely compromised. It is unclear whether his wariness about pursuing major league talent for his club was rooted in a disapproval of efforts to tempt players to violate the spirit of their reserve clauses or in a reluctance to commit himself to spending much of his winter away from Robba and Peoli—or perhaps in something else. But by the beginning of December 1913 the Green Sox were looking for a new manager, and Cy Young was enjoying the hills of Tuscarawas County.

Thereafter, for the rest of his long life, Cy Young's contacts with baseball were spectatorial, ceremonial, commemorative, and nostalgic. He went to several Indians games each year. He also happily participated in old-timers' games. He appeared—to mention only the most notable occasions—in Cleveland in 1921 (to mark the city's 125th birthday) and 1932 (to open the new Municipal Stadium), in Boston in 1930 (to raise funds for the Children's Hospital),[7] and in Pittsburgh in 1933 (to honor Honus Wagner). But there were many others, for these events were as popular with fans as with the old-timers themselves. Young also continued his involvement in charity games. In 1923 he made a brief mound appearance in a match-up between old-timers and sandlotters to raise money for the Medical Protective Fund of the Cleveland Amateur Baseball and Athletic Association. Ten years later a team of Tuscarawas County all-stars met Walter Johnson's Cleveland Indians in a benefit game at the Tuscarawas County fair.[8] Finally, throughout the years Young stayed in touch with close friends from playing days—especially with his valued battery-mates, Chief Zimmer and Lou Criger. In fact, the Boston old-timers' game of 1930 drew him because one of its goals was to raise money to help disabled veterans like Criger.

Baseball engagements aside, Cy Young spent most of the first two decades of his retirement secluded from the scrutiny of the press. With the help of a hired hand he raised potatoes and tended his sheep, hogs, and chickens. He also hunted and bred dogs, living the life of a modest gentle-man farmer. For a while he enjoyed occasional lunches with Davis Haw-ley at the Union Club in Cleveland. He sometimes traveled as far afield as New York City, Chicago, St. Paul, or Kansas City. More regularly he welcomed visitors to his Peoli home and showed off a mantelpiece laden with mementos of his playing days: trophies, loving cups, a bat, and two baseballs—one from the 1895 Temple Cup series and one from his five hundredth victory. He remained a visible citizen of Tuscarawas County, moving steadily upward through Masonic degrees and regularly coach-ing local youngsters (including a teen-aged Woody Hayes, who later went on to fame as a football coach). A lifelong Republican who had literally leapt with excitement in the middle of a game on hearing in 1896 that Ohioan William McKinley had secured the party's nomination, he was elected to the county party's Central Committee in 1930.[9]

Meanwhile, the older generation of Youngs and Millers slowly passed away. Robba's father, Robert Miller, moved in with the Youngs at some point after his wife's death in 1903 and died in Peoli in 1917. Cy Young's mother, Nancy Young, had died two years earlier from an unidentified stomach ailment, and after her death McKinzie Young Jr. moved rest-lessly about, sometimes returning to Gilmore but often staying with his nearby children, Emma (Young) Ripley in Tippecanoe and Cy Young in Peoli. In 1928, during a stay with his famous son, the eighty-five-year-old Civil War veteran succumbed to the ravages of diabetes and age.

It is hard to get a fix on Robba Young in the years of her husband's re-tirement. She continued for a while to enjoy hunting, and she maintained a correspondence with her husband's siblings, nephews, and nieces. To many friends and acquaintances she was simply "Mrs. Cy." But there is no evidence that she traveled with her husband to the various baseball occasions that he graced after his retirement. And there is a far more striking omission. In the 1910 census, interviewees were asked if they had any children, living or dead. Robba Young replied in the negative.[10] In light of the couple's tragic loss just three years earlier, this is an unset-tling response, and it leaves us room to speculate about the surges of denial or despair that may have visited her in her later years. However that may be (and I readily admit that I may be over-reaching), it is known that she began to suffer from symptoms of uremia in the mid-1920s. Cy Young's decision in 1931 to forgo his usual autumn hunting trip was per-haps a sign that Robba Young's condition was deteriorating, and she was only sixty when, on January 25, 1933, she died. Her death certificate cited a blocked bile duct as the immediate cause of death, with kidney and heart problems as contributing factors.[11] Cy Young had loved his wife. Now he was alone.

Not only that. By the early 1930s, he was living in straitened circumstances. This may come as a surprise, since in his playing days Cy Young was held up as an example of the prudent professional athlete, investing in real estate and amassing a modest fortune. "I have enough money," he declared on retiring in 1912, "to last me throughout the rest of my life."[12] One report attributed Young's difficulties to the collapse of a bank in Dover, Ohio, where he had deposited his money.[13] Since bank failures during the Depression were widespread, that explanation remains possible, although an investigation of banks near Peoli uncovered none that reneged on commitments to depositors during the early 1930s.[14] I think it likelier that the explanation is less dramatic.

Once he retired from baseball, Cy Young discovered that he lacked an aptitude for making money. "I'm no great shakes as a farmer," he said in 1932, adding that "there is no 'business' in a ball player after he quits the game. I guess we're too used to being told what to do by a manager and too used to following the rules of the old ball game to make good in other lines of work after we get too old for baseball."[15] Three years later he added that an investment in an unidentified Cleveland company "isn't doing anything now."[16] In 1943 he offered his bleakest explanation for his situation: "I guess I'm living too long."[17] Perhaps his habitual conservatism served him poorly in an era when farmers who were unable to adjust their visions of marketing and technology often met with financial failure; by one account, for example, he never purchased a tractor in his lifetime.[18] Then again, perhaps he simply encountered bad luck; the summer of 1930, for example, saw the most severe drought in the recorded history of Tuscarawas County. In any case, I think that Young's own testimony lends credence to the view that his economic difficulties early in the 1930s were results not of the collapse of a financial institution but of his long-term inability to make money from farming.

Robba's death shattered the regularity of Cy Young's life and led him to make some decisions that he himself quickly acknowledged to have been ill-advised. In the spring of 1935, just a week before his sixty-eighth birthday, he sold his Peoli home for $6,400, a sum that was $600 less than he had paid for it in 1904. "Somehow, after she died I didn't want to live there any more," he later said.[19] Then he traveled to Augusta, Georgia, to begin working out with a group of retired baseball players who proposed to make money by touring the country and playing exhibition games for ticket-purchasing fans. Young was, of course, too old to play hard, but he was to pitch one inning in each game as an enticement to spectators. This hare-brained scheme foundered almost immediately. And when it did, Young did not even have all the proceeds from the sale of his farm to fall back on because, before returning to Tuscarawas County in June of 1935, he had already used much of it to provide food and transportation for the baseball veterans he was touring with. His only significant remaining asset was the stock in Cuyahoga Savings and Loan, worth about $9,000.

Young was, of course, a generous man. But his readiness to assist his fellow veterans, even at the cost of his own meager wealth, suggests that he may have felt some responsibility for their predicament since, as the only former star in the group, he was to be a magnet for money. On his return to Tuscarawas County Cy Young explained his actions by noting that "I was alone and footloose. . . . It was a good chance to see the country down south—sort of an outing." He was determined to discredit rumors that he now was impoverished. "Don't you go saying," he declared, "Cy Young needs charity."[20] The stance was characteristic. But proud as his claim might ring, his return to the county found him without a home, working as a clerk in a retail store in Newcomerstown and, when he could no longer afford accommodations in a local hotel, living with a local couple, John and Ruth Benedum. His only regular income, in the amount of about $450 per year, came from stock dividends.[21] Still, even if Cy Young's days of financial independence were over, the invitation to join the Benedums closed a brief unhappy period in Cy Young's life and allowed him slowly to recover his moorings.

The Benedums had lived with the Youngs in the early 1930s and perhaps earlier. John Benedum was a foreman for the state highway department. Ruth Benedum had attended Robba Young during her years of illness. About the time that Cy Young sold his house, the Benedums moved into a large farmhouse a quarter mile farther out of town. They were much younger than the Youngs: in the fall of 1935, roughly when Cy Young moved in with them, Ruth gave birth to a daughter named Jane. Cy Young earned his keep by doing chores on the Benedum farm.[22] After a few years he added child care to his responsibilities, and the relationship between the man in his seventies and the girl in grade school blossomed into such a remarkable friendship that John Benedum later hypothesized that Jane came to serve as the daughter Cy Young had lost in 1907. Although Young's new living arrangements were attractive, it took him several years to accept their full implications. In 1938, he accepted the assistant managership of Putnam's Hotel in Boston, experimenting with independent life in the city that had feted him in his glory days.[23] But he soon discovered that the Hub held little enchantment for a man of rural tastes who was entering his eighth decade: he returned to Newcomerstown in the fall of that year and for the rest of his life made his home with the Benedums.

And his life again became a good and ordered one. Outdoor work on the Benedum farm helped to keep him healthy: "I'm still in good shape," he happily reported at the age of seventy-six.[24] When not working, he spent much of his time in Newcomerstown, sometimes wandering about and talking with acquaintances but often drinking whiskey in the convivial all-male environment of the Elks club. In 1937 the Ohio legislature named him an assistant sergeant-at-arms, a duty that required minimal time and effort and brought in some additional income.[25] Curious young reporters sought him out in his new Peoli home to listen to his anecdotes and commentary; old players sometimes dropped by too, including Tris Speaker and Joe Bush. He began to move back into the wider world of baseball. Early in 1938, for example, he joined Rogers Hornsby on the instructional staff of the Al Doan baseball school in Hot Springs. His return to the Arkansas town after an absence of thirty years was triumphantly celebrated (with a parade and a key to the city), and he was saluted for his loyalty to the spa and thanked for bringing national attention to the therapeutic value of the town's thermal waters.[26] When passing quieter time in Ohio he discovered, like many other fans, that radio was a medium made for baseball, and he listened regularly to games from Cleveland, Pittsburgh, or Cincinnati. He was often invited to attend major league games and was invariably treated with honor by the host club. When Cincinnati's Johnny Vander Meer, having pitched back-to-back no-hitters, sought to surpass Young's record for consecutive hitless innings in 1938, the record-holder was present to watch the young Red pitcher fall short. Meanwhile, his round of non-playing appearances at old-timers' games took him as far afield as Detroit and New York, where he delighted in sharing observations and memories with veterans from his own days while fascinating the younger generation of players and fans with his tales.

And to top it all off, the late 1930s witnessed Cy Young's election and induction into the Hall of Fame.

The plan to create a commemorative museum for baseball was determinatively influenced by bad history. The Mills Report of 1908 had concluded—with no basis—that baseball had been invented in 1839 at Cooperstown, New York. Despite its flaws, the report received the imprimatur of organized baseball, whose leaders were eager to confirm that America's game had authentically and exclusively American origins. If one accepted the Mills date, then by the early 1930s the centennial year of baseball was approaching, and calling for some sort of celebration. If one accepted the Mills site, then the location for the central celebratory event seemed obvious. And so, to honor the outstanding figures in baseball history, organizers set about to build a Hall of Fame that would be ready to receive visitors by 1939. As the construction project moved ahead, so too did plans for identifying the honorees. Two groups of baseball writers were polled to choose the initial members of the Hall, one group having special responsibility for old-timers, and in 1936 the first class was announced: Ty Cobb, Walter Johnson, Christy Mathewson, Babe Ruth, and Honus Wagner. The following year the second class was chosen. Its three members—all, coincidentally, associated with Cleveland—were Larry Lajoie, Tris Speaker, and Cy Young. (If it seems odd that the winningest pitcher of all time failed to qualify in the first vote, the difficulty may have rested with the voting procedures. The organizers neglected to specify how "old-timer" was to be defined, and while Cy Young did well in both polls in 1936—and was the only veteran who did—he also fell well short of the requisite 75 percent in both elections.) The outcomes of two additional elections in 1938 and 1939 brought Grover Cleveland Alexander, Eddie Collins, Willie Keeler, and George Sisler forward to complete the roster of the twelve charter inductees.[27] Keeler and Mathewson were dead, but Cy Young and the others gathered in Cooperstown on June 12, 1939, for the official opening of the hall.

Preparations for the big day had occasionally been slipshod, as evidenced by the scroll that identified the honorees. To Cy Young's considerable amusement, it gave "Tecumseh" instead of "True" as his middle name, an error arising from a researcher's failure to recognize as a sobriquet the nickname given to Young by his Boston teammates at the opening of the century (he was the "chief" of the team) and then widely adopted by the Boston press. But there were other sights at Cooperstown that probably warmed Young's heart, including several items—a baseball, a bat, a uniform, a painting of himself (by Abbot Thayer of New Hampshire), and some photographs—that he had already donated to the hall. Of all the greats who were importuned to contribute memorabilia to the new museum, Cy Young was the first and easily the most cooperative donor.[28] Of course, since he had neither wife nor children, he had less reason than many of his colleagues to retain the souvenirs of his career. Still, the gift bespoke his characteristic helpfulness.

In the formal ceremony that launched the enterprise each honoree took his turn in stepping out through the front door of the hall to deliver brief remarks. Introduced as "the old grand daddy of them all," Cy Young was the fifth to came forward. "Folks," he began, "I'm like the other boys that preceded me." He then continued:

> I glad to be here today—the quirkiness of his language is re-corded in the transcript—in honor of this sanctuary, this Hall of Fame, that I was able to go though 22-odd years and do what I did and to have my name on the records. I'm very glad to be here nothing pleases me better then to be about and see and know that the young generation today is following our footsteps going along throughout our land. One of the greatest games on earth, I don't think and I do hope and wish that 100 years from now the game will still be greater. I thank you very much.[29]

Of the various speakers that day only Eddie Collins and Babe Ruth managed to rise much above stammers in their remarks, and Ruth was kind enough to mention "my old friend Cy Young" in associating himself with the hope that baseball would endure for another century. But parsing the remarks of inarticulate men whose greatness resides in physical exploits is beside the point, except perhaps as a reminder that good speaking skills were not a requisite for the game's early heroes. Deep and sincere gratitude was the common thread that ran through the remarks of all the honorees that day.

Induction into the Hall of Fame certified Cy Young as one of baseball's "immortals"—as the twelve were often called—and meant that his views on baseball's past and present received considerable attention. He was frequently sought out for interviews and invited to speak at clubs and dinners. Like most people who are asked to respond to the same small set of questions at each public appearance, Young honed a repertory of anecdotes and responses. The most common question was, who was the best hitter you played against? Quite consistently Young mentioned four men and gave pride of place to Ty Cobb, whose abilities to bunt, to hit to all fields, and to outguess the pitcher elevated him above Willie Keeler,

Larry Lajoie, and Honus Wagner. "Cobb was," he said directly, "the great-est batter I ever pitched to."[30]

On at least two occasions he offered his all-time line-ups. In both cases the outfield consisted of Ty Cobb, Babe Ruth, and Tris Speaker, and the left side of the infield featured Jimmy Collins and Honus Wagner. But he shifted from Cap Anson to Lou Gehrig at first base and from Larry Lajoie to Eddie Collins at second base, and for the position of catcher he changed from a tie among Bill Dickey, Lou Criger, and Chief Zimmer (there's loy-alty for you) to the single selection of Roger Bresnahan, an odd choice since he scarcely ever saw his work. Walter Johnson, Rube Waddell, and Ed Walsh made both his pitching staffs, but on his earlier team he filled out a four-man complement with Addie Joss, while on his later team he installed Grover Cleveland Alexander and himself as part of a five-man staff. Aside from Christy Mathewson, notable omissions include Jesse Burkett, Kid Nichols, and Amos Rusie. But even in his playing days Young believed that the quality of baseball players was steadily improv-ing, and his dismissal of the best of the 1890s probably reflects that judg-ment.[31] In fact, in a 1947 letter to Robert Smith, Young used stunningly faint praise to damn Burkett and Hugh Duffy (who had batted .440 in 1894); they were, he allowed, "better than the average."[32]

As an observer of the current game, Cy Young was no captive of ro-manticized nostalgia. His comparison of pitching in the present and the past was quite sober. He noted that pitchers in his day had been expected to work more frequently and to pitch more innings than the pitchers of the 1930s and 1940s. And he added that their travel and living accommo-dations had been wretched. But he also noted that pitchers in his day had enjoyed the benefits of a larger strike zone, doctored baseballs, and more distant outfield fences to cushion their mistakes. On one occasion he even said that modern pitchers, unfairly disadvantaged by the purported liveli-ness of the ball, could only "pitch and pray."[33] Although he regretted that salaries had been low in his day, he expressed no resentment—except in the instances of players "more interested in their salaries than in the condition of their bodies"—that current stars could command far higher paychecks than he ever did.[34] He even approved of night baseball, though in moderation.[35] On the stars of the 1930s and 1940s he was common-sensical. When asked how he would pitch to Joe Dimaggio, he replied, "Young man, I don't know," explaining that he had seen him only from the stands, not the pitcher's box. "I'd have to do that to be able to answer your question."[36] When asked in March of 1947 how Ted Williams would do in the coming season, he posed a cagey counterquestion: "What did he do in the [1946] World Series?"[37] Among the hurlers whom he admired, Carl Hubbell ("a great pitcher, a very great pitcher"), Johnny Sain ("he's a lot like some of us old-timers"), and Bob Feller ("the best pitcher I've seen among the modern boys") won particular praise.[38] Young accepted that the game he had excelled at was changing. "It's all a natural evolution of the sport," he told writer Hy Turkin in 1945, "and it's been healthy progress."[39]

When talking about himself, Cy Young was unostentatiously proud about his career. In 1938, for example, when a youngster asked him if he had really been a major league pitcher, he replied—smiling, I presume—"Yes, son. And I hope you won't mind if I put it this way. I probably won more big league games than you'll ever see."[40] But the passage of time had rendered his memory increasingly inaccurate about the facts that defined that career. Of the runaway 1903 pennant race he once said "we went right down to the wire to do it."[41] On one occasion when he reminisced about his perfect game, he said that Frank Chance rather than Candy LaChance was his first baseman; on another occasion he described the final out of the game, which had been a lofty outfield fly by Rube Waddell, as "a sizzler, but right at an infielder"; on yet another occasion he attributed his success in the game—remember: he had led the league in victories for three straight years—to the fact that "the American League was pretty young then, and the hitters didn't know what I had."[42] Though he took pride in his twenty-inning duel with Rube Waddell the next year, in one interview Young mistakenly placed Waddell on the Red Sox.[43] Young himself was the source of the oft-cited "fact" that in "my last big league game I was beaten 1–0 by a kid named Grover Cleveland Alexander"; in truth, Young started six more games after this great outing.[44] I think it's fair to treat these misstatements as ingratiating hints of Young's effort to make sense of his past, and we can probably write their factual inadequacies off to the memory problems that bedevil us all as we get older. After all, anybody who took pleasure in discussing games he had lost—and both the second Waddell game and the Alexander game so qualified—wasn't primarily concerned with deceiving. In fact, Young's commentary on the baseball scene sometimes tended to the wry; when Cleveland celebrated Mel Harder's two hundredth career victory with a party, Cy Young won honors for the best remark of the evening when, after noting that he had not been feted for his two hundredth, three hundredth, four hundredth, or five hundredth victory, he said, "I guess those weren't party-giving times."[45]

Cy Young experienced many memorable birthday celebrations during his lifetime. In his later playing days his teammates had regularly taken time off from spring training to honor him, and in his old age the annual milestone again captured attention. On his seventy-fifth birthday, for example, he received cards from all across the country, an outpouring triggered by editorial encouragement from the *Sporting News*. "They've all made me very happy," he declared on that occasion.[46] But none of the celebrations matched the festivities associated with his eightieth birthday in 1947. The plans began when the civic leaders in Newcomerstown decided to turn the day into a grand honoring of the town's most famous citizen.[47] Then Bill Veeck, owner of the Cleveland Indians, decided to stage a dramatic show of gratitude for Cy Young's work by inviting all of Newcomerstown to an Indians game.

The town's birthday party was held on March 29, 1947. Young himself had signed more than 1,000 programs that were distributed on the occasion, and most of the town turned out for the celebration.[48] Friends spoke warmly about their valued neighbor; Governor Thomas Herbert brought congratulations from the state; two baseball friends from the 1890s, Jack Darrah and George Westlake, shared thoughts with the honoree about the past; Waite Hoyt and Sam Jones represented a more recent generation of veterans; Connie Mack sent greetings and a check; Bill Veeck was on hand to extend the invitation to the town and to muse about "how we [the Indians] could use another pitcher like him now";[49] and his neighbors in Newcomerstown awarded the veteran a cream-colored Kaiser sedan. Aside from an apt riposte when asked if he wanted to cut the cake— "Give me an axe, and I will"—Young had little to say throughout the ceremonies.[50] But accounts report that he wept.

The trip to Cleveland took place on Wednesday, June 11. Almost every business in Newcomerstown closed; a train hired by Bill Veeck transported roughly a thousand residents north to Cleveland, while perhaps another thirty-five hundred people traveled by car. In the presence of such old teammates as Bill Bradley, Elmer Flick, and Jack Graney, Cy Young was given a set of luggage, a car heater, and a car radio. Only Bob Feller's 3–0 loss marred the day.

A few days after his eightieth birthday, Cy Young replied to a letter of greetings from his childhood friend Grant Kramer. "All I can tell you about myself," he wrote, "is that I am well and hearty at 80. Can still do a fair days work."[51] The description was reasonably accurate, but early on in his ninth decade Cy Young began to decline. His weight had long since dropped from the levels of his playing days, and between 1942 and 1956 it slipped further, from 178 to 150 pounds.[52] As his legs stiffened and weakened, he relied more and more on his cane. As his eyes faltered, he came increasingly to depend on his eyeglasses and his magnifying glass to follow the sports pages and on Jane Benedum to read his correspondence for him. He abandoned the habit of rising early, preferring now to stay in bed until about 8:00 A.M. He also gave up driving his car. He still worked outdoors, still hunted, still played with his beloved dogs, still walked the knobby hills of Tuscarawas County. When feeling crotchety, he would describe his beloved collie Judy as "smarter than some people."[53] But more and more he found pleasure in such sedentary activities as card-playing, television-watching, and porch-sitting. His memberships in the Masons, the Shriners, the Elks, the Eagles, the Moose, the Rotary, and the Lions gave him lots of opportunities for male camaraderie and pool-hall afternoons. Between his pipe and his chewing tobacco, he had the leaf near his mouth most of the day. He also took to drinking somewhat more heavily as he aged.[54] And he thought about Robba. "From up there on the [Benedum] porch," he told one reporter wistfully, "I can look down on the little churchyard where Bobby is buried."[55] One person who knew him in his old age recalls him as essentially a "gentle" man.

Early in 1950 he became seriously ill for the first time in his life, spending two weeks in the hospital with hepatitis. "I think I got cards and letters from people in about every state," he happily reported.[56] In 1953, declaring that "I don't feel quite up to it," he declined an invitation to dine with President Dwight Eisenhower, even though Ike was the first Republican to live in the White House since the days when Robba was alive.[57] Though another person recalled him as "grumpy," it appears that he did not suffer from depression in his final years. The letters kept flowing in, as new fans and old sought to make contact with the winningest pitcher of all time. He tried to answer them all, though as he grew older Jane Benedum composed many of the replies, leaving them for Young to sign. When Jane turned fourteen she also served as his chauffeur on shorter trips. She was still too young to have a driver's license, but the authorities gave her a special license for local excursions.

Toward its close, Cy Young's life had a number of good moments. In recognition of the flow of mail that he received, the United States Post

Office decided that it would keep the tiny Peoli station open. New friendships developed, including a correspondence with Lefty Grove. In April 1950 he was interviewed on NBC's *We, the People,* and in September 1952 he traveled to Chicago with Jane Benedum to appear on *Ask Me Another,* a televised game show featuring sports celebrities.[58] In 1951 he represented the Cleveland Naps when Addie Joss was posthumously inducted into the Wisconsin Sports Hall of Fame. Throughout his life Cy Young had enjoyed coaching young boys, and he began supporting the developing Little League movement after 1949. In succeeding years he traveled throughout Ohio to throw out first pitches at Little League games, and he sometimes visited Williamsport, Pennsylvania, for the Little League World Series. In recognition of his contributions to the Little League, in 1953 he was made a lifetime member of the organization. And throughout his final years Cy Young remained a hero at home. On May 28, 1950, with three thousand people present, Newcomerstown dedicated its handsome new recreational area as the "Cy Young Park." The honoree was "visibly affected by the tribute."[59]

His best moments, however, may have come when he participated in events that brought him back together with his former ball-playing colleagues. Always a fan favorite, he appeared at Yankee Stadium events in 1947 and 1953 to raise money for the Babe Ruth Foundation and to commemorate the fiftieth anniversary of the first World Series, and a 1955 dedication at Pittsburgh's Forbes Field of a statue of Honus Wagner. He attended anniversary celebrations of both the National League (its seventy-fifth) and the American League (its fiftieth) in 1951. He traveled to Cooperstown as often as possible for the annual induction ceremonies. These various reunions of old-timers offered no compensation—"you'd think they could give an old fella $75 or so," he once quipped—but they afforded him the chance to renew acquaintances with friends from a half century earlier.[60] And a visit to Cleveland's Municipal Stadium in April 1954 offered posterity a grand trophy: the evocative photograph of an eighty-seven-year-old Young leaning against his walking stick in the shadows of the vastest ballpark in baseball, his back to the camera, peering out at young men who were preparing to play the game he had once been master of.

In the spring of 1955, after returning from the celebration for Honus Wagner in Pittsburgh, Cy Young began to complain of occasional chest discomfort. His physician soon ventured the diagnosis of arteriosclerosis. Young resisted allowing the problem to change his pattern of life—he remained to the end a heavy eater, with a fondness for buckwheat cakes and sausage—and in particular he made a point of attending the midsummer Hall of Fame induction ceremonies and the Little League World Series. But as Ruth Benedum later said, by the fall he was "just gradually slipping."[61] On Thursday, November 3, he felt so ill that a doctor visited the Benedum house and arranged for an ambulance to take Young to the hospital for tests the next day. Young ate supper that evening and soon retired. He awoke during the night, however, with the fixed conviction that he was soon going to die. He roused Ruth Benedum to go through with her again and again the arrangements for what was to be done after his death. The two talked until the sun rose on November 4, and then Ruth Benedum prepared him a big breakfast. He could not, however, hold it down. Restless, he moved to the kitchen door, stood taking in what would be his last look at the Tuscarawas hill country, returned to his rocking chair, and quietly died just as the ambulance pulled into the Benedum driveway.[62] The death certificate cited "coronary occlusion" as the cause of death.[63] His place of death was five miles away from his place of birth.

Cy Young's body was on view at a local funeral home over the weekend and visited by close to two thousand people. Both the Masons and the Elks conducted services for their deceased member. The formal funeral was held on Monday, November 7, at the small Methodist Church in Peoli. It was presided over by George Shurtz, a local-area clergyman who was an old friend of Young's. Although as a young man Young had been so respectful of religious convention that his contract had specified that he need not play on the Sabbath, he later became more relaxed about his habits of worship, attending services infrequently. He had not, however, abandoned the faith he had been raised in. According to Jane Benedum, "Cy had everything ready between him and his Master."[64] Among those who attended the funeral were Tris Speaker, Sam Jones, Steve O'Neill, Billy Southworth, Cy Young's very old friend George Westlake, and his much more recent friend Bob Feller. Shurtz praised Young for his character ("staunch as the hills that surround him and sturdy as the oaks he walked under") and his ability (he "synchronized his arm, eyes, and heart not only to enshrine his name in the Hall of Fame, but in the hearts of his fellow men."). After the service he was buried next to Robba in the cemetery adjacent to the church. A monument featuring a baseball marks the spot today.[65]

Cy Young's estate consisted basically of 135 shares of Cuyahoga Savings and Loan stock, ultimately sold for $20,000. In accordance with his will, drafted in 1950, this estate was divided equally among the three Benedums.[66] This allocation meant that neither of Young's surviving siblings, Alonzo Young or Ella Ripley, would benefit financially from his death. Ripley was sufficiently exercised by Young's ignoring of his blood relatives that she challenged the document in court. She was, however, in ill health and in a nursing home when she undertook her campaign, and when she died, her case lost force. In April 1957 the three Benedums were declared heirs, and the distribution occurred promptly thereafter.

Meanwhile, as word of Cy Young's passing spread across the country, the baseball world took prompt note. Ed Walsh spoke for many when he called him "the greatest pitcher of all times." Elmer Flick linked him with Kid Nichols as one of the two "greatest pitchers I ever saw." Larry Lajoie called him "one of the greatest old men in baseball." Ty Cobb described him as "a wonderful guy." George Trautmann, the President of the Minor Leagues, called him "the greatest of the great." Tris Speaker credited his own career to the fact that back in 1907 a forty-year-old legend "took an interest in me." In the *Sporting News* Fred Lieb placed him among "the immortals of baseball" and predicted that his total of 511 lifetime wins "probably will remain the all-time high."[67] But the fullest honor of all came the following year when, on the recommendation of Ford Frick, Commissioner of Baseball, Cy Young's name was attached to the new award that would be given annually to the best pitcher in baseball.

And that raises the key question: Was the award aptly named? Was Cy Young, in Ed Walsh's words, the greatest pitcher of all times?

The question is interesting because, owing to the linkage between his name and the award, lots of people today (including many players unschooled in baseball history and unaware of names like Charley Radbourn, Kid Nichols, and Lefty Grove) quite naturally regard him as the best ever. In that sense, his name has acquired the aura that still attaches to Babe Ruth's. But when the award was founded, there was talk of naming it after Walter Johnson, Christy Mathewson, or Grover Cleveland Alexander. Cy Young's name was finally chosen not because he was widely regarded as superior to the others but because only one player was to be honored each year and, of the four possibilities, only Cy Young had been a hero in both leagues.[68] Thus, Cy Young received his enduring fame essentially as a consequence of a quirk in his career. Had the initial plan for the award encompassed a winner in each league (which has been the practice since 1967), three significant results would likely have fol-

lowed. First, we would now be marveling at the number of Christy Ma-
thewsons garnered by Greg Maddux and the number of Walter Johnsons
won by Roger Clemens. Second, a major question for sportswriters would
be, which of those two brilliant old-timers was, of all the hurlers who
have ever toiled, the greatest? Third, Cy Young would be regarded as one
of those quasi-mythical giants from baseball's prehistoric days, clearly a
worthy but chiefly a relic from the era before the modern dispensation.

For those who believe that Cy Young was the greatest of all pitchers
there is one central fact to point to—Cy Young won 511 games during
his major league career, easily the highest total of all.[69] Even segments of
that total are impressive. He won 290 games in the National League and
221 in the American League; he won 285 at home and 226 on the road;
he won 195 in his twenties, 241 in his thirties, and 75 in his forties. Since
winning games is what baseball is all about, the person who wins the
most is clearly the best. Q.E.D. If in retort someone says—and the point
would have merit—that victory totals are an imperfect statistic for mea-
suring a pitcher's ability since they reflect in part the ability of the team
he hurled for, then the Cy Young supporter is apt to reply by referring
to a statistic that most fans have never heard of: wins above team
(WAT).[70] That Cy Young was better than his teams has, of course, long
been known; across his career his clubs won 62 percent of their games
when he was the pitcher of record and only 49 percent when anyone else
earned the decision. WAT is a statistic designed to quantify the number
of wins that a pitcher garners during a career above the figure one would
expect for an average hurler on that pitcher's team(s). (To avoid a common misunderstanding, I need to add that while only a pitcher who has
a long career can hope to achieve a high number, lengthy tenure is not
sufficient to assure a high WAT since below-average seasons generate
negative numbers.) Here too Cy Young has the highest career total of all:
99.7. For purposes of comparison Walter Johnson is credited with 90.0
(he's second), and among more recent pitchers with completed careers we
find Tom Seaver at 58.9, Warren Spahn at 45.8, and Steve Carlton at 33.5.
So the case for Cy Young's designation as the greatest of all pitchers can
readily rest on the one or both variations of the contention that he won
more games for his clubs than anyone else.

Two objections to that conclusion have been advanced. The first is
based on the fact that, by and large, observers who had the benefit of
watching Cy Young play did not think he was even the best pitcher of his
own day. And if he was not as good as, say, Kid Nichols or Amos Rusie

or Christy Mathewson or Walter Johnson, how could he be the best of all time? John McGraw, for example, named all-time pitching staffs at least twice. In 1911 he placed Three-Finger Brown, John Clarkson, Christy Mathewson, Nap Rucker, and Amos Rusie on the team; in 1923 he selected Clarkson, Walter Johnson, Addie Joss, Mathewson, Sadie McMahon, and Rube Waddell. Larry Lajoie, when asked to rank the pitchers he had faced, chose Johnson as the best and Young as fifteenth.[71] Charles Comiskey named five pitchers as the best ever: Bob Caruthers, Clark Griffith, Christy Mathewson, Charley Radbourn, and Ed Walsh. The *Sporting News* chose Kid Nichols as the best pitcher of the 1890s. Teammates from Young's prime often failed to rank him first: George Cuppy said Bill Hutchison and Rusie were the best; Ed McKean and Jack O'Connor nominated Rusie; Jimmy McAleer picked Johnson; Chief Zimmer—even Chief Zimmer—preferred Clarkson. Not everyone from this era slighted Young. Jimmy Collins placed him on a six-man staff, along with Jack Chesbro, Bill Dinneen, Addie Joss, Walter Johnson, and Ed Walsh. Joss allowed as how Young might be the best. And both Dinneen and Griffith declared unequivocally that Young was best of all.[72] But the pattern is clear: most of those who knew his work best and were qualified to judge it thought him very good but not the greatest.

Other measurements make similar points. Though his career was longer than Grover Cleveland Alexander's, Walter Johnson's, or Christy Mathewson's, he threw fewer shutouts than they. Though celebrated as a control pitcher, he walked batters more frequently than Babe Adams, Deacon Phillippe, or Addie Joss. He stands nowhere near the best in lifetime success at holding opponents to a low batting average, nowhere near the best in keeping runners off the bases, nowhere near the best in lifetime earned run average, nowhere near the best in lifetime winning percentage.[73]

Quite clearly, then, what made Cy Young unique—the "best," if this is how we choose to measure and define that term—was his capacity to be very good over a long period of time. Although he pitched for twenty-two years, only rarely was he the best hurler in a single season. One estimate, for example, suggests that he would have won the award that later bore his name only four times: in 1892, 1901, 1902, and 1903.[74] Not bad, but not outstanding either, considering that he spent twenty-two years in the majors. Only once—the period covered by the peculiar seasons of 1901 and 1902—was he clearly the best pitcher in baseball for as much as a two-year span. He was not the winningest major league pitcher during the first half of his career; Kid Nichols was. He was not the win-ningest major league pitcher during the second half of his career; Christy Mathewson was. And while he won more games than any other pitcher during the central decade of his career (1896–1905), in only two of those seasons did he top his league in victories. In head-to-head match-ups against contemporary mound stars he was not notably successful. Against Nichols he won 8 and lost 10; against Rube Waddell he won 6 and lost 7. And so, to summarize the point, if contemporaries did not think him the best in his own day, how can we possibly regard him as the best of all time?

The second line of objection is grounded in the contention that the quality of players has risen dramatically since Young's day. According to this argument, players who were great eighty years ago would only be pretty good (or maybe worse) today. It might of course be asked, since head-to-head match-ups between players from widely separated genera-tions are impossible, where the claim about the steady improvement of quality comes from. In part it is based on analogy. Virtually everyone agrees that the best basketball and football players of today are distinctly superior to the best of fifty years ago. Why should not the same conclu-sion hold for baseball? And in part it is based on inferences drawn from demography. The pool of talent is more extensive today than it was in Cy Young's time, not only because the country itself is far more populous but also because African Americans were excluded from the majors in his day and players of foreign birth (except for persons born in the United Kingdom) rarely seen. With a significantly larger pool to draw from, it may be inferred that the quality of those who now make it to the top is distinctly superior.

I believe that there are problems with pressing either of these argu-ments about the inevitability of improvement too far. Let's consider the first contention. The analogy with football and basketball is doubly im-perfect; first, because the motor skills that define baseball ability are more multifaceted than those required in the other two sports and therefore less readily honed and sharpened through simple refinements in train-ing routines; and second, because sheer bulking up, though often helpful to football and basketball players, is advantageous only to a few baseball players. As to the second contention, any argument grounded in the ex-pansion of the raw demographic pool must also take into account the fact that football, basketball, tennis, golf, and perhaps even soccer and hockey are now attractive rivals to baseball, capable of pulling athletically gifted young men into alternative sports careers. Which is not to say that I reject these arguments entirely. Rather I'm inclined to believe that the qualifying threshold for admission to the major leagues has been raised, which implies that the journeymen of ninety years ago would probably have trouble making a major league roster today. But that stipulation has no consequences for the small set of players who were the giants of baseball a century ago. These stars—Ty Cobb, Willie Keeler, Tris Speaker, Larry Lajoie, Honus Wagner, Walter Johnson, Kid Nichols, and of course Cy Young—would still shine if, by some miracle, they could be resurrected in our own age.

Two considerations oblige us to treat Young's career with enormous respect. First, there is the sheer cumulative weight of the effort he turned in. Not only did he win more games than anyone else, he compiled more innings pitched than any other hurler (7,356⅔ innings). This total exceeds by 24 percent the figure of his closest challenger, Pud Galvin (5,941⅓). That's a wider percentage gap than his 511 victories represents over Walter Johnson's 417 and is probably an even more unsurpassable figure than his victory total. There is also the quality of his performance in what for many players are called the over-the-hill years. He still holds the record for the most victories by a man aged thirty-four (33), aged thirty-five (32) aged thirty-six (28), aged thirty-seven (26), aged forty (21), and aged forty-one (21). Also, he played against future Hall of Famers from a range of eras. At the opening of his career he won a 7–1 victory from Pud Galvin, who had launched his professional career even before the National League existed. At the close of his career he lost his 1–0 match-up against the young Grover Cleveland Alexander, who lasted in the majors until 1930. He pitched to Cap Anson, who had played in 1871, and to Eddie Collins, who retired after the 1930 season. Although we rightly regard Charley Radbourn, Tim Keefe, and Mickey Welch on the one hand and Walter Johnson, Rube Waddell, and Eddie Plank on the other as representing two very different eras in baseball (and pitching) history, Young dueled with them all. Finally, there is the sheer number of years he was among the best. He first led the league in shutouts in 1892; he won his last shutout title—his seventh (a record he shares with Alexander)—in 1904. And this is even more impressive: his first 20-victory season came in 1891, and his last came seventeen years later, in 1908. That's a record span. In all, he posted fifteen 20-victory seasons, two more than runners-up Christy Mathewson and Warren Spahn. And that does not count the problematic reckoning of the 1900 season. Cy Young was an outstanding pitcher during three full baseball generations.

The second consideration is that Cy Young chalked up his remarkable record of protracted success while coping with a stream of alterations in the way baseball was played. There were changes in the rules, most significantly the great discontinuity of 1893 that lengthened the pitching distance, but also the adoption of the foul strike rule in 1903. There were shifts in the definition of bunts and balks, the emergence of a raised mound for the pitcher, the deepening of pitching staffs, the adoption of fielder's gloves, the evolving concept of scientific baseball. It was because the game was almost constantly in very visible transition that Cy Young labored so hard to add deliveries to his repertory. And it is a mark of his success in making the requisite adjustments that he was a triumphant pitcher both in the year in which major league batting averages reached their all-time high (.309 in 1894) and in the year in which they reached what was their all-time low (.239 in 1908) until the 1968 season snuck in beneath it. In short, Cy Young lasted as long as he did not simply because he was blessed with a tough body and durable arm but also because he used his intelligence to study, adapt, and learn.[75] He was one of the smartest pitchers in baseball history.

So, again, was Cy Young the greatest pitcher of all times? We don't know, of course. There's no way—*pace* all the sabermetricians in the audience—that we can even out all the changes in equipment, in playing rules, in strike zone dimensions, in ground rules, in travel circumstances, in ball parks, in times of play, in pitches, in strategy, in training practices, in coaching assistance, in umpiring, in protection of injured players, in media attention, in roster sizes, in housing circumstances, and in off-season activities that have occurred over the years. And that means that there is no way we can compare the distilled pitching essence of Cy Young to the distilled pitching essences of Walter Johnson, Lefty Grove, Bob Feller, Tom Seaver, or Greg Maddux. Moreover, much depends on how you define "greatest." Are you talking about absolute dominance for a fairly short span of time—peak value, as it is often called? Or are you talking about enduring success over a wide span of years? Or are you perhaps blending these two measures in some unspoken formula? By whatever definition one operates, Cy Young is clearly a candidate for the honor. And the greater the weight you give to the sustaining of excellence over a long period of time, and the more you are willing to assume that a man who had proved himself smart and adaptable in his own day would continue to show those traits in a later era, the stronger Cy Young's candidacy becomes.

APPENDIX ONE

✂

Cy Young's Salary History

At various points in the book I have assigned specific annual salaries to Cy Young. In most cases the figures are guesses, derived from the often inconsistent sports columns of his day. The need to speculate arises from the fact that salary information was not public in Young's time. Baseball writers, to be sure, often spoke as if they knew the true figures. But on that subject John Clarkson provides us with a wise reminder: "When anybody talks about players' salaries he does not know what he is talking about."[1]

Fortunately, we are not totally at sea. For three of Young's playing seasons, his annual contracts have survived.[2] The salary figures they provide are our three baseline numbers: $1,430 for the 1891 season, $4,000 for the 1906 season, and $4,000 again for the 1909 season. (The last of these three contracts was signed with the Boston Red Sox. Although Young was subsequently traded to the Cleveland Naps for the season, the new club was presumably obliged to pay him the sum that the old club had contracted for.) In order to fill in the figures for Young's other nineteen seasons we must rely on contemporary reports in the press and on inferences we can draw from them.

Let's begin at the beginning. Various reports put Young's compensation in 1890, when he came up to the Spiders toward the end of the season, at $75 a month—presumably $150 for the remainder of that year.[3]

For 1891 we have the contract figure of $1,430. (That peculiar additional $30 was probably included as the club's way of absorbing the cost of Young's uniforms, an expense that was ordinarily passed on to the player in this era.) Young performed splendidly in 1891, and if a press account is accurate, the club rewarded his good work by agreeing to provide him "extra compensation" whenever he pitched out of his regular turn in the rotation.[4]

For 1892, I must guess. But we can be confident that Young received another raise, both because he complained about being underpaid 1891 and because Elmer Bates, a sportswriter covering the Spiders, reported that he would get "a handsome increase in salary" for 1892.[5] I think that we will not be far from wrong if we place his salary at about $2,000.

The disappearance of the American Association allowed the National League owners to embrace a policy of salary retrenchment during the 1892 season, and a salary cap of $2,400 per player was imposed. Nevertheless, even in an era of wage reduction Young's ability could not be denied, and because the club's 1893 payroll list inadvertently fell into the hands of Chief Zimmer and was then passed on to the press, it became public that Young's salary rose to $2,300.

In the early months of 1894, Cy Young mounted a rare display of unhappiness at his club's salary offer, and as late as the fourth week of March he still had not signed for the imminent season. The reason for his resistance lay in information (disclosed when Chief Zimmer got his hands on that 1893 payroll list) that John Clarkson, contrary to assurances Young had received from the club, had been paid $200 more than Young the previous year.[6] Young promptly demanded parity with Clarkson. Frank Robison complained that "it's a pretty poor time of year to talk about increasing salaries," but he apparently relented.[7] The precise level of Young's salary in 1894 is unknown, but it is likely that Robison put Young on an equal footing with Clarkson, with both receiving $2,400.

Through the 1898 season Cy Young's nominal salary probably stayed at $2,400. I base this conclusion on the facts that $2,400 remained the stated salary cap for the league, and that in the absence of an alternative circuit, players had no other market in which to sell their skills. In November of 1898 the press reported that no Spider made more than $2,400.[8] It is likely, however, that the club actually paid Cy Young several hundred dollars more in some of these years, since the extending of sub rosa subsidies and gifts to stars was a common practice to keep them happy in an era of intense salary constraint.

When Cy Young and most of his teammates moved to St. Louis for 1899, Young used the opportunity to demand a raise. He was emboldened by the consideration that St. Louis was likely to be more profitable than Cleveland for the cash-strapped Robisons, and by press accounts telling how Kid Nichols had invoked the lengthening of the schedule in 1898 to press successfully for a salary increase well above the cap.[9] A local press account stated that Young received a raise for 1899.[10] I suspect it took him to about $3,000, the figure linked with Nichols' salary for the previous year.[11] Another reason for postulating $3,000 as Young's salary figure for 1899 is that the same amount is cited in a brief biography of Young as his salary for 1900.[12]

Assuming that $3,000 was the correct figure for 1899, it is difficult to believe that Frank Robison would have raised Young's salary in 1900 after his good but not outstanding season, and it is almost as unlikely that he would have reduced it at a time when rumors of a new league were gaining credibility. I am left to conclude that the 1900 salary remained at about $3,000.

Just before the 1901 season Cy Young signed with the new Boston American League club. There are differing reports about the figure he settled for as he headed for Boston, but Ira Smith's determination that the salary was $3,500 seems reasonable. Young's own testimony at the time—"I am getting more money in Boston than Robison gave me"—is evidence of a raise.[13] But in light of his age, it is unlikely that he commanded a salary at Larry Lajoie's or Jimmy Collins's level.

For 1902 Cy Young could expect a significant raise—and he received one. Its level is unknown, but with Bill Dinneen jumping to the Boston Americans for at least $4,800, it seems likely that Young's salary in 1902 stood at $5,000 or above.[14] Since he declared late in the season that his National League salary had been only half his current salary, he may in fact have received as much as $6,000 in 1902.[15] In any case, for the first time in his career he was receiving more compensation than the best-paid players of the late 1880s.

For 1903 through 1905, Cy Young received $6,000 a year, the highest annual salary he ever commanded. I draw the figure from a 1904 article that described him as having a three-year commitment from Boston at that level.[16] There was also a report that he spurned an offer of $5,000 from the Boston Beaneaters.[17]

The salary listed in the 1906 contract brings us back from informed speculation to ascertainable fact: after his disappointing 1905 season, Cy Young accepted a cut to $4,000. That his salary had been reduced was public knowledge, with *Sporting Life* commenting that President Taylor had reduced the salary of every player and that "Criger, Young, and Dinneen had been cut heaviest."[18] It is possible that Young resisted a club effort to impose an even more severe reduction, for according to one account he returned the initial contract proffer with "Not enough" written on it.[19]

Since we know that Cy Young still commanded $4,000 in 1909, it seems reasonable to suppose that his annual salary in the intervening seasons of 1907 and 1908 held steady at $4,000.

For the final two years of Young's career I know of no reported salary figures. That his wages declined by the end seems likely. But we should probably not imagine the decline to have been prompt or precipitous. A press report in 1910 speculated that he was still the highest-paid pitcher in the American League (almost surely not an accurate assertion), a press report from August 1911 used his high salary to explain Cleveland's decision to drop him, and still another from September 1911 claimed that the Boston Nationals were paying him well.[20] I suspect that he may still have received $4,000 in 1910 and that in 1911 he received at least $2,000. After all, Charles Somers owed a great deal to Cy Young.

A chart summarizes my conclusions and guesses about Cy Young's annual compensation:

1890	$ 150
1891	$1,430
1892	$2,000
1893	$2,300
1894	$2,400+
1895	$2,400+
1896	$2,400+
1897	$2,400+
1898	$2,400+
1899	$3,000
1900	$3,000
1901	$3,500
1902	$5,000+
1903	$6,000
1904	$6,000
1905	$6,000
1906	$4,000
1907	$4,000
1908	$4,000
1909	$4,000
1910	$4,000
1911	$2,000

To be fair in this analysis I need to draw attention to two important data that dramatically contradict my conclusions and to explain why I have chosen to ignore them. First, there is the *Sporting Life* report that Cy Young's 1900 contract promised him $4,000.[21] I reject this assertion in favor of my $3,000 figure because to credit it would involve granting him an implausibly large raise for the year and, even more important, remove the financial incentive for his decision to jump to the American League in 1901. Second, there is Young's own later claim that $4,400 or $4,500 was the highest salary he ever received.[22] Despite its source, the claim is implausible because it requires us to believe that Young accepted lower salaries than either Bill Dinneen or Jesse Tannehill could command from the very same man who employed Young.[23] Moreover, since one of these statements came from late in Young's life—and I suspect the undatable one did as well—I see them as reflecting the wobbling memory of an old man.

As Cy Young recognized, he was well paid for his day. From 1894 on, no Spider (except Patsy Tebeau, who also managed) received more money than he (though Jesse Burkett was almost surely paid at an equivalent level). From 1902 on, no Boston player (except player-manager Jimmy Collins) was paid more. Elsewhere in baseball a few players commanded higher salaries. Jack Chesbro and Larry Lajoie, for example, may have received $8,000 as early as 1903; Bobby Wallace reached $6,500 by 1906; Honus Wagner was earning $10,000 by 1908.[24] Surely there were a few others. But Cy Young was near the top, receiving approximately the honor he was due—for his day.

And what about our own day? A scholarly study of 1992 suggested that were Cy Young around in the 1990s, he would command an annual salary of about $9,500,000.[25]

Cy Young's Greatest Games

Lists like this one are intensely subjective. I've enjoyed trying to identify Cy Young's finest efforts, and I thought the reader would enjoy knowing my choices for the greatest outings of a great career. I've selected a baker's dozen because, having picked my own twelve, I felt I could not ignore Young's own sense of the matter. See number 13. Positions in the ranking are themselves somewhat arbitrary. The call on number 1, of course, strikes me as easy. How could anyone disagree? And I'm sure that number 2 was better than number 10. But is number 5 really better than number 6? Or number 4 better than number 7? Those are tougher calls. I hope the reader will have fun second-guessing me.

Number 1:   May 5, 1904   Boston 3, Philadelphia 0   9 innings
This is Cy Young's perfect game. He later said that from his very first pitch that day he knew he'd be able to put the ball where he wanted it. His mound opponent was Rube Waddell, and the Philadelphia Athletics were a formidable team. But Young tamed them, fanning 8. This was the first perfect game in American League history and the first in the majors since the pivot distance had been moved back to 60 and 6 in 1893.

Number 2:   June 30, 1908   Boston 8, New York 0   9 innings
Has a pitcher in his forties ever hurled a better game? Cy Young walked the first Highlander to face him, Lou Criger promptly gunned him down, and Young meanwhile retired the next 26 batters in order, crafting the third no-hitter of his career. A master of wiliness in his last years, Young struck out only 2. This game made Young the toast of the baseball nation.

Number 3:   September 18, 1897   Cleveland 6, Cincinnati 0   9 innings
Critics carped that Cy Young got a break from the official scorer on a ball

that Bobby Wallace threw away. Others, however, disagreed, and Wallace himself declared the error call to have been correct. In any case, Young's first no-hit effort—also the first by anyone in four years in the major league—was a brilliant accomplishment against a fine Cincinnati team.

Number 4:   October 17, 1892   Cleveland 0, Boston 0   11 innings
The playoff plans for the split season pitted the winners of the first half (Boston) against the winners of the second half (Cleveland). Boasting 71 victories between them, Cy Young and Jack Stivetts dueled brilliantly in the opening encounter until darkness ended a scoreless game. Young yielded only 4 hits to one of the great dynasty teams of the nineteenth century. The game quickly earned celebrity as one of baseball's all-time great pitching duels.

Number 5:   May 11, 1904   Boston 1, Detroit 0   15 innings
Has a major league pitcher ever been sharper? (See the date of number 1 above.) In his first appearance on the mound since his perfect game, Cy Young held Detroit scoreless for 13 innings, yielding only 5 hits (though walking an unusually high number of 4). He collected 3 hits himself and fielded brilliantly. When in the seventh inning Detroit made its first hit, Young's unparalleled string of 24 consecutive hitless innings finally ended.

Number 6:   July 23, 1896   Cleveland 2, Philadelphia 0   9 innings
Only a clean single by Ed Delahanty with 2 out in the ninth inning prevented Cy Young from spinning his first no-hitter in this game. As it was, he had to settle for a splendid one-hit shutout. He walked but 1, struck out 3, and pitched the best game of the year in the National League.

Number 7:   May 30, 1908   Boston 6, Washington 0   9 innings
Throughout his career Cy Young had Washington's number, perhaps not surprisingly, since the Senators were almost perennially among the majors' worst teams. The 1908 version of the Senators was quite typically punchless. Still, a one-hitter is a one-hitter. Striking out 7 and walking none, Young was serving springtime notice that age had not withered the craftsman's abilities.

Number 8:   October 8, 1904   Boston 1, New York 0   7 innings
Though shortened by darkness, this was a magnificent effort—the third and last of three consecutive shutouts that Cy Young pitched at the end

of the 1904 season as he led Boston in its tight pennant race with New York. Relying more on guile than speed, Young walked none and kept Boston's chief rival scoreless in a game that put Boston one and a half games in front of New York rather than half a game behind.

Number 9:   July 4, 1905   Philadelphia 4, Boston 2   20 innings
Even a losing effort can be a great game. This is the second of the trio of Cy Young's epic battles with Rube Waddell that is on this list; at its time it was the longest game in American League history. Young walked no one and struck out 9. Two errors—one by Young himself—helped Philadelphia score 2 unearned runs in the top of the twentieth inning to win. Waddell celebrated the victory by doing flip-flops as he left the field.

Number 10:   September 9, 1907   Boston 0, Philadelphia 0   13 innings
Here is the third game in the Young-Waddell rivalry to make the list. For 13 innings the two masters tossed goose eggs. Cy Young had good stuff, giving up only 6 hits while striking out 8 before darkness brought the game to a close. If Christy Mathewson and Three-Finger Brown supplied the most celebrated pitching duels in the National League in these years, Young and Waddell provided the equivalent service to the junior circuit.

Number 11:   July 1, 1903   Boston 1, Chicago 0   10 innings
On several occasions during his career Cy Young found a groove of compelling excellence that endured over several remarkable starts. This game capped the 1903 version of that groove, being the last of four consecutive shutouts and also the final game of a still unequaled string of three consecutive 1–0 victories. Young yielded 6 hits and struck out only 1 batter, but he walked none.

Number 12:   July 16, 1895   Cleveland 1, Baltimore 0   9 innings
In 1895 Baltimore batted at a .324 pace and won the pennant. In this game, Cy Young became the first pitcher of the season to hold the mighty Orioles scoreless. He allowed only 4 hits while giving Baltimore a foretaste of what awaited them in the Temple Cup competition in October.

Number 13:   June 24, 1892   Cleveland 3, St. Louis 3   16 innings
In 1904 Young identified this game as one of the three most memorable games he had pitched.[1] I find the judgment odd but feel that I can't ignore

it. Not wanting to dislodge any of my own favorite dozen, I am taking the easy way out—expanding the list to a baker's dozen. Moreover, this duel with Ted Breitenstein just might belong on its own. After all, Young gave up only 5 hits in 16 innings, and 2 of St. Louis' 3 runs were unearned.

511 Wins?

Strange as it may seem, there is still disagreement over how many games Cy Young won.[1] You won't, to be sure, detect hints of uncertainty in the most authoritative works. Baseball's two chief reference books, *The Baseball Encyclopedia* and *Total Baseball*, accept the figure of 511, which is (not entirely coincidentally) the total celebrated when Young was inducted into the Hall of Fame in 1939.[2] We may call 511 the canonical figure. But early record books sometimes credited him with 508 lifetime victories.[3] Some people today prefer 510.[4] And as I will try to show, there are reasons for arguing that the figure could be 512 or even 513. The whole dispute adds a wry footnote to Young's oft-quoted throwaway line that although he was proud at having gained 511 victories, "I won one they didn't give me credit for."[5]

This disagreement does not, of course, call into doubt that Cy Young won more major league games than any other pitcher. After all, confusion about who should be deemed the pitcher of record in any game can arise only if more than one hurler takes the mound for a team, and since Young's club won 477 times when he pitched a complete game, there can be no dispute that he is the winning pitcher in each of those contests.[6] That figure easily exceeds Walter Johnson's 417 wins. The logical possibility of doubt exists only for the additional 60 games which Young's team won but for which he *shared* hurling responsibilities. The canonical count awards 34 of these games to Young, 29 through relief appearances and 5 from those rare occasions when he started but did not finish a victorious game.

One source of the confusion is that before 1950—and this too may surprise the reader—there was no "official" rule for designating who the pitcher of record was. That means that, though the practice of ascribing wins and losses to pitchers had been around since the 1880s as another of Henry Chadwick's statistical innovations, the rules for making that determination had not been codified. Scoring practice had thus rested on the common sense of the scorer to adjudicate in those rare instances where more than one hurler had a claim. Using this latitude, scorers sometimes awarded victories to starters who completed fewer than five innings (if they left the game with large leads) or to the relief pitchers who in their judgment had turned in the best performances even if they hadn't been in the game when the winning runs (or unrelinquished leads) were secured.[7] In 1950 and 1951 the rules committee finally legislated principles for determining the pitchers of record, specifying (among other things) that: (1) a starting pitcher, in order to be credited with a victory, needed to stay in the game through at least five innings; (2) if a starter failed to last the requisite five innings but left with a lead that was kept, and if there was more than one relief pitcher, the victory would be awarded to the reliever who was deemed to have done the best work; and (3) if a lead was lost after the starter left the game and then was later regained, the victory would be awarded to the reliever who was in the game when the unrelinquished lead was secured.

The question then arose: what implications did these new rules have for pre-1950 records? That is, should those earlier records be reexamined and adjusted in accordance with the new rules? In 1968 a special baseball record committee met to address this question. It decided that all pitching records from 1901 through 1949 should stand as received, but that for the years 1876–1900 the new rules would be applied. This decision may at first glance seem odd. Why, after all, should one era's records be accepted and another's not? And why should the era further from current practice and hence less easily revisited be subjected to the new rules?

The answer to both questions lies in the fact that the play sheets for games before 1901 do not exist. All that we have of an official nature for the nineteenth century are aggregate players records, compiled (presumably) from no-longer-extant game records.[8] Thus, while we can be confident that we know how scoring rules were applied in the twentieth century (even in the absence of officially binding rules), we lack that confidence for the nineteenth century. Moreover, despite the work of Leonard Gettelson (see note 7, above), the committee suspected that a disorderly ad hoc approach governed scoring decisions before 1901. Convinced that sound record-keeping required the imposition of an order upon the data, it imposed the order of the modern world. And besides, for an era when starters usually finished, a reexamination of won-lost decisions was deemed unlikely to upset many apple carts.

In the 1970s several researchers undertook the task of examining each of Cy Young's 906 games. Their responsibility was to decide, by the application of criteria appropriate to the era under examination, whether he had won the game, lost the game, or simply appeared in the game. The most important of these scholars was Frank Williams. For the pre-1901 seasons Williams sought to compensate for the absence of official game records (and in the process to recover what had happened as accurately as possible) by consulting the rich array of nineteenth-century newspaper accounts and box scores now available to us. His conclusions, which form the basis of many columns of figures published in both *Total Baseball* and *The Baseball Encyclopedia*, include the determination that Young—as had long been claimed—won 511 games.[9]

Some of the particular discoveries uncovered by the researchers are notable. First of all, three victories that had long appeared in summaries of Young's annual performances—and hence in his career total—seemed patently inadmissible. The first, resulting from a game played on September 3, 1890, was unacceptable because the contest turned out to have been an exhibition match, not a regulation game. (This discovery had the incidental effect of reducing Young's victory total in his rookie year from double to single digits.)[10] The second expunged victory was discovered by a close examination of the 1900 season. The various baseball guides of the day credited Young with a 20–18 (occasionally a 20–16) record. But an analysis of his appearances for the season generated a record of 19–19. Since both records tally to 36 games, the easiest explanation for the discrepancy is that someone at the time mistakenly credited a game to Young's win column when it should have been assigned to his loss column.[11] The third illegitimate win emerged from scrutiny of the 1907 season. For many years Young had been credited with 22 victories during the year, but a study of game sheets revealed that he had been designated the winner only 21 times. The discrepancy was probably accounted for when Frank Williams discovered that someone had inexplicably squeezed an extra "w"—shorthand for "win"—between the scrawled lines on Young's official summary sheet, allowing anyone who made calculations directly from the summary sheet to count out 22 victories for Young.[12] When the appropriate adjustment was made, Young's canonical record for 1907 stood at 21–15, not 22–15.

But what the left hand took away from Young's victory total, the right hand gave back, for the intense scrutiny of Young's record also uncovered three wins not credited to his permanent record. One arose from the game of July 31, 1894, for Young, in late relief, was the pitcher of record when Cleveland scored the winning runs. Apparently he was not awarded the victory in his own day since his postseason published total of 25 wins makes sense only if this game is excluded. But by the 1950 rules the win was Young's, and so his 1894 total was raised to 26. Two other lost wins were uncovered when researchers looked at the 1901 season and discovered a counting error. Cy Young had generally been assigned 31 wins for the year. But as it turned out, that figure had apparently referred only to victories in games he had started, omitting two relief wins (June 14 and September 16) that official scorers had awarded him at the time. And so, after all the juggling, a gain of three offset a loss of three.[13]

And now the reader may be wondering where any opportunity lies for disagreement? It resides in the decision by the special committee to accept the judgments of scorers in the second half of Cy Young's career while potentially challenging them—even in the instances when we know them—for the first half. Consider three games:

1. On April 24, 1891, Young pitched the final 3 innings in a 6–5 Cleveland victory. At the time Henry Chadwick himself awarded him a win. Had the game been played after 1900, Young would have kept the win. But because we apply the 1950 rule to games played before 1901, the official record credits Young only with a save.
2. On April 30, 1904, Young entered a game early with Boston ahead and pitched 7 innings of hitless relief. Despite Young's brilliant performance, the scorer awarded the game to the starting pitcher. And because we accept the views of scorers for the post-1900 period, that judgment stands, even though by today's scoring rules Young would be credited with the victory.
3. On April 11, 1907, Young pitched the first 8 innings of a game that Boston won in 14 innings. Even though Young was long gone when Boston finally prevailed, the scorer awarded the game to Young. And because we treat post-1901 scorers' views as unchallengeable, we award the game to Young, even though today the victory would go to the pitcher of record in the fourteenth inning.

These games are reminders that the effort to be systematic in assessing the work of early players has created anomalies of its own. There is reason to be somewhat uneasy about this situation. First, it is inherently messy to give the benefit of the doubt to scorers from one era while denying it to scorers from another. I realize that the distinction derives from the fact that we know *all* of the scorers' judgments from the 1901–11 period and only some of them for 1890–1900. But rather than reject known decisions from the earlier period it might make better sense to impose the 1950 rule only to those games for which the scorers' decisions are unknown. Second, because the figure of 511 has acquired a luster of its own—becoming one of the seven wonders of the baseball world—there has sometimes been a tendency to find some combination of annual figures that will add up to 511. (This is not, I hasten to add, Frank Williams's method; he is scrupulous, systematic, and clear.)

In light of the absence of game sheets for the years prior to 1901 there is no clean way to adjudicate the matter. And I can understand the desire to be consistent in assessing careers of players from earlier eras. My point is simply that the effort to secure consistency of one sort rests on tolerating an inconsistency of another sort. The safest conclusion is to state that Young won between 508 and 513 games and that 511 is the figure that posterity has agreed to accept. In this book I have regularly used the canonical figures because they are convenient, because (whatever their minor problems) they are either correct or very close to correct, and because even the rudimentary sort of statistical presentations I have here attempted require data which are precise.[14] Besides, Cy Young is so far out of everyone else's ballpark—surely an appropriate metaphor—that disagreement on his exact totals is beside the point. But the reader should recall that 511 is to some degree an arbitrary number, the product of laborious research by a small group of dedicated workers, but reflecting a deliberate choice about definitions and a healthy reverence for baseball's honored numbers.

NOTES

Preface

1. For examples, see Charles C. Alexander, *Ty Cobb* (New York: Oxford University Press, 1984) and Robert W. Creamer, *Babe: The Legend Comes to Life* (New York: Simon and Schuster, 1974).

1. 1867–1890: *Life before Glory*

1. His medical bag is on display at the Temperance Tavern Museum in Newcomerstown, Ohio.

2. In writing this sketch of Cy Young's ancestors, I have relied on the Young family history (in manuscript) written by Linnie Wells and McKinzie Young Jr., on military documents supplied me by Doris Baker, and on the following published works: *Combination Map of Tuscarawas County, Ohio* (Philadelphia: Everts, 1875); *1840 Census and Index Tuscarawas County Ohio* (New Philadelphia, Ohio: Tuscarawas County Genealogical Society, 1994); Charles A. Hanna, *Historical Collections of Harrison County, in the State of Ohio* (New York: n.p., 1900); *A History of Tuscarawas County, Ohio* (Chicago: Warner, Beers, 1884); *Index for 1875–1908 Combination Atlas Map of Tuscarawas County Ohio* (New Philadelphia, Ohio: Tuscarawas County Genealogical Society, 1980); and *Tuscarawas County Cemetery Book VI* (New Philadelphia, Ohio: Tuscarawas County Genealogical Society, n.d.).

3. Fred Lieb reminds us that many ballplayers in Young's day, including Honus Wagner and Larry Lajoie, had little schooling. *Baseball as I Have Known It* (New York: Coward, McCann, and Geoghegan, 1977), 266.

4. *Cleveland Plain Dealer*, November 5, 1955.

5. Arthur Daley, *Times at Bat: A Half-Century of Baseball* (New York: Random House, 1950), 7.

6. Bill Shelton, "Cy Young and His Record: They Never Grow Old," *Baseball Magazine* 90 (May 1953): 30.

7. Unidentified clipping from 1899, Cy Young scrapbook BL-356-1939, National Baseball Hall of Fame and Museum, Cooperstown, N.Y.

8. " 'Cy' Young's Debut," *Webster County Argus Weekly*, July 21, 1905; Cy Young's letter of thanks in 1911 to the birthday well-wishers, published in the *Guide Rock Signal Weekly*, n.d.; his letter in 1955 is dated February 1. All were made available to me by the Webster County [Nebraska] Historical Museum.

9. *Sporting Life*, April 29, 1905.

10. Ralph Romig, *Cy Young: Baseball's Legendary Giant* (Ohio Hills, Ohio, 1964), 10.

11. Cy Young file, undated typed sheet, Hall of Fame.

12. *Cadiz Sentinel*, August 8, 1889. I don't know if the team remained undefeated throughout the season, and I don't know which team won the championship series.

13. Shelton, "Cy Young," 30.

14. *Sporting News*, December 10, 1892. I think the claim found in one newspaper that Dent also played for Leesburg in 1889 implausible. That town lies too far away, in the southwestern quadrant of Ohio.

15. Several important accounts of this turning point in Young's career identify the representative as George Moreland. See Lewis, *Indians*, 22; Romig, *Cy Young*, 1; Walsh, *Baseball's Greatest Lineup*, 282. This statement is incorrect. It's true that there was a George Moreland at this time; he was instrumental in the discovery of Honus Wagner and perhaps of Rube Waddell, and he later wrote *Balldom*. But he never claimed credit for discovering or signing Cy Young. See *Sporting News*, March 24, 1900; *Cleveland Leader*, October 26, 1910. In 1905 a James Moreland claimed credit for bringing Young to Canton and offered the oft-cited story about his trips to Gilmore to persuade a reluctant McKinzie Young to allow his son to sign. *Sporting News*, December 9, 1905. Though there are manifest errors in this published account, the core of the tale might be true, and the coincidence of surnames might explain how the fairly well-known George replaced the obscure James in the communication of the tale. But I have not found anybody with the name of Moreland associated with the Canton club—and thus I can't confirm that James Moreland's story was any truer than the conventional George Moreland story.

16. Cy Young told this story to Gordon Cobbledick, writer for the *Cleveland Plain Dealer*. One version of it can be found in Christy Walsh, *Baseball's Greatest Lineup* (New York: A. S. Barnes, 1952), 282.

17. Glenn Dickey, *The History of National League Baseball since 1876* (New York: Stein & Day, 1979), 35. In later years, Cy Young told various versions of the story.

18. *Canton Evening Repository*, April 28, 1890.

19. *Canton Evening Repository*, April 10, 1890. As part of the publicity buildup, the paper questioned whether any catcher on the Canton team was capable of handling Young's speed.

20. Two articles discuss Cy Young's work with Canton in 1890: James Holl, "Cyclone Comes to Canton," available through SABR Research Library; and Alvin Peterjohn, "Cy Young's First Year," *Baseball Research Journal* 5 (1976): 83–89.

21. *Canton Evening Repository*, July 26, 1890. The words are presumably the reporter's paraphrase of whatever Young really said.

22. Miller is not the only man to have later asserted that he discovered Cy Young. Similar claims came from Eddie Aschenbach and Jack Darrah. I credit Miller's claim primarily because Cleveland sportswriter Elmer Bates supports it. *Sporting Life*, January 8, 1898.

23. *Sporting News*, December 9, 1905.

24. The source for the figure of $300 is Guy Hiner, son of the acting secretary of the Canton club. Guy Hiner to A. E. Dillehey, March 5, 1947, Temperance Tavern Museum, Newcomerstown, Ohio. Just after Canton concluded with Cleveland, Pittsburgh offered $500 for Young.

25. Clarence Young, "Cy Young, as a $2,400-a-Year Star, Offered $2,000 Bribe," *Baseball Digest* 9 (April 1950): 22.

26. *Cleveland Plain Dealer*, March 10, 1896. A variation of that story has him trying to leave the city even before the game, certain that he was bound to fail as a major league pitcher. *Sporting News*, September 23, 1897. I find this version implausible.

2. *1890–1892: The Cyclone Blows into Town*

1. On Robison, see "Robison's Career," *Sporting News*, February 18, 1899.
2. This was a double duel, for one of the backers of the Cleveland entry in the Players League was Albert Johnson, a rival streetcar magnate.
3. During the 1890 season the Spiders drew 47,478 home fans while the Players League entry drew 58,430. Even combined, the two figures would have been on the low end for a major league club. Robert Tiemann, "Some Nineteenth-Century Attendance Figures," 1–2, available through SABR Research Library.
4. *Cleveland Plain Dealer*, August 7, 1890.
5. *Cleveland Leader and Herald*, August 7, 1890.
6. One version of Young's own account is included in Walsh, *Baseball's Greatest Lineup*, 285; another account from Young appeared in *Sporting News*, November 12, 1904; Ed McKean's contribution appeared in *Sporting News*, March 21, 1896; Stanley Robison's account appeared in Alfred Spink, *The National Game* (St. Louis: National Game Publishing, 1911), 306; Charles Mears's recollection was printed in *Sporting News*, February 27, 1892.
7. *Sporting News*, August 16, 1890.
8. *Sporting Life*, July 18, 1891.
9. *Sporting News*, November 12, 1904. Another strand of the story has Young being measured for a uniform on his arrival in Cleveland, Secretary George Howe then telling the tailor to hold off on making it until the rookie had pitched, and several directors rushing to the tailor's shop after the game on August 6 to authorize him to go ahead. *Sporting Life*, June 17, 1899.
10. Walsh, *Baseball's Greatest Lineup*, 285.
11. *Cleveland Leader and Herald*, August 28, 1890.
12. In appendix 3 I discuss the controversies and complications involved in trying to count the number of games that Cy Young won.
13. Corrected to .900 by modern historians.
14. George Davis was also a member of the 1890 Spiders. But within a few years he would be traded away, and the Giants would be the beneficiaries of his great talents.
15. Virtually forgotten today, Childs stood behind only Dan Brouthers, John McGraw, and Billy Hamilton in his ability to get on base in the 1890s.
16. *Cleveland Plain Dealer*, April 8, 1891, quoting *New York Daily Continent*.
17. *Sporting News*, November 8, 1890.
18. Among the teams the Spiders played was the Cuban Giants, one of the finest African American squads of the day. (Such games between major league clubs and strong black clubs were unusual but not unknown as segregation descended on the diamond in the closing decades of the nineteenth century.) The Spiders won the game, 15–1. This is the only occasion I know of in Young's life when his team played against a black team, though, since Henry Gruber pitched the entire game, Young himself had no occasion to take the field.
19. *Sporting Life*, May 9, 1891.

20. *Sporting Life*, July 25, 1891. As another mark of his growing celebrity, in mid-1891 the Waldo M. Claflin baseball shoe company added his name to the list of players who recommended the company's product.

21. *Sporting Life*, September 26, 1891. The words are the reporter's.

22. John J. Grabowski, *Sports in Cleveland: An Illustrated History* (Bloomington: Indiana University Press, 1992), 12; Robert L. Tiemann and Mark Rucker, eds., *Nineteenth-Century Stars* (Kansas City, Mo.: Society for American Baseball Research, 1989), 124.

23. *Sporting Life*, June 27, 1891.

24. *Sporting News*, October 10, 1891.

25. *Sporting News*, February 21, 1891.

26. See, e.g., *Sporting Life*, March 19, 1892; *Sporting News*, December 17, 1904. I assume such tales are false.

27. The reserve clause, included in each player's contract for year X, obliged the player to play for that same team (unless his contract was sold or reassigned) in year X+1 or not to play at all. It meant that players could not shop around for bids for their services.

28. Young and Cuppy won 381 games between 1892 and 1899. In second place was the duo of Kid Nichols and Jack Stivetts, with 350. In their prime, however—1892 through 1897—the Boston pair were more successful, with 319 wins to Young and Cuppy's 310.

29. *Cleveland Plain Dealer*, April 10, 1892.

30. *Sporting Life*, March 19, 1892.

31. *Reach's Official Baseball Guide 1892*, 53. Young's total of 27 victories in 1891 is the fifth-highest total ever posted by a pitcher who didn't throw a shutout.

32. *Sporting News*, April 30, 1892; *Cleveland Plain Dealer*, April 30, 1892.

33. *Cleveland Plain Dealer*, June 7, 1892.

34. *Sporting News*, June 18, 1892.

35. *Cleveland Plain Dealer*, April 21, 1892.

36. I'm not sure I agree with Young's judgment, but it was certainly a splendid effort, and out of deference to Cy Young's own judgment—for who should know better?—I have placed it thirteenth among the baker's dozen of Young's greatest games in appendix 2.

37. *Cleveland Plain Dealer*, August 30, 1892.

38. *Sporting News*, October 22, 1892.

39. As plans for postseason play took shape, some observers proposed playing the series in San Francisco, where the midfall weather would be better than in the Northeast. When several players protested, the decision was made to stay in major league territory—three games in Cleveland, three in Boston, and (if needed) three in New York.

40. *Sporting News*, October 22, 1892.

41. *Sporting News*, January 16, 1904. I almost agree: that's why I have included the game in appendix 2 as Young's fourth-greatest. See also Robert L. Tiemann, "The 1892 Heroics of Jack Stivetts," from SABR Research Library.

42. Jerry Lansche, *Glory Fades Away: The Nineteenth-Century World Series Rediscovered* (Dallas: Taylor, 1991), 222.

43. In addition to Lansche, *Glory Fades*, discussions of the World Series of 1892 may be found in Frank Williams, "The First League Championship Series–1892," *Grandstand Baseball Annual* 5 (1989): 99–111; L. David Roberts, *Insider's Baseball: The Finer Points of the Game, as Examined by the Society for American Baseball Research* (New York:

Charles Scribner's Sons, 1983), 19–22; and Dean A. Sullivan, ed., *Early Innings: A Documentary History of Baseball* (Lincoln: University of Nebraska Press, 1995), 220–24.

44. Lansche, *Glory Fades*, 223.
45. Most record books still give Hutchison 37 victories in 1892. But recent research has reduced that figure to 36, thus allowing Young to share the honor of being the league's winningest pitcher.
46. *Cleveland Plain Dealer*, August 30, 1892.
47. Brad Willson, "The Love Story of a Baseball Legend," *Baseball Digest* 34 (November 1975): 72. The words are Cy Young's, but from many years later.

3. The Birth of the Modern Pitching Regime

1. Robert F. Burk, *Never Just a Game: Players, Owners, and American Baseball to 1920* (Chapel Hill: University of North Carolina Press, 1994), 135, states it as probable that eleven of the twelve National League clubs lost money in 1892.
2. Robison (and perhaps Patsy Tebeau) believed that a staff of Clarkson, Cuppy, and Young would be able to handle a change better than most clubs' pitching corps.
3. I borrow that useful term from Robert E. Shipley, "Baseball Axiom No. 22," *Baseball Research Journal* 23 (1994): 45.
4. There was a third important consequence of the rule change, advantageous to the pitcher and probably unintended. Because it did not prohibit raising the area from which the pitcher made his delivery, it allowed for the creation over the next few years of the now-familiar mound. And in fact—we know surprisingly little about this—the mound may already have been appearing.
5. *Cleveland Plain Dealer*, April 12, 1893.
6. Craig Wright and Tom House, *The Diamond Appraised* (New York: Simon and Schuster, 1989), 155.
7. Bill Rubenstein, "Major League Pitching Kings, 1890–1900," in *Grandstand Baseball Annual: Pitching W-L Records NL 1890–1899 Issue no. 1* (Long Beach, Calif.: Printmasters, 1996), 8.
8. These are modern figures. Contemporary calculations arrived at slightly different totals, but the lesson was the same.
9. *Sporting News*, November 30, 1895.
10. Garrett Kelleher, "More Than a Kid: The Story of Kid Gleason," *Baseball Research Journal* 17 (1988): 80.
11. Incredibly, Hutchison had exceeded 600 in 1892, with 627 innings pitched.
12. *Sporting Life*, September 9, 1893.
13. *Cleveland Plain Dealer*, March 31, 1895; John Phillips, *The 1895 Spiders: Temple Cup Champions* (Cabin John, Md.: Capital Publishing, 1990), n.p. (March 25).
14. *Sporting News*, March 2, 1895; *Sporting News*, February 9, 1895.
15. Over a decade later W. M. Rankin quoted Joe McGinnity advancing the heterodox view that the rule change, by giving a pitched ball five additional feet in which to break, had actually helped pitchers. He was not in the majors in 1893, however, and his judgment may really reflect the tactical adjustment that rising pitching stars like Clark Griffith and himself had to make to earn their way in the National League. *New York Clipper*, November 17, 1906.

16. William Curran, *Strikeout: A Celebration of the Art of Pitching* (New York: Crown Publishers, 1995), 91.

4. *1893–1895: Success at Sixty and Six*

1. *Cleveland Plain Dealer*, April 2, 1893.
2. *Sporting News*, December 17, 1892.
3. *Sporting News*, December 17, 1892.
4. It was rumored that Hawley and Howe had disapproved of the purchase of John Clarkson's contract.
5. *St. Louis Post-Dispatch*, February 21, 1900.
6. *Sporting Life*, April 29, 1893; *Sporting News*, April 8, 1893.
7. *Sporting Life*, May 6, 1893.
8. *Cleveland Plain Dealer*, May 3, 1893.
9. *Cleveland Plain Dealer*, July 4, 1893.
10. *Cleveland Plain Dealer*, July 22, 1893.
11. Note the contrast with the apparently similar game of May 21, 1892, that I mentioned in the previous chapter. On the earlier occasion the St. Louis Browns had not arrived at the ballpark on time. The umpire directed Cy Young to throw one pitch and then declared the game forfeit. Because the game had not gone five innings, it did not figure into the players' records. As a consequence, the Spiders won 93 games in 1892 but the sum of pitching victories amounts only to 92.
12. Happily, for 1893 there is no quarrel between the records of the time and the retrospective calculations of today; on October 14 *Sporting Life* reported that Young had posted a 34–16 record.
13. *Sporting News*, July 29, 1893.
14. On the 1893 Spiders, see John Phillips, *Buck Ewing and the 1893 Spiders* (Cabin John, Md.: Capital Publishing, 1992). See also Robert L. Tiemann, "The National League in 1893," *Baseball Research Journal* 22 (1993): 38–41.
15. *Sporting News*, December 30, 1893.
16. Cincinnati won.
17. See David Q. Voigt, "1894!: The Modern Game's Greatest Hitting Explosion," *Baseball Research Journal* 23 (1994): 82–84.
18. *Sporting News*, March 17, 1894.
19. *Sporting News*, May 5, 1894.
20. *Sporting News*, May 26, 1894.
21. This was a terrible stretch for Cleveland. On July 4 both Rusie and Young were bombed, but the Giants won 12–10. On July 5 Boston crushed the Spiders 22–7, as a despairing Tebeau, eager to ease the pressure on a battered staff, sent Burkett and Virtue to the mound. On July 6 Cuppy lost to Boston 19–6. On July 7 Young lost to Boston 16–10.
22. *Cleveland Plain Dealer*, August 21, 1894.
23. The two teams played a doubleheader; Kelley was 9 for 9.
24. As a sign of what the offense was like in 1894, on July 10 Young had been the beneficiary of a 23-run outburst against Washington.
25. Wright and House, *Diamond Appraised*, 157–58.
26. *Cleveland Plain Dealer*, September 14, 1894.

27. On the Spiders' season, see John Phillips, *Cleveland Baseball, the 1894 Spiders* (Cabin John, Md.: Capital Publishing [ca. 1991]).
28. *Cleveland Plain Dealer*, March 15, 1895; *Sporting News*, April 6, 1895.
29. *Sporting Life*, April 27, 1895; *Sporting News*, May 4, 1895.
30. Nig Cuppy (with symptoms like Young's), Cupid Childs (a groin injury), Harry Blake (a "rupture"), and Patsy Tebeau (symptoms like Young's) were all among the halt and/or lame as the season opened.
31. Mike Sullivan said that "if we are lucky he's likely to stay with us the whole season. If we don't do well . . . the mascot will have tough sledding." *Cleveland Plain Dealer*, April 18, 1895.
32. This index was called "average earned runs by game per opponent." The principle sounds simple enough, but the figures provided are mystifying. Young came in at 3.78. By comparison Phil Knell (of Cleveland) was best with 1.00, Pink Hawley was 5th at 1.77, Amos Rusie was 11th at 2.21, and Kid Nichols was 29th at 3.50. *Sporting News*, June 15, 1895.
33. *Cleveland Plain Dealer*, June 12, 1895.
34. *Sporting Life*, June 22, 1895.
35. This game is listed in appendix 2 as Cy Young's twelfth greatest game. The Orioles' lineup included Hughie Jennings (.386 for the season), Willie Keeler (.377), John McGraw (.369), and Joe Kelley (.365).
36. *Sporting Life*, July 6, 1895; *Sporting Life*, July 13, 1895.
37. *Sporting News*, July 27, 1895.
38. Phillips, *1895 Cleveland Spiders*, n.p. (September 26).
39. Clyde Shaffer, "Nation's Fans Flood Cy Young," unidentified newspaper clipping, in George Westlake album, Temperance Tavern Museum, Newcomerstown, Ohio.
40. Unidentified clipping in Cy Young file, Hall of Fame. Alternate versions can be found in Cy Young scrapbook BL-358-1939 (125), Hall of Fame, and the *Sporting News*, November 24, 1910.
41. In one respect *race* is a misleading term to attach to the close of this season. Owing to scheduling anomalies and bad weather, the Spiders played only two games during the final ten days of the season while Baltimore played seven. The effect was that Cleveland, one-ten-thousandth of a percentage point behind on September 22, was immobile while Baltimore glided inexorably away.
42. I'm choosing my words carefully. The postseason play of the 1880s did not, in fact, attract fans. As for the Temple Cup competition, it should not be confused with the 1892 postseason series between Boston and Cleveland. The foundation for the discontinued 1892 experiment was the unique split season: the championship series of that year had pitted the winner of the first season against the winner of the second season.
43. The word was used by the Temple Cup Committee. Phillips, *1895 Cleveland Spiders*, n.p. (September 4).
44. By the official calculations of 1895 Burkett's batting average stood even higher, at .423. It is modern research that has corrected it to the lower but still startling figure of .409.
45. John McGraw, *My Thirty Years in Baseball* (New York: Boni and Liverright, 1923), 159; *Sporting News*, October 5, 1895.
46. Phillips, *1895 Cleveland Spiders*, n.p. (October 6).
47. Walsh, *Baseball's Greatest Lineup*, 288.

48. Other accounts of the 1895 Temple Cup match may be found in Lansche, *Glory Fades;* Phillips, *1895 Cleveland Spiders;* and Burt Solomon, *Where They Ain't: The Fabled Life and Untimely Death of the Original Baltimore Orioles. The Team That Gave Birth to Modern Baseball* (New York: Free Press, 1999), 98–99. See also Frank J. Williams, "Temple Cup Series Thoughts," *Grandstand Baseball Annual* 11 (1995): 129. A book that cannot be recommended is John McGraw's ghostwritten *My Thirty Years.* It is a sign of the disregard for accuracy which poisoned so much early baseball writing that the publisher allowed McGraw's work to go forward even though it stated that Baltimore had contended with Boston for the 1895 Cup and had won.

49. *Sporting Life*, October 19, 1895. *Spalding's Official Baseball Guide 1896* has a useful description of the party. See also *Sporting News*, October 19, 1895.

50. The account in Nig Cuppy's. John Phillips, however, has noticed references in the account which raise questions about Cuppy's dating. *Uncle Nick's Birthday Party* (Cabin John, Md.: Capital Publishing, 1991), 81.

51. *Sporting Life*, October 26, 1895, reported that he could make $15 to $25 per game.

52. *Sporting News*, October 19, 1895.

53. Most contemporary sources gave him only 33 victories. That was still a league-leading total.

54. Nichols and Rusie each had 92.

55. *Sporting News*, October 19, 1895.

5. 1896–1898: A Durable Man

1. *Sporting News*, February 29, 1896.

2. See especially John Phillips, *The Riotous 1896 Cleveland Spiders* (Perry, Ga.: Capital Publishing, 1997).

3. *Sporting News*, July 11, 1896; *Sporting Life*, July 18, 1896.

4. *Sporting News*, July 4, 1896.

5. *Sporting Life*, August 22, 1896.

6. I found this tale in an obituary prepared in 1940 for the event of Cy Young's death. Cy Young file Hall of Fame.

7. *Sporting Life*, May 2, 1896.

8. *Sporting Life*, May 9, 1896.

9. *Sporting News*, August 1, 1896. I have included the game in appendix 2 as the sixth-greatest of Young's career.

10. McCormick won 265 games during a major league career that saw service on six clubs.

11. *Sporting Life*, quoting the *Cleveland Leader*, presents Young's own account of his initial surprise at and subsequent copying of Cuppy's action. May 15, 1909.

12. Elton Chamberlain and Cy Swaim, the other two preseason pitching hopes, were inconsequential. Bobby Wallace, however, provided unexpected pitching help.

13. Childs also starred afield, accepting almost 150 more chances than any other second baseman. All things considered, his performance in 1896 was the finest by any second baseman of the decade.

14. The matter was not finally resolved until after the Temple Cup competition, but the

outlines of a settlement were clear at least a month earlier. The four offending Spiders were ultimately obliged to pay fines of $10 each.

15. *Sporting Life*, October 17, 1896.
16. In addition to Phillips, *1896 Cleveland Spiders*, an account of the Temple Cup games may be found in Lansche, *Glory Fades*, 277–85, and Solomon, *Where They Ain't*, 108–10.
17. The strikeout title was a gift from Amos Rusie, who sat out the entire 1896 season in a salary dispute with the New York Giant owner and thereby abdicated his crown as strikeout king.
18. Phillips, *1896 Cleveland Spiders*, 35.
19. The *Spalding Guide* put it at 21–16; the *Boston Herald* put it at 22–17.
20. *Sporting Life*, July 3, 1897.
21. John Phillips, *Chief Sockalexis and the 1897 Cleveland Indians* (Perry, Ga.: Capital Publishing, 1991), n.p. (May 15).
22. One account, for example, noted that Young did not like being roughed up by batters and flashed "the yellow feather." Phillips, *Sockalexis*, n.p. (June 4).
23. *Sporting Life*, September 25, 1897.
24. Unidentified clipping (dated 1903), in scrapbook BL-354-1939, Hall of Fame.
25. I have included the game—the first of three career no-hitters chalked up by Young— in appendix 2 as his third-greatest game.
26. *Sporting News*, October 23, 1897.
27. *Cleveland Plain Dealer*, March 14, 1897.
28. *Cleveland Plain Dealer*, March 23, 1897.
29. Many fans—perhaps even more than the 9,500 admitted—were turned away for want of space.
30. Only 115,250 paid to see the Spiders play in Cleveland; even the miserable St. Louis Browns, who won only 29 games all year, drew 136,400 at home.
31. McAleer later changed his mind and returned to Cleveland in 1898.
32. *Sporting News*, August 14, 1897.
33. *Sporting News*, November 6, 1897.
34. *Sporting News*, October 9, 1897; the *Sporting News*, December 25, 1897; *Sporting Life*, November 6, 1897.
35. *Sporting Life*, February 12, 1898.
36. The facts in this paragraph come from an article in the *Cleveland Plain Dealer*, March 11, 1898.
37. The words come from a player on another team. *Cleveland Plain Dealer*, March 21, 1898.
38. *Sporting News*, April 9, 1898.
39. *Sporting Life*, June 18, 1898.
40. *Cleveland Plain Dealer*, March 23, 1897. The story has other complexities. Because Robison had hired nonunion labor to make improvements at the ballpark, Cleveland unions struck back by declaring a boycott of Spider games. Still, this situation in 1898 cannot explain feeble attendance in earlier years.
41. Robison's anger was justified. A court later held that Hanna had improperly acquired stock worth $1 million from Robison in a stock fraud scheme.
42. Among the twelve clubs in the National League, Cleveland stood last in attendance in 1898 and 1897, and second to last in 1896, 1895, and 1894.

43. They were not, however, the Orphans. That term was reserved for the Chicago Cubs, bereft for the first time in their history of the presence of Pop Anson.

44. Burkett's day of mastery was not yet over. One additional batting title lay ahead (in 1901). And his average over the nine years from 1893 to 1901 was .379. Only Ty Cobb and Rogers Hornsby have posted better nine-year marks. All three benefitted from playing some of their careers in high-offense eras.

45. *Sporting Life*, November 5, 1898.

46. That's the modern count. *Sporting Life* put the record at 26–13 (October 29, 1898), while *Sporting News* came up with 25–14 (November 5, 1898).

47. *Sporting News*, May 7, 1898.

48. *Cleveland Plain Dealer*, September 27, 1898.

6. 1899–1900: St. Louis Blues

1. This statement excludes teams that played in seasons shorter than 80 games.

2. *Sporting News*, February 24, 1900.

3. *St. Louis Post Dispatch*, April 10, 1899.

4. *St. Louis Post Dispatch*, April 3, 1899.

5. I use "home" advisedly. Though his team bore the name of Cleveland, Frank Robison continued the practice adopted halfway through 1898 of playing as many games on the road as possible. Thus the "Exiles" wound up playing between 24 and 42 games at home (it depends on what truly counts as a home field) and between 112 and 130 on the road. On the infamous 1899 Spiders, see J. Thomas Hetrick, *Misfits! The Cleveland Spiders in 1899* (Jefferson, N.C.: McFarland, 1991), and John Phillips, *The 99 Spiders: The Story of the Worst Baseball Team That Ever Played in the Major Leagues* (Cabin John, Md.: Capital Publishing, 1988).

6. *Sporting News*, May 6, 1899.

7. *Sporting News*, May 20, 1899. Sports poetry was common in the publications of the day.

8. The adoption of red stockings in 1899, another break from the past (the team had worn brown stockings), led fairly quickly to the club's enduring nickname of "Cardinals." But throughout Young's two years in St. Louis "Perfectos" was the commonest usage.

9. *Sporting Life*, June 24, 1899.

10. John Phillips, *The Spiders: Who Was Who* (Cabin John, Md.: Capital Publishing, 1991), n.p.

11. *Sporting Life*, September 2, 1899; *Sporting Life*, July 27, 1899.

12. *Sporting News*, September 2, 1899.

13. *St. Louis Post Dispatch*, August 25, 1899.

14. *Sporting News*, November 18, 1899; *Sporting Life*, October 28, 1899; Tiemann, "Nineteenth-Century Attendance," 2.

15. *Sporting News*, November 4, 1899; *Sporting Life*, October 28, 1899.

16. See appendix 3 for details.

17. Cy Young was not a consistent hitter, but he could occasionally hit with great power as his 1893 home run in Washington had shown. A home run stroked out in New York on July 14, 1899, was reported to be the longest hit of the year in the Polo Grounds.

18. *Sporting News*, September 2, 1899.
19. Phillips, *Who Was Who*, n.p.
20. *St. Louis Post Dispatch*, September 24, 1899.
21. Phillips, *Who Was Who*, n.p.
22. *Sporting News*, May 12, 1900.
23. For a fuller discussion, see Bob Bailey, "Four Teams Out: The NL Reduction of 1900," *Baseball Research Journal* 19 (1990): 95–98.
24. *Sporting News*, February 24, 1900.
25. Undated clipping in Cy Young file, Hall of Fame.
26. *St. Louis Post Dispatch*, April 15, 1900.
27. Young, McGraw, Robinson (admittedly a courtesy member of the Hall), Burkett, and Wallace.
28. McGraw later claimed he received $9,500 in 1900 (*My Thirty Years*, 123); a contemporary report put his remuneration at over $8,000—a salary of $5,000 augmented by a share of the purchase price ($3,000) and a stipend to pay for a keeper of his Baltimore saloon ($250–$500) (*Sporting News*, January 19, 1901).
29. *Sporting Life*, July 14, 1900.
30. One press account called the problem a "floating rib." Another called it "pleurisy." Still others said it was "rheumatism." Early in the season Young dodged the possibility of a far more serious injury. A line drive hit his glove with such force that it drove the mitt into his face and "staggered me for a few seconds. . . . It was the narrowest escape I have had during my career on the rubber." Unidentified clipping, Cy Young scrapbook BL-356-1939 (88), Hall of Fame.
31. *Sporting News*, September 8, 1900.
32. *Sporting News*, December 1, 1900.
33. The National League's average for bases on balls per game fell from 5.40 to 5.33. This represented the seventh consecutive year of decline. Young himself once again led the league in posting the fewest bases on balls per nine innings. His figure of 1.01 was an improvement on the 1.07 of 1899 but higher than the dazzling .98 of 1898.
34. *Sporting News*, August 25, 1900.
35. *Sporting News*, January 5, 1901; *Spalding Guide 1901*.
36. See appendix 3 for a discussion of alternative explanations.
37. The term is attributed to Chief Zimmer, a leader of the players' movement. *Sporting News*, January 19, 1901.
38. The text of Francis Richter's newspaper account of the meeting is printed in Sullivan, *Early Innings*, 252–55.
39. One report says that John McGraw would have attended had he not been injured.
40. *Sporting Life*, August 4, 1900.
41. *Sporting Life*, October 20, 1900.
42. *Sporting Life*, October 27, 1900.
43. Undated clipping in file BL-354-1939, Hall of Fame.
44. *Sporting Life*, April 13, 1901.
45. The St. Louis club lost $40,000 in 1900. As a consequence, the Robison brothers faced a serious cash flow problem late in 1900. Still, the only explanation I've seen for the timing of Frank Robison's explosion is that, having spent the summer of 1900 in Cleveland recuperating from illness, he did not follow the Perfectos closely during

the season and was unprepared for the transformations he discovered when he finally turned his attention back to the team.

46. On Ban Johnson, see Eugene Murdock, *Ban Johnson: Czar of Baseball* (Westport, Conn.: Greenwood Press, 1986).

47. The chief reason that some players had already locked themselves in, even as rumors of a new league swept the baseball press, was that, in need of money, they had signed 1901 contracts early so that they could receive advances.

48. *Sporting News*, November 17, 1900.

49. *Sporting News*, March 9, 1901.

50. Undated clipping in file BL-354-1939, Hall of Fame.

51. *Sporting Life*, March 10, 1900.

52. On Criger, see Pete Cava and Paul Sandin, "Criger—as in Trigger," from SABR Research Library.

53. Undated clipping in file BL-354-1939, Hall of Fame.

7. *Snapshot of a Private Man*

1. Note the spelling. Although her tombstone spells her name "Roba," the spelling she used in her lifetime—on her wedding invitation, for example—was "Robba."

2. Unidentified clipping (marked "Feb. 20") in file BL-356-1939, Hall of Fame.

3. Walsh, *Baseball's Greatest Lineup*, 290.

4. Past efforts to piece this story together have been complicated by Cy Young's age-muddled recollection from 1947 that the farm that Robba and he retired to after his baseball career had been inherited from his own grandfather, not purchased from the estate of Robba's grandfather. Willson, "Love Story," 72.

5. Tuscarawas County Court House, Deed Record 156 (552).

6. The house is currently owned by an Amish family who prefers that people not photograph it.

7. During the Cubs–White Sox World Series of that year, Cy Young had the telegrapher in Newcomerstown phone him with inning-by-inning reports of the game as they came over the telegraph machine. *Sporting News*, January 26, 1907.

8. In 1900, Young went on record as saying ball players wished the season didn't keep them away from home so long. I'm not confident he spoke for most players, but he certainly spoke for himself. *Sporting News*, November 19, 1900.

9. *Sporting News*, February 25, 1905.

10. *Sporting News*, February 18, 1899; unidentified clipping from 1908, Cy Young file, Hall of Fame.

11. *Sporting News*, April 14; *Sporting Life*, May 11, 1907; *Cleveland Plain Dealer*, March 14, 1892.

12. *Sporting News*, April 7, 1894.

13. *Sporting Life*, October 28, 1899.

14. *Cleveland Plain Dealer*, September 16, 1890.

15. This estimate comes from 1897. *Sporting News*, April 7, 1897.

16. The figure of 230 pounds comes from the *St. Louis Post Dispatch*, May 7, 1900. It is a mark of how uncertain this information about weight is that the same paper, on first

seeing the new St. Louis player in the spring of 1899, listed his weight as 170 pounds. April 14, 1899.

17. The 1903 figure of 218 comes from the *Boston Globe*, April 6, 1904.

18. *Boston Globe*, October 15, 1903.

19. *Sporting Life*, September 2, 1893.

20. Unidentified clipping from 1901, file BL-354-1939, Hall of Fame; *Sporting News*, August 17, 1901.

21. Unidentified clipping, file BL-354-1939, Hall of Fame.

22. *Cleveland Plain Dealer*, March 6, 1896.

23. It was their respective poultry exhibits, not their baseball interests, that brought Cy Young, Honus Wagner, and Larry Lajoie briefly together at the end of 1909! *Sporting News*, January 6, 1910.

24. Phillips, *Who Was Who*, n.p.

25. Frederick G. Lieb, *The Boston Red Sox* (New York: G. P. Putnam's Sons, 1947), 27.

26. *Sporting Life*, April 10, 1909.

27. Jacob Morse, "The Story of 'Cy' Young," *Baseball Magazine* 1 (September 1908): 44. Many years later Dorothy Marshall, president of the Temperance Tavern Museum in Newcomerstown, Ohio, said that "he wasn't a very good writer. He wasn't a schoolteacher or anything." Jim Massie, "Oh, Could Young Pitch," undated clipping from the *Columbus Dispatch*, Cy Young file, Hall of Fame.

28. One person who spoke to me of his memories of Cy Young called him "very intelligent," and Jane Benedum Meuhlen, who as a young girl spent much time with him in the 1940s, recalled how he "helped with my homework, though he never graduated from high school himself." *Newcomerstown News*, October 6, 1993.

29. *Sporting Life*, April 4, 1908.

30. Unidentified newspaper clipping in Cy Young scrapbook (BL-358-1939, p. 58), Hall of Fame. Young turned down a proffered reward but declared he might accept Mr. Slemaker's invitation to go hunting.

31. *Sporting Life*, July 11, 1891.

32. *Sporting Life*, November 25, 1893.

33. *Sporting Life*, November 11, 1899.

34. *Sporting News*, August 16, 1902.

35. *Sporting News*, February 25, 1909.

36. Morse, "Story," 45.

37. *Sporting News*, January 21, 1905.

38. *Sporting Life*, February 10, 1912.

39. *Sporting News*, April 8, 1909.

40. Letter from George Harding, to Temperance Tavern Museum, Newcomerstown, Ohio.

41. Unidentified clipping, W. S. Farnsworth folder, Hall of Fame; George Sullivan, *The Pictorial History of the Boston Red Sox* (Indianapolis: Bobbs-Merrill, 1979), 34; Gerald Astor, *The Baseball Hall of Fame 50th Anniversary Book* (New York: Prentice-Hall, 1988), 92.

42. Wright and House, *Diamond Appraised*, 157; Donald Honig, *Baseball America: The Heroes of the Game and the Time of Their Glory* (New York: Macmillan, 1985), 67.

43. Unidentified clipping, Cy Young file, Hall of Fame.

44. *Sporting Life*, April 13, 1901.

45. *Sporting News*, February 25, 1909.
46. *Sporting Life*, July 18, 1908.

8. 1901–1902: *The Toast of Boston*

1. Frederick Ivor-Campbell, Robert L. Tiemann, and Mark Rucker, eds., *Baseball's First Stars* (Cleveland: Society for American Baseball Research, 1996), 2:34. By some accounts Collins received more than $10,000 in 1901, partly as a result of a profit-sharing agreement.
2. *Sporting Life*, May 4, 1901.
3. Walsh, *Baseball's Greatest Lineup*, 291.
4. *Sporting Life*, April 13, 1901.
5. See Cy Young file BL-354-1939, Hall of Fame.
6. Unidentified clipping in file BL-354-1939, Hall of Fame.
7. In his ghostwritten biography John McGraw ranks Criger—"an everyday, hard-working catcher that always could be depended upon"—right behind Ray Schalk as the finest catcher of the first two decades of the American League. *My Thirty Years*, 232.
8. Morse, "Story," 42.
9. While the other seven clubs in the American League were regularly identified by the cities they represented—e.g., the "Bostons," the "Detroits"—the Philadelphia team was ordinarily styled "the Athletics," even in the standings.
10. *Sporting Life*, June 15, 1901.
11. Lieb, *Red Sox*, 21.
12. *Boston Globe*, June 30, 1901.
13. *Sporting Life*, June 22, 1901.
14. *Sporting Life*, July 20, 1901.
15. The prior six were Jim Galvin, Tim Keefe, John Clarkson, Charley Radbourn, Mickey Welch, and Kid Nichols.
16. Unidentified clipping, Cy Young file, Hall of Fame.
17. Boston's record in games in which Cy Young was not the pitcher of record was 46 wins and 47 losses.
18. Joseph Wayman notes that both Boston and Chicago finished the season with four postponed or tied games not made up. Thus it is theoretically possible that, had the full schedule been completed (which is the procedure that would be followed today), Boston would have tied for the pennant. But it is also possible that they would have wound up in third place. "Updates and Corrections," *Grandstand Baseball Annual* 12 (1996): 18.
19. *Sporting News*, October 5, 1901.
20. For a fuller account of Boston's season, see Charles W. Bevis, "The 1901 Boston Americans," *National Pastime* 10 (1990): 27–32.
21. For an account of the confusion, see appendix 3.
22. *Sporting Life*, September 14, 1901.
23. Undercutting the league average by more than two runs is very unusual. It was not accomplished again until 1930, when Dazzy Vance and Lefty Grove both did it. More recently, Greg Maddux has (as of this writing) achieved the feat twice.
24. *Sporting Life*, June 22, 1901.

25. He was also the biggest. At six feet, two inches he was exceeded in height by only three major league pitchers, none able to win more than 7 games. Only tubby Charley Hickman, listed at 215 pounds, rivaled him in weight.

26. He was hurt by a suspension that kept him out of action in August, but he was already trailing Young's pace when put on the sidelines.

27. *Sporting News*, February 22, 1902. Young had been trying to master the change of pace for at least five years.

28. Unidentified clipping in Cy Young file, Hall of Fame.

29. The Harvard nine had a good season, completing its schedule with a 6–5 victory over Yale. The press noted that Cy Young should take some pride in the achievement.

30. *Sporting Life*, March 1, 1902; *Sporting News*, March 1, 1902. It is a sign of how casual sportswriting was in this era that many of the words attributed to Cy Young in the *Sporting News* piece are attributed to Robba Young in an unidentified piece dated February 20, 1902, in file BL-356-1939, Hall of Fame.

31. *Sporting News*, March 22, 1902.

32. *Sporting Life*, May 3, 1902; *Sporting Life*, June 21, 1902; *Sporting News*, June 28, 1902.

33. Young, "$2,400-a-Year Star," 23.

34. *Sporting Life*, August 2, 1902.

35. See Joe Scott, "Rube Waddell," *National Pastime* 10 (1990): 72–74.

36. Exceeded only by Walter Johnson's 68 victories in 1912–13. Joe McGinnity's 66 victories in 1903–4 in the National League marks the only other twentieth-century occasion for bettering Young's achievement. But there's this additional consideration. In both of Young's seasons the schedule called for 140 games per team. Johnson pitched in the era of 154 game schedules. McGinnity won 31 with a 140-game schedule, 35 with a 154-game schedule.

37. Bill Bernhard won 11 straight.

38. Al Orth led, with 1.11.

39. *Sporting Life*, June 21, 1902.

40. Lee Allen, *The American League Story* (New York: Hill and Wang, 1962), 24.

41. *Sporting Life*, October 18, 1902.

42. Dale Gear was both secretary of the PPA and part owner and manager of the Kansas City franchise in the independent American Association. Reports of financial irregularities also surfaced.

43. Tim Murnane reported before the 1902 season that the Boston Americans' payroll was $40,000, exceeded only by the Baltimore Orioles' payroll of $43,000. *Sporting Life*, April 26, 1902.

44. See Frank Williams, "Post-Season Interleague Series," *Grandstand Baseball Annual* 4 (1988): 137, for more information.

45. In calling the series a disappointment I follow Dennis DeValeria and Jeanne DeValeria, *Honus Wagner: A Biography* (New York: Henry Holt, 1996), 105–7. The *Reach Guide* for 1903 makes the contrary claim that the games were "well attended," allowing the players to divide "quite a large sum" (33).

9. The Triumph of Bifederal Baseball

1. *Sporting News*, December 13, 1902.

2. Note that I say "squads," not teams. Baltimore had been a very successful franchise

in the 1890s. It was dropped from the league not because its squad no longer existed, but because that squad now played for Brooklyn. Baltimore, like Cleveland, was a victim of syndicate baseball. See Solomon, *Where They Ain't*, 137–57.

3. The sixteen were almost entirely eastern and midwestern. Only San Francisco (340,000) was west of St. Louis.

4. The proposed rule envisioned drawing a straight line across the entire playing field through first and third bases. Foul balls landing on the plate-side of the line would be strikes; foul balls landing on the outfield-side would be inconsequential.

5. *Sporting News*, March 1, 1902.

6. *Sporting Life*, May 25, 1901; *Sporting Life*, March 7, 1903. The paraphrase of Young's words in the latter piece has him lamenting the fact that "the batsman stands so little show." The expression is oblique, bordering on the cryptic, but its thrust is clear.

7. *New York Clipper*, October 22, 1904.

8. Johnny Evers, a proponent of the inside game, wrote that baseball—which he called "a scientific pastime"—could be "reduced to exact figures." John Evers and Hugh Fullerton, *Touching Base: The Science of Baseball* (Chicago: Reilly and Britton, 1910), 13.

9. After the 1903 season there were intracity matches in Chicago, Philadelphia, and St. Louis, and an intrastate match in Ohio.

10. 1903–1904. *The King of Pitchers*

1. Jimmy Jones, "Baseball Observes 72nd Anniversary," *Mercerian* 49 (March 1963), 10. When Mercer played Boston in exhibition games, Young ordinarily pitched for Mercer. His Boston teammates hit him hard, but we may presume he was easing himself into shape. Young was said to be "proud" of the work of his collegiate charges. *Macon Telegraph*, April 2, 1903.

2. *Sporting News*, April 25, 1903.

3. *Sporting News*, December 20, 1902.

4. Having secured Keeler, the American League now boasted, save for two Pittsburgh Pirates, every major league batting champion from 1895 onward.

5. Lieb, *Red Sox*, 38.

6. *1904 Spalding Guide*, 130, 139.

7. *Sporting News*, March 25, 1905.

8. In the American League in 1903 strikeouts increased by 70 percent over 1902. In the National League in 1901 they had increased by 57 percent over 1900.

9. I've included this game in a appendix 2 as Young's eleventh-greatest game.

10. As quoted in the *Sporting News*, September 26, 1903.

11. Noted by Charles Mears, as early as 1892. *Sporting News*, April 2, 1892.

12. *Sporting Life*, September 5, 1903.

13. He was also moving high on the list of career losses. His final appearance of the season brought him his two hundredth lifetime defeat. But Jim Whitney (204), Mickey Welch (210), Jim McCormick (214), Tony Mullane (220), Tim Keefe (225), Gus Weyhing (232), and Pud Galvin (308) still ranked higher. Only great pitchers last long enough to lose a lot of games. Young was winning them at an even faster rate than he was losing them.

14. *Sporting Life*, September 12, 1903.

15. Doheny was committed to a mental institution during the World Series.

16. Young was characteristically terse when Collins told him he'd open the Series. "All right," he reportedly replied, "I will try to be there." *Boston Globe*, October 1, 1903.

17. The two errors stuck in Young's memory. Many years later, reminiscing about the first modern World Series game, Young spoke of the two errors. "I'm not knocking him down, mind you. . . . It was just one of those days." Shelton, "Cy Young," 54.

18. Lowell Reidenbaugh picked this game as the fourth most significant in baseball history. *Baseball's 100 Greatest Games* (St. Louis: Sporting News Publishing Company, 1986), 246.

19. Shelton, "Cy Young," 54.

20. Unidentified newspaper clipping in file BL-354-1939, Hall of Fame.

21. The first stanza ran: "Honus, why do you hit so badly. / Take a back seat and sit down. / Honus, at bat you look so sadly, / Hey, why don't you get out of town." Glenn Dickey, *The History of World Series since 1903* (New York: Stein & Day, 1984), 19. For more on the Royal Rooters, see Stephen Hardy, *How Boston Played: Sport, Recreation, and Community 1865–1915* (Boston: Northeastern University Press, 1992), 188.

22. Unidentified clipping, file BL-354-1939, Hall of Fame.

23. Shelton, "Cy Young," 54.

24. Unidentified clipping in file BL-354-1939, Hall of Fame. The *Boston Globe*, perhaps drawing on the same interview, has Young saying, "I feel in first-class shape, and it will be the aim of my life to win this game." October 10, 1903.

25. A play-by-play account of the 1903 World Series can be found in Richard M. Cohen and David S. Neft, *The World Series: A Complete Play-by-Play of Every Game, 1903–1985* (New York: Collier, 1986), 3–7.

26. Shelton, "Cy Young," 54.

27. And he appeared as well in the unique divided-season championship series of 1892.

28. *Sporting Life*, October 17, 1903. Cf. Barney Dreyfuss: "We are beaten, but I know that our team is the stronger." *Sporting News*, October 23, 1903.

29. See also Richard Hack, "Four Series Surprises," *Sports History* (January 1989): 40–53.

30. The reason the affidavit was relevant to McGraw, several of whose Giants were accused of trying to bribe an opposing player late in the 1924 season, was that (according to Criger) McGraw had been the man who (in 1901, not 1903) had introduced the prospective World Series bribers to Criger.

31. *New York Times*, October 4, 1924.

32. Young, "$2,400-a-Year Star," 22–23. Cy Young made the statement to Brad Willson in 1947; Willson published the story in 1950. "Love Story," 71–73.

33. For example, newspaper accounts tell of Jimmy Sebring betting $50 on the Pirates in one game, of Sam Leever betting $100 on the Pirates in another, of Barney Dreyfuss having lost $7,000 on the Series, of $10,000 having passed hands in the Pirates' hotel before the first game, and of $50,000 having been wagered on the opener in Boston.

34. Lowell L. Blaisdell, "Trouble and Jack Taylor," *National Pastime* 16 (1996): 133.

35. Baseball's boosters later cited the fact that the Series went only eight games as proof that major league baseball wasn't crooked. *Sporting Life*, October 24, 1903; *Sporting News*, January 14, 1905.

36. *Sporting News*, March 19, 1904. In fact, Hughes didn't even suit up for the remaining games. By one contemporary account, he had blown his reputation with Collins in the third game by being "too sporty." *Boston Globe*, October 8, 1903.

37. Lee Allen, *The Hot Stove League* (1955; reprint, New York: Amereon House, n.d.), 185.

38. Dickey, *History of the World Series*, 21.

39. Undated clipping in file BL-354-1939, Hall of Fame.

40. Young was in the second year of a three-year contract in 1904; as he was probably receiving $6,000, he had no complaint. Dinneen, however, was unhappy that Killilea was trying to get him to accept a salary reduction (on the order of from $4,000 to $3,500) even though he had been Boston's mound star in the recent World Series.

41. *Boston Globe*, March 27, 1904.

42. I have included this game in appendix 2 as Young's fifth-greatest effort.

43. Lieb, *Red Sox*, 54.

44. Unidentified clipping, Cy Young file, Hall of Fame.

45. Shaffer, "Nation's Fans," Temperance Tavern Museum, Newcomerstown, Ohio; Shelton, "Cy Young," 52.

46. Young, "$2,400-a-Year Star," 23.

47. Cy Young, "First—Learn Control of Ball," *SABR Review of Books* 1 (1986): 59; reprinted from *How to Pitch* (1912).

48. *Boston Globe* (afternoon ed.), May 6, 1904.

49. Lieb, *Red Sox*, 54.

50. *Boston Globe* (morning ed.), May 6, 1904.

51. *Boston Globe* (morning ed.), May 6, 1904.

52. *Sporting Life*, May 14, 1904.

53. *Sporting Life*, May 25, 1904.

54. For a box score, see Ronald A. Mayer, *Perfect: Biographies and Lifetime Statistics of 14 Pitchers of "Perfect" Baseball Games, with Summaries and Boxscores* (Jefferson, N.C.: McFarland, 1991).

55. By alternative counts, Young pitched either 23 consecutive hitless innings or 25⅓ hitless innings. Either would still be the record. The lower figure is produced if one doesn't count the first inning of Young's relief appearance on April 30; the reason for not including that inning would be that, though Young's inning involved his retiring three straight batters without giving up a hit, the game inning in fact had hits in it. The higher figure results from tagging on to the core count of 24 innings the hitless outs (i.e., the partial innings) that Young recorded at each end of the string. A dramatic way of underscoring the achievement is to note that Young secured 76 straight outs without yielding a base hit. See "Clarifying Some Records: Cy Young's Streak of Hitless Innings," *Baseball Research Journal* 7 (1978): 103–4.

56. Lowell Reidenbaugh, *Baseball's 25 Greatest Pennant Races* (St. Louis: Sporting News Publishing Company, 1987), ranks it sixth.

57. *Sporting News*, August 20, 1904.

58. Given the importance of the contest—a matter of first or second place with two games left—and the way in which it capped an October in which he allowed not a single run, I have listed it as Young's eighth-greatest game in appendix 2. (I am inclined to think that Young's three consecutive shutouts at the close of the 1904 season bear reasonable comparison to Christy Mathewson's famous and identical feat in the 1905 World Series. It is true that all of Mathewson's games lasted 9 innings, and that

he delivered his 3 victories over the course of 6 days. But the pressure on Young grew greater as time passed, whereas for Matty it eased, since the Giants enjoyed a 3-to-1 advantage in games by the time he chalked up his third triumph.)

59. Unidentified clipping, Cy Young file, Hall of Fame.
60. Dickey, *History of the World Series*, 21.
61. *Sporting Life*, October 15, 1904.
62. *Sporting Life*, October 22, 1904.

11. The Foundations of Success

1. *Cleveland Leader and Herald*, September 11, 1890.
2. From the *Boston Globe*, quoted in the *Cleveland Plain Dealer*, June 5, 1891. During a game in August Boston continually complained that Young's delivery was actually illegal. *Cleveland Plain Dealer*, August 29, 1891.
3. From the *Boston News*, quoted in the *Cleveland Plain Dealer*, July 24, 1892.
4. *Sporting News*, October 10, 1891; *Cleveland Plain Dealer*, May 9, 1891.
5. Unidentified clipping in Cy Young scrapbook BL-358-1939 (70), Hall of Fame.
6. Christy Mathewson [and John N. Wheeler], *Pitching in a Pinch, or, Baseball from the Inside* (reprint, Lincoln: University of Nebraska Press, 1994), 87–88.
7. *Sporting News*, March 2, 1911.
8. In 1903, for example, Young "used a fine underhand raise to good effect." *Boston Globe*, April 25, 1903.
9. *Sporting Life*, July 18, 1891. Over a decade later Joe Kelley spoke of Young on "the raised pitcher's box" as a "giant towering over a batsman." *Sporting News*, March 7, 1903.
10. See, e.g., *St. Louis Post Dispatch*, September 23, 1899; unidentified clippings in file BL-356-1939, Hall of Fame. William Patten and J. Walker McSpadden, eds., *The Book of Baseball: The National Game from the Earliest Days to the Present Season* (New York: P. F. Collier, 1911), 62.
11. Denton True (Cy) Young, "How to Become a Good Pitcher," in Alfred H. Spink, *The National Game* (St. Louis: National Game Publishing, 1910 [1911]), 391.
12. Evers and Fullerton, *Touching Base*, 103.
13. *Sporting Life*, March 31, 1900.
14. Undated clipping from *The Cleveland News*, Cy Young file, Hall of Fame.
15. Joel Pisetzner, "Cy Young: His Name Remains a Symbol of Greatness," *Baseball Digest* 40 (July 1981): 86.
16. Phillips, *Birthday Party*, 26.
17. *Sporting News*, December 24, 1904.
18. In the interval between Rusie's prime and Waddell's settled arrival Young might have been fastest. At least, that's what an unidentified Pirate thought. *Cleveland Plain Dealer*, March 21, 1898.
19. Young, "$2,400-a-Year Star," 22.
20. Martin Quigley, *The Crooked Pitch: The Curveball in American Baseball History* (New York: Algonquin, 1984), 70.
21. *Cleveland Plain Dealer*, August 10, 1890.
22. *Cleveland Plain Dealer*, August 5, 1893.
23. *Sporting News*, December 25, 1897.

24. *Sporting News*, June 16, 1906.
25. Telephone conversation with Feller, May 12, 1999. Conversation with Don Kohl, June 10, 1999. John Thorn and John Holway, *The Pitcher* (New York: Prentice-Hall, 1987), 13, assert that Young called the delivery his "curve."
26. Gary Spoerle, "John Clarkson: Early Ironman," *Vintage and Classic Baseball Collector 2* (June 1995): 55.
27. Gerard Petrone, *When Baseball Was Young* (San Diego: Musty Attic Archives), 108; *Sporting Life*, July 5, 1902.
28. Cy Young interview with Jack Ledden of *Cleveland News*, undated clipping, Cy Young file, Hall of Fame.
29. Phillips, *Birthday Party*, 25.
30. Sometimes Young himself is the historian's worst ally. " 'Cy' Young said the other day . . . that he never used a curve ball until he came to the Boston Americans." *Sporting Life*, April 16, 1910.
31. *Sporting Life*, March 27, 1897.
32. *Sporting Life*, March 31, 1900.
33. *Sporting News*, June 13, 1896.
34. This game is discussed in chapter 9.
35. *Sporting News*, June 21, 1945.
36. *Sporting Life*, March 22, 1902.
37. *Sporting Life*, April 5, 1902.
38. *Sporting Life*, April 4, 1908.
39. *Boston Globe*, August 6, 1901.
40. *Sporting Life*, April 22, 1905.
41. *Sporting Life*, June 3, 1905.
42. *Sporting Life*, July 30, 1910.
43. *Sporting News*, April 2, 1908.
44. Wright and House speculate that fastball pitchers have longer careers than wily pitchers because, when their deliveries begin to lose zip as they age, they can develop alternatives. Cy Young clearly is evidence of that theory. *Diamond Appraised*, 190.
45. I am using, and in some cases adjusting, calculations made by Thorn and Holway, *Pitcher*, 43.
46. Burton Hawkins, "A Chat with Cy Young," *Baseball Digest 2* (October 1943): 25.
47. Unidentified clipping, Cy Young file, Hall of Fame.
48. Unidentified clipping, Cy Young file, Hall of Fame.
49. Young, "First—Learn Control," 58; Denton True (Cy) Young, "How I Learned to Pitch," *Baseball Magazine 1* (September 1908): 15; Young, "Good Pitcher," 391.
50. Young, "First—Learn Control," 58–59.
51. "Many of Records Set by Denton T. Young Will Never Be Broken," *Coshocton [Ohio] Tribune*, May 31, 1964.
52. *Cleveland Plain Dealer*, August 10, 1890.
53. *Sporting Life*, August 22, 1903. The words are probably Francis Richter's.
54. Young, "Good Pitcher," 391–92.
55. *Cleveland Plain Dealer*, September 27, 1897.
56. John D. McCallum, *Ty Cobb* (New York: Praeger Publishers, 1975), 45.
57. *Sporting Life*, May 13, 1893.
58. I draw these inferences in part from the numerous cartoon depictions of games from these pre-sports photography days.

59. *Sporting News*, January 21, 1905. But not always. An unidentified member of the St. Louis Cardinals said early in 1901 that "Young is inclined to be nervous when the other fellows' bats are manufacturing base hits off his delivery." *Sporting News*, March 23, 1901. Given the timing, the remark might have been prompted by interleague tensions. But Young himself once admitted to Gordon Cobbledick that he sometimes needed a rebuke from Lou Criger to get him to snap out of a funk. Unidentified clipping, Cy Young file, Hall of Fame.

60. McCallum, *Cobb*, 57.

61. Phillips, *Birthday Party*, 83–84.

62. *Sporting News*, January 26, 1907.

63. Walt Wilson, "Early Batteries," in *Grandstand Baseball Annual: Pitching WL Records NL 1890–1899 Issue no. 1* (Long Beach, Calif.: Printmasters, 1996), 27.

64. Unidentified clipping from ca. 1947, Cy Young file, Hall of Fame.

65. *Sporting News*, October 22, 1892.

66. *St. Louis Post Dispatch*, May 2, 1899.

67. Unidentified cutting, November 5, 1908, Cy Young file, Hall of Fame.

68. Mathewson, *Pitching in a Pinch*, page after p. 107.

69. Thorn and Holway, *Pitcher*, 58.

70. Young, "How I Learned to Pitch," 14.

71. Young, "How I Learned to Pitch," 14.

72. Phillips, *Birthday Party*, 32.

73. Unidentified clipping, Cy Young file, Hall of Fame.

74. Unidentified clipping, Cy Young scrapbook BL-356-1939, Hall of Fame.

75. Dickey, *National League*, 36.

76. Young, "How I Learned to Pitch," 14.

77. Ibid.

78. *Sporting News*, December 9, 1905.

79. *Sporting Life*, March 20, 1909.

12. 1905–1908: *Old Cy Young*

1. *Sporting News*, March 11, 1905.

2. There was variation among the record books of the day. The *Reach Guide* (55) and *Sporting Life* (December 16, 1905) agreed with current reckoning, but the *Spalding Guide* (121) put his record at 16–18, and the *Sporting News* (October 28, 1905) came in at 17–19.

3. *Sporting News*, November 25, 1905.

4. *Sporting Life*, March 19, 1910.

5. *Sporting News*, January 6, 1906.

6. Lieb, *Red Sox*, 65. I've included this game in appendix 2 as Young's ninth-best career effort.

7. *Sporting Life*, November 4, 1905.

8. *Sporting News*, January 20, 1906.

9. The Boston club was, on average, the oldest in the American League every year from 1903 to 1906. Tom Ruane, posting on SABR-L, July 21, 1998.

10. *Sporting News*, May 2, 1912.

11. The other years that saw 7-game losing streaks were 1894 and 1897.

12. *Sporting News*, June 16, 1906.
13. *Sporting News*, September 22, 1906.
14. *Sporting News*, March 9, 1907.
15. Dick Thompson, "Chick and Jake Stahl: Were They Brothers?" SABR Research Library, 2.
16. *Sporting News*, April 6, 1907. To me, the words, if they are authentic, sound rather like a conflation from at least two occasions. In June the Americans played an exhibition game with Providence to raise money for Stahl's widow; the players also contributed $125 to the cause from their own pockets. The following April the entire team visited Stahl's grave site.
17. Three years later, in praise of Hughie Jennings, manager of Detroit, Young voiced his strong preference for "a fighting manager." *Sporting News*, August 25, 1910.
18. *Sporting News*, April 6, 1907.
19. See, for example, Jacob Morse in *Sporting Life*, April 20, 1907.
20. Patsy Donovan was also technically a playing manager in 1907, inserting himself in one game.
21. See appendix 3 for more on the season opener. By the scoring rules of today Young would not have been adjudged the winner.
22. Lieb, *Red Sox*, 74.
23. *Sporting Life*, June 1, 1907.
24. I have included this game in appendix 2 as the tenth-greatest of Young's career. It is the third Young-Waddell match-up to make the list.
25. *Boston Globe*, July 31, 1907.
26. *Boston Globe*, August 10, 1907.
27. *Sporting Life*, September 14, 1907.
28. *Sporting News*, December 15, 1907.
29. *Sporting News*, October 17, 1907.
30. See Williams, "Post-Season," 123–24.
31. *Sporting News*, January 2, 1908.
32. *Sporting Life*, April 11, 1908.
33. I have included this game in appendix 2 as Young's seventh-greatest.
34. *New York Times*, July 1, 1908.
35. *Sporting News*, February 11, 1909.
36. I have included this game in appendix 2 as Young's second-greatest effort, outranked only by the perfect game of 1904.
37. The All-Stars won, 3–2, in 11 innings. Young pitched the first 2 for Boston.
38. This cup is on display at the Hall of Fame in Cooperstown.
39. *Boston Globe*, August 14, 1908.
40. *Sporting News*, August 20, 1908. For comparison, on July 17, 1908, Pittsburgh had honored Honus Wagner with an expensive watch and a game rack. The largest previous appreciation gift I have found is the $3,500 given by Cincinnati fans to Bid McPhee in 1897.
41. Young beat Washington 7–3, but Johnson, who came in in relief, was not the losing pitcher.
42. *Sporting Life*, May 16, 1908.
43. Unidentified clipping, Cy Young file, Hall of Fame.
44. *Sporting Life*, October 10, 1908.
45. This representative quotation comes from *Sporting Life*, January 4, 1908.

46. Criger published a letter of outrage in the Boston papers and negotiated to get a part of his sales price for himself.
47. *Sporting News*, February 4, 1909.
48. *Sporting Life*, February 27, 1909.
49. *Grandstand Baseball Annual, Special Issue 2* (1992): 116.
50. *Sporting News*, February 25, 1909.

13. True Nobility

1. *Sporting Life*, July 18, 1908.
2. *Sporting Life*, July 11, 1908.
3. *New York Times*, July 1, 1908.
4. *Sporting News*, July 9, 1908.
5. *Sporting Life*, July 11, 1908.
6. *Baseball Magazine* 1 (August 1908): 32.
7. *Sporting Life*, August 22, 1908.
8. *Baseball Magazine* 1 (September 1908): 13–16, 38–45.
9. Morse, "Story," 41.
10. *Sporting Life*, July 30, 1910; *Sporting Life*, August 14, 1909.
11. *Sporting News*, July 22, 1909. The advertising copy spoke of the two men being "caught by the camera in their new uniforms [for 1909] as they greeted each other [when their clubs] clashed for the first time this season. There will be a big demand for copies of this supplement." Young's likeness also appeared on baseball cards distributed by the American Caramel Company and the Sporting Life Publishing Company in his final playing years.
12. Spink, *National Game*, 164; Patten and McSpadden, *Book of Baseball*, 77; *Baseball Magazine* 7 (October 1911), n.p.
13. *Sporting News*, January 2, 1908, quoting the *Philadelphia North American*.
14. *Sporting Life*, February 22, 1908. Rice published a somewhat revised version of the poem to celebrate Young again just before the opening of the 1911 season. *Sporting Life*, March 25, 1911.
15. The words are Jacob Morse's, *Sporting Life*, May 16, 1908.
16. Unidentified clipping (ca. 1905), Cy Young file, Hall of Fame.
17. In 1926, near the end of his active career, Billy Evans told how he had once miscalled one of Young's pitches, immediately regretted his judgment, and thereby given Sam Crawford an extra swing. Crawford took advantage of the opportunity to rocket a ball to deepest center, where, to Evans's relief, Chick Stahl hauled it in with a fine catch. Young hadn't complained about the mistake and had even called off the furious Criger from berating the umpire. But after the game he approached Evans to say: "Bill, I am not so good I can spot batters like Crawford an extra strike." Evans concluded the story by noting his gratitude that the deserved rebuke was private, not public. *Wichita Daily Times*, January 8, 1926.
18. *Sporting News*, February 13, 1908.
19. Press accounts frequently linked Young with Abraham Lincoln. See, for example, *Sporting Life*, September 25, 1897.
20. The linking of Young with Indian strength and virtue had been a trope since at least 1897, when a poem titled "Cyawatha" included these lines: "Forth he [Patsy Tebeau]

brought his mighty cyclone, / Cyclone Cy, with arm of iron." Unidentified clipping in file BL-358-1939, fol. 510c, Hall of Fame.

21. *Sporting Life*, February 12, 1910.

22. See, for example, the representative usage in the *Sporting News*, June 8, 1907.

23. Some of my remarks and speculation on Christy Mathewson are drawn from William Curran's fine rhapsody, *Strikeout*, 123–29.

24. See, for example, the *Sporting News*, August 2, 1902.

14. 1909–1911: Recessional

1. So called because their manager was Napoleon (Larry) Lajoie. On the club in these years, see Franklin Lewis, *The Cleveland Indians* (New York: G. P. Putnam's Sons, 1949).

2. *Sporting News*, February 25, 1909. This is an interesting and accurate observation. Across his career Cy Young won 61 percent of his springtime decisions (April and May), 63 percent of his summertime decisions (June through August), and 60 percent of his autumn decisions (September and October).

3. Larry Lajoie used the occasion to express the hope that he (Lajoie) could play until he was forty-two. Interestingly, that's exactly the age at which he retired.

4. Ball had an inning to remember. Having completed the triple play in the top of the second, he smashed an inside-the-park home run over Tris Speaker's head in the bottom of the inning.

5. The renovations increased seating from 9,000 to 21,000 by replacing wooden grandstands with steel and concrete structures.

6. *Sporting Life*, July 30, 1910.

7. Unidentified clipping, Cy Young file, Hall of Fame.

8. *Sporting Life*, July 30, 1910.

9. *Cleveland Leader*, August 21, 1910, sec. 3 (1).

10. Young pitched in Canton on September 18, supported by a team of Nap youngsters, and hurled one game of the postseason Ohio State Series against Cincinnati, losing 5–2. The series earned him $171.31.

11. *Sporting Life*, November 19, 1910.

12. Joss told the story of how he had once almost hit Young with a pitch. "Pshaw, Addie," Young had said (according to Joss, or the writer), "that ain't no good system"—referring *not* to brushing back batters but to throwing at fellow pitchers. Joss replied that he hadn't meant to pitch so close. "I know you didn't," Cy smiled, and—Joss concluded his tale—"we became better friends than ever right then and there." *Sporting News*, December 19, 1907.

13. *1911 Reach Guide*, 260–61.

14. Patten and McSpadden, *Book of Baseball*, 155.

15. *New York Times*, March 30, 1911.

16. *Sporting News*, April 6, 1911.

17. *Sporting News*, April 6, 1911.

18. Jim Ingraham, "The Magnificent Career and Tragic Death of Addie Joss," *Baseball History* 1 (summer 1986): 28.

19. On the game, see John R. Husman, "Baseball's First All-Star Game," *Sports History* (January 1990): 8. Here is the remarkable starting lineup for the all-stars: Speaker,

of; Collins, 2b; Cobb, of; Baker, 3b; Crawford, of; Chase, 1b; Wallace, ss; Street, c; Wood, p.

20. *Sporting Life*, August 12, 1911.

21. With his loss to Chicago on June 30 Cy Young recorded his 309th career loss, surpassing Pud Galvin's total. Insofar as I can tell, the event passed unremarked.

22. *Sporting Life*, August 26, 1911; *Cleveland Leader*, August 16, 1911; unidentified clipping, Cy Young file, Hall of Fame. Although each article puts entirely different words in Young's mouth, the purports of the three interviews are very similar, and it is quite possible that there was only one interview, with each writer paraphrasing his statements.

23. The "Braves" are the former "Beaneaters." Other nicknames were in use as well during 1911.

24. *Sporting News*, August 31, 1911.

25. In his later years Cy Young sometimes said that this splendid game had been his final major league appearance—almost a passing of the torch. Some accounts of his career make the same claim. In fact, Young pitched six games after his fine duel with Alexander.

26. Young is the only one of the four to face each of the other three in an official game. But his appearance against Walter Johnson had predated 1911.

27. Jacob Morse, "Review of the Baseball Season," *Baseball Magazine* 8 (December 1911): 51.

28. *Sporting Life*, March 16, 1912.

29. Arthur D. Hittner, *Honus Wagner: The Life of Baseball's "Flying Dutchman"* (Jefferson, N.C.: McFarland, 1996), 212, quoting the *Pittsburgh Gazette Times*.

30. *Cleveland Plain Dealer*, May 25, 1912.

31. *Sporting Life*, June 8, 1912.

32. Paul F. Doherty, "Cy Young's Final Fling," *Baseball Research Journal* 8 (1979): 8–9. According to the 1958 reminiscence of the man who caught Young at this time, William Jennings Bryan attended and spoke at one of the games. Unidentified clipping, Cy Young file, Hall of Fame.

33. Unidentified clipping, Cy Young file, Hall of Fame.

34. Unidentified clipping [June, 1912], Cy Young file, Hall of Fame.

35. Hawkins, "Chat with Cy Young," 26.

36. *Sporting News*, June 6, 1906.

15. *1912–1955: Life after Glory*

1. *Sporting Life*, January 27, 1912. So far as I know, the work never appeared.

2. *Sporting Life*, September 7, 1912.

3. *Sporting Life*, February 1, 1913.

4. See Marc Okkonen, *The Federal League of 1914–1915: Baseball's Third Major League* (Pittsburgh: Society for American Baseball Research, 1989), 4–5, for more information on the league in 1913.

5. Jack O'Connor handled St. Louis, Deacon Phillippe directed Pittsburgh, and Burt Keeley directed Chicago.

6. I use that designation because the official records regard the Federal League during its two-year affiliation with organized baseball (1914–15) as a major league. In fact,

the evidence overwhelmingly suggests that it did not reach parity with the American and National Leagues in those years.

7. This was a grand occasion. Future Hall of Famers present included Frank Baker, Chief Bender, Roger Bresnahan, Fred Clarke, Ty Cobb, Eddie Collins, Jimmy Collins, Hugh Duffy, Johnny Evers, Billy Hamilton, Harry Hooper, Bill McKechnie, Edd Roush, Tris Speaker, Honus Wagner, Ed Walsh, and Cy Young.

8. Young and Johnson made brief mound appearances. The three Indians who faced Young entered the spirit of the occasion by obligingly striking out.

9. Young's enthusiasm for McKinley may be linked to the fact that McKinley claimed nearby Canton as his hometown. In the 1890s many Spiders, including Frank Robison, were Republicans. But Young's Republicanism had family roots, his father having voted for Lincoln.

10. 1910 Census, Tuscarawas County, Ohio, Washington Township, Enumeration District 153, Sheet 5B.

11. Robba Young death certificate, Ohio Historical Society, Columbus, Ohio.

12. *Cleveland Plain Dealer*, May 25, 1912.

13. Young, "$2,400-a-Year Star," 24.

14. I am grateful to James Keeler of the economics department of Kenyon College for tracking down important information for me on this point. See also Henry C. Hagloch, *The History of Tuscarawas County, Ohio, to 1956*, 2d ed. (Dover [Ohio] Historical Society, n.d.).

15. Unidentified clipping, Cy Young file, NBL, Hall of Fame.

16. *Cleveland Plain Dealer*, July 3, 1935.

17. Hawkins, "Chat with Cy Young," 25.

18. *USA Today*, November 10, 1997.

19. Unidentified clipping from 1944, Cy Young file, Hall of Fame. This is a widely quoted remark; I think that this article is its earliest appearance. Information about the sale is found in the Tuscarawas County Recorder's Office, vol. 218, p. 254.

20. *Cleveland Plain Dealer*, July 3, 1935.

21. I am grateful to Fred Hawley, grandson of Davis Hawley, for his information about Cuyahoga Savings and Loan.

22. In 1940 a 73-year-old Cy Young split two truckloads of rails and drove them to Columbus, more than 100 miles away, for fence building at the Ohio State Fair.

23. Putnam's—called "Put's" by the players—was a popular site for team partying with the Royal Rooters in 1903 and 1904.

24. Hawkins, "Chat with Cy Young," 25.

25. The Ohio Senate also gave him a meerschaum pipe.

26. I am grateful to Don Duren of Dallas for sending me materials from the *Hot Springs Sentinel-Record* and the *New York Times* about Young's 1938 visit to the spa.

27. In addition to these twelve great players, thirteen so-called "pioneers" were selected in time for the opening of the hall in 1939. Some of the thirteen were chosen for reasons unrelated to playing ability, and all but Connie Mack were dead. But any list of charter members chosen at least partly for their diamond skills that purports to be complete must include Cap Anson, Candy Cummings, Buck Ewing, John McGraw, Charley Radbourn, and Al Spalding.

28. The hall paid the transportation of the items, and Alexander Cleland, the man behind the solicitations, traveled to Peoli to expedite delivery. James A. Vlasich, *A Legend for*

the Legendary: The Origin of the Baseball Hall of Fame (Bowling Green, Ohio: Bowling Green State University Press, 1990), 45–67.

29. Transcript of "Induction Ceremonies," Hall of Fame.

30. Hawkins, "Chat with Cy Young," 26.

31. The two all-star teams may be found in Hawkins, "Chat with Cy Young," 26, and an unidentified paper from 1954 (though the team may have been named as early as 1943) in Cy Young file, Hall of Fame. In 1912 W. M. Rankin chided Cy Young for believing that "the game of baseball is better in every particular than it was twenty years ago." *New York Clipper*, April 20, 1912.

32. I'm grateful to Thomas Eakin for making a copy of this letter available to me.

33. Unidentified clipping, Cy Young's scrapbook, Temperance Tavern Museum, Newcomerstown, Ohio.

34. Vye Knox, "The Incomparable Cy Young," *Good Old Days* (1992): 21.

35. *Sporting News*, June 21, 1945.

36. Unidentified clipping, Cy Young file, Hall of Fame.

37. Unidentified clipping, Cy Young file, Hall of Fame. Williams had performed poorly in the World Series.

38. *New York Times*, February 27, 1938, 5: 10; Rich Westcott, *Masters of the Diamond* (Jefferson, NC: McFarland Publishers, 1994), 110; Hawkins, "Chat with Cy Young," 25.

39. *Sporting News*, June 21, 1945.

40. Ed Rummill was interviewing Young at the time of, and thus is the source of, this famous exchange. Unidentified clipping, Cy Young file, Hall of Fame.

41. Shelton, "Cy Young," 52.

42. Young, "$2,400-a-Year Star," 23; Hawkins, "Chat with Cy Young," 26; Pisetzner, "Cy Young," 87.

43. Daley, *Times at Bat*, 6.

44. Knox, "Incomparable Cy," 22.

45. *Washington Post*, May 25, 1944.

46. Shaffer, "Nation's Fans," n.p.

47. Technically, Cy Young still lived in Peoli. But Newcomerstown, 11 miles away, was the place where he went to visit friends and was increasingly identified as the hometown of Cy Young.

48. Young turned down a suggestion that his signature be simulated by a stamp; he insisted on providing authentic autographs. The story of the programs is told by Ralph Romig. It does not appear in his biography of Young but rather in an unidentified cutting based on an interview with Romig, found in the Cy Young file in the Hall of Fame.

49. *New York Times*, March 31, 1947.

50. Unidentified clipping, Cy Young file, Hall of Fame; Romig, *Cy Young*, 106.

51. I am grateful to Jay Willey for making a copy of this letter available to me.

52. The 1942 figure comes from his driver's license (in the possession of Charles Leech); the 1956 figure comes from an unidentified clipping, Cy Young file, Hall of Fame.

53. Undated piece from 1954 in *Cleveland Plain Dealer*, Cy Young file, Hall of Fame.

54. When asked how he lived so long, he replied: "I drink red whiskey every day." Pisetzner, "Cy Young," 86.

55. Willson, "Love Story," 72.

56. *Newcomerstown News*, March 30, 1950.

57. *Congressional Record*, appendix, June 5, 1953, A3421.

58. Telefax communication from Jonathon Rosenthal, The Museum of Television and Radio, July 21, 1998. Despite tales that Young appeared on *What's My Line?* or *I've Got a Secret*, Rosenthal could find no evidence of his participation in either show.

59. *New York Times*, May 29, 1950. The park and monument still stand.

60. Bob Broeg, *Superstars of Baseball* (St. Louis: The Sporting News, 1971), 286.

61. *Newcomerstown News*, November 10, 1955.

62. I am grateful to Jane Benedum Meuhlen for the information about Cy Young's last hours. She was in nursing school in Columbus at the time and heard the story from her mother.

63. A copy of the death certificate is held by the National Baseball Hall of Fame and Museum, Cooperstown, New York. In 1975 Ruth Benedum wrote Clifford Kachline at the Hall of Fame to explain that even though the certificate listed Newcomerstown as the place of death, the Benedum home was in Peoli.

64. Telephone conversation with Jane Benedum Meuhlen, June 17, 1996.

65. The last time I visited the grave site, in June 1999, I found four scuffed baseballs resting on the lower ledge of the monument. Scrawled on each of the balls was some version of a request that Cy Young assist the baseball career ambitions of the writer. Is it possible that Cy Young is becoming a nondenominational patron saint of aspiring pitchers?

66. He also owned two cars—a 1952 Chrysler valued at $900 and a 1937 Dodge valued at $25—and a checking account containing $5,800. There are complications in the tale of the stock shares that I have not been able to sort out. In particular, I am dubious that he acquired the stock in the 1930s and 1940s. In short, though my reconstruction covers some of the received information, it does not cover it all.

67. All of these quotations come from the *Sporting News*, November 16, 1955.

68. Joseph Wayman, "Cy Young Award," in *Grandstand Baseball Annual: Pitching: W-L Records NL 1890–1899 Issue No. 1* (Long Beach, Calif.: Printmasters, ca. 1996): 61.

69. Young is also the winningest career pitcher in all of organized baseball, with 526 victories (including his 15 at Canton in 1890). Joe McGinnity is second at 482, Kid Nichols third at 444.

70. See Thorn, Palmer, and Gershman, *Total Baseball*, 2551 for details.

71. Perhaps not surprisingly. Lajoie batted .379 lifetime off of Young. J. M. Murphy, "Napoleon Lajoie—Modern Baseball's First Superstar," *National Pastime* 7 (spring 1988): 71. By contrast, Ty Cobb hit .329 off of Young. McCallum, *Cobb*, 218.

72. *New York Clipper*, December 12, 1911; McGraw, *My Thirty Years*, 212; *Sporting Life*, January 3, 1914; *Sporting Life*, December 30, 1911; *Sporting News*, January 22, 1898; *Sporting News*, December 30, 1905; *Sporting News*, December 12, 1896; *Sporting Life*, April 14, 1906; *Sporting Life*, September 30, 1901; *Sporting Life*, August 31, 1907; unidentified clipping, Cy Young file, Hall of Fame; *Sporting News*, February 23, 1911; Cava and Sandin, "Criger," 8; *Sporting Life*, March 6, 1909.

73. Thorn and Holway, *Pitcher*, 250–53. Even when figures are normalized, Cy Young falls short of the lead. See David Bloom, "Lifetime Relative ERA," *By the Numbers* 4 (April 1992): 9; Bill Deane, "Normalized Winning Percentage," *Baseball Research Journal* 25 (1996): 44.

74. Thorn and Holway, *Pitcher*, 282.

75. Guy Waterman, "The Iron Men of Baseball," *Baseball Research Journal* 25 (1996): 59,

concludes that Cy Young was the most durable of all hurlers inasmuch as he went 14 straight years (1891–1904) without dropping out of the regular rotation for any significant amount of time. Christy Mathewson is second at 12, Walter Johnson third at 11, Jim Bunning, Gaylord Perry, and Kid Nichols tied for fourth at 10.

Appendix 1: Salary History

1. *Cleveland Plain Dealer*, April 12, 1893.
2. Cy Young file, Hall of Fame and Museum.
3. Romig, *Cy Young*, 13.
4. *Sporting Life*, July 25, 1891.
5. *Sporting Life*, September 9, 1891, and October 10, 1891.
6. *Sporting News*, March 24, 1894.
7. *Cleveland Plain Dealer*, March 21, 1894.
8. *Sporting News*, November 5, 1898.
9. *Sporting Life*, February 11, 1899.
10. *St. Louis Post Dispatch*, March 30, 1899.
11. *Cleveland Plain Dealer*, March 23, 1898.
12. Ira Smith, *Baseball's Famous Pitchers* (New York: A. S. Barnes, 1954), 33.
13. *Sporting Life*, April 13, 1901.
14. *Sporting Life*, January 18, 1902. (See *Sporting Life*, January 11, 1902.)
15. *Sporting News*, August 16, 1902.
16. *Sporting News*, December 10, 1904. Without identifying his sources, Ralph Romig also concludes that $6,000 was the highest salary Young received. Romig, however, assigns the figure to 1908. *Cy Young*, 90.
17. *Sporting News*, September 20, 1902.
18. *Sporting Life*, January 6, 1906.
19. Petrone, *When Baseball was Young*, 108. President Taylor later claimed that, in the face of player resistance, he had backed away from all cuts. That wasn't true. *Sporting Life*, February 3, 1906.
20. *Sporting Life*, April 9, 1910; *Cleveland Leader*, August 16, 1911; *Sporting Life*, September 16, 1911.
21. *Sporting Life*, October 7, 1899.
22. The claim of $4,400 was made in an undated Zanesville, Ohio, newspaper in 1947, as Cy Young's eightieth birthday approached; the claim of $4,500 appeared in an undated, unidentified newspaper cutting. Both are in the Cy Young file, Hall of Fame.
23. As noted above, Dinneen was paid $4,800 in 1902; Tannehill received $5,300 in 1904. (*Sporting Life*, January 7, 1905.)
24. *Sporting Life*, February 7, 1903; *Sporting Life*, August 16, 1902; *Sporting News*, August 18, 1906; DeValeria and DeValeria, *Wagner*, 176.
25. Lawrence Hadley, Elizabeth Gustafson, and Mary Jo Thierry, "Who Would be the Highest Paid Baseball Player?," *Baseball Research Journal* 21 (1992): 92.

Appendix 2: Greatest Games

1. Unidentified clipping [from 1904], Cy Young file, Hall of Fame.

Appendix 3: 511 Wins?

1. I am grateful to Joe Wayman and Frank Williams for critiquing this appendix in its draft form. I hope they will not be too disappointed that I accepted only some of their valuable suggestions.
2. Though the hall arrived at the same total, it sometimes used different annual figures from those found in modern reference books.
3. George L. Moreland, *Balldom: The Britannica of Baseball* (New York: Balldom Publishing Company, 1914; reprint Horton Publishing Company, 1989), 283. The figure of 508 was used by Grantland Rice in "Big 3 of the Mound," *Collier's* 75 (April 11, 1925): 22.
4. Thorn and Holway, *Pitcher.* The figure 510 is found frequently in the Young files at the National Baseball Hall of Fame and Museum in Cooperstown, New York.
5. Broeg, *Superstars*, 286. Frank Williams believes that Young had the game of April 30, 1904, in mind when he said this. Williams letter to author, August 3, 1998.
6. Similarly, he is undoubtedly the losing pitcher in 256 complete games losses. Beyond these 733 complete games that he either won or lost, Young pitched another 16 complete games, 15 of which were ties and 1 of which was a one-pitch forfeit win for the Spiders that, by the quirky rules now agreed on, counts as a complete game for the pitcher but not as a victory.
7. Leonard Gettelson was the first to distill the implicit rules by which nineteenth-century scorers operated. Joseph Wayman has refined those conclusions in a splendid and valuable article. "Pitching Win-Loss Guidelines," *Grandstand Baseball Annual: Pitching W-L Records NL 1890–1899 Issue no. 1* (n.d.): 98–107.
8. The difficulty of recovering the sequence of events of a particular game played over a century ago can be daunting. Since no official game sheets exist for the pre-1901 period, information must be gathered indirectly from contemporary accounts. But newspaper stories contradict each other, and published box scores contain mistakes.
9. And from his angle of vision, that was a good outcome. At one point, when he thought that the evidence suggested that a figure of 510 rather than 511 would be the accurate one, he feared that mere facts would not suffice to persuade those who preside over baseball's most sacred statistics to authorize a change. He said to Joe Wayman: "Don't think that I did not realize that nobody but nobody is going to change that record." *Grandstand Baseball Annual: Special 2* (1992): 12. Happily, he didn't have to request a change. Williams reports that Cy Young's nineteenth-century record is the same, whether calculated by Gettelson's rules or the 1950 rules.
10. Joseph Wayman, "Cy Young's Two Questionable Games, 1890," *Grandstand Baseball Annual* 10 (1994): 11–12.
11. I have said "easiest" because there is at least one alternative possibility. On May 16 Young left a tie game after pitching 7⅔ innings, and his club ultimately won. It is possible that this game was awarded to Young (such practice was not unknown). Joe Wayman is inclined to this view. And because the recount dropped Young below the 20-win threshold and broke up his "record" run of 14 straight 20-win seasons. Wayman also designates the game of May 16 as the most important of Young's controversial decisions. (*Grandstand Baseball Annual: Pitching W-L Records*, 101.) However, as Frank Williams has argued, this alternative explanation solves only the error in the

"win" column and therefore requires one additional move—accounting for the inaccurate figure of 18 in Young's "lose" column. And that's harder to do.

12. Frank Williams, "All the Record Books are Wrong," *National Pastime* 1 (1982): 59. I should add that I think of Frank Williams as a Tycho Brahe awaiting his Kepler.

13. To repeat: this is a simplified version of a more complicated story. Questions have been raised about more than a dozen of Cy Young's wins or nonwins.

14. Some of the same arguments can be made for the career loss figure of 316. I've ignored that total here because 316 has acquired no automatic recognition status among fans.

BIBLIOGRAPHY

Unpublished Sources

Interviews

Craigo, E. Allen. Telephone conversation with author, March 10, 1998.
Daily, Miller, and Irene Ransom. Interview by author, Mount Vernon, Ohio, January 29, 1997.
Feller, Bob. Telephone conversation with author, May 12, 1999.
Hawley, Fred. Telephone conversations with author, June 9, 1997; June 25, 1998.
Kohl, Don. Interview by author, Newcomerstown, Ohio, June 10, 1999.
Leech, Charles. Interview by author, Gambier, Ohio, July 31, 1996.
Meuhlen, Jane Benedum. Telephone conversation with author, June 17, 1996.
Ransom, Robert. Interview by author, Mount Vernon, Ohio, January 14, 1997.
Robinson, Dale. Telephone conversation with author, November 23, 1996.
Romig, Ralph H. Interview by author, New Philadelphia, Ohio, November 5, 1996.
Wayman, Joe. Telephone conversation with author, August 21, 1998.

Correspondence

Baker, Doris J. Letters to author, August 5, 1996; January 2, 1997; "History of the Young Family."
Eakin, Thomas C. Letter to author, January 6, 1997.
Wayman, Joseph. Letters to author, February 25, 1998, March 26, 1998; July 20, 1998; July 28, 1998; August 14, 1998.
Willey, Jay. Letter to author, June 19, 1997.
Williams, Frank. July 26, 1996, August 4, 1996, March 27, 1997, April 16, 1997, June 6, 1997; June 25, 1997, July 19, 1998; August 3, 1998, September 26, 1998.

Private Papers

CLEVELAND PUBLIC LIBRARY, CLEVELAND, OHIO
Mears Collection.

HARRISON COUNTY (OHIO) COURT HOUSE
Young, Denton. Probate records, 1832.

Bibliography

NATIONAL BASEBALL HALL OF FAME AND MUSEUM, COOPERSTOWN, NEW YORK

Young, Cy. Contracts, 1891, 1906, 1909.

————. Annual performance data [ICIs and Day-by-Days].

————. Three scrapbooks: BL-354-1939, BL-356-1939, BL-358-1939.

————. Two unnamed folders.

OHIO BASEBALL HALL OF FAME, SHAKER HEIGHTS, OHIO

Gaffney, James. Cy Young's release from baseball, 1912.

Young, Cy. Letter to Red Smith, January 31, 1948.

List of pall bearers at Cy Young's funeral, 1955.

Material from Cy Young Centennial, Newcomerstown, Ohio, 1967.

OHIO HISTORICAL SOCIETY

Young, Denton True (Cy). Death certificate.

Young, Robba. Death certificate.

TEMPERANCE TAVERN MUSEUM, NEWCOMERSTOWN, OHIO

Photo album of Robba Miller Young's family.

Photo album of McKinzie Young.

"Cy Young's Scrapbook" Clippings album assembled to memorialize George Westlake, 1887–93, 1917–18, 1940–47.

Untitled clipping album to memorialize George Westlake.

TUSCARAWAS COUNTY (OHIO) COURT HOUSE

Young Sr., McKinzie, McKinzie Young Jr., and Denton True (Cy) Young. Probate records.

Land purchase records in the Recorder's Office.

WEBSTER COUNTY HISTORICAL MUSEUM, RED CLOUD, NEBRASKA

Letters from Cy Young, April 11, 1911, and February 1, 1955.

SABR RESEARCH LIBRARY

Boynton, Bob "Time-of-Game Signposts Along Memory Lane" (1993).

Cava, Pete, and Paul Sandin "Criger—as in Triggers" (1993).

Derby, Richard E. "The Race" [American League 1908].

Gilbert, Bill. "Is the Triple Milestone Pitcher Extinct?" (1995).

Holl, James P. "The Cyclone Comes to Canton."

Lanigan, Ernie. "Other Temple Cup Dope."

Thompson, Dick. "Chick and Jake Stahl: Were They Brothers?" (1987).

Tiemann, Robert L. "Cy Young's Shutout Games For and Against."

————. "The 1892 Heroics of Jack Stivetts."

————. "Major League Winning Streaks of 12 or More Games."

————. "Some Nineteenth-Century Attendance Figures" (1987).

Wayman, Joseph M. "Final National League 1899 Standings."

PUBLISHED SOURCES

Books

Alexander, Charles C. *John McGraw*. New York: Viking Press, 1988.
———. *Our Game: An American Baseball History*. New York: Henry Holt, 1991.
———. *Ty Cobb*. New York: Oxford University Press, 1984.
Allen, Lee. *The American League Story*. New York: Hill and Wang, 1962.
———. *The Hot Stove League*. New York: A. S. Barnes & Co., 1955. Reprint, Mattituck, N.Y.: Amereon House, n.d.
Anson, Adrian C. *A Ball Player's Career*. Chicago: Era Publishing Co., 1900.
Astor, Gerald. *The Baseball Hall of Fame 50th Anniversary Book*. New York: Prentice-Hall, 1988.
Axelson, Gustaf W. *"Commy": The Life Story of Charles A. Comiskey*. Chicago: Reilly and Lee, 1919.
Bak, Richard. *Ty Cobb: His Tumultuous Life and Times*. Dallas: Taylor Publishing Co., 1994.
Barrow, Edward Grant, with James Kahn. *My Fifty Years in Baseball*. New York: Coward, McCann, 1951.
Bartlett, Arthur. *Baseball and Mr. Spalding*. New York: Farrar, Straus and Young, 1951.
A Baseball Century: The First 100 Years of the National League. New York: Macmillan, 1976.
Benson, John, and Tony Blengino. *Baseball's Top 100: The Best Individual Seasons of All Time*. Wilton, Conn.: Diamond Library, 1995.
Benson, Michael. *Ballparks of North America*. Jefferson, N.C.: McFarland & Co., 1989.
Berry, Henry, and Harold Berry. *Boston Red Sox: The Complete Record of Red Sox Baseball*. New York: Macmillan, 1984.
Bjarkman, Peter, ed. *Encyclopedia of Major League Baseball Team Histories: The National League*. Westport, Conn.: Greenwood Press, 1991.
Broeg, Bob. *Superstars of Baseball*. St. Louis: The Sporting News Publishing Co., 1971.
Broeg, Bob, and William J. Miller, Jr. *Baseball from a Different Angle*. South Bend, Ind.: Diamond Communications, 1988.
Bruno, Joseph. *Baseball's Golden Dozen Pitchers*. Hicksville, N.Y.: Exposition Press, 1976.
Buck, Jack, John Warner Davenport, and Jeffrey Newman, *The Cardinals*. New York: Collier Books, 1983.
Burk, Robert F. *Never Just a Game: Players, Owners, and American Baseball to 1920*. Chapel Hill: University of North Carolina Press, 1994.
Campbell, Thomas F., and Edward M. Miggins, eds. *The Birth of Modern Cleveland, 1865–1930*. Cleveland: Western Reserve Historical Society, 1988.
Cappio, Alfred. *Slide Kelly, Slide*. Paterson, N.J.: Passaic County Historical Society, 1962.
Carmichael, John P., ed. *My Greatest Day in Baseball*. New York: A. S. Barnes and Co., 1945.
Carter, Craig. *Daguerreotypes*. 8th ed. St. Louis: The Sporting News Publishing Co., 1990.
Charlton, James, ed. *The Baseball Chronology: The Complete History of the Most Important Events in the Game of Baseball*. New York: Macmillan, 1991.
Church, Seymour. *Baseball: The History, Statistics and Romance of the American National Game from Its Inception to the Present Time*. San Francisco: S. R. Church, 1902; reprint, Princeton: Pyne Press, 1974.
Cobb, Ty, and Al Stump. *My Life in Baseball: The True Record*. New York: Doubleday, 1961.
Coberly, Rich. *The No-Hit Hall of Fame*. New York: Triple Play Publications, 1985.
Cohen, Eliot, ed. *My Greatest Day in Baseball*. New York: Little, Simon, 1991.

Cohen, Richard M., and David S. Neft. *The World Series: A Complete Play-by-Play of Every Game, 1903–1985.* New York: Collier, 1986.

Combination Atlas Map of Tuscarawas County, Ohio. Philadelphia: Everts and Co., 1875.

Creamer, Robert W. *Babe: The Legend Comes to Life* New York: Simon and Schuster, 1974.

Curran, William. *Mitts: A Celebration of the Art of Fielding.* New York: Morrow, 1985.

Curran, William. *Strikeout: A Celebration of the Art of Pitching.* New York: Crown Publishers, 1995.

Cy Young Centennial, 1867–1967: July 14 & 15, New Philadelphia and Newcomerstown, Ohio. [n.p.]: Cy Young Centennial Committee, 1967 and 1970.

Cy Young 125th Anniversary. [n.p.]: Tuscarawas County Old Timers Baseball Association, 1992.

Daley, Arthur. *Sports of the Times.* New York: E. P. Dutton, 1959.

———. *Times At Bat: A Half Century of Baseball.* New York: Random House, 1950.

DeValeria, Dennis, and Jeanne DeValeria. *Honus Wagner: A Biography.* New York: Henry Holt, 1996.

Dickey, Glenn. *The Great No-Hitters.* Radnor, Pa.: Chilton Book Co., 1976.

———. *The History of the American League since 1901.* New York: Stein and Day, 1981.

———. *The History of National League Baseball Since 1876.* New York: Stein & Day, 1979.

———. *The History of the World Series Since 1903.* New York: Stein & Day, 1984.

Dickson, Paul. *The Dickson Baseball Dictionary.* New York: Facts on File, 1989.

Douglas, Byrd. *The Science of Baseball.* New York: Thomas E. Wilson & Co., 1922.

Durso, Joseph. *Baseball and the American Dream.* St. Louis: The Sporting News Publishing Co., 1986.

1840 Census and Index Tuscarawas County Ohio. New Philadelphia, Ohio: Tuscarawas County Genealogical Society, 1994.

1890 Widows and Veterans Census Tuscarawas County Ohio. N.p.: Ohio Genealogical Society, n.d.

Evers, John, and Hugh Fullerton. *Touching Base: The Science of Baseball.* Chicago: Reilly & Britton Co., 1910.

Foster, John B. *How To Pitch.* Spalding's Athletic Library. New York: American Sports Publishing Co., 1917.

Frick, Ford. *Games, Asterisks, and People: Memoirs of a Lucky Fan.* New York: Crown Publishers, 1973.

Gies, Joseph, and Robert H. Shoemaker. *Stars of the Series: A Complete History of the World Series.* New York: Thomas Y. Crowell, 1965.

Ginsburg, Daniel E. *The Fix is In: A History of Baseball Gambling and Game Fixing Scandals.* Jefferson, N.C.: McFarland & Co., 1995.

Grabowski, John J. *Sports in Cleveland: An Illustrated History.* Bloomington, Ind.: Indiana University Press, 1992.

Grayson, Harry. *They Played the Game: The Story of Baseball Greats.* New York: A. S. Barnes, 1946.

Hagloch, Henry C. *The History of Tuscarawas County, Ohio, to 1956.* 2d ed. N.p.: Dover Historical Society, n.d.

Hanna, Charles A. *Historical Collections of Harrison County, in the State of Ohio.* New York: n.p., 1900.

Hardy, Stephen. *How Boston Played: Sport, Recreation and Community, 1865–1915.* Boston: Northeastern University Press, 1992.

Hetrick, J. Thomas. *Misfits!: The Cleveland Spiders in 1899*. Jefferson, N.C.: McFarland Publishers, 1991.

A History of Tuscarawas County, Ohio. Chicago: Warner, Beers & Co., 1884.

Hittner, Arthur D. *Honus Wagner: The Life of Baseball's "Flying Dutchman."* Jefferson, N.C.: McFarland, 1996.

Honig, Donald. *The American League: An Illustrated History*. Rev. ed. New York: Crown Publishing, 1987.

———. *Baseball America: The Heroes of the Game and the Time of Their Glory*. New York: Macmillan, 1985.

———. *The Greatest Pitchers of All Time*. New York: Crown Publishers, 1988.

———. *The World Series: An Illustrated History from 1903 to the Present*. New York: Crown, 1986.

Honig, Donald, and Lawrence Ritter. *The 100 Greatest Baseball Players of All Time*. New York: Crown Publishers, 1981.

Hoppel, Joe. *The Series: An Illustrated History of Baseball's Postseason Showcase*. St. Louis: The Sporting News Publishing Co., 1988.

Hurt, R. Douglas. *The Ohio Frontier: Crucible of the Old Northwest, 1720–1830*. Bloomington, Ind.: Indiana University Press, 1996.

Index for 1875–1908 Combination Atlas Map of Tuscarawas County Ohio. New Philadelphia, Ohio: Tuscarawas County Genealogical Society, 1980.

Ivor-Campbell, Frederick, Robert L. Tiemann, and Mark Rucker, eds. *Baseball's First Stars*. vol. 2. Cleveland: Society for American Baseball Research, 1996.

James, Bill. *The Bill James Guide to Baseball Managers from 1870 to Today*. New York: Scribner, 1997.

Kaese, Harold. *The Boston Braves*. New York: G. P. Putnam's Sons, 1948.

Kavanaugh, Jack. *Honus Wagner*. New York: Chelsea House, 1994.

Koppett, Leonard. *The New Thinking Fan's Guide to Baseball*. New York: Simon and Schuster, 1991.

Lanigan, Ernest. *The Baseball Cyclopedia*. New York: The Baseball Magazine Co., 1922. Reprint, Horton Publishing Co., 1988.

Lansche, Jerry. *Glory Fades Away: The Nineteenth-Century World Series Rediscovered*. Dallas: Taylor, 1991.

Levine, Peter. *A. G. Spalding and the Rise of Baseball: The Promise of American Sport*. New York: Oxford University Press, 1985.

Lewis, Franklin. *The Cleveland Indians*. New York: G. P. Putnam's Sons, 1949.

Lieb, Frederick G. *Baseball As I Have Known It*. New York: Coward, Mccann, and Geoghegan, 1977.

———. *The Baseball Story*. New York: G. P. Putnam's Sons, 1950.

———. *The Boston Red Sox*. New York: G. P. Putnam's Sons, 1947.

———. *The St. Louis Cardinals: The Story of a Great Baseball Club*. New York: G. P. Putnam's Sons, 1944.

———. *The Story of the World Series: An Informal History*. New York: G. P. Putnam's Sons, 1949.

Longert, Scott. *Addie Joss: King of the Pitchers*. Cleveland: Society for American Baseball Research, 1998.

Lowenfish, Lee, and Tony Lupien. *The Imperfect Diamond: The Story of Baseball's Reserve System and the Men Who Fought to Change It*. New York: Stein and Day, 1980.

Lowry, Phillip J. *Green Cathedrals.* Cooperstown, N.Y.: Society for American Baseball Research, 1986.

Macht, Norman L. *Cy Young.* New York: Chelsea House Publishers, 1992.

Mack, Connie. *My 66 Years in the Big Leagues.* Philadelphia: John C. Winston Co., 1950.

Mathewson, Christy [and John N. Wheeler]. *Pitching in a Pinch, or, Baseball from the Inside.* 1917. Reprint, Lincoln: University of Nebraska Press, 1994.

Mayer, Ronald A. *Perfect: Biographies and Lifetime Statistics of 14 Pitchers of "Perfect" Baseball Games, with Summaries and Boxscores.* Jefferson, N.C.: McFarland & Co., 1991.

McCallum, John D. *Ty Cobb.* New York: Praeger Publishers, 1975.

McGraw, John J. *My Thirty Years in Baseball.* New York: Boni and Liverright, 1923.

Meany, Tom. *Baseball's Greatest Pitchers.* New York: A. S. Barnes, 1953.

Moreland, George L. *Balldom: "The Britannica of Baseball."* New York: Balldom Publishing Co., 1914. Reprint, Horton Publishing Co., 1989.

Murdock, Eugene. *Ban Johnson: Czar of Baseball.* Westport, Conn.: Greenwood Press, 1986.

Neft, David, and Richard Cohen. *The Sports Encyclopedia: Baseball.* New York: St. Martin's Press, 1986.

Nemec, David. *The Great Encyclopedia of 19th-Century Major League Baseball.* New York: Donald I. Fine Books, 1997.

Obojski, Robert. *Great Moments of the Playoffs and World Series.* New York: Sterling, 1988.

Okkonen, Marc. *The Federal League of 1914–1915: Baseball's Third Major League.* Pittsburgh: Society for American Baseball Research, 1989.

Okrent, Dan, and Harris Lewine, eds. *The Ultimate Baseball Book.* Boston: Houghton Mifflin, 1984.

Patten, William, and J. Walker McSpadden, eds. *The Book of Baseball: The National Game from the Earliest Days to the Present Season.* New York: P. F. Collier and Son, 1911.

Petrone, Gerard. *When Baseball Was Young.* San Diego: Musty Attic Archives, 1994.

Phillips, John. *Buck Ewing and the 1893 Spiders.* Cabin John, Md.: Capital Publishing, 1992.

———. *Chief Sockalexis and the 1897 Cleveland Indians.* Perry, Ga.: Capital Publishing Co., 1991.

———. *Cleveland Baseball, the 1894 Spiders.* Cabin John, Md.: Capital Publishing, ca. 1991.

———. *The 1898 Cleveland Spiders.* Cabin John, Md.: Capital Publishing, 1997.

———. *The 1895 Cleveland Spiders: Temple Cup Champions.* Cabin John, Md.: Capital Publishing, 1990.

———. *The 99 Spiders: The Story of the Worst Baseball Team that Ever Played in the Major Leagues.* Cabin John, Md.: Capital Publishing, 1988.

———. *The Riotous 1896 Cleveland Spiders.* Perry, Ga.: Capital Publishing Co., 1997.

———. *The Spiders: Who Was Who.* Cabin John, Md.: Capital Publishing, 1991.

———. *Uncle Nick's Birthday Party.* Cabin John, Md.: Capital Publishing, 1991.

———. *Who Was Who in Cleveland Baseball, 1901–10.* Cabin John, Md.: Capital Publishing, 1989.

Quigley, Martin. *The Crooked Pitch: The Curveball in American Baseball History.* New York: Algonquin Books, 1984.

Rader, Benjamin. *Baseball: A History of America's Game.* Urbana: University of Illinois Press, 1992.

Reichler, Joseph. *Baseball's Unforgettable Games.* New York: Ronald Press Co., 1960.

———. *The World Series: A 75th Anniversary.* New York: Simon and Schuster, 1978.

Reidenbaugh, Lowell. *Baseball's 100 Greatest Games.* St. Louis: The Sporting News Publishing Co., 1986.

————. *Baseball's 25 Greatest Pennant Races*. St. Louis: The Sporting News Publishing Co., 1987.

Rhodes, Edwin S. *The First Centennial Atlas of Tuscarawas County, Ohio*. New Philadelphia, Ohio: Tuscarawas Centennial Association, 1908.

Rice, Grantland. *The Tumult and Shouting: My Life in Sport*. New York: A. S. Barnes and Co., 1954.

Richter, Francis C. *A Brief History of Baseball*. Philadelphia: Sporting Life Publishing Co., 1909.

————. *Richter's History and Records of Baseball: The American Nation's Chief Sport*. Philadelphia: Richter Publishing Co., 1914.

Rickey, Branch, and Robert Riger. *The American Diamond*. New York: Simon and Schuster, 1965.

Riess, Steven A. *City Games: The Evolution of American Urban Society and the Rise of Sports*. Urbana, Ill.: University of Illinois Press, 1989.

————. *Touching Base: Professional Baseball and American Culture in the Progressive Era*. Westport, Conn.: Greenwood Press, 1980.

Ritter, Lawrence. *The Glory of Their Times*. New York: Macmillan, 1966.

————. *Lost Ballparks: A Celebration of Baseball's Legendary Fields*. New York: Viking Penguin, 1992.

Roberts, L. David, ed. *Insider's Baseball: The Finer Points of the Game, as Examined by the Society for American Baseball Research*. New York: Charles Scribner's Sons, 1983.

Robinson, Ray. *Matty: An American Hero: Christy Mathewson of the New York Giants*. New York: Oxford University Press, 1993.

Roff, Elwood A. *Base Ball and Base Ball Players*. Chicago: E. A. Roff, 1912.

Romig, Ralph. *Cy Young: Baseball's Legendary Giant*. [n.p.]: Ohio Hills, 1964.

Schneider, Russell J. *The Cleveland Indians Encyclopedia*. Philadelphia: Temple University Press, 1996.

Schoor, Gene. *A History of the World Series*. New York: William Morrow, 1990.

Selzer, Jack. *Baseball in the Nineteenth Century: An Overview*. Manhattan, Kans.: Society for American Baseball Research (1986).

Seymour, Harold. *Baseball: The Early Years*. New York: Oxford University Press, 1960.

————. *Baseball: The Golden Age*. New York: Oxford University Press, 1971.

Smith, Ira. *Baseball's Famous Pitchers*. New York: A. S. Barnes, 1954.

Smith, Red, ed. *The New York Times Book of Baseball History*. New York: Arno Press, 1977.

Smith, Robert. *Baseball*. New York: Simon and Schuster, 1970.

————. *World Series: The Games and the Players*. Garden City, N.Y.: Doubleday, 1967.

Solomon, Burt. *The Baseball Timeline: The Day-by-Day History of Baseball from Valley Forge to the Present Day*. New York: Avon, 1997.

————. *Where They Ain't: The Fabled Life and Untimely Death of the Original Baltimore Orioles, The Team That Gave Birth To Modern Baseball*. New York: Free Press, 1999.

Spalding, A. G. *Baseball: America's National Game*. New York: American Sports, 1911. Reprint, Samm Coombs and Bob West, eds. San Francisco: Halo Books, 1991.

Spink, Alfred H. *The National Game*. St. Louis: National Game Publishing Company, 1910.

Stevens, David. *Baseball's Radical for All Seasons: A Biography of John Montgomery Ward*. Lanham, Md.: Scarecrow Press, 1998.

Stump, Al. *Cobb: A Biography*. Chapel Hill, N.C.: Algonquin Books, 1994.

Sullivan, Dean A., ed. *Early Innings: A Documentary History of Baseball, 1825–1908*. Lincoln: University of Nebraska Press, 1995.

Sullivan, George. *The Pictorial History of the Boston Red Sox*. Indianapolis: Bobbs-Merrill, 1979.

Thorn, John, ed. *The Armchair Book of Baseball*. New York: Charles Scribner's Sons, 1985.

Thorn, John, and John Holway. *The Pitcher*. New York: Prentice-Hall, 1987.

Thorn, John, and Pete Palmer. *The Hidden Game of Baseball: A Revolutionary Approach to Baseball and Its Statistics*. Garden City, N.Y.: Doubleday, 1984.

Thorn, John, and Pete Palmer, with Michael Gershman. *Total Baseball*. 4th ed. New York: Viking Press, 1995.

Thorn, John, *et al. Total Indians*. New York: Penguin, 1996.

Tiemann, Robert L. *Cardinal Classics: Outstanding Games from Each of the St. Louis Baseball Club's 100 Seasons*. St. Louis: Baseball Histories, 1982.

Tiemann, Robert L., and Mark Rucker, eds. *Nineteenth-Century Stars*. Kansas City, Mo.: The Society for American Baseball Research, 1989.

Tuscarawas County Cemetery Book VI. New Philadelphia, Ohio: Tuscarawas County Genealogical Society, Inc., n.d.

United States Department of Commerce. *Statistical Abstracts of the United States 1907*. Washington, D.C., Government Printing Office, 1908.

Van Tassell, David D., ed., and John J. Grabowski, man. ed. *The Dictionary of Cleveland Biography*. Bloomington: Indiana University Press, 1996.

———. *The Encyclopedia of Cleveland History*. Bloomington, IN: Indiana University Press, 1996.

Vecchione, Joseph J., ed. *The New York Times Book of Sports Legends*. New York: Times Books, 1991.

Vlasich, James A. *A Legend for the Legendary: The Origin of the Baseball Hall of Fame*. Bowling Green, Ohio: Bowling Green State University Press, 1990.

Voigt, David Quentin. *American Baseball:* Vol. 1: *From Gentleman's Sport to the Commissioner System*. University Park: Pennsylvania State University Press, 1983. Reprint, Norman, OK: University of Oklahoma Press, 1966.

———. *American Baseball:* Vol. 2: *From the Commissioners to Continental Expansion*. University Park, PA: University of Pennsylvania Press, 1893. Reprint, Norman: University of Oklahoma Press, 1970.

———. *The League That Failed*. Lanham, Md.: Scarecrow Press, 1998.

Walsh, Christy, ed. *Baseball's Greatest Lineup*. New York: A. S. Barnes, 1952.

Wayman, Joseph M. *Grandstand Baseball Annual: Pitching W-L Records NL 1890–1899 Issue #1*. Long Beach, CA: PrintMasters, 1996.

———. *Grandstand Baseball Annual: Special 2: Frank Williams Issue*. Hollywood, Calif.: The Copy Place, 1992.

Westcott, Rich. *Masters of the Diamond*. Jefferson, N.C.: McFarland, 1994.

Wolff, Rick. *The Baseball Encyclopedia*. 9th ed. New York: Macmillan, 1993.

Wright, Craig, and Tom House. *The Diamond Appraised*. New York: Simon and Schuster, 1989.

Periodicals

Alexander, Charles. "Triple Play: Cleveland's Hall of Fame Triumvirate." *Timeline* 9, no. 2 (April–May 1992): 2–17.

"All-Time Top Pitching Winners Against Quality of Opposition." *Grandstand Baseball Annual* 11 (1995): 8–9.

Alvarez, Mark. "An Interview with Smokey Joe Wood." *Baseball Research Journal* 16 (1987): 53–56.

Arms, Louis Lee. "The Bobby Wallace Story." *Sporting News*, March 31, 1954, 13–14; April 7, 1954, 15–16.

Bailey, Bob. "Four Teams Out: The NL Reduction of 1900." *Baseball Research Journal* 19 (1990): 45–48.

"Baseball in the Nineteenth Century: A Special Pictorial Issue." *National Pastime* 3 (spring 1984).

Bevis, Charles W. "The 1901 Boston Americans." *National Pastime* 10 (1990): 27–32.

Blaisdell, Lowell L. "Trouble and Jack Taylor." *National Pastime* 16 (1996): 132–36.

Bloom, David. "Lifetime Relative ERA." *By the Numbers* 4 (April 1992): 8–10.

Boren, Stephen D., and Thomas Boren. "Pitcher Player-Managers: An Unusual Combination." *Baseball Research Journal* 22 (1993): 89–92.

Bowles, Frank P. "Statistics and Fair Play: The Oliver System." *National Pastime* 4 (spring 1985): 74–81.

Broeg, Bob. "Durable Ace Cy Young—A 511-Game Winner." *Sporting News*, April 17, 1971, 18–19.

Bryson, Bill. "No-Windup Big in 1868, Too!" *Baseball Digest*, January–February 1957, 31.

Carey, Max, as told to Jack Kofoed. "The 20 Greatest Pitchers." *Baseball Digest*, November–December 1956, 37–46.

"Clarifying Some of the Records: Cy Young's Streak of Hitless Innings." *Baseball Research Journal* 7 (1978): 103–4.

Cooper, Desmond. "The Canton 'Cyclone.'" *Ohio Magazine* (July 1968): 40–41.

"Cy Young." *Baseball Magazine* 7 (October 1911).

"Cy Young Remembered with Statue in Boston," *Newcomerstown [Ohio] News*, October 6, 1993.

"Cy Young's Debut: Great Baseball Pitcher Got His Start in Webster County." *Webster County [Nebraska] Argus Weekly*, July 21, 1905.

"Cy Young's String of Hitless Innings." *Baseball Research Journal* (1978): 103.

Deane, Bill. "Normalized Winning Percentage." *Baseball Research Journal* 25 (1996): 44–46.

Doherty, Paul F. "Cy Young's Final Fling." *Baseball Research Journal* 8 (1979): 6–8.

D'Vys, George Whitefield. "Old 'Cy' Young." *Baseball Magazine* 1 (August 1908): 32–33.

Egenriether, Richard. "Chris Von der Ahe: Baseball's Pioneering Huckster." *Baseball Research Journal* 18 (1989): 27–31.

Eldred, Rich. "Umpiring in the 1890's." *Baseball Research Journal* 18 (1989): 75–78.

Feldman, Jay. "The Rise and Fall of Louis Sockalexis." *Baseball Research Journal* 15 (1986): 39–42.

Finlan, Stephen. "Evaluating Pitchers' Won-Lost Records." *Baseball Research Journal* 18 (1989): 20–24.

Fleitz, David L. "Cy Young." *Toledo Magazine: The Sunday Blade* July 29, 1990: 42–46.

———. "Going to Bat for a Friend." *Oldtyme Baseball News* 3 (4): 8.

Foster, Mark S. "Foul Ball: The Cleveland Spiders" Farcical Final Season of 1899. *Baseball History* 1 (summer 1986): 4–14.

Gibson, Campbell. "Competitive Imbalance: A Study of the Major Leagues from 1876 through 1993." *Baseball Research Journal* 24 (1995): 153–56.

Gilbert, Bill. "Triple Milestone Pitchers." *Baseball Research Journal* 25 (1996): 90–92.

Hack, Richard. "Four Series Surprises." *Sports History* (January 1989): 40–53.

Hadley, Lawrence, Elizabeth Gustafson, and Mary Jo Thierry. "Who Would be the Highest Paid Baseball Player?" *The Baseball Research Journal* 21 (1992): 86–92.

Hawkins, Burton. "A Chat with Cy Young." *Baseball Digest* 2 (October 1943): 25–26.

"Honor Cy Young." *Good Will News* 4 (March 1947): 2.

Husman, John R. "Baseball's First All-Star Game." *Sports History* (January 1990): 8+.

Ingraham, Jim. "The Magnificent Career and Tragic Death of Addie Joss." *Baseball History* 1, 2 (summer 1986): 15–31.

"Iron Man." *Time* 66 (November 14, 1955): 66+.

Jones, Jimmy. "Baseball Observes 72nd Anniversary." *Mercerian* 49 (March 1963): 10–11.

Katz, Lawrence S. "When Immortals Returned to the Minors." *Baseball Research Journal* 19 (1990): 33–35.

Kaufman, Alan S., and James C. Kaufman. "Dominant Pitchers: II." *National Pastime* 24 (1995): 47–52.

Kelleher, Garrett. "More Than a Kid: The Story of Kid Gleason." *Baseball Research Journal* 17 (1988): 79–81.

Kermisch, Al. "From a Researcher's Notebook." *Baseball Research Journal* 22 (1993): 111–12.

———. "From a Researcher's Notebook." *Baseball Research Journal* 24 (1995): 162–64.

Kimmel, Michael S. "Baseball and the Reconstruction of American Masculinity, 1880–1920." *Baseball History* 3 (1990): 98–112.

Klein, Moss. "The Unsinkable Cy Young." *Sporting News*, June 10, 1991, 13.

Knox, Vye. "The Incomparable Cy Young." *Good Old Days* (1992): 18–22.

Koefod, J. C. "The Greatest Pitcher in Baseball History." *Baseball Magazine* 29 (October 1922): 499–501+.

Koppett, Leonard. "Greatest Pitcher of Them All." *Baseball Digest* 24 (February 1965): 35–42.

Kuenster, Bob. "Here are Majors' All-Time Best Right-Handed Pitchers." *Baseball Digest* (March 1995): 54–63.

Lahmers, Ken. "Cy Young: Story of a Baseball Great." *Newcomerstown [Ohio] News*, July 12, 1978.

"Legend Born: 100 Years Ago, Cy Young Started in Cleveland." *Cleveland Plain Dealer*, August 6, 1990, D:12.

Lewis, Franklin. "Was Cy Young Greatest? We'll Never Know." *Baseball Digest* 15 (January–February 1956): 85–86.

"Many Records Set by Denton T. Young Will Never Be Broken." *Coshocton [Ohio] Tribune* May 31, 1964.

Massie, Jim. "Oh, Could Young Pitch." *Columbus Dispatch*, undated, Cy Young folder, National Baseball Library, Cooperstown, N.Y.

McCormack, John. "Bring Back the Spitter? Yes!" *Baseball Research Journal* 20 (1991): 14+.

Miller, Jim. "The Old Orioles' First Pennant." *National Pastime* 10 (1990): 49–53.

Miller, Ray. "Pre-1900 NL Franchise Movement." *National Pastime* 17 (1997): 57–61.

Morse, Jacob. "Review of the Baseball Season." *Baseball Magazine* 8 (December 1911): 47–52.

———. "The Story of 'Cy' Young." *Baseball Magazine* 1 (September 1908): 38–45.

Mulligan, Hugh A. "Red Cloud History Enriched by Baseball Luminaries." *Lincoln [Nebraska] Star* May 7, 1982.

Murphy, J. M. "Napoleon Lajoie—Modern Baseball's First Superstar." *National Pastime* 7 (spring 1988): 5–77.

"Names: Connie Mack and Cy Young." *Grandstand Baseball Annual* 10 (1994): 5.

"Obituary." *Newsweek*, November 14, 1955, 78.

Okkonen, Marc. "Team Nicknames 1900–1910." *Baseball Research Journal* 27 (1998): 37–39.

"An Old Indian Comes to Town." *Friends* (September 1954): 2–3.

Peterjohn, Alvin. "Cy Young's First Year." *Baseball Research Journal* 5 (1976): 83–89.

Phillips, John. "Temple Cup Series Epilogue." *Grandstand Baseball Annual* 11 (1995): 131–32.

Pickard, Chuck. "These Pitchers Allowed Fewest Base Runners per Nine Innings." *Baseball Digest*, May 1986, 22–24.

———. "These Pitchers Have Best Power Proficiency Rating." *Baseball Digest*, April 1989, 82–85.

Pietrusza, David. "Sliding Billy Hamilton." *Baseball Research Journal* 20 (1991): 30–32.

Pisetzner, Joel. "Cy Young: His Name Remains a Symbol of Greatness." *Baseball Digest* 40 (July 1981): 85–87.

Polhamus, Jim. "Pitchers With Ten Winning Seasons." *Baseball Research Journal* 13 (1984): 9–11.

Rice, Grantland. "Beyond Reach." *Collier's*, June 30, 1928, 10+.

———. "Big 3 of the Mound." *Collier's*, April 11, 1925, 22+.

"Robison's Career." *Sporting News* (February 18, 1899): 4.

Ruiz, William. "Near-Perfect Games." *Baseball Research Journal* 20 (1991): 46–50.

Scott, Joe. "Rube Waddell." *National Pastime* 10 (1990): 72–74.

Shaffer, Clyde. "Nation's Fans Flood Cy Young." Unidentified newspaper clipping, March 29, 1942. George Westlake Album, Temperance Tavern Museum, Newcomerstown, Ohio.

Shannon, Bill. "The American League's Lost Season [1900]." *Grandstand Baseball Annual* 10 (1994): 34–37.

Shelton, Bill. "Cy Young and His Record: They Never Grow Old." *Baseball Magazine* 90 (May 1953): 28–30+.

Shipley, Robert E. "Baseball Axiom No. 22." *Baseball Research Journal* 23 (1994): 44–50.

———. "Goose Eggs: Career Shutout Masters." *Baseball Research Journal* 16 (1987): 48–50.

Shouler, Kenneth. "Maintaining a 20-Win Pace is a Mark of Pitching Greatness." *Baseball Digest*, November 1993, 40–41.

Simons, Herbert. "Perfect Game Encores." *Baseball Digest*, January–February 1957, 13–18.

Skagg, Charles H, and Howard C. Skagg. "Control Pitching—A Learned Behavior." *Baseball Research Journal* 21 (1992): 73–77.

Spoerle, Gary. "John Clarkson: Early Ironman." *Vintage & Classic Baseball Collector* 2 (June 1995): 48–49+.

———. "Buck Ewing: Thinking Man's Player." *Vintage & Classic Baseball Collector* 4 (December 1995): 4–5.

Stout, Glenn. "The Grand Exalted Ruler of Rooters' Row." *Sox Fan News* (August 1986): 18+.

Stout, Steve. "Haddix Visited (Cy) Young." *Urbana Daily Citizen* (1992).

Suehsdorf, A. D. "Frank Selee, Dynasty Builder." *National Pastime* 4 (winter 1985): 35–41.

Thom, John. "These Pitchers Posted Most Net Wins in a Season." *Baseball Digest*, March 1992, 26–28.

Tiemann, Robert L. "Denton True Young (Cy)." In *Baseball's First Stars*, vol. 2. Cleveland: Society for American Baseball Research (1996): 179–80.

———. "The Forgotten Winning Streak of 1891." *Baseball Research Journal* 18 (1989): 2–5.

———. "The National League in 1893." *Baseball Research Journal* 22 (1993): 38–41.

Trachtenberg, Leo. "Wee Willie Keeler: Fame and Failure." *National Pastime* 13 (1993): 57–61.

Voigt, David Q. "1894! The Modern Game's Greatest Hitting Explosion." *Baseball Research Journal* 23 (1994): 82–84.

Waterman, Guy. "The Iron Men of Baseball." *Baseball Research Journal* 25 (1996): 56–60.

Wayman, Joseph M. "American League Status 1900." *Grandstand Baseball Annual* 10 (1994): 38–41.

———. "Amos Wilson Rusie: 19th-Century Fireball Ace." *Grandstand Baseball Annual* 10 (1994): 48–50.

———. "Cy Young's 21 Wins and Lifetime Decisions." *Grandstand Baseball Annual* 10 (1994): 12.

———. "Cy Young's Two Questionable Games, 1890." *Grandstand Baseball Annual* 10 (1994): 11.

———. "GBA Correspondence Interview: Frank J. Williams." *Grandstand Baseball Annual: Special 2: Frank J. Williams Issue* (1992): 7–12.

———. "Interleague Championship Series Pitching Records. 1901–1920." *Grandstand Baseball Annual: Special 2: Frank J. Williams Issue* (1992): 52–56.

———. "Joe Wood Revisited." *Grandstand Baseball Annual: Special 2: Frank J. Williams Issue* (1992): 111–31.

———. "Radbourn 1884 and Young 1900, Wins?" *Grandstand Baseball Annual* 14 (1998): 39–46.

———. "Updates and Corrections." *Grandstand Baseball Annual* 11 (1995): 15–16.

———. "Updates and Corrections." *Grandstand Baseball Annual* 12 (1996): 18–19.

Williams, Frank J. "All the Record Books are Wrong." *National Pastime* 1 (fall 1982): 50–62.

———. "The Boston Beaneaters, 1898 NL Champions." *Grandstand Baseball Annual* 12 (1996): 115–28.

———. "The Boston Beaneaters, 1897 NL Champions." *Grandstand Baseball Annual* 11 (1995): 98–128.

———. "The First League Championship Series—1892." *Grandstand Baseball Annual* 5 (1989): 99–111.

———. "Post-Season Interleague Series, 1901–1920." *Grandstand Baseball Annual* 4 (1988): 115–43.

———. "Temple Cup Series Thoughts." *Grandstand Baseball Annual* 11 (1995): 129–30.

———. "A Tribute to Smoky Joe Wood." *Grandstand Baseball Annual: Special 2: Frank J. Williams Issue* (1992): 108–110.

———. "Winning and Losing Streaks of Eight or More Games by American League Pitchers, 1901–1919." *Grandstand Baseball Annual* 10 (1994): 115–17.

Willson, Brad. "The Love Story of a Baseball Legend." *Baseball Digest* 34 (November 1975): 71–73.

Wilson, Walt. "Early Batteries." *Grandstand Baseball Annual: Pitching WL Records NL 1890–1899 Issue no. 1* (1996): 27.

Young, Clarence. "Cy Young, as $2,400-a-Year Star, Offered $20,000 Bribe." *Baseball Digest* 9 (April 1950): 21–24.

Young, Denton True (Cy). "First—Learn Control of Ball." *SABR Review of Books* 1 (1986): 58–59. Reprint from *How to Pitch* (1912).

———. "How I Learned to Pitch." *Baseball Magazine* 1 (September 1908): 13–15.

———. "How to Become a Good Pitcher." In Alfred H. Spink. *The National Game*. St. Louis: National Game Publishing Co. 1910, 391–92.

Newspapers

The Boston Globe (Boston, Massachusetts), 1901–8, 1911.

Cadiz Sentinel (Cadiz, Ohio), March–October 1889.

Cleveland Leader, 1909–11.

Cleveland Plain Dealer, 1890–98, 1909–11.

Evening Repository (Canton, Ohio), March–July 1890.

Leader and Herald (Cleveland, Ohio), 1896–98.

Newcomerstown News [and Index] (Newcomerstown, Ohio).

New York Clipper (New York City), 1904–12.

New York Times (New York City), 1890–1912.

St. Louis Post Dispatch, 1899–1900.

Sentinel Record (Hot Springs, Arkansas), February 1938.

Sporting Life (Philadelphia, Pennsylvania), 1890–1912.

Sporting News (St. Louis, Missouri), 1890–1912.

INDEX